We were at a conference on leadership Johnson shared with me his plan to write a book on leadership. I was a bit apprehensive and said to myself: "No! Not another western book on leadership!" Now as I read the full manuscript I feel grateful to God and admiration of Dr Johnson's work.

This book is a unique contribution not only in its global scope, which is really impressive, but by skillfully weaving together missing and multiple voices even if these voices may vary sometimes in tone and melody. However, at their crescendo these voices do provide global concepts, insights, values and models of what genuine and humble leadership should look like in our age. This book is like a deep valley where we can clearly hear and enjoy the sweet echoes of leadership voices coming from both the global south and the global north.

Riad Kassis, PhD
Director, Langham Scholars Ministry, Langham Partnership
International Director, International Council for
Evangelical Theological Education

Missing Voices: Learning to Lead beyond Our Horizons should be required for any pastor, teacher, or lay leader who aspires to understand, respond to, and work alongside others in our multi-cultural worldwide Christian family. John Johnson encourages us to listen first so that we understand our different cultural expressions of leadership. Then he leads us on an exploration of how leaders from many cultures can bring both their strengths and their weaknesses together to forge dynamic partnerships committed to the work of Christ in the world.

Paul Borthwick, DMin
Author
Senior Consultant, Development Associates International

Millions of people have migrated around the world in the last few decades. Easterners are moving West and Westerners are moving East at a very rapid pace. Thomas Friedman has written that the world is flat and Harvard Professor John Kotter tells us that organizations cannot meet the fast-moving demands of our society. Western leaders are moving to other cultures with multinational companies and churches are being filled with those of other cultures. Dr Johnson has captured this well in this signature work. Beginning by outlining theories of leadership and moving to a variety of global perspectives, he returns to search for a strong cultural and theological basis for how to lead in such a world, with clear success in so doing. This is a study that is long overdue and brings clarity to how to lead in our "flat" world. A must-read for all Christian leaders.

Bud Lindstrand
Former CEO, Moda Health Care
Instructor in Business Ethics, University of Northwestern,
Roseville, Minnesota, USA

Combining broad reading of contemporary writing on leadership with keen biblical insight and diverse voices from numerous cultures and regions, John Johnson provides a fresh, readable and profound perspective for leaders who want to navigate the increasing complexity of our twenty-first century, globalized world. Both emerging and experienced leaders from any nation can benefit from this conversation between leadership theory, experienced global practitioners, and Scripture.

David W. Bennett, DMin, PhD
Global Associate Director for Collaboration and Content,
Lausanne Movement

Missing Voices

Missing Voices

Learning to Lead beyond Our Horizons

John E. Johnson,
with Global Contributors

GLOBAL LIBRARY

© 2019 John E. Johnson

Published 2019 by Langham Global Library
An imprint of Langham Publishing
www.langhampublishing.org

Langham Publishing and its imprints are a ministry of Langham Partnership

Langham Partnership
PO Box 296, Carlisle, Cumbria, CA3 9WZ, UK
www.langham.org

Isbns:
978-1-78368-563-9 Print
978-1-78368-564-6 Epub
978-1-78368-565-3 Mobi
978-1-78368-566-0 PDF

British Library Cataloguing-in-Publication Data
A catalogue record for this book is available from the British Library

ISBN: 978-1-78368-563-9

Cover & Book Design: projectluz.com

This book is dedicated to Alex and Grant, and the rest of our band of brothers, who challenged me to lead beyond my horizon.

CONTENTS

Foreword

Any astute observer of the church worldwide would realize that there is a crisis relating to leadership within the church. Among the many reasons for this is the fact that most churches in both the western and non-western world, have been greatly influenced by models of leadership that are closer to the culture in which they operate than to the Scriptures. Addressing this issue biblically and practically is one of the most urgent needs the church faces in my part of the world and, I believe, elsewhere too.

That is what this book does, and it does so by following a unique format. With the skill of an expert on the topic of global leadership, John Johnson presents contemporary thinking and thoughtful reflections on key leadership issues. Then he has been able to harness and make available for us the riches from the thinking and experience of a wide spectrum of leaders from all over the world. An added value of this book is that these voices (and I personally know, or know about, many of them) are acknowledged leaders, with reputations for integrity, and proven track records of biblically shaped leadership.

The life of the church in the Majority World has been immeasurably enriched by riches from the western world through literature and other media. We are grateful for that contribution and must continue to be enriched in this way. But the church worldwide needs to hear from the Christians in the Majority World also. There are unique riches there which can bless the universal church. We need each other. Our theology of the body of Christ demands a partnership in all fields of Christian endeavour. Much partnership is taking place these days in the fields of mission strategy and practice. But we also need partnership in Christian thinking covering the different segments of theology, including the theology of leadership.

Let me list three reasons why thinking from the Majority World will be of great value to the church worldwide.

- All Christian truth is cruciform coming from a theology of the cross of Christ and from a belief that obedience to Christ cannot be divorced from taking up a cross of suffering. Suffering and material deprivation can foster deep thinking about God's truth which Christians living in the affluent west could easily miss. As suffering and persecution are realities in most churches in Majority World nations, these churches are uniquely positioned to enrich the church with deep, health-giving, cruciform truth.

- In many parts of the western world churches are in decline and are losing the positions of influence they once had. In response to this some Christian communities, trying to not cause offense to outsiders, are soft-peddling radical Christian essentials and losing their cutting edge. Others are trying to assert that their views are the official values of the nation and should therefore be enforced. Sadly, many are pursuing these paths in ways that are viewed by outsiders as intolerant and arrogant.

  Christians in the West can be emboldened and instructed by hearing the voices from churches where growth and vitality is evidenced in the midst of persecution. There are helpful models of winsome witness amidst hardship.

  Their vibrant experiences of growth and of God's power have contributed a unique flavour to their interpretation of and approach to God's truth. When Christians experience God powerfully at work among them their eyes are opened afresh to discovering certain biblical truths, especially about the ability of God. Those discoveries could bring new light and encouragement to Christians who are discouraged by being in churches which are in decline.

- One reason for the reduced output in terms of literature and scholarly thinking from poorer nations is the inability of their Christian community to afford separating out people to be specialists and writers of serious scholarly material. Capable people are so busy doing the work of ministry that they find it difficult to devote time exclusively to their specialities and to putting into writing the rich insights they have gained from their study and experiences in ministry. Yet this apparent obstacle may contribute to one of the most important contributions these churches can make to the body of Christ. There is an urgent need for integration in theology and practice. Penetrative insight comes through thinking that takes theory and applies it to life. Such integration is difficult to find in today's specialized world. In the history of the church some of the most influential thinkers were brilliant theologians and were grassroots practitioners at the same time. Examples of such are Augustine, Martin Luther, John Calvin, Jonathan Edwards, John Wesley and Charles Finney.

  The commitment of leaders to efficiency can push them to engage in such a strong program of pursuing measurable results (intellectual and practical) that they can become lazy about integrating the serious thinking and with the practical realities of grassroots work. People in our part of the world are forced to focus on their chosen field of specialization and expertise out of a background of a generalist lifestyle and ministry-style. We cannot afford pure specialists. Our output may be much less in terms of volume, but hopefully the struggle to be an integrated person will have produced penetrative insight which will be health-giving to the church. Many brilliant minds in the Majority World have moved to the West, lured by prospects of a more "productive" output in their areas of specialization. In doing so, they may have sacrificed penetrative insight on the altar of productivity.

Besides, I think people in many of our nations have a more conducive cultural environment for integration than people in western countries. We may have a more holistic (integrated) approach to life as opposed to a more compartmentalized approach in the West.

All this makes it imperative that the contribution of Majority World Christians should be made available to the wider church. However, as implied above, a lack of time, the burden of multiple responsibilities, and a lack of resources make it more difficult for our people to publish their thinking. We are grateful to Langham Partnership for its different endeavours to encourage publications from Majority World Christians. The unique format of this book serves admirably to enable Christians worldwide to hear some of these *Missing Voices*.

Ajith Fernando
Teaching Director, Youth for Christ, Sri Lanka
Author, Discipling in a Multicultural World (2019)

Acknowledgments

Wendell Berry, the agrarian novelist, once said these words: "Isn't it something, how we get what we need at just the right time? The right book comes along at just the right time. The right friend comes along at just the right time. The right conversation comes along at just the right time. It's grace." Russell Moore, a leader in the Southern Baptist movement, recalled these words in an article he wrote for *Christianity Today*.[1]

I hope this is true of this book. I have written it out of a conviction that a book on global leadership is necessary. I want this to be a book that fills a void. It is my audacious hope that it will address a global need, as well as fill a theological gap in leadership studies. Most of all, my wish is that it has come along at just the right time for you.

I have many to thank for their help, beginning with my family. As with my previous book, they have allowed me to take cover and escape in order to complete this project. I am especially grateful for my wife, Heather.

I appreciate Western Seminary, which is dedicated to leadership studies and global education. Most of all, I appreciate that it encourages its professors to write.

Corporate and missional leaders, as well as theologians, have advised me along the way: Tim Harmon, Bud Lindstrand, Riad Kassis, Paul Borthwick, David Bennett, Enoch Wan, Skip Centioli, Mikel Neumann, Karen Fancher, Galen Currah, Ben Spotts, Steve Stephens, and Mark Heddinger. Without their excellent minds and servant hearts, I could not have done this.

I am especially grateful for Langham Publishers, and Vivian Doub in particular.

---

1. Moore, "How Frederick Buechner Blessed My Life," 46.

Before We Begin: An Introduction

In his book *Leading across Cultures*, James Plueddemann imagines a situation where a dozen blind people are locked in a large room, bumping into one another. Eventually, they begin to establish signals to prevent so many collisions. They begin to build community. And after some time, a dozen more blind people enter, people who had previously worked out a system of signals in another context. These two groups run into each other, causing criticism and frustration. Each group thinks the other uncultured. Eventually, the two cultures work out a new system.

The Aim of This Book

Part of the purpose of this work is to bring a diverse group of global leaders together so that we can look beyond our horizons, decode our cultural differences, work past our misunderstandings and disapprovals, and reframe the subject of leadership. The aim is to develop what some have referred to as "contextual intelligence." To remove our blinders. To open our ears and hear the missing voices. This is essential if we hope to understand leadership and avoid the cultural traps that come with narrow assumptions. If you want to expand your vista, this book is for you.

My objective, however, runs deeper. I am writing out of a conviction that successful leadership also requires an awareness of – and a deference to – a divine voice. We will be far stronger leaders if we "de-compartmentalize" the local and global, as well as the secular and spiritual.

There is a present, critical need to enlarge our thinking and discover cultural and theological voices, especially for those entering into and those presently engaged in ministry. Followers of Jesus celebrate a gospel that transcends all barriers – gender, age, ethnicity – but even here we run into one another. We assume our approach to leading is the right approach. We look to resources on leadership that reinforce our assumptions about what it means to lead. But no one perspective is right – only different.

This is especially true in the West, where typical publications are culturally biased with Eurocentric/American influences. Most leadership books represent that which is WEIRD (Western, Educated, Industrialized, Rich, Democratic).

Prompted by the modern worldview, traditional leadership books have assumed that these voices are improving the human condition and bringing order to a disorderly world.[1] They assume that they can create better organizations through rational business processes. They are sure they are the experts when it comes to leadership. Just look at the books on our business shelves. It is the West and the rest.

To be fair, these voices have brought significant contributions to our understanding of leadership. They are the voices we hear. However, they are insufficient on their own. There is a cultural bias that infuses many of them, and a larger divine narrative tends to be left out. They can act like cataracts, clouding our clarity. We can end up with misguided assumptions about who leaders are and how leaders should lead. To the Majority World, some of the thinking regarding communication, power, or use of time might actually seem *weird*, if not bizarre.

The Need for This Book

From a Cultural Side

I was born into a monocultural setting just east of San Diego. My neighborhood was mostly blue collar, middle class, and white. My international travel was confined to a few trips south of the border to Tijuana. I hardly made it out of California. University and seminary studies began to expose me to more cultures, but it wasn't until I began my pastoral work in Portland, Oregon, and taught abroad in Manila, that my world opened up.

Ever since that first trip, I am restless if I do not engage cross-culturally. Whether it is dancing with Nigerians in a morning worship, taking a fifteen-hour train ride across northern India, sipping coffee in a Bedouin tent in Lebanon, trekking through a jungle in Borneo, or preaching to congregants in Aleppo, I can't get enough. Each time I engage in a different culture, and teach leadership, I grow beyond my narrow assumptions. My thinking expands. I see another dimension of God's creative work and I become a better leader.

I have been a lead pastor for over thirty-three years, seven of them in Europe (where my board chair was South African, and board members were composed of Japanese, Dutch, German, American, and Nigerian). It has been my privilege to lead two strong multicultural churches for the majority of these years. I have also been a professor in a seminary, and teaching leadership has

---

1. Myers, *Engaging Globalization*, 54.

been a passion. It is a subject I have taught, and continue to teach, both at home and abroad.

In every case, I am struck by the absence of a sound leadership book that engages multiple global voices, builds on a Christian worldview, and applies this to the twenty-first-century age – an age marked by a growing paganism, globalization, huge people movements, technological advances, and a growing shift of Christianity from north to south. Nearly three-quarters of the world's evangelicals live outside of the United States and Europe. This rapid move in global Christianity toward the Majority World mandates that we do some fresh thinking here. I hope that this book will fill that gap.

If leadership is to be effective, there are commonalities and differences we must acknowledge and learn how to navigate. The following list shows how some noted anthropologists, social psychologists, and international business teachers, such as Edward T. Hall, Geert Hofstede, Robert J. House, James Plueddemann, and Erin Meyer, have outlined them.[2] Given globalization, and recognizing that cultures tend to be an incoherent jumble of influences picked up from all over the world, these are not tight boxes. There are universals and culture-based differences, as well as general norms, we should be aware of.

Differences in How We Value Relationships versus Tasks

In some cultures, the human connection is far more important than human achievement. Leadership focuses on the human dynamics – the state of morale, the heart of the people, and the level of trust. People are not units. They have names, and their names represent families, tribes, and other associations. Harmony, cooperation, and flexibility are paramount. Attention is given to ancestors.

In other cultures, greater weight is given to assigned tasks and achievable goals. Trust is built through efficiency and productivity. People are important, but value is placed upon performance. Things are linear and direct. Core words include execution, implementation, and goal achievement. Attention is given to events.

Differences in How We Communicate

Communication is contextual and complex. In what some define as "high context culture," the focus is on the more immediate. People pay attention to the concrete world around them (e.g. atmosphere, smells, expressions, and

---

2. See Hall, *Beyond Culture*; Hofstede, Hofstede, and Minkov, *Cultures and Organizations*; Meyer, *Culture Map*; and the work of Robert J. House and the GLOBE research program.

body language). Everything communicates something significant.[3] Interaction between people is less verbal; messaging is more subtle, implicit, nuanced, and layered. A leader gives attention to the physical cues – the clothes one wears, the place where one sits, and the way one greets. One listens for tones, observes postures, and notices how one says something.

In a "low context culture," greater weight is given to the spoken. Leadership is more about verbalizing concepts and ideas. Communication is more overt and precise. People take things at face value.

Differences in How We View Authority and Power

In what has been categorized as a "low power distance culture," people assume a more egalitarian approach to social relations. There is less of a gap between follower and leader. People view the leader as one among equals, having minimal status or privilege. There is a preference for a consultative, participative, democratic decision-making style of leading. Interpersonal relationships are more horizontal and less formal. In America, as an example, it is a bottom-up society, in which leaders draw their power not from themselves or their office, but from the people.[4]

In "high power distance cultures," deference to and respect for the leader require a certain distancing. Leaders and followers accept that the leader has more authority, status, and special privileges than others. Leadership is top-down, hierarchical, with a more directive style. In some cases, one could use the word "paternalistic." A national or tribal leader is viewed as a father to his family. People "sing" to their leader.

Leaders draw their power from themselves or their position. In some hierarchical contexts (Japan being an exception), the leader is accorded the right to make unilateral decisions (such as in some African and Latino contexts). Those who question authority are hindering rather than investing in the process. Challenging leadership can amount to dishonor and disloyalty.

Differences in How We View Community versus Individualism

Few cultural values are more fascinating (or frustrating) for leaders in the global church than individualism and collectivism.[5] This may be the most important attribute distinguishing cultures.

---

3. Plueddemann, *Leading across Cultures*, 78.

4. Gergen, *Eyewitness to Power*, 82.

5. Plueddemann, *Leading across Cultures*, 114.

In collectivism, higher value is placed on interdependence, community, and family. The interest of the group prevails over the interest of the individual. Social harmony, not personal preference, is what matters. Sin and failure have both personal and corporate ramifications. Preaching is directed to the community and less to the individual.

Dominating American and certain European cultures is an individualism in which a person is taught to be independent, do things for oneself, and seek personal freedom. Decisions are based on what benefits the person rather than the group. Personal self-respect is the driver. Nepotism is inappropriate; joining is optional. Having your own space is important; group loyalty and collective interests are less necessary. The hermeneutic employed to scriptural truths has an individual focus and application.[6]

Differences in How We Handle Conflict

Some cultures are predominantly governed by guilt/innocence; others by shame/honor; and others by fear/power.[7] In varying degrees, all worldviews consist of one of these three constructs. Leaders must recognize and adjust, especially if they hope to manage disagreements.

In a culture governed by guilt/innocence, conflict is more acceptable. Those who have crossed the line and violated accepted norms are guilty. In this case, open challenge and direct confrontation are expected. It is important to determine where there is wrong. One must take responsibility, accept the consequences, seek reconciliation, and move on. Leaders here are more inclined to be candid as they deal with the issues.

A culture governed by shame/honor tends to avoid conflict for fear of losing face. Leaders must realize that the pursuit of respect, honor, and status frames every facet of life. One must live up to the ideals of the community and avoid shame at all costs. Shame means a relationship is broken. A person has lost face, and this personal disgrace might extend to one's family. It leads to exclusion and rejection.

The community uses shame as a powerful motivator for keeping people in line. In more extreme cases, dominating others is a way of bringing shame, and revenge can become a means of removing shame. In any conflict, one aims to save face and avoid any direct confrontation that might cause embarrassment. Communication is more subtle and indirect.[8]

---

6. Rah, *Next Evangelicalism*, 34.
7. See Muller, *Honor and Shame*.
8. Webber, "Reflections," 9.

Jayson Georges captures the difference in the first two cultures with this statement: "Guilt says, 'I made a mistake, so I should confess,' but shame says, 'I am a mistake, so I should hide.'"[9] The first focuses on what you did; the second focuses on who you are. The first cuts to the chase; the second is more of a dance.

Some cultures, particularly tribal cultures like those in Africa, are governed by fear/power. Discerning leaders recognize that conflicts are less about proving guilt or wielding shame, and more about exerting power, winning the conflict. Those in authority tend to use fear to gain one's submission and compliance.

Differences in How We Approach Scripture

Each culture will bring its worldview, its values, its way of perceiving and thinking, and its experiences into its interpretation of a text. Those of us in the West are often blind to interpretations that the original audience and readers in other cultures see naturally.[10] It is important to recognize that no one culture has the final word on proper hermeneutics. Even if we come to the same interpretation of the passage at hand, our application may vary. Branson and Martinez note, "the biggest tension will often not be with the text itself but with the implications of the text for our lives today."[11]

Summary

Appreciating these differences can be useful in understanding and appreciating cultural values. Given the variances, effective leaders will listen for the similarities and disparities, as well as overarching patterns, that exist across various cultures.[12] This book will illustrate differences, recognizing that no one culture should act from a position of dominance.

We all come to learn from and listen to one another with an empathetic ear. What is a strength in one culture may be a barrier in another. This requires the "bracketing" of one's perceptions and emotions in order to problem solve and enter into the world of another.[13] It will require a humility that acknowledges the weaknesses of our own cultural biases, while seeking out the strengths and contributions of others.

---

9. Georges and Baker, *Ministering*, 37.

10. Richards and O'Brien, *Misreading Scripture with Western Eyes*, loc. 123.

11. Branson and Martinez, *Churches, Cultures, and Leadership*, 184.

12. Livermore, *Expand Your Borders*, 7.

13. Branson and Martinez, *Churches, Cultures, and Leadership*, 199.

The need is urgent. Bryant Myers, professor of transformational leadership, describes our world as one where going global has become "supercharged."[14] The leaders of tomorrow's multicultural communities will need the necessary skills to help people learn the signals, recognize their blind spots, learn the values of others, read the contexts, and adapt. They will also need to help people see that embracing other voices is to everyone's advantage.

The voices in this book are not exhaustive, but the hope is that readers will gain a more expansive understanding of leadership, as well as find themselves in the dialogue. For our purposes, we have recruited voices from the following regions of the world: Latin America, Europe, Africa, Asia, India, and the Middle East.

From a Theological Side

Coming to grips with leadership requires that we discern the mind of God. Leadership is inescapably theological. Without a theology of leadership, we will make a number of false assumptions about the nature of human beings, the place of power, the basis of morality, and the role of leaders. We might succumb to false witnesses and create false idols. *We might assume this is about us.*

It is God, however, who makes and calls leaders to carry out his purpose. Leadership is his idea, not ours.

There are different ways of going about developing a theology of leadership. None are easy. Theology is thinking hard about what God has taught about himself and all things in relation to himself. It is not about deploying God's name simply to add support to one's pet ideas.[15] I will resist the temptation to compile proof texts. Instead, I will take a biblical-theological approach (as I understand it), focusing on selected portions of the biblical narrative that I believe represent the whole of Scripture.

The intent is to look beyond our immediate range of perception, out beyond other cultural horizons, and determine a divine perspective on the leadership topics identified and discussed in this book.[16] While I don't presume to sum up all that the Bible has to say about these topics, I nonetheless believe that the passages I have highlighted supply a helpful distillation of its teaching.

---

14. Myers, *Engaging Globalization*, 4.

15. Vanhoozer, "Letter to an Aspiring Theologian," 28.

16. I understand that biblical theology is understood in various ways. A helpful resource is Klink and Lockett, *Understanding Biblical Theology*. My approach is closer to their fifth approach, though I incorporate elements of their second approach, "Biblical Theology as Redemption."

I acknowledge my own thought is embedded in the values and language of my American culture. As Plueddemann warns, it is easy to assume that our limited, culture-bound assumptions about leadership are biblical. There is the danger of proof texting our cultural biases.[17] Nonetheless, in the end, my hope is that the biblical-theological reflections provided in these sections will help to anchor convictions as to what leadership, ideally, ought to look like.

A post-Christian West, as well as the growing connectivity of cultures, makes the need more urgent. All manner of entities – currencies, customs, commodities, and communicable diseases – circulate around the world with enormous speed.[18] The future staff of an engineering group or a pastoral team will be more diverse – both ethnically and theologically – than ever.

The Approach of This Book

Leadership is first about *becoming*. The initial five chapters will give attention to who leaders are. We will look at leadership definitions in chapter 1. This is not easy. There is a lot to this subject. Everyone seems to have his or her own way of defining. In chapter 2, we will enter the debate regarding the need for leadership. Can the world – the church – get by without leaders, or will it be hopelessly lost without them? There are strong voices on both sides. In chapter 3, we will wrestle with the question of acquisition. Is leadership inherent or acquired over time? Or is there another answer? Chapter 4 delves into the issue of character. Does it matter if a leader holds to a set of moral values, and if so, what are they? Chapter 5 explores the competencies essential to effective leadership. Are there skills that all leaders, regardless of culture, must have in order to lead?

The second section will focus on leadership and *implementation*. How do leaders get things done? In chapter 6, we will look at the function of teams and the relationship they have to a leader. Is there value in building teams? Why are so many so unhealthy? Chapters 7 through 8 describe the essential task of leaders – to be missional, visionary, strategic, and tactical. Are these Western concepts, or do they reflect the way God works? Could it be that without all four, a leader is merely going through the motions, and the people one leads will drift and languish?

The third part of the book deals with global leadership that *endures*. Chapter 9 examines the subject of change. If leaders bring lasting transformation,

---

17. See Plueddemann, *Leading across Cultures*, chapter 4.
18. Barendsen and Gardner, "Three Elements of Good Leadership," 269.

what are the laws of change they must adopt? In chapter 10 we will face the inevitable byproduct of change – conflict. What do I do when my leadership is challenged? How do leaders survive and navigate through the storms? Finally, we will talk about the inescapable: the leader and transition. How do I know when it is time to leave? How do I know when it is time to stay? What's required to leave behind a legacy?

Within each chapter, we will look at leadership from three contexts: First, we will do a brief survey, bringing together some of the best thinkers on leadership. These are the voices we hear. The aim is to determine a collective theory on each leadership theme. Growing up in American culture, I acknowledge that most of my reading and leadership training has been from a Western perspective. I will bring my own experiences and stories and also draw from my own cross-cultural experiences.

Second, in each chapter we will view leadership from a broader, global perspective, giving attention to a diversity of global voices we need to hear. In some cases, global leaders will make a written contribution. In others, they will be interviewed. The aim is to discover how leadership is practiced in different cultural contexts. Without a macro awareness, we will assume certain biases that skew the nature and manner of leadership.

Finally, each chapter will end by looking more expansively, listening for a biblical-theological voice. The emphasis will be on the grand narrative of Scripture, focusing on selected texts that, in my view, uniquely illustrate a biblical view of that chapter's topic. The goal is to determine what God has to say about leadership. As noted, there is no perspective that matters more. We must hear these words.

As we begin, and as we encounter the various voices and integrate theological foundations, let us come with a posture to hear and learn. Some of these geo-cultures were doing leadership long before those in the West came into existence. And God was doing leadership long before anyone ever existed. Let's do this with the aim of developing a broader approach to leadership, as well as of becoming the leaders so necessary to the mission of the church.

Part I

Becoming a Global Leader for Twenty-First-Century Ministry

"A large chair does not make a king."
Sudanese proverb

1

Get a Grip on Who You Are

The straight-up aim of this book is to shape future leaders. This is a book designed to sharpen your leadership skills and make you a better version of yourself. It's critical. In his groundbreaking work of 1978, *Leadership*, James MacGregor Burns noted that leadership is one of the keynotes of our time.[1] How much more so today! Contemporary analysts warn that the forces of history and powerful elements of human nature are bringing us back to precarious times[2] – times in which we feel the absence of leadership, or at least a certain despair over the leaders we have. We hunger for compelling and creative leadership. We need leaders who come with a relevant agenda, who will create islands of sanity in the midst of wildly disruptive seas.[3] This is where you come in.

It is my conviction that the best leaders are those who are well informed on the subject. They have not only studied what is immediately at hand; they have determined to cross the cultural divide and explore how others view leadership. More, they believe that what God has to say on the subject matters, so they are passionate to think theologically. After all, redemption and spiritual restoration are the largest leadership projects in the world. Working for human flourishing is the leader's highest endeavor.

Exploring leadership is an arduous task; its complexity requires intentional, focused effort. But this pales in comparison to being a leader. Stephen King likens the difficult task of writing fiction to crossing the Atlantic Ocean in a bathtub.[4] It is a metaphor that can also be applied to those charged to lead (though one might replace the bathtub with a bucket!). Leading people forward, regardless of the culture, can sometimes feel hopeless and impossible.

---

1. Burns, *Leadership*, 451.
2. See Kagan, *Jungle Grows Back*.
3. Wheatley, *Who Do We Choose to Be?*, 9.
4. King, *On Writing*, 209.

There are skills to learn, rules to grasp, cultures to understand, and habits to overcome. One is not a born visionary any more than one suddenly becomes a skilled tactician. Leading teams is a course in itself. Managing change or transitioning successfully will require a fair amount of counsel, reading, and research. And handling conflict? Better not go with your gut!

So where does one begin? Most leadership books begin with definitions. This makes sense. Leaders who are determined to lead need to understand what leadership means. But there is a problem, as Stogdill notes: "There are almost as many definitions as there are people trying to define it."[5] What exactly is leadership? Is it some magical power or spiritual gift conferred at birth, giving one an elevated status? Does it require the right charisma or job description? How does one know if one has it? What do familiar voices say? What do different global leaders assume when it comes to leadership definitions – and who is right? And, by the way, what does God have to say on the subject?

The Voices We Hear

In 1989, Warren Bennis, a professor at the University of Southern California (and revered as the godfather of modern leadership literature), wrote *On Becoming a Leader*. My running partner gave it to me as a gift. It was the first book on leadership I read, and it launched me on a lifetime journey of studying the subject. I began to ask questions, starting with "What is leadership?" and "Is there a definition that has universal agreement?" Other questions quickly followed: "What distinguishes a leader from a non-leader?" "Am I a leader?" "Would others concur?" How do others see you?

As I began to read everything I could on the subject, this much became clear: there is no universally accepted meaning of the word.[6] Leadership is one of the most observed and least understood phenomena on earth. Burns concludes that most leaders are not leading because a number have not the faintest concept of what leadership is about.[7]

Educator Dave Ulrich underscores the complications that come with mastering the subject, likening leadership to the inner workings of a computer. It is a complex set of relationships, systems, and processes that few fully master.[8] Even Bennis acknowledges in his introduction that the study of leadership isn't

---

5. Quoted from Stogdill, *Handbook of Leadership*, 7.
6. See Burns, Shoup, and Simmons, *Organizational Leadership*, 10.
7. Burns, *Leadership*, 451.
8. Ulrich, "Credibility x Capability," 210.

as exact as other disciplines. It is not a science that can be mastered through standardized training. Leadership is more of an art; it is difficult to define, but you know it when you see it.[9]

I saw it in my first cross-country coach. He called me out of a crowd of freshman students, and I literally followed him for four years, running nearly one hundred miles a week. There was a command in his voice, a direction to his steps, and a vision of what he wanted to accomplish. It was also evident in my spiritual godfather, who inspired me to consider ministry as a profession. It was a passing invitation on a spring evening, but I could not shake it. My life course took a huge turn. I went to his home and said, "Here I am."

Leadership was in the bones of many of the expats I pastored in the Netherlands. Here were these up-and-comers, sent across the ocean to expand the reach of their corporations. They were directional and tenacious, and I felt like I was in the company of the committed.

Still, leadership is hard to put into words and define in one sentence.

Definitions range from the simple to the complex. Simple: "Influence toward goals." Complex: "Leadership is a dynamic process over an extended period of time in various situations in which a leader utilizing leadership resources and by specific leadership behaviors, influences the thoughts and activities of followers toward accomplishment of aims usually mutually beneficial for leaders, followers, and the macro context of which they are a part."[10]

This second one reminds me of a review I recently read: "He never says in a sentence what he can say in a long paragraph." Here are a sample of other definitions, some more concise than others, which highlight the multidimensional nature of leadership:

- "A leader is a dealer in hope" – Napoleon Bonaparte[11]
- "Leadership is the art of accomplishing more than the science of management says is possible" – Colin Powell[12]
- "Leadership is the art of the future" – Leonard Sweet[13]
- "Leadership is the act of making a difference" – Michael Useem[14]

9. De Pree, *Leadership Jazz*, xi.
10. Clinton, *Making of a Leader*, 213.
11. Forbes, "21 Quotable Definitions."
12. Harari, *Leadership Secrets of Colin Powell*, 13.
13. Sweet, *Summoned to Lead*, 11.
14. Useem, *Leadership Moment*, 4.

- "Leadership activity is aligning people by translating vision and values into understandable and attainable acts" – Bernice Ledbetter[15]
- "Leadership is mobilizing others toward a goal shared by the leader and followers" – Garry Wills[16]
- "Leadership is the capacity to translate vision into reality" – Warren Bennis[17]
- "The only definition of a leader is someone who has followers" – Peter Drucker[18]

Whew! And this is a small list. Why does this word inspire so many definitions?

Different Factors Make Defining Leadership a Challenge

Northouse says of leadership, "leadership has presented a major challenge to practitioners and researchers interested in studying the nature of leadership. It is a highly valued phenomenon that is very complex."[19] This explains why none of the statements appears to be complete on its own.[20]

Context Influences Definition

If you isolate leadership from its setting, definitions become impossible.[21] Leadership does not work in a vacuum. In his book *Certain Trumpets*, Garry Wills analyzes leadership within sixteen different contexts, concluding that leadership is not "a single thing."[22] Each "sound" of leadership differs, depending upon the kind of person and kind of leadership required.

Step into the athletic world, and even within this setting there are different ways to define leadership. Leadership on the field and leadership on the court look different. At the Paris Open, Rafael Nadal's tennis coach, Toni Nadal, might lead with only the slightest movement of his finger (if he can get away with it); at Wrigley Field, a baseball manager demonstrates leadership by yelling

---

15. Quoted in Lingenfelter, *Leading Cross-Culturally*, 15.
16. Garry Wills, *Certain Trumpets*, 17.
17. Cited in Kruse, "What Is Leadership?"
18. Drucker, "Not Enough Generals," xii.
19. Northouse, *Leadership*, 11.
20. See the Introduction to Bennis, *On Becoming a Leader*.
21. Ledbetter, Banks, and Greenhalgh, *Reviewing Leadership*, 14.
22. Wills, *Certain Trumpets*, 20.

at an umpire, kicking a base, and getting tossed out of the game. One coach's definition might derive from the relationship; another's, from the goal.

Move into the corporate context of leaders like PepsiCo's Indra Nooyi and Apple's Tim Cook, and leadership is about pressing people to maximize their performance, increase the profits of the corporation, and beat the competition. There is no room for small changes to small things (incrementalism). Terms and phrases like efficiency, tasks, productivity, organizational management, creating value for the customer and the shareholder, accountability, and results create leadership's meaning.

The political world requires a different definition of leadership. No matter the global context, political leadership is about governing, guiding, and mustering the necessary support to carry out policies. Definitions take into account a fair amount of bureaucracy. Those called to this context are often complex figures, further complicating descriptions.

Consider biographer William Manchester's opening account of Winston Churchill, a man who was, in Manchester's estimation, England's most singular statesman. He was "a brilliant, domineering, intuitive, inconsiderate, self-centered, emotional, generous, ruthless, visionary, megalomaniacal, and heroic genius who inspires fear, devotion, rage, and admiration among his peers."[23] Or reflect upon speechwriter Ray Price's description of American President Richard Nixon: "Exceptionally considerate, caring, sentimental, generous of spirit, kind . . . angry, vindictive, ill-tempered, and mean spirited."[24] So much for simple classifications.

Political leadership requires an ability to both go it alone and reach across the aisle. Diplomacy and persuasion are core skills. As Wills puts it, the audience has to be worked with many thousands of strings, and the strings must be kept from tangling.[25] Governing also requires the shrewd use of power. Witness current world leaders like Syria's Bashar al-Assad, Nigeria's Muhammadu Buhari, or Germany's Angela Merkel. Leaders of nations have to be ambitious, adept at climbing to the top, and skillful in persuading others to give them more control.[26] Some are small-time figures; others are larger than life. It was once said of American President Theodore Roosevelt, "You got to the White House, you shake hands with Roosevelt and hear him talk – and then

---

23. Manchester, *Last Lion*, 3.
24. Quoted in Thomas, *Being Nixon*, loc. 9600.
25. Wills, *Certain Trumpets*, 33.
26. Caro, *Years of Lyndon Johnson*, 19.

you go home to wring the personality out of your clothes."[27] Historians might be tasked to interpret the world, but political leaders are called to change it.

Unlike other leadership contexts, where the power of a leader grows over time (e.g. a university president, a CEO, a head of a union), the power of political leadership can evaporate quickly. In American political culture, the widest window of opportunity is the first hundred days.[28] Hence, in this definition of leadership, efficiency and urgency have to be part of the description. Leaders dare not be slow in discerning the expectations of their constituents and carrying out an appropriate agenda.

In the military world, where dedication, service, honor, courage, and warriorship are prized, the definitions of leadership are more hierarchical and heroic. Those who lead, be they acting American Secretary of Defense Patrick Shanahan or Russian General Anatoliy Serdyukov, must process large amounts of information, think systemically, develop situational awareness, lead valiantly in chaotic situations, and use their intuition.[29] They must shape followers who will not question their command but carry out the mission with military precision.

What about the nonprofit world? What defines a religious leader? Is there any difference between the leadership required to lead a church and the leadership needed to run a corporation or lead an army? Some years ago, Eugene Peterson wrote a stinging rebuke directed at pastors who had left their calling and metamorphosed into other kinds of leaders (like CEOs), leaders ill-equipped to serve the church.[30]

A pastor's essential role is to give expression to the faith and keep the community attentive to God. This is at the core of spiritual leadership. One is set apart for a vocation of shepherding souls, not managing an institution. One's best leadership is more private than public, not devoted to managing the organization but committed to prayer, reading Scripture, and giving spiritual direction.[31]

As these few examples demonstrate, context goes a long way toward defining leadership. In his analysis of leaders, Michael Useem, a professor of management, notes that leadership acquires nearly as many incarnations as there are analysts and consultants.[32] Whatever your objective – be it winning a

---

27. Morris, *Rise of Theodore Roosevelt*, xxxi.
28. Gergen, *Eyewitness to Power*, 350.
29. Wheatley, *Who Do We Choose to Be?*, 57.
30. See Peterson, *Working the Angles*.
31. Peterson, 2.
32. Useem, *Leadership Moment*, 4.

football game, earning a profit, winning a war, governing a nation, or leading a church – it requires a certain kind of leader and a different definition of leadership. Hence, if you distill leadership definitions to one sentence, things will get confused.

Conditions Influence Definition

It's not only the context that shapes a definition of leadership. The state of affairs at a particular moment will influence leadership's description.[33] Is a nation at peace, or has it been attacked? Time and place and conditions matter. John Adair, the world's first professor of leadership, once noted: "It is difficult to be a great leader in Luxembourg in a time of peace."[34] Peacetime and wartime require different kinds of leaders.

In her chapter "Peacetime Management and Wartime Leadership," consultant Judith Bardwick notes that peacetime leaders tend toward the status quo. Peacetime *management* might be a more accurate description. In war, leadership is anything but focused on the status quo. Leaders are out in front, creating strategies, bringing change, and generating confidence.[35]

Robert Gates, while serving as US Secretary of Defense, observed that military leadership and success in war are not the same as those required in peacetime. He writes, "In war, boldness, adaptability, creativity, sometimes ignoring the rules, risk taking, and ruthlessness are essential for success." He adds, "These are not characteristics that will get an officer very far in peacetime."[36]

Circumstances create leaders, as well as the type of leaders. What would William of Orange or the Duke of Marlborough have been without Louis XIV, Pitt without Napoleon, Washington without George III, and Lincoln without the slave interest?[37] Who would Churchill have become without the Boer War? In Churchill's case, the conflict offered him an irresistible opportunity for personal glory, and it catapulted him into the House of Commons.[38]

Ever-changing times shift definitions. Younger, emerging leaders tend to view existing leadership definitions and forms as archaic and inadequate. In some global contexts, authoritarian styles have given way to a more egalitarian

---

33. Ledbetter, Banks, and Greenhalgh, *Reviewing Leadership*, 5.
34. Quoted in Roberts, *Hitler and Churchill*, loc. 409.
35. Bardwick, "Peacetime Management and Wartime Leadership," 134.
36. Gates, *Duty*, 576.
37. Hayward, *Greatness*, 165.
38. Millard, *Hero of the Empire*, 164.

approach. The turbulence of economic upheaval and world wars in the first half of the twentieth century required an authoritarian style of leadership. Leaders tended to impose their will on followers, inducing obedience and respect. Men like Czar Nicholas, Winston Churchill, Douglas MacArthur, Josip Tito, and Mahatma Gandhi were some of these larger than life leaders.

In the post-world war era, the circumstances have changed. The desire and need for strong, authoritative leaders have altered. Moving into the twenty-first century, leadership has become less commanding and more collegial, be it in Norway or Japan. Those following the "Boomer" generation are suspicious of traditional forms of authority, all of which is affecting how leadership is defined and carried out.

In some global settings, the coach has replaced the general. Other contemporary metaphors include symphony conductor (conducts by being conducted), air traffic controller (essential but invisible), or narrator (listens and allows for creativity).[39]

Leadership definitions must take into account that there is less emphasis on professional performance and more emphasis on participation.[40] A leader today is less a tour guide, more a fellow traveler joining others on the journey. Leaders today have a lower profile and carry a shorter lead.[41]

Cultures Influence Definition

While there are certain commonalities, different ethnicities have their own perspectives on leadership's meaning. In Africa and the Middle East, the sheikocratic leadership style is prevalent. It has strong paternalistic components, fitting within a tribal culture. Raised in this context, one will have a different definition from someone who has grown up in northern Europe, or nearby Israel, where egalitarian values define most leaders.

Researching the development of Chinese church leaders, Otto Lui concludes that culture is decisive in shaping the expectations of the leader, as well as the pattern of leadership development.[42] In cultures with a respect for age, position, titles, education, and defined social hierarchies (Asia, Africa, Latin America), followers tend to place leaders on pedestals. In this "high power distance" relationship, they expect their leaders to make unilateral decisions. In almost every case, they yield to the will of their leaders.

---

39. Hjalmarson, "Kingdom Leadership."
40. Gibbs, *Leadership Next*, 24.
41. Murray, "After the Revolt."
42. Lui, *Development of Chinese Church Leaders*, 271.

On the other hand, in cultures characterized by "low power distance" (those mainly in the West), followers expect leaders to involve them in the decision-making process. Everyone shares in the power and authority. Outcomes are a result of collaboration.

Multiple definitions and expectations of leadership are certain to lead to confusion and misunderstanding. Underneath are different cultural values about leadership.[43] One will need to decode and chart a wise course. In her book *The Culture Map*, Erin Meyer identifies eight areas leaders must navigate: Communication, Evaluating, Persuading, Leading, Deciding, Trusting, Disagreeing, and Scheduling.[44] Knowing how people define leaders is the starting point.

I discovered this in the Netherlands, where I pastored an international church. Some thirty-five different nationalities came together for worship every Sunday. I soon realized that there were multiple assumptions about my role as a congregational leader.

Hardly a month went by in those seven years when I did not commit some leadership faux pas. For some, I was too autocratic and overbearing ("Who is he to suggest we refine our mission and vision statements?"). For others, I was too passive and complacent ("When is he going to step out and lead?"). Some preferred a more functional leader; others a more relational leader.

Tensions and anxieties stalked my path. In some homes I visited, there were both deference and reverence. It stood to reason. Their cultures were more paternal and communal. In other meetings, I was received but somewhat ignored. In yet others, I could sense there was an ongoing "feud" between leader and followers. Their idea of a good leadership book would have had the title *The Unstoppable Power of Leaderless Organizations*. The Dutch valued linear-time, while the Antilleans lived in a world of flexible-time, and this impacted their leadership assumptions. And so it went.

In leading multiple cultures, I learned that there are no superior or inferior cultural approaches to – or definitions of – leadership. Survival depended upon being both an egalitarian and a hierarchical leader. Ultimately, it meant learning to lead in different ways in order to motivate and mobilize groups dissimilar from those back home.

---

43. Plueddemann, 71.
44. Meyer, *Culture Map*, 15–16.

Traits, Personalities, and Styles Influence Definition

If contexts, conditions, and cultures are not enough to confuse one's definition, let's throw in a leader's particular traits. Trait studies have sought to identify those characteristics that distinguish leaders from non-leaders. In the American culture in which I grew up, those in the upper echelons of leadership tend to be dominant, self-confident, and goal-oriented. Tracking those who have been successful in business, consultants like Jim Collins note that those leaders have an inner intensity, a massive determination, and a dedication to making anything that is touched be the best it can possibly be.[45]

Standout leaders tend to have ultra-gregarious personalities. They make the noise and dominate the scene. Steve Jobs of Apple was an American success story. He led a high-tech revolution, and he did it with a mercurial personality. His presence could demoralize or inspire. Jobs was the type who had zero tolerance for those who underperformed. His bombastic style of leadership attracted some and distanced others. Some found his mannerism daring; others found it repulsive. Some could not handle his withering words; others withstood them. Those who endured actually thrived and did things they never dreamed possible.

But these traits are not universally appreciated. A mercurial personality might work in a task-oriented culture, but it will set things back in a relationship-based society.

What does work? In his research of current leadership styles in the North African church, Farida Saidi concludes that there is no standard list of personality traits that define a leader.[46] Some are flaming extroverts; others are shy, retiring introverts who avoid public speeches and prefer to lock themselves in their offices. Some are impulsive; others are methodical and calculating. Certain leaders are austere, while others are ostentatious. A number of leaders are tough and ruthless (e.g. Attila the Hun – "Heads I win; tails you lose"); others are the sensitive, nurturing type, determined that everyone wins. In one global context, you find a leader who is modest and self-effacing; in another, a leader who is incredibly vain. Pope John Paul II refused to bring glory to himself. Churchill's idea of a fine meal was to dine well and discuss a serious topic – "with myself as a chief conversationalist."[47] Driven by a sense

---

45. Collins, *Good to Great*, 25.
46. Saidi, *Study of Current Leadership Styles*, 14.
47. Manchester, *Last Lion*, 17.

of destiny, one journalist described Churchill as "a person of titanic self-regard that occasionally verged on the half-mad."[48]

No wonder finding a definition agreeable to all is impossible. Leader types are all over the map. Or are they? After many years as a management consultant, Drucker concluded that leadership personalities, styles, and traits do not actually exist at all.[49] In the end, it depends upon what the situation demands. However, he made this ironic observation: "The one and only *personality trait* the effective ones I have encountered did have in common was something they did *not* have: they had little or no 'charisma' and little use either for the term or for what it signifies."[50]

Worldview Influences Definition

Finally, the diversity of worldviews complicates a working definition of leadership. A worldview is a complex and multifaceted fabric of beliefs. A worldview includes one's assumptions about reality, God, humanity, history, morality, concept of time, relationship roles, humanity's place and purpose in relation to the world, and death. These inform how one leads.

In much of the West, theism and naturalism dominate, with deism serving as an isthmus between these two continents.[51] As a result, leadership is more an issue of function, of directing others toward clear goals and execution. Efficiency, predictability, and control are valued in a leader. Time is a commodity to be segmented and used.

In the East, pantheistic monism, Eastern mysticism, and Confucianism are prevailing worldviews. Leadership development is viewed as a process of personal growth, which develops the human nature into its fullest potential.[52] Living harmoniously is a core value, and achieving a moral life is a chief aim. Here, the practice of a leader is less functional and more relational. The goal is to develop followers into morally perfect humans. One's inner life matters far more than one's management skills.

In parts of the world under a totalitarian worldview, devoid of God and liberty, compliance is a key part of how one defines leaders and followers. Collaboration and consensus are largely absent. Those who rule are power wielders determined to centralize control.

---

48. Noonan, "Churchill's Adversaries Weren't His Enemies."
49. Drucker, "Not Enough Generals," xi.
50. Drucker, xii.
51. Sire, *Universe Next Door*, 53.
52. Lui, *Development of Chinese Church Leaders*, 79.

Coming to a Definition – or at Least a Consensus

Our brief survey confirms what we stated from the beginning: there is simply no universally accepted definition of leadership. It's not for lack of research; it may be more a lack of agreement on what matters and what doesn't. Still, I would propose there are at least three elements that contexts, conditions, cultures, styles, and worldviews affirm:

Leaders Have Followers

The cliché is true – "The best test of leadership is whether or not anyone is following."[53] You can be a chief, a hero, a head of clan, a general, a captain, an owner, a conqueror, a sage, a king, an imam, an emperor, a shaman, a president, a CEO, a coach, a priest, *or whatever* – but if no one is following, you are not a leader.

Leaders cannot exist independent of followers.[54] Many of the best writers on leadership affirm this somewhere in their opening words. Recall Peter Drucker's words quoted earlier: "The only definition of a leader is someone who has followers."[55] John Maxwell, who has sold nearly twenty million books on the subject, remarks: "He who thinks he leads, but has no followers, is only taking a walk."[56] Kouzes and Posner, co-authors of some of the most important books on leadership, concur: "A person with no constituents is not a leader."[57] According to Burns, followership gets to the very definition of leadership: "I define leadership as leaders inducing followers to act for certain goals that represent the values and the motivations – the wants and needs, the aspirations and expectations – *of both leaders and followers*."[58]

In sum, the test of a leader is not temperament or virtue, giftedness or vision, but the ability to acquire followers. Leaders take people with them. They have to. A single person cannot achieve a great vision.

Lui calls the influence of followers in Eastern culture "decisive," making the development of followers a top priority in leadership.[59] In every context, effective leaders consciously manage the dynamics of their relationship. They

53. Ledbetter, Banks, and Greenhalgh, *Reviewing Leadership*, 11.
54. Burns, *Leadership*, 77.
55. Drucker, "Not Enough Generals," xii.
56. Maxwell, *21 Irrefutable Laws*, 20.
57. Kouzes and Posner, *Leadership Challenge*, 11.
58. Burns, *Leadership*, 18.
59. Lui, *Development of Chinese Church Leaders*, 77.

give significant energy to recruiting, equipping, and inspiring followers to fulfill their mutual goals. Leaders focus on the things that attract followers:

- constancy (they stay the course)
- congruity (they walk the talk)
- reliability (they are there when it counts)
- integrity (they honor their commitment)
- competence (they know what they are doing)
- compassion (they are exceptional listeners)
- discernment (they see life through the eyes of their followers)
- team (they aim for a mutually determinative activity)
- character (they pay attention to the condition of their hearts)

In similar fashion, leaders pay attention to what repels followers:

- inconsistency (constantly shifting)
- hypocrisy (not walking the talk)
- undependability (not there when needed)
- immorality (lacking character)
- deception (forsaking truth-telling)
- ineptitude (not up to the task)
- heartlessness (goals at the expense of relationships)
- imperceptiveness (unable to see what leaders must see)
- self-centeredness (in a word, a narcissist)

In their relationship to followers, leaders exercise different styles of leadership. Some are more transactional, while others are more transformational.[60] Transactional leaders fulfill the needs of followers through the exchange of interests. Benefits are exchanged for loyalty, jobs are exchanged for votes.

On the other hand, transformational leaders recognize the needs of followers and seek to meet these by elevating their potential. Leaders and followers raise one another to higher levels of motivation and morality. Under the right leadership, followers can become leaders, outrunning those they followed.

Alexander the Great was a transformational leader who unified a nation around his vision. He was attentive to the confidence levels of those he led; he paid constant attention to morale. Alexander lifted his followers to their better selves. He made his followers believe they could conquer anyone; hence they were willing to go over a cliff for him.

---

60. Burns, *Leadership*: see Parts 3 and 4.

The American President Franklin D. Roosevelt was a transactional leader who gave his followers the benefit of his time. He confided in them, as well as consulted with them. He did not ignore or talk down. He was smart enough to sense what the people wanted, and he knew how to find common ground. In exchange, they gave both their time and their loyalty.

Because followers are at different stages, multiple approaches to leading are necessary. In her book on followership, Barb Kellerman classifies four kinds of followers – bystanders, participants, activists, and diehards.[61] Paul Hersey and Ken Blanchard use different language, but agree that leaders should make their behavior contingent upon the followers and their state of readiness.[62] One's style of leading is determined by the willingness and ableness of followers. Servant leadership is another model that is oriented toward the interests of followers.[63] Words like sacrifice, empathy, foresight, listening, and commitment to growth characterize their leading.[64]

There are moments a leader may have to go it alone, but these are rare. John F. Kennedy, a former American president, studied leaders in Congress who occasionally defied their constituents.[65] Ironically, Kennedy praised them at the very point where they ceased to be leaders.[66] But they remained leaders, for their boldness to lead above popularity eventually led to a greater followership.

Leaders Have Influence

Here's a second element that goes to the core of leadership's meaning: leaders impact. They are integral players, often with outsized personalities and forceful actions, who change the landscape. To use Wheatley's new science terminology, leaders fill the space by creating a "leadership field." This "field" serves as a vital effect – that is, influence – on followers.[67] Influence works its way into followers, raising aspirations and provoking actions.

Rost, in his *Leadership for the Twenty-First Century*, refers to leadership as "an influence relationship."[68] Likewise, Peter Northouse describes leadership as "a process whereby an individual *influences* a group of individuals to achieve

---

61. See Kellerman, *Followership*.

62. See Paul Hersey and Ken Blanchard, *Management of Organizational Behavior.*

63. Note Ledbetter, Banks, and Greenhalgh, *Reviewing Leadership*, 13; and Branson and Martinez, *Churches, Cultures, and Leadership*, 108.

64. Greenleaf, *On Becoming a Servant Leader*, 33–35.

65. Kennedy, *Profiles in Courage*, 10.

66. Wills, *Certain Trumpets*, 23.

67. Wheatley, *Who Do We Choose to Be?*, 55–56.

68. Rost, *Leadership for the Twenty-First Century*, 104.

a common goal."[69] Influence is the sine qua non of leadership. "Without influence, leadership does not exist."[70] Influence outpaces other things, including authority. John Maxwell sums up leadership's definition in one word: influence. Leadership is nothing more and nothing less.[71]

In the conclusion of his classic on leadership, Burns writes, "The most lasting and pervasive leadership of all is intangible and non-institutional. It is the leadership of *influence* fostered by ideas embodied in social or religious or artistic movements, in books, in great seminal documents, in the memory of great lives greatly lived."[72] Warren Bennis adds that the basis of leadership is the capacity of the leader to change the mindset, the framework, of another person; in a word, "influence."[73]

In his book *Spiritual Leadership*, J. Oswald Sanders begins his fourth chapter with the words, "Leadership is influence, the ability of one person to influence others to follow his or her lead. Famous leaders have known this."[74] Bobby Clinton describes leadership as a dynamic process in which one influences the thoughts and actions of followers toward the accomplishment of aims beneficial for leaders, followers, and the macro context of which they are a part.[75]

Atatürk is an impressive example. He founded modern Turkey because he was an influential and forceful leader. He clarified within himself his personal goals, identified those he determined to lead, and overcame whatever obstacles were found in his path. He changed his world. His words and actions carried weight. His initiatives brought about a cultural revolution, a democratic structure, and an internal order. He put religion in a more subservient place, creating an "Islam-within-secularism." He divided the Allies and defeated the last Sultan. Under his influence, Turkey became self-reliant. A backward economy became the world's seventeenth largest economy, and an inconsequential nation became a regional power.[76] What a difference-maker!

Winston Churchill's leadership is also a model of influence. At significant moments in history, he imposed his imagination and his will upon his fellow citizens. In time of war, he idealized his followers with such intensity that in

---

69. Northouse, *Leadership*, 3.
70. Northouse, 3.
71. Maxwell, *21 Irrefutable Laws*, 13.
72. Burns, *Leadership*, 454.
73. Quoted in Tichy, *Leadership Engine*, 42.
74. Sanders, *Spiritual Leadership*, 27.
75. Clinton, *Making of a Leader*, 14.
76. Mango, *Atatürk*, 532–539.

the end they approached his ideal and began to see themselves as he saw them. In doing so, he transformed cowards into brave men.[77] That's influence born of leadership.

In the end, it's not status or position that makes a difference. Influential leaders carry a certain gravitas – a force in the eye, a power in one's voice, and a dynamism in one's bearing.[78] They hold the views they espouse, and they can make their case. Another English leader comes to mind: Margaret Thatcher. Her force of will and her resolute, righteous convictions compelled a nation to follow. Her words carried weight, and her actions changed her world. Henrietta Mears was another influencer. She was a remarkable teacher and formidable leader because she made a significant impression on the lives of people like Bill Bright and Billy Graham.[79] Billy Graham remains a symbol of godly leadership for Americans because he influenced many influencers, including numerous American presidents.

Leaders Have a Direction

Followers. Influence. But there is one more characteristic that is true of all leaders. Without it, the first two gain little traction. Those who lead set forth a clear, steady path into the future. In his *Understanding Leadership*, Tom Marshall begins by stating that the first essential characteristic of leaders is that they are going somewhere.[80] They are always on the way, and the main work of leadership is to mobilize people toward that way. Leaders are not content to preserve the inherited institution; they intend to lead a vision-based and mission-focused community forward.[81] Without some result, some end point, there is little support for leadership.[82]

Again, Northouse's words bear repeating: "The component common to nearly all of the classifications is that leadership is an influence process that assists groups of individuals toward goal attainment."[83] Leaders are those out in front, having a particular direction, a compelling cause, a clear vision, and certain goals. They are forward looking, asking the question, "What is next?" They set a course, which helps to create followers.

---

77. Manchester, *Last Lion*, 454.
78. Morrow, "Gravitas Factor," 94.
79. See Roe, *Dream Big*.
80. Marshall, *Understanding Leadership*, 9.
81. Gibbs, *Leadership Next*, 38.
82. Grint, *Leadership*, 8.
83. Northouse, *Leadership*, 11.

It might be a physical destination and physical results. Think of Ernest Shackleton, the Antarctic explorer, who was able to lead his men to safety because he could mobilize their wills in a single direction and toward a defined end. Napoleon was successful as a military leader because he was directional. He motivated his armies with the words "Fight toward the supplies." It might also be a spiritual direction leading to spiritual results. Martin Luther nailed his ninety-five theses on the door of a Wittenberg church, and it served to start the Reformation.

In the end, if one considers oneself to be a leader, but does not work within the framework of a mission and a vision and tangible goals, one is deceiving oneself. Followers look to leaders who have a compelling cause, who set out goals that are mutually shared and mutually owned.[84]

Summarizing What We Hear

Bringing these initial voices together provides a starting point for defining leadership. They are incomplete in themselves, but they help us toward a working definition of leadership: *A leader is someone who has followers who follow because a leader has a sense of direction and is influencing people to move in that path.*

The Voices We Need To Hear

As helpful as this initial analysis might be, our voices have been largely Western. How would a leader in the East, Japan in particular, define leadership? I sought out a ministry leader and author, Takeshi Takazawa, who has served in numerous leadership roles. He is currently involved in leadership development in Japan and parts of Asia.

The Voice of Takeshi Takazawa, Asian Director, Asian Access/Japan

I am a Japanese national. I was born and raised in Tokyo, Japan. I continue to work in Japan, as well as other parts of Asia. I am committed to developing leaders, both in church and in non-church settings. I have been grappling with issues of leadership for over thirty years.

Asia is a diverse area divided into smaller geographical regions such as East Asia, Southeast Asia, Central Asia, South Asia, and West Asia (a.k.a. the

---

84. Wills, *Certain Trumpets*, 17.

Middle East). Context does impact our understanding of leadership and how it is expressed. It is different from culture to culture and region to region. While there are many cultural similarities across Asia, there are also regional differences that influence our perceptions and our practices.

Because of this, it would be presumptuous for me to claim to have the "Asian" perspective, but I can say that my assessment comes strongly from East Asia. East Asian countries (China, Hong Kong, Japan, North and South Korea, and Taiwan) are high context cultures with shared history and development. This is evident in our philosophical and religious roots, our writing systems, our cultural practices, and our values.

Defining Leadership

How do Japanese people define leadership? Are there similarities with what Western research and practices have discovered? In the first place, East Asian cultures do not start with definitions. Definitions do not have the same importance.

For the West, it is helpful to begin with a definition. This is important to an intellectual understanding of leadership, which then leads to practice. This may be an overgeneralization, but it seems to begin with an understanding (head) that then moves to action (hand). Reflection brings it back to the head for refinement, moving it back to practice that is more effective. In this repetitive cycle, it eventually becomes part of a person (heart).

For those of us in the East, understanding leadership begins with practice (hands). Actions are what inform the heart. Hence, our approach to leadership is different. We value heart and integration more than a mental understanding. This can also be seen in our word for knowledge and information, *kokoroe* (心得), which is made up of the character for heart (心) and the character for gain/grasp (得). Additionally, we often feel that when we define something it loses its meaning, as words are limiting and inadequate to describe what is actually there.

Other voices in the East affirm this approach. Maiqi Ma, writing on leadership, says, "We also need to understand that whereas Western languages are phonetic with one or more brief definitions for each word, the Chinese language is based on characters often described in a metaphorical story. This leads to a Western approach towards decision-making that is more analytical compared to the Chinese which is more holistic."[85]

---

85. Ma, "Leadership in China," 3.

So how do we transfer concepts without explicitly defining them? Since we are a high context culture, we prefer to describe how something may look in different contexts and from there we infer what it is. Descriptions force us to interact and think about what is being described. They become part of an internalized understanding.

We may struggle to define "life," but even a child can intuitively tell the difference between something that is alive and something that is not. It is this sense of intuitive understanding that is valued over verbal definitions. The existence of life does not depend on one's ability to define it. The same is true of leadership.

Instead of giving definitions, we describe different aspects of a concept indirectly. We do this through narratives, proverbs, poems, sayings, and stories. As an example, when leadership is taught to children, it might begin with the stories of three military leaders, the ones who unified the nation of Japan. The first was Nobunaga Oda (1534–1582). The second was the servant to Oda, Hideyoshi Toyotomi (1536–1598). He rose to power, and then he betrayed Oda to become the shogun. The third leader was Leyasu Tokugawa (1543–1616). He fought and overturned Toyotomi. He started the Edo period which lasted through his clan for seventeen generations (1603–1865).

Their comparison is expressed in a poem describing how these three leaders would get a songbird to sing. The poem goes like this:

> Oda: Little songbird, if you don't sing I will kill you, little songbird.
> Toyotomi: Little songbird, if you don't sing I will make you sing, little songbird.
> Tokugawa: Little songbird, if you don't sing I will wait until you sing, little songbird.

Through this story and poem, not only is leadership recognized, but the order is also understood as impacting the meaning. Without passion and quick action (Oda), the country wouldn't have been unified. Without strategy (Toyotomi), he would not have ascended to be the nation's leader. And without patience and long-term thinking (Tokugawa), a lasting system to establish the nation would not have arisen.

Looking at Concepts of Leadership

As you can see, we understand through our hearts and through our descriptions. Before I look more deeply at what leadership looks like to us, I would like to mention some of the strong assumptions we hold about leadership.

The first is that leadership happens in the context of a leader's life. When we think of leadership, we always think of leaders. We focus on the leader and not on the abstract concept of leadership. We have a strong sense that it is not worthwhile to focus on leadership when the leader is the issue. Second, virtue is of central importance. Even though we may not define leadership directly, we do have strong concepts of who a leader is and who we expect a leader to be.

The founder of Panasonic, Konosuke Matsushita (1894–1989), created the post-World War II Japanese model of leadership. He started the Matsushita Institute of Government and Management. One of his textbooks, *Real Leader's Requirements* (1974), unpacks 102 requirements for leaders. Each one deals with a virtue rather than with a technique. The first requirement is that leaders accept everything as it is.[86] In other words, it is not about what the leader likes or dislikes. What the leader accepts is the starting point, which is the good and bad of all people. Leaders must acknowledge and accept this reality.

Mr Matsushita's final requirement in the book is that a leader must be the most humble and most grateful person.[87] (This reminds me of Max De Pree's saying that "the first responsibility of a leader is to define reality and the last is to say thank you."[88]) While the approach may be different, there are commonalities between the ideal Japanese and ideal Western leader.

It is not that the concepts of leadership discussed earlier – followers, influence, and direction – are unimportant. But they need to be understood in a high context culture, specifically Japan and East Asia. This will lead to a better perception of what we mean by leadership.

Followers

East Asian cultures strongly value vertical relationships. There are leaders and there are followers. In school, we call those in the grade ahead of us *senpai* (先輩), the one who comes before, and those in the grade below call us *senpai*. We are a vertical society. We honor those who are older or more experienced than us, whether they are positionally the top leaders or not. We are constantly aware of who is ahead and who is behind. It is ingrained in our language. The speech we use to speak to *senpai* is deferential, while the language we speak as *senpai* is not.

We are also highly communal cultures. Therefore, leadership is never about one person; it always includes followers. Followers create leaders. Leadership

---

86. Konosuke Matsushita, *Real Leader's Requirements*, 18.
87. Matsushita, 220.
88. De Pree, *Leadership Is an Art*, 11.

and followership are two sides of the same coin. They are held together in community. We are all followers. There are generations before us that we follow. This is not about blindly following the past but a conscious awareness of those before us. We have a deep respect for them and a strong sense that we are building on their work and have much to learn from them.

In the Western view, there isn't the same value placed on followers and/ or followership. Greater emphasis is given to individual leaders. Leadership is something that is separate from the group. It is carried inside the leader, and the leader brings it to wherever it is needed. Leadership starts and ends with that leader. This is very different from East Asian thinking. In Asia, leadership happens amongst people and community, and it continues beyond the leader's life.

One of my North American friends was a manager of a US Fortune 500 company. He wanted to honor one of his Japanese project leaders for his excellent performance. The project leader begged my friend not to single him out, as the project would not have been successful apart from his team. He turned down the offered award and the bonus. He said that he would receive it only if everyone else on his team did as well. This underscores the communal perspective. Leadership cannot be isolated apart from the group.

Influence

To be a leader is to have influence. Influence, however, is determined by the followers. It goes back to the level of trust between the leader and the group. While the leader is in a position above, it is not as a ruler over, but as the person responsible for the group. It is understood that the leader's job is to take care of and look out for the followers. Influence comes from trust in the leader's ability to do so. The greater the trust, the greater the influence.

The essence of influence is virtue or worthiness of character. People follow the example of the leader and the leader is expected to be worthy of being followed. We have an expression that says that leaders are raised by watching the back of the leader in front of them.

Influence comes directly from character and how you live. In his book *Bushido*, and its discussion on the education of young samurai, Inazo Nitobe notes that a leader's chief aim is character. People whose minds are simply stored with information find no great admirers.[89] When a leader possesses virtue, we trust the leader and influence happens. When someone is all talk and no character, that person has little to no influence on the group.

---

89. Nitobe, *Bushido*, 68.

Masakatsu Hayashi, who has twenty years of experience training leaders with Toyota, says that the essence of leader development is acquiring character. Without character, it does not matter if people have incredible skills and talents. You can't use them to lead others. The fifth CEO of Toyota, Mr Eiji Toyoda, who made Toyota a worldwide company, shares a similar philosophy: "If humans are not 'made' or developed themselves, then they can't make things. In order to make high quality products, they focus on high quality people."[90]

Direction

Leaders have direction. In Japanese, the word most often used for leader is *shidousha* (指導者).These three characters depict a finger (指) which refers to pointing, then guidance (導), and lastly a person (者). A leader for us is someone who points in a certain direction and guides us there. Leaders take their followers from one place to another.

Where does this direction come from? The context is time and continuity. We cannot ignore the past since the present is a direct result of the past. Our nations are thousands of years old. We cannot grasp a goal or a vision that is not connected to our history since the present consists of past decisions. The context shapes the person, and thus history shapes the leader.

All leaders think in terms of spans of time and eras. We expect leaders to have a strong consciousness of the past, present, and future. In the Modern Japanese translation of his book, Yukichi Fukuzawa (the founder of Keio University and honored on our 10,000 yen bill) states that "our task is to leave the legacy of our life for the future generations to build on."[91]

We look at the generations before us and think about the impact of their leadership on us. We also think about our impact on the generations to come. We expect our leaders to have a strong awareness of the gravity of leadership as well as of their place in a long and continuing history. Direction is the continuation of influence and followership. It is rooted in our history and in our responsibility to future generations that will become our history.

Lessons from an Asian World

In reflecting on Takeshi's contribution, it is clear that an Asian voice resets the start point. A definition of leadership does not begin with the comparative study of theories. Leadership is defined, first of all, by the lives of leaders.

---

90. Quoted in Hayashi, *Genba o nameruna AsaShuppan*, 40, author's translation.
91. Fukuzawa, *Gendaigoyaku Gakumonnosussume ChikuwaShinsho*, 125.

Much like looking at the different facets of a diamond that reflects the light, different lives show different aspects of leadership. Universal leadership concepts shine differently through the lives of leaders in differing contexts. These become the working material for defining a leader.

The Voices of Mark Greene, Executive Director, The London Institute for Contemporary Christianity, UK, and Alex Kulpecz, Executive Chairman of Kerogen Exploration, a North American Oil and Gas Company

Mark Greene and Alex Kulpecz represent Western voices, ones we have heard in the first section. Nonetheless, I include them here because we sometimes miss the voices of ministry and corporate leaders in dialogue.

Mark and Alex operate in different worlds, one a nonprofit and one a profit. Leadership looks different. In common, the leaders carry the weight of leadership responsibilities. They have also enjoyed a long friendship. When I met them in London, they reflected on leadership definitions and other leadership themes.

How do you define leadership?
Greene: Leadership is often reduced to mere influence. Anyone who influences is a leader. But I believe that leadership is more than influence. Leadership involves organizational decision making. Leaders spur others to action, transcending mere intellectual assent.

Here in the UK, I work closely with churches. Some people occupy positions of leadership, but this does not mean they have the gift of leadership. Indeed, there has been a very damaging conflation of positional leadership and actual ability, meaning that many churches find themselves ill led by pastors. They may be brilliantly gifted in all kinds of ways, but not necessarily as organizational or community leaders.

Kulpecz: In the corporate world where I have worked for most of my life, I have found that defining leadership is difficult. There is a complexity to leadership, as already noted. That said, you know leadership when you see it. What do you see? Someone with passion, someone thoroughly committed to the common good, and someone who draws people to one another and the mission.

What could church leadership learn from corporate leadership?
Kulpecz: Corporate leadership tends to bring a discipline to ideas and results. I have been deeply involved in the church and its leadership, and discipline is

often missing. Corporate leaders do not – in fact they cannot – make excuses for a lack of performance. But churches do this all too often.

What could corporate leadership learn from church leadership?
Greene: I am not sure corporate leadership can learn very much from ministry leaders. I have not found that the best ministry leaders are any better at leading than the best corporate leaders.

A biblical view of leadership emphasizes servanthood, character, and care for people. The best church leadership, as well as the best military, political, and corporate leadership, models these. Authors like Jim Collins and Fred Kiel affirm this. Humility and service are critical to effective leadership, no matter the context. But there are costs. Believers in the workplace who bring a moral framework and a respect for the dignity of human worth will conflict with those driven by a financial bottom line.

What distinguishes a British leader?
Greene: That may be easier for an American to answer. What I do see in our iconic, historical leaders is a unique combination of bulldog determination and reserve. Men like Ernest Shackleton and Winston Churchill come to mind. Margaret Thatcher was tenacious and determined, and somewhat reserved, but not so generous to those who disagreed with her.

Our contemporary icons tend to be of a different mix. Today we think of leaders like Richard Branson, who distinguish themselves by their entrepreneurial, can-do spirit. They are David vs Goliath kind of characters.

What distinguishes an American leader?
Kulpecz: The first thing that comes to mind is a rugged sort of toughness. In American culture, successful leaders need a thick skin and a hardened exterior to survive the rough and tumble of leadership. Effective leaders make the difficult decisions, no matter how they might make people feel. Like the Brits, American leaders value tenacity. They don't give up. They are not inclined to think they will fail.

How important are teams?
Kulpecz: Teams are critical to effective leadership. Capable leaders build teams and work for synergy. Given a more egalitarian structure, leadership requires involvement on everyone's part.

Greene: It is the same in our culture. Teams are vital. No one gets anywhere, no one accomplishes anything of significance, and no one's leadership is sustained without them.

How do leaders deal with conflict?

Kulpecz: Leaders in an American corporate world tend to get things out into the open. Working relationships are vital, so things are not left unsaid (most of the time).

Greene: It depends upon the type of conflict. Is it rooted in strategic differences? It might be a personality clash. It could be ornery competitiveness. In general, however, good leaders aren't afraid of differences. If there are disagreements, leaders tend to deal with them promptly, with hope and without judgment.

Lessons from a Corporate and a Ministry World

Listening simultaneously to these two leadership voices can be of great benefit. There is much to learn from them both, even if they sometimes clash. I have seen this firsthand, as I have led ministries in which most of the congregants were corporate leaders. Sometimes, those in ministry demonstrate a certain naiveté, believing that everything they need to know about leadership is found in the Bible. They miss the fact that corporate leaders live in a world of disciplines and metrics, strategies and goals, and they have much to teach ministry.

Likewise, those in the corporate world can learn from ministry leaders that what matters more than efficiency and performance is relationships and respect. Leaders who are tough and tenacious have their place, but only if love and service drive their lives.

The Voice We Must Hear

Hearing other cultural voices widens our grasp of leadership. Discerning the voice of God expands our imagination. We move into spaces new and unexplored. We transcend our own conceptions.

One might ask, "Does God have any answers to this question of leadership definition? Does he make any contribution? Is God even interested?" These are fair questions, even though many are not asking them. Few leaders think theologically. This includes some ministers and priests! Most leaders have been educated in other fields where psychology, sociology, and business theory dominate, and the discipline of theology is relegated to divinity schools and religious subjects.

It is, however, about more than educational background. An increasing number of people are pushing back against the notion that there are solid, enduring truths. But then it is in our nature to ignore, even suppress, the truth of God. Though the existence of God and his power and nature – and wisdom – are revealed in nature and the human conscience, we have a tendency to be more impressed with our own knowledge, our own ideas about everything, including leadership (Rom 1:18–19).

Why Theology Matters

Theologians describe theology as an aspect of thought and conversation for all who live and breathe, who wrestle and fear, who hope and pray[92] – and, I would add, who lead and guide. Theology frames all of life's subjects, including leadership. It takes us back to God.

We were created for the purpose of knowing God and his ways. It is wisdom to listen to his voice. The God of Scripture is the one true God, and his Word is authoritative for all endeavors, including leading. Leadership may draw from secular theories of leading, but ultimately all forms of leadership take their cue from who God is and what he reveals.

Throughout this book, you will discover (I hope!) that God has much to say about leadership. It might expand your leadership assumptions. It has expanded mine. It fills in the space. Some years ago, when Catholic priest and professor Henri Nouwen was asked to speak about leadership to a gathering of leaders in Washington, DC, he began with these words: "Without solid theological reflection, future leaders will be little more than pseudo-psychologists, pseudo-sociologists, and pseudo-social workers."[93] A divine perspective will enable us to become genuine leaders.

What Theology Tells Us

The first thing we discover is that the mind and will of God do not contradict many of the truths previously posited.

Leadership Takes on Many Complementary Shapes

Abraham is a patriarch over a people; Joseph is a civil officer in a pagan court; Moses is a shepherd with no outward rank or position; Joshua is a military general in a wilderness; Samuel and Deborah are judges representing a theocracy; and Nehemiah serves as a governor. Little wonder there is no exact equivalent to the word "leader" in the Hebrew Bible.

---

92. Kapic, *Little Book for New Theologians*, 16.
93. Nouwen, *In the Name of Jesus*, 65.

It's the same in the New Testament. God gives the church gifted leaders, each office a variation of the other. The church is led by apostles, prophets, evangelists, pastors, and teachers (Eph 4:11). Elsewhere, we find the term "elders" used to describe church leaders (cf. Titus 1:5). Each one has its own shade of meaning. Peter and Paul are apostles who establish a vision for the church; prophets like Agabus come with a centering word from God for the community; Philip the evangelist is carried along by the Spirit, sharing the gospel; Timothy is a pastor who serves among the elders; and Apollos opens up the Scriptures and corrects the body of Christ.

What Scripture illustrates is that diverse leaders complete and correct one another.[94] Leaders need this finishing work. Scripture does not idealize or eulogize. The writers do not airbrush their subjects. We see their strengths as well as their weaknesses. All leaders have feet of clay. David is a warrior king, but Joab is assigned to correct his course (2 Sam 19:7). Kings like Uzziah serve to lead and protect the nation, but prophets emerge to keep their feet to the fire. They speak with words of revelatory force, challenging royalty's settled assumptions of power and authority. Nathan rebukes David, Elijah criticizes Ahab, and Hanani confronts Asa.

Sages are created as another leadership office, and they serve to guide the monarch with authoritative wisdom (Prov 25:1–2). God has preserved their words to counsel us. Priests are raised up to keep the king attentive to God (1 Sam 14:3). Without their support, the king loses his divine right to rule.

In the New Testament, the various offices of leadership serve a similar role, complementing and completing. They are always in creative and dissonant tension with one another. Together, these different roles are essential for the formation of authentic and faithful communities.[95]

Leadership Has Many Contrasting Styles

There is no singular mold that biblical leaders are forced to squeeze into. Some leaders are impulsive, like Samson and Peter. Others are methodical and calculating. Nehemiah prays for months, plans carefully, and sets out to build a wall with meticulous care. Some leaders are austere, like Elijah, and others are ostentatious, like Solomon. Some are relational, like David, and others are task-oriented, like Rehoboam.

Some are vain, like Uzziah. Others are more modest, like Moses ("Now Moses was a very humble man, more humble than anyone else on the face of

---

94. Ledbetter, Banks, and Greenhalgh, *Reviewing Leadership*, 22.
95. Hirsch and Catchim, *Permanent Revolution*, loc. 410.

the earth," Num 12:3) and John the Baptist ("He must become greater; I must become less," John 3:30). Joseph is sure of himself, but Saul and Gideon are not so confident in themselves. Esther wants to keep the peace (Esth 4:11), while Paul is confrontational ("I opposed him to his face," Gal 2:11).

Leadership's Essential Elements Include Followers, Influence, and Direction

In every story, leaders have followers. A true king is one whose army is with him (Prov 30:31). Without followers, a would-be leader is simply a would-be. Withdrawal of popular allegiance topples a leader (e.g. Rehoboam, 1 Kgs 12:1–20). Godly leaders are therefore attentive to their relationship with followers.

Leaders have influence. The strength of Joshua's leadership persuades an army to submit to circumcision before entering battle (Josh 5:2–12). That's influence! Under the encouragement of reformers like Asa and Josiah, a nation comes back to God (1 Kgs 15; 2 Kgs 22). Early church leaders like Peter and John turn the world upside down. Their words still transform lives.

Leaders in Scripture are also directional. Moses points Israel to the promised land and gives a vision of peace and prosperity; Joshua's whole life is forward thinking; David envisions the moment the presence of God will return and compel the people to build the temple; Josiah points people to the fear of God; and Nehemiah is able to effectively lead because he is resolved to carry out his mission to build the wall. And Paul has his eyes on the ends of the earth, calling his followers to press on to lay hold of why they were laid hold of by Christ (Rom 15:24; Phil 3:12).

God Is the Essence of Leadership

Here is where theology takes us further than most leadership classes and cultures. Few leadership books will acknowledge this, but leadership definitions begin with God. He is the source of leadership. Leadership is his idea. He alone has influence over everything that has come into being (Gen 1–2).

At times God leads as a suzerain dispensing his law. At other times, he manifests his authority and power as a judge. He has the commanding power of a warrior, the compassionate voice of a shepherd, and the tender love of a mother.

God's Son, Jesus, is the visible incarnation of the invisible God, the polestar of leadership. He and he alone perfectly models both followership ("whatever the Father does the Son also does," John 5:19) and leadership ("As the Father has sent me, I am sending you," John 20:21). Jesus oversees the temple as the perfect high priest. He speaks authoritatively to life as the Sage of sages. He declares his non-negotiable will with the voice of a prophet. He reigns as the King above all kings, the Leader above all leaders.

In every realm, he leads. He is God who speaks and acts, heading his flock as a shepherd, and, paradoxically, expressing his dominance through the identity of a servant. This gets to the definitional heart of leadership. He could have showcased his power. He could have used the sort of force that energizes a crowd, a Douglas MacArthur-type presence that fills a room. Instead, he made himself as nothing (Phil 2:5–11). He gathers his future leaders in an upper room and shows them the true nature of a leader. He takes a towel and a basin and washes the feet of his disciples, reversing all human assumptions of what it means to be a leader (John 13:3–17).[96]

No one fulfills the essential marks of a leader like Jesus. No one has had or has more followers. One day, every knee of every corporate head, leader of every nation and empire, and general of every military might will bow down to him (Phil 2:10–11). No one's influence comes close to his. His life and message still impact a world. Writers like Leighton Ford (*The Transforming Leader*) point to Jesus's strategic and visionary leadership. Robert Greenleaf, founder of the servant leadership movement, regards Jesus as the archetypal leader, the very definition of leadership.[97]

Nothing influences like servant leadership. Words like ambitious, popular, efficient, self-oriented, productive, and transactional have a secondary influence compared to words like faithful, fruitful, transformational, and God-centered. Jesus has direction and purpose in everything he does. He calls men to leave everything and fish for men (Luke 5:10). He points his followers to the future and declares that he is sending them (John 20:21).

This underscores what our Japanese voice declared. Jesus develops servant leadership in the context of following him. The disciples are servant followers and servant leaders. When they lead, they do not cease to be followers. Being a leader and a follower happens simultaneously. The disciples do not follow action steps, but they follow the person of Jesus. Paul talks about following him as he follows Jesus (1 Cor 11:1). It is a concept of followership and leadership that is holistic and dynamic in community. It is not that a person is one or the other. We are both at the same time.

---

96. Johnson, *Under an Open Heaven*, 196.
97. Ledbetter, Banks, and Greenhalgh, *Reviewing Leadership*, 108.

Leaders Are Ultimately God's Instruments

Scripture is the story of God placing men and women in positions of authority to fulfill his will and carry out his rule. This is core to leadership's definition. God is not the supporting actor in our stories; we have bit parts in his.[98] God has not positioned us in stations of authority to exercise our independent wills or create our self-determining dreams. It is not ours to determine who is higher or lower, who gets to sit at the top of the social hierarchy and who doesn't. It is not ours to decide what is natural or abnormal, unquestioned or questioned. It is not a leader's special privilege to define reality – or leadership. God determines all of these. He calls leaders to lead in light of what he decides.

Those of us who lead serve his purposes – "by intention or by accident."[99] He summons men and women to live directional lives, inviting followers to advance God's kingdom and bring about his glory (Gen 12:1; Exod 3:10; Eph 4:10–16; Col 1:24–29; Jas 1:1; 1 Pet 1:1). People might be impressed with their power, but whatever authority they claim is ultimately derived from God (Ps 75:6–7). Some may boast of their influence, but whatever power tribal chiefs, prime ministers, chief executive officers, and military generals amass God uses for his purposes. God turns the hearts of kings whichever way he wishes, like streams (Prov 21:1). Little wonder the psalmist, assessing life around him, simply declares, "The LORD reigns" (Ps 97:1).

Not only does God declare a leader's course, he also determines a leader's time and space. No matter our plans or calculations; all of our days are in God's hands. In the morning we flourish, and in the evening we fade (Ps 90:6). The evidence speaks for itself. Leadership eventually passes out of our hands. Churchill, Chiang Kai-shek, Khrushchev, Sukarno, Nixon, de Gaulle, Gandhi – and every leader before and after – slide or are pushed down the "greasy pole."[100]

Contrasting the greatness of God with the greatness of humankind, Isaiah notes that the tempest eventually carries the rulers of the earth off like stubble (Isa 40:23–24). No one is necessary but God. As one aptly said, "The graveyards are full of indispensable men." *Wise is the leader who admits that God is the writer of the story.*

Those whose lives are transformed by the gospel and the character of God exhibit God's true intentions for leadership. The apostle Paul is a proud and brutish leader, a Hebrew of Hebrews, who meets Jesus on the Damascus road. Grace works in powerful ways to redefine Paul's assumptions about what it

---

98. Vanhoozer, "Letter to an Aspiring Theologian," 31.

99. Langer, "Toward a Biblical Theology of Leadership," 68.

100. Burns, *Leadership*, 424.

means to lead (Phil 3:1–8). Leaders no longer boast of their preeminence; it's not in their MO to have confidence in the flesh. Their relationships are now marked by love and grace. Their authority is sourced in humility. If anyone should measure one's leadership qualities, let it be as a servant of Christ (1 Cor 4:1). This is how it is for those who follow Christ: *God's kingdom works on inverted principles.*

Bringing the Voices Together

So what do all of these voices tell us? If leadership is not so easy to define, it should move us to a certain humility. These voices affirm that we can be different leaders leading in different ways. We can have different styles – even different definitions. No one culture has a handle on leadership's meaning. We need to expand our imaginations, as well as our cultural and theological horizons.

And while a working definition may be useful, it's only a starting point.[101] What's important is to get a grip on who you are. Theology brings us back to earth. It's about God, not us. Our task is to be faithful to the kind of leader we are called to be; and, above all, to be consistent with our theological convictions.

The complexity of defining leadership requires flexible structures. As the church discerns ways to break out of homogeneous units and become more multicultural, there will inevitably be a clash of leadership assumptions. There will be differences in definitions. No one theory of leadership will be sufficient. A posture of mutual submission and respect will be critical.

But just how necessary is leadership? That's the subject of the next chapter.

---

101. Ledbetter, Banks, and Greenhalgh, *Reviewing Leadership*, 5.

2

Establish Your Necessity

How critical is leadership? Does the world turn on the decisions of its leaders? Some who study leadership would say everything rises and falls on those who govern. But is this true? Does leadership affect – significantly affect – organizational outcomes? Are leaders essential, irrelevant, or somewhere in between? What do different voices tell us?

The Voices We Hear

A survey of present writers on leadership can persuade us in different directions.

Leaders Can Be a Problem

Read today's news and you could become convinced that leaders are more of a hindrance than a help. Anarchist philosphers and certain libertarian thinkers argue with conviction that our underlying problems begin with the very concept of leadership.[1] We see this expressed on the streets and on the screen. Criticizing leaders, be they political, religious, or corporate, has become public sport (at least in the West). Populist revolts, largely leaderless, are expressing their disdain for those attempting to govern. There has been a loss of civility.

People do not seem to think twice before spewing their vitriolic words. Leaders are the butt of most jokes, both in front of and behind their backs. Adversaries are constantly assassinating a leader's character. Everything from manhood to IQ are questioned. It's an unruly and disrespectful world out there. To quote writer Anne Lamott, some can't help but feel "like a treadmark on the underpants of life."[2]

---

1. Roberts, *Hitler and Churchill*, loc. 307.
2. Lamott, *Bird By Bird*, 212.

45

So are leaders necessary? Can we go without them? Look at the early hunter-gatherer societies. They operated without a single formal leader. The Vikings settled in Iceland, creating an inclusive and collaborative community where everyone had an equal voice. Their influence has led to some of the most egalitarian, consensus-oriented cultures in today's world.[3]

In contrast, other cultures have found leadership to be a necessary key to societal order and harmony. If problems are to be solved, they must be pushed up the hierarchy. In places like Bangladesh, vertical trumps horizontal. People have been traditionally drawn to a guru model of leadership. The leader is everything. He holds great power, gets all of the credit, and is expected to do everything on his own.[4]

In nearby India, Jeyakaran Emmanuel notes that this has been the traditional assumption regarding many Indian pastors. They are the "intellectual guides" who "have all the power, run everything in the church, and expect the congregation to give."[5] In these contexts, the need for leadership would never be questioned. But times are changing.

Followers Are Disillusioned

The trend is away from hierarchal types with their high power distance. Many have become disheartened with the rising number of leadership failures. As I write, the Catholic Church is going through a leadership crisis of its own, one that goes all the way to the Pope. Pushing problems upwards has only created larger problems. Followers are questioning the long-held assumption that the leader is always right even when the leader is very wrong. They are more attracted to social networks than to tiered organizations.

In an age of growing social technology, leaders are no longer able to hide behind an image of unimpeachable authority. It is more difficult to create distance, to keep followers beyond their gaze and blind to their common failings.

In other eras, ambitious autocrats might have identified themselves with the gods, but their fallibility is now out there for all to see. And what people see is that too many of today's political leaders seem inept at governing. Corporate CEOs and their scandals headline the news on a regular basis; educational leaders bury their heads in the sand of administrative detail in order to avoid confrontation with real student needs; and religious leaders keep disappointing us with their moral failures. Leaders? Who needs them?

---

3. See Meyer, *Culture Map*, 128.
4. Sarkar, "Sharing Credit in a Guru-Centered World," 86.
5. Emmanuel, "Breaking through the Barriers," 208.

It reminds me of a moment years ago in Damascus. Sitting in an ancient Turkish bath, I overheard a Syrian masseuse say to my friend, "Ah, the American people I love. The American government I hate." Without skipping a beat, my friend responded, "Ah, the Syrian people I love. The Syrian government I hate." They high-fived and continued on. For them, and many others, the world would be a better place without leaders. Who needs autocratic presidents, let alone democratically elected ones?

Followers Should Have a Voice

Today's world is skeptical, mistrustful, and even cynical. In political and corporate cultures, there is a growing preference for Viking types who insist upon low power distance. It is more likely that the best knowledge might be out on the edge, out on the fringe of the organization.[6] If there are to be leaders, they should view themselves as facilitators among equals. If they want to get things done, they need to push power and problems downwards and step out of the way.[7] Only through a collaborative process, without recourse to leaders, can the world's problems be solved. Today's mantra is flatten or be flattened.

Glimpses of this style of leadership are emerging, even in the sports world. Explaining his approach to coaching (one that has led to consecutive National Basketball Association championships), Coach Steve Kerr says, "I suppose I'm a little more egalitarian in my approach . . . maybe because I was a role player myself. I feel there's a power in everybody touching the ball and everybody sharing in the offense. There's nobody who's right or wrong."[8] It's not uncommon for his players to design the plays and determine adjustments at half-time.

The same move away from dominant leadership is occurring in the church. Voices are clamoring to see a more laity-driven church. An increasing number are drawn to house churches, where the size allows for everyone to be an integral, active part of the leadership.

Everywhere one turns, disruption, disintermediation, and decentralization are becoming the orders of the day. Niall Ferguson, author of *The Square and the Tower: Networks and Power, from the Freemasons to Facebook*, characterizes our age as one in which hierarchy is at a discount, if not despised.[9] The networked crowd that rules yearns to smack down and shame every authority figure.

---

6. Brafman and Beckstrom, *The Starfish and the Spider*, 204.

7. Meyer, *Culture Map*, 116. She refers to the extreme egalitarian principles in Scandinavian culture.

8. Davis, "Steve Kerr Explained."

9. Ferguson, "In Praise of Hierarchy"; *Square and the Tower*, chapter 1.

Better to have disruption than the visible hand of order. The assumption is that a decentralized corporate culture better determines the success of an organization.

Some of this thinking goes back to an earlier work, *The Starfish and the Spider: The Unstoppable Power of Leaderless Organizations*. Its authors Ori Brafman, an organizational expert, and Rod Beckstrom, CEO and leadership consultant, believe biology has much to teach us about leadership. Like many hierarchical organizations, the spider is fully dependent on its head. If it loses its head, it dies. In contrast, the starfish doesn't have a head. Where there is the loss of a part, it regenerates into a whole new starfish.[10] The starfish is a model of decentralized leadership. It resonates with those asking, "Who needs more leadership cults?" What the world needs is less centralized leadership and more open systems – flat versus pyramid, spontaneous versus fixed. In such an ethos, the core words and phrases are "catalyst," "collaborative," and "behind the scenes."

Leaders? There's a reason why they always get "voted off the island." For all of the attention, leaders disappoint. If they have any role, it is largely symbolic, even romantic, but not substantive. Dwarfish montebanks are pulling levers and producing flames behind an imposing shaman-like façade.[11] Their command and control are what stifle creativity. To put it in "Wizard of Oz" language, instead of the Wiz we need Dorothy.[12]

Leaders Are the Solution

Questioning the need for leaders is understandable, given the present and past abuses of power. It's true, we don't need the Wiz, or any other pseudo-leader. But it's also fair to say that Dorothy will probably not engage the dreams and mobilize the energies of a people.

If we are to attempt something big and get to the right "somewhere," we need a visible head. Someone whose character commands respect, points the way, articulates a plan, and effectively leads. Such leaders have been central to every turn in history. Where would the world have been without Gandhi, Benito Juárez, Gaozu of Han, George Washington, Winston Churchill, Anwar Sadat, Yitzhak Rabin, and Nelson Mandela – to name but a few? In a better place? Likely not.

---

10. Brafman and Beckstrom, *The Starfish and the Spider*, 35.
11. Roberts, *Hitler and Churchill*, loc. 284.
12. Hjalmarson, "Kingdom Leadership."

The times make the leader, but the leader also shapes the times.

The need for leadership is affirmed across cultural lines and demonstrated in multiple contexts. Take political leadership. It required the presence of an Atatürk to reframe and remake the Turkish state. It's doubtful that leadership by committee would have sparked a revolution. A backwoods lawyer by the name of Abraham Lincoln steered America through some of its darkest days. It required his leadership for slaves to be emancipated. An Anwar Sadat rose up and said, "Enough war," knowing that it might lead to his death. He stepped across the border and signed a peace agreement with Israel, one that has survived the Arab Spring and is still intact.

David Gergen, in his assessment of political leaders from Nixon to Clinton, concludes: "Everyone who has worked in government, a corporation, a professional group, or a nonprofit knows that leadership matters. Had it not been for a Roosevelt and Churchill to rally Western democracies, civilization might have perished. At a moment of crisis, the quality of a nation's leader can be decisive."[13]

In the corporate world, most would agree that a leader at the helm is critical. Noel Tichy, a leadership consultant, notes that having a winning culture and efficient work processes are great, but leadership takes precedence over everything else.[14] Max De Pree adds: "When I ask myself about the future of an organization, this is my answer: Senior leaders *are* the future."[15]

It's no different in the religious realm. Will Willimon, who has written on pastoral leadership, states, "There is no church without leadership."[16] Where leadership is absent, ministries languish. The extensive research of George Barna would agree. The reason for weak churches goes back to one thing: weak leaders.

What is the support for their arguments? Here are some of the reasons for the necessity of leaders:

Leaders Bring Order

Without leadership, things can become chaotic. Some might glory in the mess, the freedom that generates creativity, but without an established order, anarchy usually takes over. A good leader brings stability.

---

13. Gergen, *Eyewitness to Power*, 12.
14. Tichy, *Leadership Engine*, 25.
15. De Pree, *Leadership Jazz*, 209.
16. Willimon, *Pastor*, 15.

The absence of leadership, particularly in a desperate situation, can lead to both chaos and the manifestation of people's worst behaviors. Stories like those of the Donner Party, the *Karluk* expedition, and the *Indianapolis* disaster at sea prove that when people are without leadership, the desperateness of a situation can multiply every weakness, every quirk of personality, and every flaw in character a thousandfold.[17]

I was a political science major in college. In my third year, I had one of the worst course experiences ever. The professor decided to yield his leadership to the students. We were invited to determine the syllabus and the course of the course. Confusion and bedlam ensued. For weeks, we had no idea where things were going. The professor's abdication of his leadership left the program uneven, requirements unclear. I do not remember learning anything.

Even Brafman and Beckstrom would agree that without some structure and control there will be inconsistency.[18] Leaders, particularly those grounded in ethics and skilled in leading, are essential to stability, order, and evenness. Organizational consultants like Warren Bennis have observed that leaders are not only the pivotal force behind successful organizations; they are the anchors who provide stability in a time of upheaval.[19] Hierarchical cultures, such as those in Asia, would underscore that leaders provide more than order. People with rank, and behaviors appropriate to that rank, bring a necessary harmony.

Leaders Sound the Alarm

Leaders not only bring order out of chaos, they also replace complacency with a sense of urgency. This is so necessary. Over time, people slide into comfortable patterns. I have encountered this in every church I pastored. Someone must awaken the organization. Leaders might need to stage a revolution! Leaders are those who see out ahead, make people aware of the potential crises, and stress the need to press forward. Someone has to stand up and say, "The time is now!"

If these things are not true – if there is no crisis, no chaos, no need for change – then leaders are not so necessary. A few incremental modifications will do. Peacetime management will suffice. But this is not true. It is not reality. There is always some chaos. In today's turbulent world, leaders are the necessary voices who sound the alarm and rouse followers, even if their mood

---

17. Perkins, *Leading at the Edge*, 100.
18. Brafman and Beckstrom, *The Starfish and the Spider*, 191.
19. Bennis, *On Becoming a Leader*, 2.

is not to be disturbed. Even if there is pushback. People tend not to embrace leaders with their siren calls to break from the past.[20]

Leaders Give Direction

Once leaders awaken constituents, they move to point the way. Behind every significant movement is a visionary leader, someone with a built-in gyroscope.

Having splashed cold water on people's directionless complacency, leaders point the way forward. They direct the flow of energy and help an organization develop a picture of the future. This is why educator Stephen Covey refers to leaders as "pathfinders." They give a guiding purpose and a strategic pathway.[21]

Churchill understood this necessity. As a student, he had memorized these lines:

Who is in charge of the clattering train?
The axles creak and the couplings strain;
And the pace is hot, and the points are near,
And sleep has deadened the driver's ear;
And the signals flash through the night in vain,
For death is in charge of the clattering train.[22]

These words stayed with him in the 1930s, when sleep had deadened England's ears to the rising Nazi threat. An eroding empire was without direction. The nation needed a leader to rouse it and direct a course. Someone needed to take charge of the clattering train.

Leaders Make Things Happen

Leaders not only are important to the waking up and giving direction; they also initiate the movement. They catalyze efforts. Leaders point the way and move wills toward a collective responsibility. They make sure decisions are made, either by deciding or by bringing the team to collaborate and determine the course. But even with the latter, the team still needs a leader. On their own, collectives are poor at decision making.[23]

Noel Tichy writes: "It's true that one person alone can't change the world, or even a moderate-sized organization. It takes the concentrated energy, ideas,

---

20. Bardwick, "Peacetime Management and Wartime Leadership," 132.
21. Covey, "Three Roles of the Leader," 152.
22. Edwin J. Milliken, "Death and His Brother Sleep," quoted in Manchester, *Last Lion*, 148.
23. Grint, *Leadership*, 126.

and enthusiasm of many people. But without a leader, the movement doesn't get started. It dies for lack of direction or momentum."[24]

Leaders know when it is time for action.

Leaders Bring Results

Decisive action leads to outcomes. In the corporate realm, research shows that strong and effective leaders are behind superior business results.

In their article "Leadership as a Brand," Ulrich and Smallwood begin with two simple words: "Leaders matter."[25] Executive leaders can turn a fledgling company into a viable competitor. Where would Apple be today without a Steve Jobs – or General Electric without Jack Welch? What would have happened to Intel if Andy Grove had not responded to new realities and led the effort to leave the memory chip business? What would Sony look like if there had not been an Akio Morita? What would the political outcome have been in El Salvador if Alfredo Christiani had not stepped out?

Tenacious leaders set goals, leading to successful organizations – ones that bear fruit.

Leaders Keep Things Going

Initial results are great, but organizations need a constant supply of leaders with ideas, values, energy, and edge. True leadership sustains the movement. Without leaders, people prematurely celebrate success. Momentum slows. The end point gets lost in a haze of confusion.

Leonard Sweet describes leaders as those who close the deals of history. They are the boulders that arrest the drift, the pied pipers behind whom people follow the music.[26] One can talk reengineering, but at the difficult point of execution and continuance it requires a leader. Without leaders, the status quo stays in place. With leadership, things keep pushing forward.

Leadership coach Marshall Goldsmith popularized the quote, "What got you here won't get you there." At critical moments, these words spur me to press on. It's like the words my pastor once wrote on the opening page of a book he gave to me during my first year of seminary: "Keep on keeping on."

These are leadership words. They compel leaders to anticipate the inevitable atrophy and keep creating new s-curves at the inflection. If this does not happen, the organizations we lead will become institutions of misdirected resources,

---

24. Tichy, *Leadership Engine*, 25.
25. Ulrich and Smallwood, "Leadership as a Brand," 141.
26. Note Leonard Sweet's concise but compelling book on leadership, *Summoned to Lead*.

massive ineffectiveness, and squandered opportunities. A gravitational force will begin to pull downwards.

This happened in 1973 in Israel. The nation was in a lull. For six years, things stopped moving forward. Leadership was overly confident – and absent – after a successful victory in the Six-Day War of 1967. The nation had assumed an invincibility. The surprise attack of resentful Arab nations caught the country's leadership sleeping at the helm. This led to the deadliest war in Israel's history. Victory came, but at a high price. It led to the end of the prime minister's leadership, and of his place in history.

Leaders save us because they have an eye for laxity, a nose for stale air. They can discern the *kairos*, the moment where divine opportunity breaks into visible reality.[27] Leaders understand that ideas and methods get old and people get distracted. Only leaders are sufficient to keep the organization evolving in an increasingly fast-paced world.

Leaders Shape the Values

Organizations reflect the moral tone of the leader, and this is critical. More important than results and momentum is the institution's value system.[28] A number of forces converge to create the culture, but no one influences the moral framework like a leader. Leaders are necessary to an institution's integrity – period!

British historian John Keegan noted that the political history of the twentieth century could be found in the biographies of six men: Lenin, Stalin, Hitler, Mao Tse-tung, Roosevelt, and Churchill. As their hearts went, so went the nations.[29] Some lived monstrous lives; others chose a virtuous path. The impact of their leadership lives on.

Adolf Hitler is said to have inscribed these words in one of the gas ovens in Auschwitz: "I want to raise a generation of young men devoid of a conscience – imperious, relentless, and cruel." He did, and nearly eighty years later, a nation still suffers with the scars.

Stalin was a combination of ruthlessness and paranoia. In his biography on the despotic leader, Simon Sebag Montefiore describes the decades of Stalin's terrifying rule and then notes the present consequences: "Modern Russia has

---

27. Fleming, *Leadership Wisdom from Unlikely Voices*, 37.
28. Brafman and Beckstrom, *The Starfish and the Spider*, 13.
29. Gergen, *Eyewitness to Power*, 12.

not yet faced up to its past; there has been no redemption, which perhaps still casts a shadow over its development of civil society."[30]

Assessing the moral impact of a leader, Kouzes and Posner write, "Without leaders, constituents have no energizer to ignite their passions, no exemplar to follow, and no compass by which to be guided."[31] Leaders with moral convictions become the backbone of a virtuous society.[32] We will look at this further in the chapter on character.

Summarizing What We Hear

While we can rail against leaders, create a resistance, and question our need for them, the arguments for leaders outweigh the negatives. Leaders harm and disappoint. But they also bring stability, sound the warning, point the way, instigate the movement, bring outcomes, sustain the momentum, and shape the ideals. Without them we would enter a state of confusion and paralysis.

The Voices We Need to Hear

How do other cultures assess the need for leaders? How does a society that has had to learn survival, or one that has known nothing but war, value leaders? The first is an interview with a Jewish leader based in Tel Aviv. The second is a contribution from a Serbian leader. Both are respected for their creativity and forward thinking.

The Voice of Dan Sered, Chief Operations Officer, Jews for Jesus

First, how do Israelis view the importance of leadership?
Given that Israel is an army culture, we believe leaders and leadership are vital. Someone must be at the front to lead.

What's behind this culture?
Survival is the backdrop to how Israelis approach life. There is a joke that we often tell about Jewish holidays. It goes like this: "Do you want to know the story behind every Jewish holiday? It's simple. They tried to kill us. We won. Let's eat!"

---

30. Montefiore, *Stalin*, xx.
31. Kouzes and Posner, *Leadership Challenge*, 30.
32. Meyer, *Culture Map*, 132.

We have a history that includes Pharaoh, Haman, Hitler, and the Holocaust. We live in a world today where numerous nations are committed to our destruction. Enemies surround us. A leader is needed who will protect the nation. This matters more than anything else. We must have one who conveys strength, someone who will defend at all costs. This is why many of Israel's political leaders have been war heroes.

Leaders must be held in high respect. Is this true?
Not necessarily. Unlike in other cultures, leaders are not accorded respect simply because of their position. They must earn it. Position does not matter so much.

How does this play out?
Here is an example. Teachers in public school are typically referred to by their first name. It is common to challenge, even talk back to, an instructor. If you want respect, you have to have a reputation that is developed over time. Respect must be earned. Unfortunately, in today's Israel, there is less and less esteem for leaders. There is a growing cynicism. It is hard to find a leader to admire and follow. Too many are fraudulent.

How do leaders get to the top?
It's important to note that a good leader is one who, first, starts at the bottom. Those who rise to the top are those who have a history of being servants. This is certainly true in the Israeli Defense Force. One does not become an officer unless one has first been an excellent private.

This being said, those who rise to the top need to create and sustain a network. In Israel, we refer to this as *protektzia*. It's all about who you know. Right leaders start at the bottom, but over time they develop the right connections. However, it is also fair to say that the truly exceptional leaders in Israel are those who get there, not merely because of who they knew, but because of outstanding character.

Getting to the pinnacle also requires that one be tenacious. The immediate mindset is "take no prisoners." Winning is everything. Conflict is less about working toward reconciliation and agreement, but about coming out on top.

Leaders are necessary; are teams?
Yes, but remember that ours is a culture with a tribal mentality. This defines much of Middle Eastern culture. There is less individualism. People in tribes yell. They are passionate. The one who is loudest tends to be served first. This translates over into teams. Even here, people scream. Everyone is used to this.

A leader has to have skin as thick as an elephant's. If a team has any hope of accomplishing its mission, leadership is critical. Remember, the kibbutz model really helped Israel survive as a state.

Lessons from a Jewish World

As Dan notes, the Jewish people have a long history of great leaders, from biblical times to the present. It is no coincidence that when you look at the number of people who have won Nobel Prizes, there is a high percentage of Jewish prizewinners relative to the percentage of Jewish people in the world. Israel is a small country, but it is a world leader in start-ups.

What explains this? Maybe it is their history of survival, requiring that everyone develop some leadership capabilities. There are more leaders than followers, and that is a model worth emulating. The challenges we face will demand cultures in which everyone plays some leadership role.

There is a strong need both to respect our leaders and to require that they merit that respect. This can be a healthy alternative to cultures where followers are mere sycophants, giving their loyalty to whoever simply has the position.

The Voice of Samuil Petrovski, Serbian National Director of the International Fellowship of Evangelical Students

Like Israel, there has been a survivalist mentality in Eastern Europe, but there are different leadership dynamics. I asked Samuil Petrovski, a highly respected leader in numerous fields, to contribute to this discussion on leaders and their necessity.

A Brief History

Ours has been a world of kings, tsars, dukes, bishops, communist dictators – and significant problems. We have been annexed by the Ottomans, disrupted by the Hapsburg Empire, overrun by Axis powers, and impacted by numerous Yugoslav wars. Our is a history of upheaval, unpredictability, and domination.

The Need for Leaders

Given our history, there has been a long-held assumption that leaders are essential to survival. Leaders are the ones who are competent, the strong types with authoritarian personalities. We have tended to view them as messianic. They are the ones above who bring the order, sound the alarm, and sustain the movement. They also make the decisions others are afraid to make. They are the only ones brave enough, stable enough, and capable enough to solve big and small problems. They have had the power, and followers have learned to fear and respect them.

The Nature of Leading

To maintain their control, leaders work to maintain a strong image. To convince people of their necessity, leaders in the Balkans tend to macro- and micro-manage. Collaboration and consensus have not been part of the vocabulary. Leaders are hesitant to share or delegate power. This comes from fear of losing power or from an assumption that they alone are capable of making the right decisions. Consequently, many operate as one-man shows.

If leaders create teams, it is expected that team members be "yes-men." Team members are discouraged from having independent ideas, ones in contradiction of the leader. Leaders expect a blind loyalty. Anything less is betrayal. Such members will be marked as enemies, or persons the leader will eventually replace.

In our Eastern European context, leaders have tended to keep their distance. They cannot show their emotions, as followers would see this as a sign of weakness, a softness people will take advantage of. People may not see leaders as so necessary. Distance is part of maintaining a sense of need on the part of followers. Leaders are not typically close to their followers or members of their teams. Keeping their distance helps protect them from criticism. Distance protects leaders from having their weaknesses exposed, their character flaws revealed. As a result, followers hold on to myths and misconceptions. They are content to see only the posture and charisma, remaining blind to the deep personal and moral cracks.

The Cost of Disruption

In much of leadership, there are deep fault lines that lie hidden. Much of this has to do with the lack of opportunities for character to develop. Leaders have had to give most of their energy to survival. In my region, there has been a major war every fifty years. As mentioned, different empires through the centuries have fought for power. To endure, leaders have had to rule with a strong fist, doing everything to ensure they are not overthrown. There has been little time for the soul. Deficient of moral integrity, leaders have made disastrous decisions, leading their people into one destructive war after another. As a result, they could fairly serve as a chapter in R. T. Howard's book *Warmongers: How Leaders and Their Unnecessary Wars Have Wrecked the Modern World*. They have sacrificed their own people rather than lose face or position. Even in the church, leaders have betrayed their historical background and religious heritage. In the famous novel *The Bridge on the Drina*, writer Ivo Andrić describes how Christian leaders changed their religion to Islam to gain positions in the Ottoman Empire. Yet people have held on to their leaders.

Another consequence of our violent history has been the failure to prepare future leaders. Because existing leaders tend to be suspicious, little effort has been given to leadership development. This was especially the case in the former Yugoslavia during the reign of Marshal Josip Broz Tito. He established himself as someone too formidable to be challenged. He viewed himself as president for life, giving little attention to who might be his successor.

This is another part of maintaining distance, and it has isolated leaders from reality. They often assume people are praising them for their big and important decisions, but behind their backs, people often criticize. Leaders expect people to show them ongoing honor, but as soon as those leaders are overthrown (for there is seldom a peaceful transition), they are forgotten. Needed one moment, they are unnecessary in the next. People switch their attention and loyalty over to the leader who follows.

Summary

I have painted a rather negative, though realistic, picture of leadership in the Balkans. People have held to the need for leaders because there would be chaos without them – even if many are unprincipled and obsessed with power. But there have also been many outstanding leaders, servant leaders with solid character and strong presence. And there is no question regarding our need for them.

Still, there is much work to be done to restore people's confidence. We are suffering the fruit of dysfunctional leadership, and this has influenced every sector of leadership, including in the church and supporting ministries. Because of insecurities, the need for trained and competent leadership is huge. Through proper education and training, with international exposure, we will be able to develop better leaders, leaders who think of their team members as assets and not as competitors.

To develop a leadership structure that is less hierarchical and authoritarian, this education will need to move beyond theory and into practice. We will need to learn through practical examples, interactive teaching, and brainstorming. Leaders will need to close the distance with their teams, sharing their knowledge and experience, as well as their lives. They will need to build confidence in emerging leaders. Too many in the next generation are afraid to make decisions, paralyzing their potential.

These are our challenges, but they are not unique. I see this across the rest of the world, including Western countries. If we are to convince people of the need for leadership, we must be intentional in making better leaders.

Lessons from a Serbian World

What do we learn from Samuil? Despite their imperfections, leaders have established their need by being voices of conviction. They are not so concerned with popularity. They are not lost in their niceness. They do not say what people want to hear. They hold to certainties driven by their strong sense of purpose, and they are not afraid to use their power to enforce them. This makes them respected – and necessary.

The Voice We Must Hear

So far, we have established that leaders are necessary. There are multiple reasons for them, and most cultures affirm these. Leadership is a necessary part of creation. But what does our theology tell us? Does God need leaders? The answer is mixed.

Leaders Are Unnecessary

Leaders aren't necessary – at least, not to God. God is, by definition, self-sufficient. He needs no one and nothing to accomplish his will:

> Heaven is my throne,
> and the earth is my footstool.
> Where is the house you will build for me?
> Where will my resting place be?
> Has not my hand made all these things,
> and so they came into being?
> (Isa 66:1–2)

God has established his throne in heaven, and his kingdom rules over all (Ps 103:19). He is a leader who doesn't even need a world to be God.

Given his perfect leadership, God told the people of Israel early on that they did not need an earthly leader. They had him. He warned that leaders would exploit the people and take what they had (1 Sam 8:10–18). But Israel persisted in their clamoring. Rejecting God's leadership is our way.

Verses like Proverbs 30:27 suggest that leaders are not so necessary. The Old Testament sage (aka, professional life watcher) admired creatures who could go without a ruler: "Locusts have no king, yet they advance together in ranks." They accomplish their objectives with unsettling efficiency, and do so without a king or queen. Is the insect world telling us something? Is this an affirmation that decentralized leadership may have a certain amount of chaos, but the absence of a dominant head allows for individual creativity, initiative, and amazing results? Is this wisdom?

And what about Jesus? He entered a world of well-established hierarchies, both religious and political, not to affirm but to disrupt. He mocked those who believed they were entitled and privileged, those who loved the lead role (Matt 6:5–6). He corrected those of his disciples who wanted to be like the world's leaders – those who love the power and status of rank (Luke 22:24–26). He shifted the formal order of top-down priests to a network of believer priests (1 Pet 2:9). He made it possible for all to have equal access in Christ, where all distinctions of gender, ethnicity, and rank are removed (see Gal 3:28). We can do what was once the prerogative of the religious hierarchy.

Are these passages sufficient to cast a shadow on a leader's importance? No.

Leaders Are Necessary

While God does not need leaders, we do. To interpret Scripture otherwise would miss the larger point. That God adapted his purposes and acquiesced sufficiently to allow Israel a king underscores this. He ended up incorporating the monarchy into his revelation of himself. Kingship was soon to be a major theme of the Old Testament, a necessary office in the life of Israel.

Throughout the narrative, Scripture affirms the same reasons listed earlier.

Leaders Bring Order

Where there is no divinely imposed order, there is chaos. This is clear from the beginning (Gen 1:1–2). After bringing something from nothing, the divine leader of the universe brought form out of formlessness and image out of an imageless mass. He creates leaders for the same purpose.

Without the strong presence of a leader, there has always been disorder. In the absence of Moses, Israel descended into revelry and chaos (Exod 32:1). It is a leader who keeps evil in check and brings stability to a land. The wise could also see this (Prov 20:8, 26; 29:4). Even in the case of Agur, the sage might have marveled at the way leaderless locusts march in unison, but there is more to leadership than movement. These same leaderless creatures are carried away by the wind, driven by their appetites, and leave behind devastation.

Is it any wonder that the sordid events described in the book of Judges came during a leaderless time? Note the writer's final statement: "In those days Israel had no king; everyone did as they saw fit" (21:25). Ultimate individuality leads to disarray and turmoil. Only when God raises up godly leaders is there hope of restoring solidity. "By justice a *king* gives a country stability" (Prov 29:4). Only when there is proper governance is there strength. Hence Paul's admonition, "Let every person be subject to the governing authorities" (Rom 13:1).

It is noteworthy that whenever God judges a nation, one of the more severe judgments is the removal of its leadership and the emergence of societal disorder. Isaiah warned a people who had spoken and acted against the Lord that he would replace its leaders with anarchy (Isa 3:1–3). When he did so, the people would become desperate, turning to anyone who might lead ("You have a cloak, you be our leader; take charge of this heap of ruins!" Isa 3:6).

Leaders Give Direction

Scripture also affirms that leaderless people are confused people. Consider the words of Proverbs: "For lack of guidance a nation falls," (11:14). They descend into violence. Or think of these words from Matthew: "When he saw the crowds, he had compassion on them, because they were harassed and helpless, like sheep without a shepherd" (9:36). Without good leadership, people have no direction or protection. In contrast, where there are leaders who guide as God intends, people flourish (2 Chr 15:15). Where there is a shepherd, people lie down in security (Ps 23:1–3).

In the church, God raises up gifted leaders to equip the saints. Leaders direct the saints to do ministry (Eph 4:11–13). They guide people to the ultimate end point – to reach the stature of the fullness of Christ (v. 16). This is the core goal of leadership. God has given the church "developmentalists" to develop people.[33]

Leaders Make Things Happen and Bring Results

In the wilderness, Moses pointed the way, generated the movement, and people were liberated from taskmasters. Under the strategic leadership of Joshua, the land found rest. The Spirit filled Saul, and the dread of the Lord came upon the people. They emerged as one people and struck the Ammonites (1 Sam 11:1–11). At the end of his life, David reflected upon what happens when a

---

33. Plueddemann, *Leading across Cultures*, 179.

king is just and fears God: the people thrive (2 Sam 23:3–4). Behind all of this is God who makes things happen. It's with his help that we can advance against a troop and scale a wall (22:29–30).

Leaders Shape the Values

Scripture underscores the effect a leader's principles have on followers. This is why God seeks out leaders after his own heart, and he places them in leadership to shape a people (1 Sam 13:14). Where there is no godly leadership, idolatry and godlessness prevail (see Judg 19:1; 1 Kgs 12:28–30). The sage in Proverbs observes that as the leaders go, so go the followers: "If a leader listens to lies, all his officials become wicked" (Prov 29:12). Depraved leaders like Ahab and Manasseh brought corruption, instability, and downfall (2 Kgs 21:9). The ultimate blame for a troubled nation rests on the person at the top. However, the opposite is also true. Godly leaders like Asa, Jehoshaphat, Uzziah, Hezekiah, and Josiah brought reform, stability, and peace. A righteous leader can set a righteous course for a nation.

Leaders Sound the Alarm

Throughout the biblical account, leaders step into self-satisfied situations, awaken people, and stage their own revolutions. Think Noah, Moses, Josiah, Jeremiah, Jesus, and Paul.

Each one removed the blinders so that people could see reality and the need for change. Noah warned the world of imminent judgment. Moses summoned Israel to leave Egypt in haste. Josiah discovered God's words and informed Israel that judgment was coming. Jeremiah alerted Israel of their need to pack their bags and leave before the train of judgment arrived. Jesus warned Capernaum and Bethsaida of judgment if they did not respond to the grace he revealed. And Paul exposed pagan Athens to the weightlessness of its idols and warned of a judgment to come.

Scripture tells us there is an unseen war going on (Eph 6:10–18). There are invisible enemies determined to destroy lives and upend the mission of God. God sent his Spirit at Pentecost to create a prophetic community. While the church often forgets its identity, it is God's voice commissioned to sound the alarm. A sense of urgency is needed.[34] This is why God sends prophets. They stand at the gates and call for needed change.

Such leadership has its risks. Moses faced a recalcitrant people who preferred life in Egypt; Elijah faced a king's wrath for disrupting people's

---

34. See Kotter, *Sense of Urgency.*

comfort; Jeremiah was mocked and beaten for suggesting the people should leave home; and in Athens, Paul was ridiculed. Still, their courage made a difference. Ours, too, will make a difference.

But it is more. There is a need for leaders that is often overlooked or ignored.

Leaders Carry Out God's Purpose

At every strategic point in history, God, in his wisdom, has chosen to employ leaders to carry out his sovereign purposes. This is the greatest argument for leaders. What makes leaders necessary is that God chooses to work through them.

Scripture tells us that God looks for one who will stand in the gap and lead (Ezek 22:30). In unpredictable ways, he moves to and fro, raising up leaders out of nowhere (e.g. Moses, Gideon, Paul). When God finds a person willing to yield to his purposes, that person is "used to the limit."[35] Consider the following examples:

- When he made creation, he appointed a man to rule for him.
- When he decided to save a world, he called Noah.
- When he chose to call forth a nation, he enlisted Abraham.
- When he determined to rescue his people from Pharaoh's grip, he appeared to Moses.
- When he decided to take the land, he told Joshua to arise.
- When he chose to create a dynasty of leaders who would perpetually reign, he anointed David.
- When he resolved to build a wall, he sent a report to Nehemiah.
- When he elected to protect his exiles, he challenged Esther to step up.
- When he expanded his redemptive work to Jew and Gentile, he turned Paul's world upside down.

God does not need leaders, but he chooses to work through them. As we often discover, decisions by committee don't always work well. Moses took the lead and commanded Israel to go into the land: "Go up and take possession of it as the LORD, the God of your ancestors, told you" (Deut 1:21). But Israel chose a more collaborative approach: "Let *us* send men ahead to spy out the land for us and bring back a report about the route we are able to take and the towns we will come to" (v. 22). Was this a lack of faith, or a refusal to recognize their need to be under leadership – or both? In the end, they ignored the leader

---

35. Sanders, *Spiritual Leadership*, 17.

God had sent, made entering the land their decision, and lost the privilege of entrance.

Bringing the Voices Together

Are leaders necessary? If there is no intent to work in partnership with followers, no discipline to live a godly life, and no effort to establish a common mission and vision, then leaders might become the problem rather than the solution. But where goals and initiatives are shared, and leadership is distributed to the outermost edges of the circle to unleash the power of shared responsibility, leaders remain essential.[36] As Niall Ferguson notes, "History has taught us to revere hierarchy as preferable to anarchy, and to prefer the time-honored hierarchs to upstart usurpers."[37]

Even in their counsel to organizations, Brafman and Beckstrom acknowledge that the decentralized structure illustrated by the starfish cannot replace the hierarchy of the spider. Healthy institutions are a hybrid – a spider structurally, with power pushed down. This allows leaders to broaden their focus, seeing both the trees and the forest. And this is essential, especially in an age struggling with a leadership deficit in nearly every sector and institution.

Are Christian leaders necessary? More than ever. In some cultures, like my own, Christianity has become the "repugnant cultural other." People view faith less and less as truth, and more and more as magical thinking. Evangelicals are denigrated as irrational, even dangerous. Part of this is the times. Part of it is the lack of leadership.

These are days that demand a new and vibrant leadership: leaders who have deep and unwavering convictions that align with truth, who live their words, and who are expansive in their vision. Only then will the church, and other institutions, refind their footing. But what makes a leader?

---

36. Hesselbein, "The 'How to Be' Leader," 122.
37. Ferguson, "In Praise of Hierarchy."

3

Lead, Follow, or Get Out of the Way

In an article on leadership, *Time* magazine contributor Joel Stein wrote, "I get deeply insulted when people say, 'Lead, follow, or get out of the way!' My entire career has consisted of getting *in* the way."[1]

Which is it with you? Are you more comfortable letting someone else take the lead? Or do you find yourself in the definitional qualities of a leader described in chapter 1? Does the need for leadership outlined in chapter 2 resonate with you? Or are you simply in the way? Maybe you are not sure.

How does one even become a leader? That's the question we are seeking to answer in this chapter. Some would say leadership is a rite of passage. The task of leading is something passed down from one generation to the next. Others would say leadership is the result of birth. Leadership is a God-given gift. Many would claim that leadership is something anyone can learn after diligent study – like reading this book! – and observation. Others believe it is the result of a summons. At strategic moments, leaders are called to lead. Others better get out of the way. Who is right?

The Voices We Hear
Leadership Is Inherited

Mount Paektu straddles the border separating North Korea and China. For centuries, Koreans have revered the site as their spiritual home. Therefore, it is not surprising that in the crater of this active volcano is a body of water with the name Heaven Lake. Many believe that leaders, past and present, have come from this mountain. They have been anointed from above, divinely empowered

---

1. Stein, "What I Learned," 70.

to lead. The Kim dynasty has ruled with this conviction. This is why Kim Jong-un views himself as uniquely blessed with vision, diplomatic savvy, and military genius. This is his destiny.

No wonder he keeps the world on edge!

Some regard Kim as some fratricidal despot living in a bizarro fantasy world.[2] Maybe, but Kim sees it otherwise. Like his father, Kim Jong-il, and those before him, Kim Jong-un holds that each successive head of state has been favored with mystical, magical powers of leadership.[3]

Other world leaders – particularly paternalistic leaders – have made similar assumptions about their own leadership, and the leadership to follow. Leadership is a matter of birthright, passed from one idealized human to the next. It's not what you have accomplished, but where you are from.

Leadership Is Innate

Others may not be able to point to some body of water or some leadership legacy, but they believe they are born to lead. They noticed it on the playground when they were young. Kids tended to follow and vote them into leadership positions.

I was the class milk monitor in second grade, one of the patrol boy lieutenants in fifth grade, junior high vice president in eighth grade, class president in ninth grade, and student body president in twelfth grade. Leadership was a natural expression. As Leonard Sweet puts it, leadership comes with one's "psychological territory."[4] Leadership is part of a person's inner being.

Philosopher Thomas Carlyle was one of the first modern leadership scholars. He promoted a "Great Man" theory of leadership which was popular in the 1900s. It assumed that great leaders do not emerge through inheritance or education, but through "individual raw," that is, natural talent – talent with a "will to power." Examples of such leaders include Martin Luther, Frederick the Great, Oliver Cromwell, and Napoleon Bonaparte – each of whom was born with little except the natural will and ability to lead.[5]

Contemporary writers have made similar arguments. Calvin Miller, in his *Empowered Leader*, writes that leadership owns leaders. It is not gained by studying books; it is encoded in one's DNA. A crisis may call it out, but it

---

2. Dowd, "Will the Blowhard Blow Us Up?"

3. Bowden, "Worst Problem on Earth," 67.

4. Sweet, *Summoned to Lead*, 13.

5. Grint, *Leadership*, 53.

is never produced by a crisis.[6] Presidential advisor David Gergen came to a similar conclusion. After studying numerous leaders on the world stage, he concluded, "It certainly appears that many of the best of the past century – Churchill, the Roosevelts, Gandhi, Mandela, Golda Meir, Martin Luther King, Jr. – had leadership in their bones."[7]

A trait approach to leadership also underscores this position. There are identifiable *innate* qualities that are possessed by great social, political, and military leaders. These inborn traits separate leaders and non-leaders. Among them are drive, charisma, intelligence, masculinity, dominance, self-confidence, and determination.[8] Those with the right stuff lead the way.

Leadership Is Learned

Most voices seem to side with the ancient Athenians, who believed that leadership comes when one pursues a number of disciplines. Applying oneself to rigorous study, attaining the right liberal arts education, and training in rigorous physical disciplines are foundational to becoming a leader. Mix these with private, reflective learning, as well as character building, and sophisticated leaders will emerge.[9]

Most leadership experts would agree. Anyone can be trained to lead. Leadership is not some élite club for those with the right genes. It is less inherent, more functional. All of us can cultivate the art over time. Communication professor Peter Northouse refers to leadership as a process, one that can be learned and is available to everyone.[10] Others stress that nurture is much more important than nature.

Warren Bennis was among the first modern scholars to teach that leadership is not a set of genetic characteristics, but the result of a lifelong course of learning.[11] All of us have the capacity for leadership, but it requires the will to become one.

Other leadership theorists agree. *The Leadership Challenge*, by Kouzes and Posner, is one of the best-selling leadership books of all time. It unpacks five core practices common to extraordinary leaders, practices available to *anyone*

---

6. Miller, *Empowered Leader*, 9.
7. Gergen, *Eyewitness to Power*, 13.
8. See chapter 1 and discussion of a trait approach to leadership; Northouse, *Leadership*.
9. Grint, *Eyewitness to Power*, 56.
10. Northouse, *Leadership*, 11.
11. George, *Discover Your True North*, vii.

who accepts the challenge.[12] The authors set out to destroy what they call "the most pernicious myth about leadership," the idea that leadership is reserved for only a few. Leadership is not conveyed in a gene or some secret code.[13] Leadership is not about an innate personality; it's about learned behavior. And it is available to anyone willing to invest time in the subject. There would be more leaders if we grasped the fact leadership can be learned.

There are multiple ways to learn and master leadership. It may come by reading books or attending various conferences. It may develop as one observes other leaders and acquires their ways. Serious students watch how they command attention and inspire people to follow. Michael Useem notes in his book on leadership that one of the most effective ways of preparing is by looking at what others have done.[14]

Some of our learning might be random. Bennis observes that more leaders have been made by accident or circumstance than have been made by all the leadership courses put together.[15] Learning often comes through hardship. The deserts of life can be harsh, relenting, and confusing. But the skills to lead emerge from these moments. They are a leader's crucible.[16]

In the end, one's leadership is the culmination of a lifetime of lessons. This is the point made in Bobby Clinton's *Making of a Leader*. Leadership is not acquired after completing a set of do-it-yourself correspondence courses over a semester, nor after attending a leadership summit or mastering a series of podcasts. It is a lifelong school with numerous stages, some by intention and some by chance.[17]

Through none of these methods is attaining leadership an instant process. Learning does not have a terminus point. Even if it comes through formal courses, Robert Gates cautions that education alone does not make a leader. Leadership is more about the heart than the head.[18] In the end, it comes down to self-will. By the weight of grit and determination, one becomes a leader.

---

12. Kouzes and Posner, *Leadership Challenge*, 15.
13. Kouzes and Posner, 339.
14. Useem, *Leadership Moment*, 3.
15. Bennis and Nanus, *Leaders*, 142.
16. Bennis and Thomas, *Geeks and Geezers*, 91.
17. Clinton, *Making of a Leader*, 27.
18. Gates, *Passion for Leadership*, 220.

Leadership Is a Summons

Finally, some believe that acquiring leadership is less about inheritance, genetics, or education and more about a summons. There are numerous examples of leaders who were "subpoenaed" by the circumstances or by some divine will. The leadership of Jeanne d'Arc, Oliver Cromwell, Martin Luther King, Jr., and Florence Nightingale – to name but a few – resulted from some directive outside of themselves.

There is no explanation other than the force of history's summons to leadership in the cases of Genghis Khan, George Washington, Joseph Stalin, Franklin Roosevelt, and George Patton. When John F. Kennedy was asked how he became a heroic leader, he replied: "They sank my boat." After 9/11, Mayor Rudy Giuliani went from a "has been" to a hero. He was ordered by the times to lead a city through its worst crisis.

In her introduction to *Team of Rivals*, Doris Goodwin refers to the march of events leading to the American Civil War. Without this fractured historical moment, she concludes, Abraham Lincoln would not have been remembered for his leadership.[19] The times demanded an Abraham Lincoln. They generated a level of self-confidence and inordinate risk taking, manifestations of great leadership.[20]

The main argument in Leonard Sweet's book on leadership is that the whole "leadership thing" is a demented concept. Leaders are neither born nor made; they are called into existence by the circumstances. The main requirement is listening. Leadership is hearing a summons – a vision – and stepping into one's leadership moment. Those who hear and rise to the occasion are leaders.[21]

Here are two more examples. Rick Langer, developing a biblical theology of leadership, states: "We are not leaders or followers because of gifts or abilities, but rather we are appointed to lead or follow in a particular place and time."[22] Management professor Michael Useem agrees. After looking at nine dramatic leadership stories, he concludes that leadership is all about leaders rising – or falling – to the occasion of leadership. Note his advice in the first words of his introduction: "We all need to be ready for those moments when our leadership is on the line."[23]

---

19. Goodwin, *Team of Rivals*, xix.
20. Grint, *Leadership*, 53.
21. Sweet, *Summoned to Lead*, 12.
22. Langer, "Toward a Biblical Theology of Leadership," 69.
23. Useem, *Leadership Moment*, 3.

So Who Is Right? Summarizing What We Hear

Inherited, gifted, trained, or summoned? In the foreword to *The Making of a Leader*, Leighton Ford writes: "I believe we can make either of two opposite mistakes in viewing leadership development. One is to attach a mystique to leadership that says in effect, 'God calls leaders. Leaders are born. There is nothing we can do about it.' The opposite is to say, 'Leaders are made. With the right techniques, we can produce them.'"[24]

What about inherited? Summoned? It may be that leadership is acquired through having the right bloodlines, but my observation is that most leadership is acquired through a combination of giftedness, training, and summons. Each has a necessary part in the process.

If leadership is not in one's DNA, one can take leadership only so far. I am not a gifted musician. I could spend my life going to voice lessons, but if I intend to spend my life singing, I will probably frustrate myself and disappoint others. I will consign myself to working in a limited and small space.

On the other hand, having the gift to lead may be necessary, but it does not mean I will do it well. There has to be a lifelong commitment to learning the skills of leading.

But even here, something is still missing. There has to be a summons, a call, be it internal or external, that leads to the manifestation of one's gift. We are the product of birth, giftedness, development, and occasion. When these intersect, the leadership flame burns brightest.

The Voices We Need to Hear

When other global voices weigh in, what do they add? How is the acquisition of leadership viewed in their cultures? How would a Peruvian, a South African, or a New Zealander speak to the issue?

The differences might seem small on the surface, but they are far larger than we realize. A person who has inherited leadership might assume that inherited privileges includes inherited power – maybe even some divine destiny. This might change an opposing leader's assumptions when it comes to negotiations. Could this person ever concede he or she has something to learn?

How do those in other cultures describe the gift of leadership? What about an African voice? Africa is an important region. Great men, like Origen, Clement of Alexandria, Tertullian, Plotinus, and Augustine, emerged to lead.

---

24. Leighton Ford, "Foreword," in Clinton, *Making of a Leader*, 10.

Thomas Oden notes that the intellectual contours of Christianity – academics, exegesis, dogmatics, ecumenics, monasticism, philosophy, and dialectics – developed in Africa.[25] How did their leadership arise and develop? We find clues in the following contemporary voice.

The Voice of Emmanuel Bellon, Vice President of Scholarleaders International, Executive Network, Kenya

Emmanuel Bellon has served as a professor of intercultural leadership. He is committed to developing values-based leaders and organizations for societal transformation. It is an audacious goal. His passion to discover and bring leaders together is underscored by an Ethiopian proverb he quotes: "When spider webs unite, they can tie a lion."

The following contribution underscores his desire that we secure a Majority World perspective.

Introducing Leadership in African Culture

Before exploring leadership acquisition, let me say something about leadership itself. In my Kenyan culture, a leader is someone who influences the behavior of followers. The leader does this through traditional values, beliefs, norms, attitudes, and practices. It is a leader's duty to promote mutual responsibility and growth, as well as to ensure the well-being of the followers.

All of this implies stepping up and taking action. A story is told of a chief in an African village who wanted to improve the services in his community, so he summoned some of the elders to deliberate on various ways he could achieve his goal. Among the elders was a well-educated schoolteacher. He engaged the other elders and enthusiastically motivated them to do whatever it might take to fulfill the chief's vision for the town.

After several meetings and planning, it was time to contribute to the project financially. Each elder announced what his household would give, but it was different with the educated schoolteacher. He intimated that he would provide only "moral support" to the project. This left the elders confused, asking one another, "How much is moral support?" Moral support is necessary, but without action, there can be no implementation.

Leadership is far more than words.

Management strategist Lovemore Mbigi underscores this, noting that leadership is about work as well as results. In my cultural setting, a true leader

---

25. See Oden, *How Africa Shaped the Christian Mind*.

translates vision and ideas into reality. One does not merely wax eloquent about what is needed. Action is the litmus test that differentiates those who have acquired it from those who bear the title but are unable to perform the function. Therefore, leadership goes beyond analysis, management of people, and number crunching, to action, undergirded by the meaning and purpose of leadership. So how does one become a leader?

Acquiring and Forming Leadership

Leadership in many African societies is not simply a matter of birthright. Becoming a leader is not an instant phenomenon that happens when one is conceived and comes into the world. Neither does one derive leadership from a classroom education. One does not learn it by rote. Rather, leadership acquisition is about something else.

When we think about acquiring leadership, the language we use is *traditional heritage*. One becomes a leader within the context of immediate family, familial relationships, and community leaders. Even those born into royalty are expected to go through the traditional process of socialization to acquire skills and competencies. A person may be born with innate gifts and talents to lead, but family and community have precedence. They make the leader. It begins at home.

The Role of Parents

Father and mother are the primary agents for the attainment of leadership. There is a necessary process of building precept upon precept to shape and mold a leader into a functional being. These actions are rooted in traditionally sound principles like those in the Christian Scriptures. The biblical injunctions to train up children in the way they must go, and to instruct them daily from the Word of God, reinforce the African traditional framework for the acquisition of leadership.[26]

In *The Leader's Source of Influence*, John Ng'ang'a observes that in African societies parents are the prime influencers of their children and their future. They instruct their children to navigate through life, avoiding the past mistakes of their ancestors.[27] Parents have a sovereign duty to teach values, norms, attitudes, and practices that undergird leadership. In this manner, parents are both the agents and the source of acquiring leadership.

---

26. Prov 22:6; Deut 11:19.
27. Ng'ang'a, *Leader's Source of Influence*, 18.

While mothers prepare children to live and lead in the community, fathers focus on their professional development. This includes farming, hunting, construction of houses, and fishing. Boys tend to spend more time with their fathers. They are encouraged to appreciate and assume societal responsibilities and leadership as they mature. Mothers have a broader role, teaching acceptable social morality in everyday life to both sons and daughters. They also train their daughters about the role of a wife, mother, and entrepreneur.[28]

During their children's adolescent years, parents give greater focus to character traits and life skills for problem solving and leadership learning. Parents pass on foundational values and norms such as respect for elders, humility, integrity, and communication and interpersonal relations skills. They discourage deviant behaviors. The aim is to reinforce community-accepted practices.[29]

Storytelling, singing, and dancing are the primary educational tools. They pass on knowledge about life at all levels and stages in many African communities. Parents use narratives to raise their children, cultivate character, and reinforce values. Through story, parents teach traditional metaphors, idiomatic expressions, and proverbs. Sometimes riddles are used to communicate vital lessons, lessons that cannot be learned any other way. All of these are necessary for leadership acquisition.[30]

Parents believe that emerging leaders who practice what they preach will be influential in society. This means learning responsibility. If leaders are to excel and avoid mediocrity, they must acquire a good work ethic. Whether the setting is rural or urban, parents must commit to instill education and hard work. The home remains the primary place for learning how to work and how to prepare to excel. This is where one learns reliability and follow-through.[31]

Ultimately, parenting involves creating self-consciousness and cultural identity. Done well, these will stay with a child for life. Though only a few will enter into formal leadership, parents expect their children to lead. This is for the well-being of the society.

The Role of Relatives

Traditional heritage goes beyond the parents. As much as fathers and mothers facilitate the acquisition of leadership, training cannot be left to them alone.

---

28. Adjei, "Education and Training," 58.

29. Adjei, 59.

30. Mbigi, *Spirit of African Leadership*, 53.

31. Muthoni, "Accelerating Women Leadership," 47.

Society has little respect for those who nurture their children on their own, apart from the larger support structure of society. It is an affront to the very values and norms one seeks to teach. Parents need the help of relatives, especially when they have difficulties instilling leadership qualities and skills.

In many African communities, relatives are an extension of the nucleus, sharing many of the roles and responsibilities of the family. Siblings, uncles and aunts, nephews and nieces, and cousins are members of the extended family. Children are free to stay with them; it is common practice for parents to place their children in the homes of relatives. There is the potential that the child will have better opportunities for leadership and professional development.

When parents identify undesirable traits in a child and realize they are ill-equipped to handle these, they will send their son or daughter to relatives for correction and proper formation.[32] If a child grows up to be an irresponsible adult, parents will feel they have failed, but relatives will take a greater portion of the blame.

All of this underscores that relatives are the second level of leadership formation in society. Relatives are the support network and resource. Parents draw from them to fulfill their goals and aspirations for their children. All available resources for formation are brought to bear to ensure that an individual acquires the needed skills to succeed and lead in life.

The distinctive of the extended family is not just in its care and generosity, but also in its promotion of democratic values. Parents and relatives dedicate themselves to creating a fair society and community where one's aspirations can find a home.[33] Faith Muthoni points out that the compassion and empathy of relatives go a long way to inspiring future leaders. They are encouraged to pursue careers that exemplify love and care for others. Relatives see this role of forming leaders in the extended family as an honorable role, one that is cherished and encouraged across the society.[34]

Like the parents, relatives also espouse values such as hard work, diligence, honesty, integrity, and delayed gratification. They do this by providing on-the-job-training. Discipline and moral behavior are encouraged, and sanctions are applied with varied forms, depending on the offense and the person who broke the tradition. Beyond parents, any relative has the responsibility to reprimand

---

32. Opuni-Frimpong, *Indigenous Knowledge and Christian Mission*, 130.

33. Opuni-Frimpong, 83.

34. Muthoni, "Accelerating Women Leadership," 48.

and sometimes discipline any child or adolescent found going astray and falling short of society's norms.[35]

Imparting these values often molds a person into a "full man" or a "full woman." This maturing process ushers one into adulthood with all its privileges and responsibilities. Therefore, the unique role of forming leaders transcends knowledge about what is right or wrong and equips the emerging leader with a sense of identity, purpose, and heart for the community that has nurtured him or her.

The Role of Elders and Community

Leadership formation goes even further than the traditional roles of parents and extended family. It involves elders and everybody in the community. It is an anomaly in many African societies for a person to think that leadership can be acquired outside the established structures and norms in the community.

In the Gikuyu community in Kenya, the power to govern is vested in the hands of the councils of elders. They are chosen from members of the community, men who have reached the age of eldership, having retired from warriorhood.[36] They serve as leaders who confer leadership on others. The elders, in league with the whole community, are responsible for the overall formation of leaders. In the Akan leadership formation patterns, traditional leaders in the community who have proven themselves to be excellent leaders are charged with the duty to form emerging leaders in society.[37]

The elders not only are accountable for the process of leadership formation; they also ensure that the community creates and owns indigenous knowledge required for successful formation. Therefore, in the quest for knowledge, individual philosophies and innovations are subservient to society.[38] The right to ownership of knowledge is not just for an individual, but for the community as a whole.

The elders do not divide indigenous knowledge into sacred and secular. Instead, they ensure that learning is integrated and holistic. They draw from this holistic knowledge to form leaders into responsible positions.[39] When both parents and relatives fail to correct a youth who engages in deviant behavior, the elders and community are the last resort. They may impose sanctions on

---

35. Adjei, "Education and Training," 59.

36. Kenyatta, *Facing Mount Kenya*, 100.

37. Opuni-Frimpong, *Indigenous Knowledge and Christian Mission*, 130.

38. Mbigi, *Spirit of African Leadership*, iv.

39. 2 Tim 2:2.

)uth. To help prevent this embarrassment, the elders commit to active involvement from the beginning. They participate in the formal socialization process such as the rites of passage during puberty. Elders devote time and energy to the training of young people, exhorting them to adhere to societal standards for moral and physical development. The aim is that they become responsible adults and leaders, speaking words and acting upon them. They will have grown to seek the interests of others. They will go out to uphold the norms and the well-being of the entire society.

The elders also give themselves to grooming future formal leaders. This requires a different level of engagement. Leaders who are tutored to be chiefs receive different socialization from those prepared to lead interest groups or community development projects. The greater the responsibility required in the community, the more rigorous the socialization and training to acquire leadership.

In Akan society in Ghana, the traditional leadership institution has maintained its leadership presence even in the post-missionary and post-independence era. The chieftaincy institution is well respected in Ghana and attracts recognition from both the state and the church.[40] The stature of the chief in the Akan leadership institution points to the level of formation required for success. Therefore the source and agent of acquisition, which are inextricably tied together, invariably determine the extent to which leadership is acquired to be a chief.

Inherent talents, and a willingness to serve in the community, determine individual merit and ability. They form the criteria for selecting leaders for certain positions. Among the Akan royals, young people in preparation for leadership must acquire specific leadership competencies, skills, and values.

Opuni-Frimpong tells us that to achieve this, the elders place an emerging leader in the chief's palace. They then charge him or her with the responsibility to perform every part of a servant's duties. Serving together with others is a pattern of Akan traditional leadership formation. As the royals get involved in the various areas of service in the palace, they learn the desirable practices and values associated with the palace life.[41] Notably, through observation, participation, interaction, and service, a royal acquires leadership.

A royal who does not participate in serving is considered proud and lazy. Such an assessment – even by ordinary servants – may disqualify one from leadership. A leader must have the support of the ordinary servants, for they

---

40. Opuni-Frimpong, *Indigenous Knowledge and Christian Mission*, 119.
41. Opuni-Frimpong, 132.

make a critical contribution to traditional governance in the palace. Emerging leaders are also subjected to confinement – an intense period of holistic training and formation – to acquire leadership skills necessary for the functions of the traditional administration in the palace, communication systems through drum language and dance patterns, and the spiritual disciplines to build emotional and spiritual capacity.[42]

Summarizing What We Hear

What have we discovered? Though the African narrative of leadership acquisition differs from region to region, they have a universal tapestry that undergirds the rationale for formation. Leadership acquisition is communal. Parents, relatives, elders, and the overall community are all vital actors. Their active participation ensures that an individual, regardless of background, is given the essential opportunity to acquire leadership. It is a lifetime engagement with many active agents, each playing their role to ensure the growth and success of others in leadership.

Although modernization and Western influence on Africa may have reduced the impact of these agents of formation, the fundamental principles and practices for the acquisition of leadership still hold unabated and strong in many traditional African societies.

Lessons from an African World

Emmanuel Bellon underscores the message of this book – cultures have voices that must be heard. Western voices have shaped the perceptions of leadership studies for centuries. The many publications on leadership from the West have, for the most part, established the norm for the study and understanding of leadership. Other cultures, however, can inform our leadership stories, experiences, and understanding of our world.

Leadership acquisition is a case in point. How one answers the question of attaining leadership differs from culture to culture. There are points of agreement, as well as areas of departure. The different angles and dimensions all contribute to broadening our understanding of leadership. Again, we must listen to them all.

When an African talks about becoming a leader, one goes beyond gifts, summons, and training. As noted in the opening of this chapter, we in the West approach leadership acquisition in those terms. It is driven, in part,

---

42. Opuni-Frimpong, 133.

by our individualistic approach to leading. We ask: How has God gifted this person? What has been his or her training? Can this person give testimony of some historical, even divine, summons? We do this, often leaving out the role of the community.

In an African culture, one that is far more collective, there are other aspects to leadership acquisition. Traditional practices, religious beliefs, and individual and communal responsibilities play a significant role. All of these are vital to the acquisition of leadership. Over time, these practices coalesce around the selection and training of leaders.

Becoming a leader is a communal process whereby people share with one another and pursue what benefits the whole. Otherwise, leaders will be set out on a course of self-centeredness. Leaders who believe they are leaders because of their individual experiences tend to use their acquisition of leadership for their own ends. Leadership is self-initiated and self-directed.

In contrast, leaders who view their acquisition of leadership as a collective process will be apt to use their leadership for the common good. They will be responsive and responsible to the people they serve. Those who have integrated the collective wisdom of home and community will view themselves as leaders among equals.[43]

What about a Latino voice? Leaders play an important role in a culture that values respect. This is a culture less impressed by doing and more impressed with being.

The Voice of Omar Gava, Founder and Director of Recursos Estratégicos Globales (Global Strategic Resourses), and Regional Director (Latin America) for People International

(Translated by Kim Gava, with some added revisions by Mark Hedinger.)

Introducing Leadership in Latino Culture

I write this section on leadership and its acquisition from my Latin American background. I'm Argentinian and a follower of Christ. In my cultural context, people with a native background are deeply rooted in their communities. They are committed to a sense of belonging. Coexistence among neighbors is important. Having all things in common is a non-negotiable value. Other

---

43. Juana Bordas has a good discussion of this in her chapter, "A Leader among Equals," in *Salsa, Soul, and Spirit*, loc. 1733.

people come first. Connection with family matters most. Our most treasured value is *la familia*.

Leadership in this setting is complex. Ingrained in society is a "high power distance" environment, where the gap between leader and followers is significant. There are understood differences in status. Followers, as a collective body, are expected to show deference to those in authority.

Much of this goes back to our history, one marked by colonialization, civil wars, radical governments, and revolutions. In Argentina, a good number of people have come from inland. They were born and raised in native cultures. They were nurtured under the leadership of local chiefs (called *cacique*, village leaders). These are the ones with authority.

Many have also grown up in Catholicism. Like other leadership structures, the church is hierarchical. People view the leader, the Pope, as infallible. This carries over to church officials. They too have both supremacy and rights over the rest of the members. The same authoritative rule that dominates Catholic faith is exercised in other faiths, like Pentecostalism. Leaders tend to rely more on their charisma (personality) than on their competencies (skill sets). Most are relatively untrained in the dynamics of organizational and systems leadership. They put simpler church systems in place, giving them more room to assert their power and control.

This leadership dynamic has permeated other leadership cultures. Since the times of conquest and colonization, the Catholic Church and the State have merged to work as one. This is a fading force in some countries, but strong bonds still exist in most. The voice of the church still has a strong influence in political and social decisions, but this has weakened due to recent scandals.

Like the church, Latin American political regimes tend to be highly autocratic. Leadership is less collegial and collaborative. Servant leadership is practically nonexistent. In addition to this, years of military influence have wielded their own power, and this has led to repression and terrorism. Those in leadership positions have acted as oligarchs and despots. More often than not, their rule has been strong and harsh. They historically have not considered the people's well-being, nor have they tried to win the people's esteem and cooperation.

Tragically, true leadership has been largely absent. There is a history of conquest and cultural oppression. Even in cases where democratic governments have replaced military dictatorships, they have led with the same structures and abuses. Corruption amongst political leaders is rampant. Oppressive leaders have exploited citizens, extorting their wealth. Many have been placed under investigation and some face trial.

Acquiring Leadership in Latino Culture
How does one become a leader in a culture like mine? This has multiple answers.

Leaders Are Summoned
Given the church's historic influence, many leaders come to assume that God summons leaders. We have been taught that God is the one who determines, gifts, and calls leaders, both within and without the church. What is applicable to the church applies to leaders in other spheres. God is the one who puts leaders in place. He does this according to his wisdom and for his purposes. Leadership is not our decision. He forms his leaders and places them in their leadership roles.

Leaders Are Gifted
This is especially true in the church. Many believe a leader is validated by his or her leadership gifts and training. It is obvious this person can lead and has the character qualities necessary for leading. Followers focus on a person's personal and family testimony. Significant questions are asked: Does this person manifest the fruit of the Spirit? What are this leader's achievements and what has been his/her previous service? Are there sound relational strengths? Can this person shepherd people?

Character matters, but in the end, one's gifting is most important. One's inherent ability to lead is the main qualification to be a leader. Those who evidence this gift are developed into mature leaders by careful study, responsible mentoring, and the nurture of a collective community. This will enable them to mentor others.

Leaders Are Those Who Pursue Leadership
Others see leadership as something less received and more taken. Whether God is involved or not, one becomes a leader by being clever, diligent, charismatic, and opportunistic. Leaders amass power, and this keeps them in their positions. Their motives for leading are less about serving the people and more about achieving fame and popularity. Humility does not fit their profile.

Followers tend to encourage this, recognizing and conferring leadership on those with dominant personalities. Latinos affirm and dutifully follow, but they may also be wearing a mask, covering the fact that their decision to follow is driven by pragmatism. They follow someone who knows how to generate growth, increase numbers, multiply finances, and build large buildings.[44]

Summarizing What We Hear

However one becomes a leader, one is accorded special privileges and prerogatives. Leaders will do everything to protect these. Part of this protection involves them wearing their own masks. It is important to give an aura of having it all together. Leaders have to appear strong.

If leaders are criticized, it is not open criticism. This would be to shame and dishonor those who lead. Hence, conflicts go unaddressed. This is why the vast majority of leaders are not very successful at dealing with conflict resolution.

Latin America needs leaders who have acquired their leadership in legitimate ways. Seizing control and forcing themselves on others is not a rightful way. We need leaders who are accorded the role because they are divinely gifted, have pursued appropriate training, and have received a divine summons. They maintain the right because they have a deep love and respect for those they lead. They are humble leaders who readily listen, who recognize their mistakes and correct themselves.

We need leaders who seek to learn, and who are intentional to surround themselves by wise mentors. We want men and women whose leadership is obvious – not because of their smooth oratory and ability to impress, or their acquisition of power, but because they have been anointed by the Spirit.

Lessons from a Latino World

Omar's observations are needful in the West. As in every culture, there has been a history of successful and unsuccessful leaders in the Latino world. But despite the failure of certain leaders, Latinos have a deep history of showing respect for, and deference to, the office. "Honor" and "esteem" are significant words in Latin American culture. No matter how a leader acquires leadership, Latinos express a certain admiration for that leader.

We must hear this voice. What does it matter if a leader has been gifted, trained, or summoned if he or she leads in a culture of disrespect? Too often we do not pause to ask: Has this person been divinely summoned? Has this leader been gifted and called for this moment? Is there a history of disciplined study that we are dismissing?

---

44. Editor's note: an example of the masks that Dr Gava refers to can be seen in Octavio Paz's essay, "Mexican Masks," in his *Labyrinth of Solitude*.

Despite a turbulent history, Latinos value the word "honor." They maintain a civility that many of us in the West have lost. Leadership in Western culture is about popularity and being liked. This is not so important in a Latino context. The desire to be loved as a leader is self-limiting. What matters is that a leader is gifted and summoned, and then respected by those he or she leads.

Finally, those who acquire leadership in Latino culture are not judged so much by their performance. American leadership tends to be mechanistic. One's success is determined by acquiring leadership and accomplishing tasks. Latin American leadership is more about acquiring leadership and building relationships, and less about achieving goals.

A few resources that might help to add texture and depth to the understanding of leadership in Latin America are: Geert Hofstede, Gert Jan Hofstede, and Michael Minkov's *Cultures and Organizations: Software of the Mind*; Justo González's *Mañana: Christian Theology from a Hispanic Perspective*; Richard Lewis's *When Cultures Collide*; and Douglas McConnell's *Cultural Insights for Christian Leaders*.

The Voice We Must Hear

Imagine standing before God and asking the question, "How does someone become a leader?" Here's what I am assuming God would say.

Becoming a Leader Is God's Prerogative

Leadership is not something we create, any more than we make the color of our hair, the shape of our nose, or the intelligence level of our brains (though plenty of people attempt to alter these). Nor is leadership an acquisition. It can't be purchased. It is not there on the shelf for those in the market for leading. God is the original cause, and leadership is God's to give. It comes out of his free will, not ours.

Scripture reveals that leadership is bestowed on leaders called to carry out the will of God. "By me kings reign and rulers issue decrees that are just" (Prov 8:15). God steps into Joshua's life and informs him that God has made him to serve as his leader (Josh 1:1–9). Of David, the prophet Isaiah writes: "See, I have made him a witness to the peoples, a ruler and commander of the peoples" (Isa 55:4; see also Ps 78:70–71). Divine presence, gravitas, and created skill sets were there in people like Joseph, Deborah, Samuel, Daniel, and Nehemiah. Leadership is of God's making.

Recognizing Leadership Is Our Responsibility

What tells us that a person is made for leadership? How does Scripture inform us? In our search, this is what we should be asking:

Have I Been Gifted?

Did God wire me to be a leader? Leadership is a gift God bestows on certain people. We are all given different capacities. The writer of Romans and 1 Corinthians likens the church to a body with different parts, each one distinguished from the others. These parts are a metaphor for gifts, each the work of the Trinity (Rom 12:4–8; 1 Cor 12:4–6). One of these extraordinary abilities is leadership. Gifts are not the result of one's choosing, but are produced in us at birth (or perhaps in extraordinary moments) *as God wills*. He endows all of us with certain talents, like leadership, and when we give our lives to God, those talents are used to accomplish his purpose, express his power, and serve the common good (1 Cor 12:7–11).

In Romans, the term for leadership is *prohistemi*. Its earliest usage speaks of one who is before or over someone. It is a gift that enables one to rule, lead, and govern, be it in the institution of the military, political government, or the church.[45] It includes the idea of guarding and protecting and is a necessary qualification of those leading the church (1 Tim 3:4, 12). If this is our gift, we are to exercise it with a sense of urgency (Rom 12:8). If you have the gift of leadership, you can't afford to be half-hearted.

In 1 Corinthians, a related term, *kubernesis*, is also used to describe the spiritual gift of leading, of mobilizing others (12:28). Some have distinguished the two words, one as emphasizing leading (*prohistemi*) and the other as emphasizing administrating (*kubernesis*). We see this in various spiritual gift surveys, but this is an artificial distinction. Both terms describe one who is in a leadership position. *Kubernao* was used of sailors in the Mediterranean (see Acts 27:11 and Rev 18:17, where the pilot of the ship is referred to as the *kubernete*).[46] This would suggest that *kubernesis* refers to one's ability to strategize and steer through rough terrain.[47] Its placement in the list of gifts (just before tongues) underscores that it is a role of steering the church and keeping things in order. It is a term related to the Latin *gubernare*, meaning to govern, guide.

---

45. Coenen, "Bishop, Presbyter, Elder," 193.

46. Coenen, 193.

47. Thiselton, *First Epistle to the Corinthians.*

Both Testaments affirm that everything necessary for wise leadership comes from God's hand. You cannot make yourself someone God has not gifted you to be. Gifts are distributed "just as he determines" (1 Cor 12:11). His gifting is there at birth and validated by the inner passion one has to lead. Others affirm it, and divine empowerment comes when one leads. There is the invisible, but real, presence of the Spirit, transforming natural leadership into something supernatural (Luke 24:49; 1 Cor 3:16).

What do you see? If God has gifted you to lead, then go, acquire followers, influence hearts, and point people in a divine direction.

But here's something else to ask:

Have I Been Summoned?

God appoints people for particular tasks at particular times. He summons as well as unsummons (Ps 75:6–7).[48] Gifts are sometimes secondary to God's appointment. This requires that leaders be attentive to their leadership moment – and seize it. They cannot procrastinate. As Erwin McManus notes, "Moments move in a timely manner, and time waits for no one. Though it may seem the case, time never stands still. And like petals of a rose, moments fall to the ground once there is no life in them."[49]

When we seize this moment, often there is a fresh influx of the Spirit. A power sends to flight fear and intimidation. God sweeps leaders up into his mission. Sometimes they are willing; sometimes they are not.

- It was there in the desert with Abraham. God summoned Abraham to lead a great nation (Gen 12:1–2).
- It was there in the wilderness with Moses. God summoned Moses to lead God's people out of Egypt (Exod 3:10).
- It was there in Joseph's dream. God summoned Joseph to reign over his people (Gen 37:5–7).
- It was there with Joshua. God summoned Joshua to take off his sandals and prepare to lead God's people into the land (Josh 3:7; 5:15).
- It was there with Gideon. God summoned him to outwit the Midianites (Judg 6:14).
- It was there with Jonathan. God led his spirit to rise and defeat the Philistines (1 Sam 14:1–15).

---

48. Langer, "Toward a Biblical Theology of Leadership," 68.

49. McManus, Seizing Your Divine Moment, 11.

- It was there with kings like Saul and David. God summoned them to be his kings (1 Sam 16:13).
- It was there with Elijah, Jeremiah, and all of the prophets. God summoned men to lead Israel to repentance (1 Kgs 18:21; Isa 6:9; Ezek 2:3; Jer 3:14).
- It was there in Galilee with the disciples. Jesus summoned emerging leaders to lead the church (John 21:15).
- It was there on the Damascus road with the apostle Paul. God summoned Paul to lead history in a new direction (Acts 9:15).

Is Leadership My Inheritance?

There are periodic examples where leadership acquisition is a matter of bloodlines. Theology makes room for this. Solomon becomes a leader of Israel because he is part of an established dynasty created by God (2 Sam 7:11–16). Having the right ancestral line enables some to inherit the office.

In certain cases, those who inherited the office demonstrated leadership. In other cases, they were dismal failures at leading. Nepotism is no guarantor of leadership. Through the line of the Omrides, godless and ineffectual leadership passed from father to son.

In the Davidic dynasty to the south, leadership also passed from father to son. In certain cases, both the office and the gift passed on. Some were good, faithful, and wise in their leadership (think Asa, Jehoshaphat, Uzziah, Hezekiah, and Josiah). They governed the nation, stewarded resources, and successfully led armies. Others were leaders in name only. While the office was passed on to them, they did not evidence divine summons, skilled training, or giftedness for leading. They were rebuked by prophets and died with little regret. One thinks of Rehoboam, Manasseh, and numerous no-names.

There is some evidence that leadership was an inherited right of priests. They represented a major authority in Israel, having an interdependent relationship with the kings. Initially, their right to acquire leadership was inherited. God appointed Aaron and his four sons to be his priests (Exod 28). Eli was promised that he *and his family* would minister before the Lord forever (1 Sam 2:30).

Godly behavior, however, trumps bloodlines, and Eli's sons forfeited the leadership passed on to them. There came a moment when leadership of the priesthood was no longer an inherited right (1 Sam 2:31–36). The same happened with the judges. Though Samuel prepared to pass leadership to his sons, their godless behavior prompted Israel to reject their leadership and turn to another source (1 Sam 8:1–5).

As for the two other major leadership offices in the Old Testament, the prophet and the sage, there is little evidence of leadership passing on through bloodlines. There was a group called "the sons of prophets," but unlike the priesthood and royal family, this guild was not hereditary. "Son," in this case, did not denote a biological relationship.

By the New Testament period, leadership acquisition had little to do with inheritance, though some hold that the authority of the apostolic office has passed from one generation to the next. There is no biblical evidence that apostolic leadership is an inherited right, and there is some uncertainty as to whether this leadership position is still operative. Qualifications for leadership in the early church had nothing to do with bloodlines. Paul mentions, "faithful to his wife," but says nothing about "son of an elder" (1 Tim 3:1–7).

How Is God Shaping Me?

Leadership does not come fully developed. Those God has created, gifted, and summoned to lead must undergo training. In almost every leadership story, preparation is a part of it. Equipping leaders to lead has always been at the heart of God's redemptive plan.[50]

In his *Leadership Secrets of the Bible*, Lorin Woolfe describes the Bible as "the greatest collection of leadership case studies ever written."[51] We are wise to learn from them and their maturing process, though it's not easy to derive great principles of leadership from the biblical models. Most are bad.[52] Learning is necessary, and school is never out. Leaders like Joseph, Moses, Joshua, David, and Paul were born leaders, but throughout their lives they were tutored in leadership development. God uses numerous tools:

God Uses Nurture

In Proverbs, fathers and mothers are called to train up children in the way they should go (Prov 22:6). Impart leadership training to those gifted to lead. Paul tells Timothy that leadership is to be modeled and imparted "in the presence of many" (2 Tim 2:2). Leadership training is a community endeavor. As we have seen, African culture seeks to reflect the communal setting of scriptural stories, where parents and community played a key role in training.

---

50. Plueddemann, *Leading across Cultures*, 55.

51. Woolfe, *Leadership Secrets from the Bible*, ix.

52. Plueddemann, *Leading across Cultures*, 66.

God Uses Difficult Circumstances

Sometimes leadership training is most effective when the conditions are harsh. David is a chapter in the "Who's Who of Leadership." God anoints him to lead and throws him into the wilderness to refine his gift (1 Sam 16:13 – 2 Sam 1:27). It's necessary. David is a mix of courageous and conniving, loyal and self-serving, architect and adulterer, sensitive and vengeful.

We are a mix as well, and sometimes the lessons come through dark nights of the soul.

Other examples that come to mind include Abraham (years of waiting); Moses (constant criticism); Joshua (defeat); Nehemiah (discouragement); Jeremiah (imprisonment); Paul (personal attack); and Peter (rebuke and shame). Are there any exceptions?

God Uses Wisdom

Proverbs is the leadership manual *par excellence*. The audience included the royal court – those who would be kings, princes, and up-and-coming diplomats. There is no comparable book that lays out the characteristics of wise leaders. The sage goes over royal leadership – everything from table manners, to the glory that comes when leaders search matters out, to how to bring stability to a land (Prov 23:1; 25:2; 29:4). Kings are instructed to keep sober so that their followers might experience justice (31:4–5).

Those leaders who give themselves to the discipline of wisdom – to the daily work of meditation, walking, reading, and reflecting – discern rhythms and patterns. They get in tune with what is self-evident – what is reality. They learn that for every cause, there is an effect (Prov 11:31). When a leader becomes self-absorbed, there is less to find absorbing. This is how life works.

God Uses the Life of Christ

Jesus's life serves as Leadership 101. Those who study his life discover some of the greatest leadership principles. This is evident in numerous books exploring the ways he led:

- Bob Briner and Ray Pritchard, *The Leadership Lessons of Jesus.*
- Laurie Beth Jones, *Jesus, CEO.*
- Michael Youssef, *The Leadership Style of Jesus.*
- Charles Manz, *The Leadership Wisdom of Jesus.*
- C. Gene Wilkes and Calvin Miller, *Jesus on Leadership.*
- Bill Robinson, *Incarnate Leadership: 5 Leadership Lessons from the Life of Jesus.*
- Ken Blanchard and Phil Hodges, *Lead like Jesus.*

In studying the life and teachings of Christ, one learns how to show compassion and serve people, lead with authority, mentor a team, be strategic and decisive, engage in conflict, and stay with the mission no matter the consequences. Ken Blanchard, a management expert, has written sixty books on leadership. He is best known for his *One Minute Manager,* but after coming to Christ, he acknowledged that Jesus had already said everything he wrote.

The message is clear: apart from development, leadership will be ineffectual. Undeveloped gifts will lie dormant. Summoned leaders will not be up to the task.

Bringing the Voices Together

How does one become a leader? With clarity and force, God tells us that leadership ultimately comes from him. He alone delegates authority. Any weight we carry is derived from him (John 19:11). But leadership must be developed. If we assume otherwise, or trivialize the gift, we run the risk of plunging into emptiness and meaninglessness.[53] Gifted leaders who submit their minds to the best possible leadership training, and train their ears to discern and respond to a divine calling, change the world. So, if you are anointed, trained, and summoned . . . lead, or get out of the way. But in your leading, establish credibility.

---

53. Barton, *Strengthening the Soul of Your Leadership,* 74.

4

If You Want to Influence Others, Make Your Character Count

Two of my colleagues in ministry have recently made poor choices. The first committed sexual immorality. He betrayed his spiritual community, not to mention his marriage. As a result, he has forfeited his job – and maybe his brilliant career. Future speaking engagements, as well as any upcoming book contracts, will likely go on hold or go away. The second colleague was exposed after enjoying the perks of a five-year embezzlement scheme. He has a long, torturous road ahead, serving time, paying off his debts, and regaining trust.

Both men have lost much. Worst of all, they have sacrificed what most leaders invest energy in acquiring: credibility.

In their book *The Truth about Leadership*, Kouzes and Posner write, "Credibility is the foundation of leadership. This is the inescapable conclusion we've come to after thirty years of asking people *around the world* what they look for and admire in a leader."[1] Followers want a leader who is solid, dependable, reliable, and trustworthy. Not a con – someone who is suspect, who might have a pathological need to be relevant and will compromise everything to acquire significance.

They want someone they can respect.

So what makes a leader credible? What gives followers reasonable grounds for believing a leader? What do leadership studies tell us?

---

1. Kouzes and Posner, *Truth about Leadership*, 15.

The Voices We Hear

Credibility requires two non-negotiables. The first is moral excellence. There is no trimming of one's principles to satisfy one's cravings, no cutting of one's conscience to fit this year's fashions.[2] Followers value those who hold themselves to the highest standards. But character alone is not enough.

Second, a leader must be competent. We want leaders who know what they are doing. Competent leaders evidence capacity and demonstrate expertise in their leading. They gain credibility as they develop and employ their leadership skills.

Let's begin with character, the focus of this chapter. Most would agree that leadership credibility starts here. If you are not convinced of the need to establish a set of principles, or do not insist on living by them, you will suffer a loss of esteem. It will not matter how much you are gifted or what title is on your door; you are an empty suit.

What Do We Mean By Character?

It's not enough to describe a person's attributes, distinguishable features, and notable traits. These are part of one's character, but character includes what is underneath, one's inner reality, the bottom line in which all behavior is rooted.[3]

Think of character as the aggregate of a person's moral qualities, and demonstrated through the values, beliefs, and choices that person makes. You see it . . .

- in how a person is moved or unmoved by injustice;
- in how a person copes with setbacks;
- in how a person deals with promotions;
- in how a person handles finances;
- in how a person controls appetites;
- in how a person treats power and authority;
- in how a person values loyalty;
- in how a person responds to criticism and personal attack.

The right choices increase one's standing.

---

2. Bennis, *On Becoming a Leader*, 41.
3. Guiness, *Character Counts*, 12.

Can A Leader Be Successful apart from Core Values?

On the surface, it appears that a leader can be successful apart from core values. In more functional cultures (especially those in the West), we sometimes trade character for performance. We are willing to overlook character flaws as long as a leader achieves. In the world of politics, an elected official might be guilty of self-aggrandizement and vulgarity, but in the end constituents give greater weight to campaign promises kept. In the corporate world, quarterly earnings are often the bottom line. Even in the religious world, a pastor's small peccadillos might be swept under the rug if attendance, growth, and personal giving are off the charts.

Even if we argue that character matters, is it critical to success? Consider the following examples. Alexander the Great created one of the world's largest empires by the age of thirty. His armies would follow him to the ends of the earth. But character? He had multiple wives, lived out a number of sexual distortions, descended into paranoia, and died, at age thirty-two, after a two-day drinking binge.[4]

Lyndon Johnson was one of America's most accomplished presidents. Yet for decades, like all too many presidents, he made up truth as he went along. Under pressure, he simply said what was necessary in order to prevail, and he seemed wholly unembarrassed when caught in a lie.[5]

History will remember Steve Jobs of Apple as one of *the* remarkable business leaders of our time. Some have likened his inventive genius to that of Thomas Edison or Henry Ford. Though Jobs set a standard for innovative leadership, he valued success over people. His passion for perfection led to abusive behavior. And Jobs's silences could be as searing as his rants. As his biographer Walter Isaacson put it, "He was not a model human boss or being, tidily packaged for emulation. Driven by demons, he could drive those around him to fury and despair."[6] And yet his accomplishments were staggering.

It doesn't seem to require principle to get to the top. In a recent article in *Harvard Business Review*, "Why Do Toxic People Get Promoted?," the author writes, "Sometimes the wrong people get promoted. They might be deceitful and unscrupulously manipulative (what psychologists call 'Machiavellian'); or impulsive and thrill-seeking without any sense of guilt (psychopathic); or egotistically preoccupied with themselves, having a sense of grandiosity, entitlement, and superiority (narcissistic). Employees with one or more of

---

4. Martin, *Ancient Greece*, 197.
5. Plantinga, *Not the Way It's Supposed to Be*, 151.
6. Isaacson, *Steve Jobs*, loc. 285.

these three personality traits, known as the 'dark triad,' are more likely to cheat, engage in fraudulent or exploitive workplace behavior, and make unethical decisions."[7] Yet they rise up through the ranks.

In the book *The Road to Character*, David Brooks, *New York Times* columnist, lays bare our tendency to measure a career by accomplishments rather than by a person's interior life: "We live in a culture that teaches us to promote and advertise ourselves and to master the skills required for success."[8] Ambition matters more than humility, empathy, and honest self-confrontation. Leaders invest themselves in what is extrinsic – numbers, control, innovative prowess, great accomplishments, surging profits, and charismatic personalities. They spend little time looking beyond the surface. Sure, there may be a fair amount of ethical baggage – rumored affairs, questionable income practices, fits of rage – but followers will turn a blind eye as long as leaders perform. For these leaders, it is more important to be remembered for what they achieved, not how they lived.

Maybe we are overselling character. Maybe a historian like Andrew Roberts is right: "Leadership – like courage and even sincerity – can be completely divorced from the concepts of good and evil."[9]

Are We Overselling or Underselling the Necessity of Character?

Let's argue that we are underselling character. The broad narrative of history affirms that leaders who give little attention to character development tend to create havoc in their worlds. Unaddressed interior corruption and turmoil eventually have a day of reckoning. Hubris, greed, corruption, cruelty, bullying, shamelessness, and appeals to people's darkest impulses come to the surface and despoil the things achieved. Such leaders lose what power and influence they gained. They eventually implode.

The overwhelming evidence underscores that leaders who are consumed with ideology, at the expense of character development, are dangerous. Ideologues are people who pretend they know a better way before they have taken care of their own chaos within.[10] Such people include Adolf Hitler, Mao-Tse-tung, Charles Manson, Jim Jones, Saddam Hussein, Osama bin Laden, and Abu Musab al-Zarqawi.

---

7. Templer, "Why Do Toxic People Get Promoted?"
8. Brooks, *Road to Character*, loc. 92.
9. Roberts, *Hitler and Churchill*, loc. 204.
10. Peterson, *12 Rules for Life*, 195.

Let's be honest. Historians do not look favorably upon these inhuman megalomaniacs. They had the essentials of leadership: followers, a directional aim, and influence. They touched many lives with their dogmas. Hitler harnessed envy and resentment to his chariot wheels, and they took him a long way.[11] But who wants to emulate someone who is morally vacant and abusive? Who needs a leader who is pompous and pretentious, a hate-filled bloodthirsty tyrant?

It's the opposite with leaders like Abraham Lincoln, Mahatma Gandhi, Winston Churchill, William Wilberforce, Pope John Paul II, Aleksandr Solzhenitsyn, Rosa Parks, Nelson Mandela, Elie Wiesel, Václav Havel, Liu Xiaobo, Malala Yousafzai, and others. Whatever ideologies they developed were built upon a moral foundation. Their dignity, their gravitas, their dreams of what might be, have inspired and stirred the imagination. They have left something behind worth remembering.

An article I read this morning about the passing of a world leader described a man who was a curious mixture of grandiosity and unaccountability. It said, "He fancied himself a great leader, but he was constitutionally incapable of accepting the burdens that great leadership entails."[12] "Constitutionally incapable" suggests an interior that received little attention. Such leadership stories are the ones we would just as soon forget.

Further, characterless leaders tend to leave a leadership vacuum. Because he failed to invest in future leadership, Alexander's empire swiftly broke up into warring states. Self-centered leaders are not inclined to invest in future leaders, given that they pour most of their energy in hanging on to what they have. In some cases, they breed a future generation that practices what's been preached. Like polluted rivers, godless leaders keep branching and re-branching into tributaries.[13] They propagate their pollution.

On the other hand, leaders who are selfless and noble, marked by fidelity and honor, are remembered. They generate energy. Rather than blind fanaticism or forced compliance, they create commitment and enthusiasm. This is why, in almost every survey on leadership, the leader's character is seen to matter. When they asked groups what they valued most in a leader, Kouzes and Posner discovered that it wasn't negotiating skills or force of personality. It was integrity.[14]

---

11. Roberts, *Hitler and Churchill*, loc. 3347.
12. Gourevitch, "Kofi Annan's Unaccountable Legacy."
13. Plantinga, *Not the Way It's Supposed to Be*, 53.
14. Kouzes and Posner, *Credibility*, 12.

People want leaders with great souls. Truthfulness rather than deception; loyalty rather than betrayal; self-effacement rather than self-promotion; compassion rather than oppression; decency rather than indecency; and sharing rather than exploitation. They need a leader who can express the values that hold a society together. They pray for a leader with the moral fiber to "lift people out of their petty preoccupations, carry them above the conflicts that tear a society apart, and unite them in the pursuit of objectives worthy of their best efforts."[15]

More and more, corporations are acknowledging a relationship between strength of character and business accomplishment.[16] People with integrity and compassion tend to outperform "self-focused CEOs." Given the large number of leader implosions, there is an increased awareness that achievement cannot come at the expense of principle.

Consider the story of American manufacturing giant Johnson & Johnson. In 1979, the CEO, James Burke, summoned his twenty strategic leaders, pointed to an internal document and proposed destroying it. It was entitled "Our Credo." It was a document originally created to underscore the values of Johnson & Johnson. It included such creeds as "a higher duty to mothers and all others who use our products." The document had been a fixture since 1943, but Burke was afraid that it was no longer a factor in the corporation's day-to-day decision making. He announced, "If we are not going to live by it, let's tear it off the wall." But he also knew that without a moral center, leaders swim in chaos.

In the end, Burke's team embraced the words. Three years later, Johnson & Johnson faced a crisis when someone tampered with one of its products. It was a tipping point. The company removed every bottle of Tylenol from every shelf of every retail outlet. They took a $100 million loss. But their gain was far greater. Their response remains the gold standard for dealing with corporate crises. It serves as a model for those leaders choosing to have core values guide their lives.

Contrast this with German automaker Volkswagen. When in 2015 the news broke that they had installed up to eleven million vehicles with software to cheat emissions regulations, the corporation ignored their failure. They carried on as if nothing was wrong. The bottom line drove the leaders. Today, Volkswagen is still working to repair a reputation that has been seriously marred, as well as recover a $25 billion loss.

---

15. John Gardner, quoted in Burns, *Leadership*, 451.
16. "Measuring the Return on Character."

Character matters.

Collins, in his book *Good to Great*, reveals that the corporations that have historically made it to the top have had one thing in common: principled leaders. Men and women with a compelling modesty. They don't talk about themselves, nor do they believe their own clippings.

The same rules apply to national leadership. Many acknowledge that history would read differently if American presidents read these words daily: "It is a great advantage to a president, and a major source of safety to the country, for him to know he is not a great man."[17] But too many have a smug certainty of their own virtue.

After serving numerous US presidents, David Gergen noted that the first lesson of leadership is that it starts from within. Even though some men, like Richard Nixon, were great strategists, and others, like Bill Clinton, were gifted tacticians, their presidencies were diminished because they could not manage the fault lines deep within their characters. Gergen's assessment is that "They were living proof that before mastering the world, a leader must achieve self-mastery."[18]

Other fields are coming to the same conviction about character. Consider the military world. Edgar Puryear, professor at Georgetown, spent thirty-five years studying military leadership and came to this conclusion: "From all of my research, it is absolutely clear that there is nothing as important in successful leadership as character."[19] American Army General Norman Schwarzkopf once said to his troops, "Leadership is a potent combination of strategy and character. But if you must be without one, be without strategy."[20] The message to his peers was clear: as go the generals, so goes the army.

True leadership begins with self-leadership.

Character is especially critical in the religious realm. Ministry is a character profession. Congregants expect their leaders to aspire to moral excellence in everything they do. There is no room for unfaithfulness or greed. Of the fifteen qualities listed for a pastor in 1 Timothy 3:1–7, all but one deal with a pastor's character. Reverence is high on the list; it is what keeps spiritual leaders from acting like gods.

Nineteenth-century English preacher, Charles Spurgeon, wrote to his students: "We are, in a certain sense, our own tools, and therefore must keep

---

17. Calvin Coolidge wrote these words.
18. Gergen, *Eyewitness to Power*, 345.
19. Puryear, *American Generalship*, 1.
20. Quoted in Maxwell, *21 Irrefutable Laws of Leadership*, 58.

ourselves in order. It will be in vain for me to stock my library, or organize societies, or project schemes, if I neglect the culture of myself."[21]

It is vital that we honestly and relentlessly evaluate, question, challenge, and improve ourselves. We must humbly admit our strengths, while realizing these can become our weaknesses. We need to honestly admit our limitations, recognizing that these are Achilles heels that will cause us to stumble if not addressed.

What Are the Essentials of Moral Excellence?

There seems to be no definitive list of moral qualities, though there have been attempts at putting one together. For Aristotle, and for the tradition that developed after him, there were four principal virtues: wisdom, justice, temperance, and courage.[22] These were considered the essence of character. Others have held that virtues begin with a natural law that all humans can know through reason. Reason is the only sensible guide and the final arbiter in determining moral values.

Over time, and with the Enlightenment and modernity, any unified sense of moral standards collapsed, especially in the West.[23] People have to decide on their own how to be. Many of our present values have been reduced to emotions and feelings. Character is about following your heart. In the end, what matters is to be true to your felt self. This, according to Bennis, is how people begin to become leaders.[24]

Some, like Kouzes and Posner, have surveyed people to bring these thoughts and feelings together, in order to determine what characterizes moral excellence. In one of their surveys, they asked some 75,000 people around the globe: "What values, personal traits, or characteristics do you look for and admire in a leader?"[25] The results did not vary demographically, organizationally, or culturally. In terms of essential values, here are some that made it to the top: honesty, fair-mindedness, courage, compassion, and loyalty.[26]

21. Spurgeon, *Lectures to My Students*, 12.
22. Hollinger, *Choosing the Good*, 130.
23. See the foreword to Prior's *On Reading Well*, loc. 65.
24. Bennis, *On Becoming a Leader*, 53.
25. Kouzes and Posner, *Leadership Challenge*, 28.
26. Kouzes and Posner, *Credibility*, 14.

What Is the Way to Principled Leadership?

If we accept that ethics matters, how does a leader cultivate moral character? How does one build such values as integrity and credibility into one's life? Can they be gained through a weekend seminar? Do authoritative pronouncements inspire character?

Every year, the US president, US Senate, state governors, and officials around the world proclaim the third week in October "CHARACTER COUNTS! Week." Here's a recent proclamation: "Now, therefore, I, Donald J. Trump, President of the United States of America, by virtue of the authority vested in me by the Constitution and the laws of the United States, do hereby proclaim October 15 through October 21, 2017, as National Character Counts Week. I call upon public officials, educators, parents, students, and all Americans to observe this week with appropriate ceremonies, activities, and programs." It seems odd to put character on the same level as other presidential pronouncements (e.g. National Tartan Day, National School Lunch Week, and National Ice Cream Month). Does a presidential proclamation do anything other than trivialize character as some seven-day observance? What about the other fifty-one weeks of the year?

There are better answers. Many would agree that character development is a process, a deep interior work. An increasing number of leadership books are urging leaders to give greater attention to this life work of becoming more self-aware. Here one finds one's moral compass, one's bearings for moving forward.[27] Bennis concedes, "When I've been most effective, I've listened to that inner voice."[28]

Probing into one's interior is not always pleasant. Those who are honest find that there are competing forces at work. Most leadership biographies acknowledge that leaders are a mix of light and dark. Evan Thomas's description of American President Richard Nixon illustrates the point: "In Nixon the light and dark strains were inextricably intertwined, impossible to disentangle. They fed each other. Nixon's strengths were his weaknesses."[29]

Likewise, Jon Meachum gives this portrayal of an earlier American leader, Thomas Jefferson: "The real Jefferson was like so many of us a bundle of contradictions, competing passions, flaws, sins, and virtues that can never be

---

27. Bill George devotes a whole book to this: *Discover Your True North.*
28. Bennis, *On Becoming a Leader,* 34.
29. Thomas, *Being Nixon,* loc. 9602.

really smoothed out into a tidy whole. The closest thing to a constant in his life was his need for power and for control."[30]

The nature of our human psychology is such that we are all a mix of strength and weakness, maturity and immaturity, other-centeredness and self-centeredness, angels and beasts. On the darker side, a leader must be aware of certain risk factors. Think of them as the Seven A's:

- Anger
- Abuse
- Arrogance
- Avarice
- Apathy
- Adultery
- Addiction[31]

Given this darker side, there needs to be a disciplined willingness to deny self. Brooks describes it as a work of "self-restraint, self-erasure and self-suspicion."[32] We have a propensity to lie to ourselves, and this undermines leadership at every level.

In the end, one has to come back to knowing one's true self. According to Bill George in his *Discover Your True North*, the way to principled leadership is to become self-aware, learn from your story, process your crucibles and setbacks, listen to feedback, and identify the values that will guide your leadership.[33] What matters is that one is true to oneself. Who wants to follow a leader who is not authentic? And authenticity, according to George, is the "gold standard" for leadership.[34]

Summarizing What We Hear

If a leader is to be credible, he or she must begin with character. Some may dismiss the importance of character, given that some leaders have been moral failures but great success stories. It goes back to how one chooses to define success. The best leaders have determined to choose and adhere to a set of core values. For many today, this begins with a healthy self-awareness. This is the

---

30. Meacham, *Thomas Jefferson*, loc. 10074.

31. From a conversation with Steve Stephens, a behavioral psychologist who works with leaders who have lost their way.

32. Iyer, "'The Road to Character' by David Brooks."

33. George, *Discover Your True North*, 118.

34. George, 1.

foundation of authenticity, which acts to guide one's moral compass. Creating this awareness, however, is not a one-week exercise; it requires a lifetime of commitment and learning.

The Voices We Need to Hear

Every culture has a set of written and unwritten core values. What is ethical in one context may be unethical in the next. Bribery might be business as usual in one place, but an unprincipled practice in the next. It goes back to the foundations upon which principles are built.

Some grow up in cultures where *being* is valued over *doing*. Character is more important than competence. But this is not the case in other parts of the globe.

How important is character in India?

The Voice of Paul Gupta, President, Hindustan Bible Institute and Global Partners, Chennai, India

Paul Gupta is leading a ministry begun by his father in 1952. HBI is one of the earliest indigenous movements created by a national. The aim has been one of developing theological leaders. His thoughts on core values are complemented by other Indian voices, including Ivan Satyavrata (Senior Pastor and Chairman, the Assembly of God Church and Mission, Kolkata, India) and David Dayalan (National Director of Asian Access/India).

The Importance of Core Values

India has a history of principled figures who have helped to shape the moral values of our culture.[35] These include Mahatma Gandhi, Swami Vivekananda, and Rabindranath Tagore, as well as more contemporary leaders like Jayaprakash Narayan, Vinoba Bhave, and Anna Hazare.

Though India is immense (one billion people and counting) and diverse (a federal union of twenty-nine states), there is agreement that values do affect how one leads.

---

35. Sources for Gupta's contribution include Babu, "Ratan Tata"; Collins and Porras, *Built to Last*; Collins, *Good to Great*; Covey, *7 Habits of Highly Effective People*; Drucker, *Management*; Elmer, *Cross-Cultural Conflict*; Friedman, *World Is Flat*; Gandhi, *Autobiography*; George, *Discover Your True North*; Gerth and Mills, *From Max Weber*; Greenleaf, *Servant Leadership*; Hunt, *Gandhi and the Nonconformists*; Huntington, *Clash of Civilizations*; Jones, *Christ of the Indian Road*; *Mahatma Gandhi*; Lingenfelter, *Leading Cross-Culturally*; Maxwell, *21 Irrefutable Laws of Leadership*; Taylor, "How Howard Schultz"; Thomson, *Gandhi and His Ashrams*.

Transformation has to be inside out, not outside in. Without it, a leader will not be able to rise above his or her circumstances. One will find oneself powerless and under the suppression and control of others. This begins at the earliest stage. Apart from character development, one's progress to adulthood will be hindered.

When a leader determines his or her core values, this same leader is able to develop a core ideology, one that guides the leader. A basic set of precepts acts like a fixed stake that is planted in the ground. It defines who we are, what we stand for, and what our lives are all about. When one's values are unclear, one's ideology is fuzzy and uncertain. Institutions and leaders begin to do things that have no connection to the purpose (or best interests) of the organization.

Common Core Values

The order of one's core values depends upon a variety of factors, such as social status, education, and cultural conditioning. Though not given in any specific order, the following represent some of the core values many Indian leaders, particularly Christian, seek to pursue:

Loyalty and Trust

India's traditional leadership is hierarchical. The wisdom of the oldest patriarch prevails. This is why loyalty to the leader supersedes one's personal interest.

Much of this is due to a religious history filled with authoritarian leaders. At the top of the religious pyramid are the high priests/pontiffs/religious heads – in the modern era, gurus. It is assumed that religious leaders are filled with the divine spirit, and they are feared because of the spiritual power they wield. The common people, including powerful political leaders, have always been subservient. They will even fall prostrate before these leaders.

In such a context, leaders expect ongoing devotion and support from their followers. Followers, in turn, look for encouragement, affirmation, and even protection from their leaders. Leaders will usually give these to them in a quid pro quo arrangement. In return for giving their loyalty, followers will turn to their leaders for protection, financial help, or power and influence to bail them out in times of crisis.

Unfortunately, this can degenerate into manipulative control on one side and an unhealthy sycophancy on the other. Followers can become passive, unwilling, and/or unable to think, act or function without someone telling them what to do. This is avoided when leaders lead with humility and seek to serve.

Courage

Leaders need to live out the courage of their convictions. Mahatma Gandhi is an example.

Gandhi led a nonviolent freedom movement that eventually liberated India from British rule. His success was due to the strength of his moral character, as well as the courage and resolve to channel his energies into a political movement. Though he grew up in a high power distance culture, where status differences shaped the social interactions between leaders and followers, he would not yield to racial bias. Hence, he was declared "Mahatma," or "Great Soul," before he was fifty years old.

A story is told of a moment when he was on a train headed to Johannesburg, South Africa. At the time, Gandhi was a proficient lawyer trained in England. He worked as a barrister to the court under the Queen of England. On his way, train officials asked him to move from the first-class cabin to the van compartment, even though he held a first-class ticket.

Obviously, racial bias was at work. His unceasing pleas and explanations about his right to travel first class went unheeded. He stood his ground but, in the end, the official threw him off the train, along with his baggage.

Throughout his journey in South Africa, Gandhi saw others experience the same racial discrimination he had faced. More troubling, he recognized that people had become apathetic about the dignity of all humanity. Even when he addressed his Indian brothers and sisters, denouncing prejudice and bigotry, he realized that they had become indifferent. They did not have the will to hold to values that recognized the worth of fellow human beings. But over time, he awakened and emboldened his followers, the *satyagrahi.*

Gandhi saw himself as a David facing Goliath. There would be no cowardice. He had no fear of governments or jails or death. His moral courage impacted the behavior and decision making of a nation.

Family and Community First

India is a collectivist culture where family is an important source of identity. Interdependence is valued over independence. Consensus is critical in our decision making. Relationships matter most. They are more important than schedules.

Effective leaders lead in light of this. They respect the bond that keeps families together. They devote themselves to going deep in community, aiming to recognize the capacities of others. It is more important to understand than to be understood.

Honor

Our culture places great weight on guarding one another's name. Shame is avoided at all costs. Saving face is important. We particularly honor the wisdom of age. The wisdom of the oldest patriarch prevails. Giving respect to him supersedes any personal interest.

Consistency

Whatever values you hold to, you should live them out. For political and corporate leaders, this means being authentic. Do what you say. For Christian leaders, this means giving more weight to following Scripture than to following Western practices. To be consistent, an Indian leader needs to identify with the culture, develop an indigenous model of serving and look at ways to be culturally relevant. Many, however, simply want to imitate the West.

In the church, there's been a historic failure to follow Jesus without being co-opted by former traditions or old biases. Sadly, Gandhi saw a racial bias in the church. Especially troubling were the many Christian leaders who failed to live out the mandates of their faith. Though Gandhi was a Hindu, he studied the Bible and was influenced by the teachings and ideals of Jesus Christ. Most of his principles of nonviolence and civil obedience – ones that led to India's independence – were derived from the Scriptures. But inconsistency in the church turned him away.

Gandhi once told the missionary E. Stanley Jones, "When the Christians in India emulate Jesus Christ, you will not have to do anything, they will all become like him." Gandhi learned from Jesus that a leader's core values matter. Helping people see their dignity can change everything. But the church's leaders failed to live these values out, impacting Gandhi's future choices.

Financial Integrity

For many of us, financial integrity is a core value. It has to be, but this is very hard. The reality is that fraud and corruption are the order of the day. Dishonesty plagues both society and the church. Pastors can sometimes be amongst those who are most guilty. Like other leaders in traditional Indian culture, they can assume a guru-shishya model, where power is hoarded and unaccountability prevails.

Justice

In our world, where poverty, injustice, environmental destruction and gender discrimination are everywhere, we need leaders who are compassionate and just. Leaders have to demonstrate this so that others will rise up and speak against these evils.

These are some of the values we pursue, though the forces challenging them can be overwhelming.

Summarizing What We Hear

Ratan Tata, one of India's leading entrepreneurs, once made the statement that what the world is looking for is role models and mentors who can lead the way so that the next generation can follow. A loss of values, however, has led to a loss of models. The emerging generation is disillusioned. Unless leaders change course, we are headed for self-destruction.

I am convinced that it is only through the intentional efforts of leaders to once again embrace truth over falsehood, and absolutism over relativism, that the world will have hope. We don't need personality-driven, charismatic leaders. What we do need are leaders who are respected, above all, for their character.

Lessons from an Indian World

Listening to these Indian voices, I am reminded of James Plueddemann's observation that cultural practices are the externals, the things we see. In between are the values, the cultural ideals that link abstract philosophy to concrete practice. Every culture has its own practices and ideals, and these will create mix-ups and tensions.[36]

The core Indian ideals outlined here do not depart from many of the values held in other cultures, including those in the West. They do reinforce the importance of relationships. A more meditative culture honors being, though India is shifting to a culture of doing, known less for its gurus and more for its entrepreneurs. Like most other collective cultures, loyalty and respect are amongst the highest ideals. In every one of my trips to India, these have stood out.

There is another part of the world where character plays a critical role in effective leadership.

---

36. Plueddemann, *Leading across Cultures*, 71. One might also add Louis Fischer's, *Gandhi: His Life and Message for the World.*

The Voice of Luis Palau, Evangelist, Luis Palau Association, Portland, Oregon

Luis Palau is a dynamic evangelist who has influenced leaders around the world. He has met with presidents and prime ministers on nearly every continent. He and his team have had the opportunity to work with thousands of churches in hundreds of cities around the world, including nine top global cities: London, Hong Kong, Singapore, Chicago, Moscow, Madrid, Mexico City, Buenos Aires, and Washington D.C. Though he is in failing health, it was my privilege to spend a couple of hours with him talking about global leadership, particularly from a Latino perspective.

What sets apart Latino leaders from other leaders?

One word that comes immediately to mind is respect. Latin American leaders honor those they lead. This is very important in Latino culture. People in this part of the world follow someone who treats them with dignity. Unlike some cultures that are tribal in nature, Latinos are nationalists. Good leaders tap into this deep regard for the nation. Peruvians pride themselves in being Peruvians; Guatemalans pride themselves in being Guatemalans; etc.

In this book, another Latin leader made the same point. Why is respect so important in this culture?

It's important to understand that our culture, more than most, has experienced poverty and pain. It is a humble culture. People love a leader who steps into a room and gives immediate attention to the marginalized. They love it when a leader touches someone on the shoulder and expresses interest in one's life. When people are shown distinction, they will go to extremes to follow this kind of leader.

Is the Latin culture hierarchical, just as the Asian and African cultures?
Yes, but with a slight difference. Latinos do not revere their leaders like the Asians tend to do with their leaders. While Africans might avoid any expression of criticism, for fear of bringing shame or being ostracized from the community, Latinos are not afraid to disagree and criticize their leaders. Latinos are expressive. Leader and follower get into one another's face. But in the end you still submit and show respect.

What else is important?
Communication. Leaders who articulate their vision especially stand out.

What skill do Latinos admire in a leader?
The skill of bringing people together. Latinos are drawn to leaders who are perceptive, who discern the hearts of their people and mobilize a movement. They want a leader who understands his limitations. Skillful leaders help people overcome their difficult past.

How important is teamwork?
Latinos want to believe they have something important to bring to a team, and they respect a leader who recognizes one's gifts and wants these gifts to flourish.

What is your sense of Latino leadership today?
There are some solid leaders, but there are too many today who want to be flamboyant. They love to show off. They are in love with power, and they have become enamored with riches. These are not true leaders.

Who have been Latino leaders you respect?
Latinos gravitate to heroes. I think of leaders like General Jose de San Martin. He was the prime leader of the southern part of South America. He was a soldier, a statesman, and a national hero. He chased out the Spaniards, and just before he died in battle he declared, "I die contented. We have overcome the enemy." I also have a deep regard for other heroes, like Simon Bolivar and Domingo Sarmiento. They stood for the oppressed. They showed respect, They honored peoples' dignity. We respect these leaders.

The Voice We Must Hear

What is the contribution of theology to this issue of character? What does Scripture say about the core values of a leader? What does it affirm? How does it fill in some of the empty spaces?

Character Matters

Scripture affirms what earlier voices have shared. Leaders' achievements are not measured by the size of their armies, the boundaries of their kingdoms or the immensity of their wealth. Character matters more than earthly success – far more than charisma, competence or accomplishment. Character comes first. Those leaders who are moral are those who gather followers around a transcendent purpose.

Character has ultimate consequences. One only has to look at the instability of Jacob's world, the thinness of Saul's leadership and the implosion of Uzziah.

Behind every disaster that beset leaders in Scripture were unprincipled hearts. Character is the part-gyroscope, part-brake that provides the leader's strongest source of bearings and restraint.[37]

Character Begins with God's Character

"Value exists from the very beginning; it is rooted in a self-existent, good God."[38] This statement is a departure from most leadership books. Our morals are not self-derived. They are not found by going deep within. If we are just dancing to our DNA – over which we have no control – how do we know we are right about anything?[39]

Any discussion of moral standards begins outside of ourselves. It starts with God. For good reason: he is the essence of character. Any acts of righteousness originate with him. He does not conform to some moral benchmark outside of himself; he is that measure.[40] He is perfectly good, righteous, and holy. He is untouched by evil (Jas 1:13).

God's Core Values Inform Our Core Values

God has created leaders to model his character, regardless of their own inclinations or cultures. God requires moral excellence for he is morally perfect. "Be holy, because I am holy" is an often-repeated command (Lev 11:44–45; 19:2; 20:7, 26; 1 Pet 1:16). This is our highest duty: to reflect God's image and align with his attributes (see Matt 5:48). He communicates them in proportion to a leader's capacity to receive them.[41]

Embracing and manifesting the character of God is the task of leadership. It is not an option. It is the difference between effectiveness and ineffectiveness, success and failure. We see this from Genesis to Revelation. God calls leaders to be principled leaders (see Josh 1:7; Ps 15; 2 Chr 15:2; Mic 6:8; Rom 12:1–2).

There is no one list of values, but there are certain ideals that stand out in Scripture. They reflect God's priorities.

---

37. Guiness, *Character Counts*, 20. Note also Gushee and Holtz, *Moral Leadership for a Divided Age*.

38. Copan, *Is God a Moral Monster?*, 214.

39. Copan, 212.

40. Tozer, *Knowledge of the Holy*, 112.

41. Oden, *Classic Christianity*, 55.

Justice

There may be no ideal that rises above justice. God loves justice; his throne is built on righteousness (Ps 89:14). He bestows what is deserved, rendering good to the good and evil to the evil. Jesus's first sermon was a statement that he had come to right the wrong, set free the oppressed and remove economic injustice (Luke 4:18–19; Ps 140:12). To do justice is what he requires of us (Mic 6:8).

God commanded his people to appoint leaders to "judge the people fairly" (Deut 16:18). More than a judicious exercise, this is to be a leader's pursuit: "Follow justice and justice alone" (v. 20). Just leaders do not show partiality or take bribes. They cannot be bought. They do not minimize right, making it secondary or subservient to expediency, achievement or personal satisfaction. To do so is to subvert the cause of righteousness.

In the organizations they lead, just leaders create an environment of equity and fairness. In matters of disagreement, they weigh all of the evidence. In the workplace, they safeguard equity in the assignment of tasks, in the opportunities to advance and in their compensation. They view anything less than a fair wage as a form of theft.

In the broader world, just leaders are passionate to erase injustice and defend the oppressed (Prov 31:1–9; 20:8). They consider it unjust to be indifferent to the human condition. Their hearts grieve when they walk the backstreets and see suffering, the kind that comes because of unjust structures. They hate the kind of misdistribution where the rich get richer on the backs of the poor. They are white-hot when it comes to forms of abuse.

With the heart of a prophet, they speak out when law courts administer law but withhold justice (see Jer 22:3–5; Zech 7:9–10). They know that God looks for leaders who do more than be religious; they act on their faith and call a fast to break the chains of wickedness, untie the ropes and set free the oppressed, feed the hungry, and clothe the naked (Isa 58:1–7). They take a stand, even if it comes at a high cost.

Unprincipled leaders have little regard for justice. They run over rights (think Ahab and Naboth's field, 1 Kgs 21). They rob the poor because they are poor. They move the boundary markers. If they act to right the wrong, they do so only when it is expedient for them (Luke 18:1–5).

Integrity

God is truth; he cannot lie. His nature makes it impossible for him to deceive (Heb 6:18). Whatever he promises, he fulfills (Num 23:19). Integrity is integral to his being. The Hebrew word is *tamam*, and it speaks to that which is complete, whole, sound, and finished. There is a perfect wholeness to God.

Its antonym is *salaph*, and it describes one who is incomplete, unsound, and twisted. It has no application to God. His nature will not allow him to bend the truth, exaggerate or understate the facts, or fail to follow through.

Integrity, therefore, is an absolute requirement of those who lead in God's name. Like a compass, it will show the way ("The integrity of the upright guides them," Prov 11:3). Leaders with integrity steer straight and walk straight. One thinks of Moses, Deborah, Nehemiah, Jeremiah, Paul, and others – leaders who refused to live crooked lives.

Integrity requires truth-telling. Because God is truth, he hates lying. Lying makes God sick (Prov 6:16–19): the language here is intestinal. It must make us sick, too. Nothing disrupts like lying. It affects our worldview, our relationships and even our health. It is the folly of follies (Prov 14:8). Leaders like Nehemiah and Paul rested their case on their integrity (Neh 5:14–18; Acts 20:32–35). Their actions backed up their words, created credibility, and earned them the trust and confidence of their constituents.[42]

In a day of fake news, when dictionaries have added "post-truth" to their word lists, our age is desperate for leaders who will speak truth. People pray for leaders who will not make up reality nor plant half-truths. We long for leaders who will stick to their convictions in every situation; leaders who realize that when trust is broken, it takes a long time to restore it. Trust is the most fragile yet the essential attribute of leadership.[43]

Other words associated with integrity include straightforwardness, dependability, predictability, credibility, and confidentiality. Here's another: consistency – inside and out. To use N. T. Wright's words, integrity means there is a pattern of thinking and acting which runs right through someone, so that wherever you cut into that person (as it were), you see the same person through and through.[44]

Integrity requires a daily discipline of heart renovation (Prov 4:23). We must be ready. Who knows where opportunities might take us? "Your talent and giftedness as a leader have the potential to take you farther than your character can sustain you. That ought to scare you."[45]

As leaders move to higher responsibilities, they must give greater and greater attention to their integrity. They must not forget this maxim: "Integrity is like oxygen. The higher you go, the less there is of it." The temptations to fall

---

42. Kouzes and Posner, *Credibility*, xvii.

43. Goodwin, "Lessons of Presidential Leadership."

44. Wright, *After You Believe*, 27.

45. Stanley, *Next Generation Leader*, 151.

increase. Money, sex, and power – these three "Horsemen of the Apocalypse" – have been responsible for the downfall of many leaders.[46] The list in Scripture starts with Samson, Eli's sons, David, Solomon, Asa, and Uzziah.

Leaders without integrity are crooked. They have a tendency to pervert what is right. Think Esau or Saul in the Old Testament, Ananias and Sapphira in the New.

Courage

I love the fact that God is fearless. He never panics. He is never overwhelmed, immobilized by dread or consumed with worry. Jesus, as the incarnate God, steps into the world and stares down evil. He confronts and sets to flight the demonic (Matt 4:10; Mark 4:35 – 5:17). He tells the devil where to go and makes it clear to the world's leaders that their threats are of no concern to him. He stills the storms and silences the crowds. Everywhere he goes, he fearlessly carries out the will of the Father. He looks fear in the eye and doesn't blink.

Part of principled leadership is to be fearless. God's first command to Joshua was to be courageous (Josh 1:9). As part of his final words, David urged Solomon to be a man of courage (1 Chr 28:20). Daniel was not afraid to say it like it was (Dan 4:17–30). Paul ordered Timothy, as a leader of the church, not to have a spirit of timidity (2 Tim 1:7). God gives his leaders a spirit of power, not anxiety. When a leader chooses to lay hold of it, that leader can be bold as a lion (Prov 28:1).

Words associated with courageous leadership include nerve, audacity, resolution, guts, resilience, resolve, and determination. Leaders will need courage to say "yes" when everyone else is saying "no," and "no" when everyone else is saying it is OK. As Peterson notes, "To stand up straight with your shoulders back means building the ark that protects the world from the flood"[47] – even if no one wants to go up the ramp.

Without courage, we are too timid to say no – for fear of disappointing. We get away from the essentials and allow others to add busyness to our lives. The disciplined pursuit of focus becomes mere lip service.[48] Leaders will need nerve to face resistance aimed at sabotaging their intentions. They will need the courage to carry on, no matter the obstacles and enemies. Leaders are called to make the long climb, to stand firm in a good purpose in the midst of

---

46. Dolan, "Called to Lead," 27.
47. Peterson, *12 Rules for Life*, 27.
48. McKeown, *Essentialism*, 132.

difficulty; to hold to convictions that do not waver; to have the kinds of hands that do not go limp in a time of trouble (Prov 24:10).

Courageous leaders are cool under fire. They are indomitable. They do not flinch. They do the right thing, regardless of what it will cost personally. They give tough yes/no answers, confront difficult problems, make unpopular decisions and challenge people to change. They step out and challenge a "seatbelt society," which is more oriented toward safety, to unbuckle and seize the adventure.[49] Without courage, we take no risks. Without risk taking, we do not grow.

To fear man is to become ensnared (Prov 29:25). To fear God is to be set free. The fear of God is what marks a leader's wisdom (1:7). It is the soul of godliness, the very equivalent to walking with God. To fear God is to honor him, revere him, and take him seriously. It is to be awed by his infinite power and beauty. Holding this as a core value, a leader is able to enter into God's intimate counsel (Ps 25:14), experience God's steadfast love (103:11) and stand with courage and confidence (Prov 14:26). Embracing the fear of the Lord is the way to overcome the fears that come with this world.

Unprincipled leaders are fearful leaders. Think Saul sitting under the pomegranate tree, too paralyzed to lead (1 Sam 14:2), and leaders running when no one is chasing (Prov 28:1). As popular psychology teaches, fear causes us to fight, flee or freeze. It leads to its own psychopathology.

Compassion

When you study the character of God, it is impossible to overlook God's love, mercy, and compassion. We are drawn to him, not only for what he has accomplished on the cross, but for how deep his love is for us (Rom 5:8). God is the essence of loyal love, *hesed* (Exod 34:6); it is what defines him – it is who he is. His love has no beginning nor end, no impurities and no limits.

We cannot grasp this love – only point to it. It is a love that is lavished on us (Rom 5:5). How great is it? Theologian F. B. Meyer put it this way: "God's love is like the Amazon River flowing down to water one daisy." It is an unconditional love, and nothing and no one can separate us from it (Rom 8:38–39).

Principled leaders – those who intend to reflect something of the Divine – have this love as part of their characters. It moderates any tendency to be performance-oriented and goal-driven. It slows a leader who is on the verge of running over feelings or ignoring those who are grieving. We might impress people with our performance numbers, our fast-paced lives and our high-

---

49. Friedman, *Failure of Nerve*, loc. 129.

minded ambitions, but if those come at the expense of mercy and grace, we lack godly principles.

Love is everybody's business (1 John 4:7), but it is the main initiative of leaders. It is the ocean we are called to swim. It means little if it is not unconditional. This is what tells the world we are, at our core, principled. Love and compassion give a leader the necessary gravitas that compels people to follow. Loving people tells our constituents that we know God and God knows us (John 13:35). We are not only about mission statements, strategies, agendas and comprehensive operational plans. Our leadership is characterized by healing, reconciliation, new life and hope.[50] We should intend to be known for bearing – rather than inflicting – pain.[51]

Here are other expressions of this divine attribute: Leaders don't weigh people down with excessive demands. People see us as includers, not excluders. It affects us when we see failure and brokenness. It breaks our hearts. We guard against anything that kills the spirit – anything cold, impersonal, or toxic. Love is our heart, and without a heart we become annoying gongs and clanging cymbals (1 Cor 13:1).

Out of such love and compassion, principled leaders remain loyal to their followers. They are always asking what is in the best interests of the whole. They obligate themselves to both the institution and the people they lead. They are committed to people beyond what people can give to the organization, refusing to reduce people to profits, dollars, seats or units. When others attack, loyal leaders have their backs. They fight for relationships. They do not easily let go.

But Scripture tells us that loyal love is rare. Many claim it, but few live it (Prov 20:6).

Unprincipled leaders are tone-deaf to human needs. Like those in the Good Samaritan story, they walk right by. Think Rehoboam, who was more in love with power than with his people (1 Kgs 12:14).

Diligence

Think about this: God is never slow, late, forgetful, haphazard, idle, sluggish or lazy. It may appear at times that he sleeps (Ps 78:65), but he is ever awake, always aware (Matt 6:26).

God has to be attentive, for he holds all things together (Col 1:17). God is never distracted or careless. If his diligence were to wane for even a second, our universe would devolve into chaos. God never wastes time and never lacks

---

50. Nouwen, *In the Name of Jesus*, 27.
51. De Pree, *Leadership Jazz*, 139.

urgency. He may seem slow, but he is never late – just patient and unhurried (2 Pet 3:9). He is always observant and focused, thorough and meticulous, deliberate and persistent.

God honors such ways in his leaders (see Prov 12:11; 10:4; 12:24; 21:5). God-honoring leaders are attentive to the task. They are not haphazard, neglecting the details. Rather, they see their leadership as a privilege to serve and a stewardship to fulfill. Time is valued as a precious asset. There is something deeply immoral about wasting the day and squandering the responsibilities given by God. Wise leaders know that time cannot be recovered.

Psychologist Angela Duckworth refers to this sort of spirit as "grit." Grit is a combination of passion and perseverance, a doggedness to go after long-term goals.[52] God refers to it as an aspect of godliness. Those who follow him have a nose for stale air. They know that what got them here won't get them there. They press the envelope, encourage innovation, and honor those who invest in a job well done. They demand excellence and discourage mediocrity. Rigor, strictness and self-control mark their organization. They know where they are going, and are intentional in getting there. They ensure that frivolous distractions do not co-opt their time, energy or mission.

These all sound like corporate values, but they go back to the person of God. Nowhere does he commend leaders who are slackers, goof-offs, long-lunchers, loafers and couch potatoes. He has no patience for those whose accomplishment is going through their emails and calling it a day. These things are immoral.

Sloth disorders the soul, eats away at one's passion and compromises one's leadership. Without passion, jobs become a wearisome routine. Leaders become content with mediocrity, have no sense of urgency and resist the efforts that come with change. And this diminishes respect.

The worst laziness happens at the center. This is a leader neglecting his or her soul. It matters little if a leader is diligent in the workplace and neglectful of the heart. Think Solomon, whose spiritual sloth brought down his leadership (1 Kgs 11:4).

Humility

There's no greater example of humility than Jesus. Co-equal with the Father and Spirit, active in creating our universe and co-eternal with the Godhead, Jesus set these aside. Unlike an egotistic governor who can't let go of his or her position, or a corporate head unwilling to release the levers of control, Jesus

---

52. Duckworth, *Grit*, 290.

did not need to hang on to his credentials. He did not come into this world to showcase his authority, make a display of his importance or manipulate and exploit those around him (Phil 2:6–8). Rather, it was a choice to forgo status, place others before self, accept correction as an opportunity to grow and wield power in the service of others.[53]

We're to have the same mind (Phil 2:5). We must. There's a lot of ego attached to leadership. All too many leaders are narcissistic, driven by their own impressiveness.[54] Like a poodle so coddled it has forgotten it is a canine, a leader can be so adulated he forgets he is human. He begins to believe he is a messiah. Bloated with an exaggerated sense of self, his arrogance leads to overreach. Power is used for personal gain.

The temptations Jesus faced in the wilderness are the same temptations faced by every leader: seeking self-gratification, doing the spectacular to get attention and pursuing the right end the wrong way (Matt 4:1–9). And all of this has damaging consequences. When rank and position go to one's head, it can even cause brain damage. Under the influence of power, leaders, according to one study, become more impulsive, less risk-aware and less adept at seeing things from other people's point of view. They cross the line and endanger the health of everyone, including themselves.[55]

Humility is freeing. It liberates us from a life driven by self-consciousness. It keeps us centered. Arrogance forgets how life works. Asa decided that political realism, geopolitical scheming and military alliances were the key to security. They led to insecurity. Full of himself, Uzziah assumed the rules no longer applied. He no longer felt he was required to stay in the lanes other kings were required to stay in. He thought he could invoke executive privilege and reinvent reality. It cost him his leadership.

The list continues. There is a long line of names in Scripture of leaders who became full of self and no longer in need of God: Hezekiah, Ahab, Nebuchadnezzar, Haman, Herod, Pilate. As Brueggemann notes, "There runs through biblical faith the foolish notion that enough of power, wealth, and knowledge can make one immune to the ways of God."[56]

Jesus was not impressed with condescending and arrogant leaders. He called them out, and he warned his disciples not to learn nor emulate their ways (Matt 23; Luke 20:46; 22:24–25). Yet these future leaders occasionally fell

---

53. Georges and Baker, *Ministering*, 207.
54. Ruth Haley Barton, *Strengthening the Soul of Your Leadership*, 110.
55. Useem, "Power Causes Brain Damage," 24.
56. See Brueggemann, *Truth Speaks to Power*.

into the trap of taking their leadership cues from the world. They argued over who was the greatest (Mark 9:34). After all, they lived in a hierarchical world of masters ruling slaves, men dominating women, and powerful kingdoms oppressing weaker ones. Leadership was all about getting to the top and having the edge. Even the religion of the day emphasized works, rank and privilege. Rabbinic writings frequently commented on the seating order in paradise.

But it is to be different with us. Our flesh will scream against this. It is the nature of leaders to want to be out in front. We are not inclined to take on a posture of irrelevance. In his book *In the Name of Jesus*, Nouwen challenges leaders to dare to let go of their relevant selves – the self that can do things, show things, prove things and build things.[57]

But are we to forgo ambition? Has God ever forbidden the desire to be a success? It doesn't impress God for leaders to settle for patchiness, to live cowardly and without aim, and to chalk it up as self-effacing. To reject greatness might be choosing to live a minimal, unimpressive life of mediocrity. There's a place to pursue greatness, but humility must drive the heart. Think of it as "humbition," ambition in the service of humility.[58]

Jesus tells us children can serve as some of our best models (Matt 18:2–5). They teach us that great leaders admit to a certain desperation, a childlike dependence. Apart from God, we can do nothing (John 15:5). Those who have been infused with true greatness are those who have come in childlike reliance – Abraham, Moses, David, Elijah, Nehemiah, Daniel, Paul.

Looking more deeply in Scripture, we discover that humility has other postures. Humility is a posture of service and submission. Humble leaders are more concerned with serving people than with their own success or recognition.[59] They subordinate themselves to their God, their followers and to the task at hand. This is a posture of indebtedness that says to followers, "I am obligated to you, I am abandoned to your needs." This is what Jesus modeled – not power games, but servant leadership.[60]

Humility is a posture of receiving. The power that comes with leadership should be earned, never grasped. Exploitative, selfish, coercive behavior unravels the fabric of the organization.[61] Receiving their call, humble leaders

57. Nouwen, *In the Name of Jesus*, 16.

58. Bill Taylor, "If Humility Is So Important, Why Are Leaders So Arrogant?"

59. George, *Discover Your True North*, 8.

60. Nouwen, *In the Name of Jesus*, 45.

61. Keltner, *Power Paradox*, 68.

invite others into the mission and vision, empowering people to carry out their roles, release their gifts and serve the group.

Humility is a posture of learning. Humble leaders know what they don't know. They acknowledge they have not arrived. There is a saying, "As long as a leader is green, he is growing. As soon as he is ripe, he will rot."

Finally, humility is a posture of imperfection, an acknowledgment of limitation. Self-effacement says, "I need you as much as you need me. I am willing to shed the notion I have to maintain an image of flawlessness. Along with others, I realize I must confess my own brokenness and express the same need for forgiveness." There is a willingness to, with those they lead, admit rather than justify mistakes. Such mutuality can be viewed by some as a weakness, a dangerous form of role confusion. But humble leaders are not threatened.

Unprincipled leaders, in contrast, are proud of their accomplishments. They assume their achievements are down to them. Think King Nebuchadnezzar (Dan 4:30).

God's Redemption Is Our Only Hope for Moral Excellence

Regarding moral leadership, the fact that God's redemption is our only hope might be the greatest theological insight of all. You won't find this in the leadership voices we typically hear. Books like *On Becoming a Leader* and *Discover Your True North* underscore that self-awareness and self-leadership are the first steps toward getting one's moral bearings. This is helpful, but it falls short. It is misguided.

Character formation does begin with heart introspection. The sage instructed his son to guard his heart above all else, for everything he does flows from it (Prov 4:23). Paul instructed Timothy to pay close attention to his life and doctrine (1 Tim 4:16). It makes sense. The human heart is the executive center of one's life.

The heart is where decisions and choices are executed. That is its function.[62] Our heart will determine our sexual thoughts and our sexual behaviors. It will determine our posture toward things: whether we are greedy or generous, honest or deceptive, coarse or gracious, arrogant or humble, foolish or wise.

There are, however, a few missing pieces – large pieces. First, knowing the heart is not enough. Left to itself, the heart is ill-equipped to guide one toward a true north. To assume one will find a true self which is innately good and can

---

62. Willard, *Renovation of the Heart*, 30.

be trusted, consulted and actualized is to ignore reality. Scripture makes this clear. We are wonderfully made in the image of God, with a certain respect for virtues. But sin has disordered the soul and disfigured our character. We are not straight arrows, but crooked timber.[63]

This explains the mass of contradictions one finds. In his book *The Character Gap*, philosopher Christian Miller confirms what we noted earlier. The heart is a "messy blend of good and evil."[64] We can be both virtuous and vicious. This radical inconsistency is especially on display in the realm of leadership. Leaders may have their titles, wealth, power and popularity, but mixed in and underneath most leaders is a tendency toward self-centeredness.

What Scripture tells us is what we already know but are hesitant to admit. In this messy blend, the darkness has far more control. In the core of our being is a sinful heart. We are not basically good and responsible. Merely following the dictates of reason, or reading the latest self-help book, will not control harmful desires.[65] Sin permeates and pollutes the whole. There is a natural bent to be full of ourselves and empty of God.

This gives leaders a great capacity for wrongdoing (Eph 2:1–3). We have the potential to both comfort and inflict suffering – suffering for the sake of suffering.[66] Cornelius Plantinga, Jr., in his groundbreaking book on sin, *Not the Way It's Supposed to Be*, describes the sin nature which runs through every leader's soul, making one's governing center internally lawless.[67] We have inherited a pathology that blinds and distorts.

The Bible uses a wide range of other terms to describe this: failure, rebellion, transgression and infidelity.[68] None of these make us worthless, but simply lost and out of place – and ill-equipped to be great leaders on our own.

We leaders are not up to being the point of reference. We cannot change things internally by mere introspection and feedback. To argue otherwise is to be like farmers who plant crops, but cannot admit the existence of weeds and insects. As Willard puts it, "We can only think to pour on more fertilizer."[69]

Our condition is the consequence of turning from God and replacing him with other gods, one of them being self. A radical innate evil has taken hold. This is what Jesus said: "For it is from within, out of a person's heart, that evil

---

63. I borrowed this from Brooks, *Road to Character.*

64. Miller, *Character Gap.*

65. Contra Matsushita's view of human nature: Kotter, *Matsushita Leadership*, 203.

66. Peterson, *12 Rules for Life*, 53.

67. Plantinga, *Not the Way It's Supposed to Be*, 48.

68. Westberg, *Renewing Moral Theology*, 93.

69. Willard, *Renovation of the Heart*, 46.

thoughts come – sexual immoralities, theft, murder, adultery, greed, malice, deceit, lewdness, envy, slander, arrogance, and folly" (Mark 7:21–22).

Given our devastating condition, there is little we can do on our own to remedy the situation. This is the other piece left out of most leadership books: it is beyond ourselves to do the repair. This is hard to admit for most leaders, West and East – but especially in an American culture of self-dependence, one David Brooks defines as the Big Me.[70] Leaders like to think they are fully capable of self-leadership.

This humanistic approach, however, is not only vain; it is intellectually dishonest. Leaders, no matter how great, carry the weight of their own defects. Our best righteousness amounts to filthy rags (Isa 64:6). Our best efforts at transformation fall short (Eph 2:8). "Humans, working out their salvation alone, are a pathetic spectacle – hopelessly defeated moralists trying to elevate themselves by their own bootstraps."[71]

Only the transformative work of Jesus can correct and empower us. Only through him do we inherit a new habit of obedience. God, out of his infinite love for us, has sent his Son to atone for our sin. Only a perfect, sinless One can undo sin's damage and save us from ourselves, shifting us from self-worship to God-worship (John 3:16). Only God can purge the interior impurities that would otherwise remain. His Spirit surfaces a self-absorption we would otherwise miss. He initiates a divine repair that exposes our motives, unmasks the things that have attached themselves to us, strips away our layers of self-deception and rationalization, and builds in us a trust and a heart for God.

This is why the gospel is good news. Os Guiness says, "In fact it is 'the best news ever' because it addresses our human condition appropriately, pertinently, and effectively as nothing else has, does, or can – and in generation after generation, culture after culture, and life after life."[72]

Yielding to God's transformative work of redemption, we are able to build our leadership around non-negotiable core values – nouns that must become verbs. With new hearts, our lives can now be reoriented and find their divine heading (Eph 2:4–10). We can be the kinds of leaders who help direct the world, on its careening trajectory, a bit more toward heaven and a bit more away from hell.[73]

---

70. Brooks, *Road to Character*, loc. 4791.

71. Albert Edward Day, "Discipline and Discovery," quoted in Job and Shawchuck, *Guide to Prayer*, 91.

72. Guiness, *Prophetic Untimeliness*, 13.

73. Peterson, *12 Rules for Life*, 62.

But it requires a daily discipline. We have to wrestle against deeply ingrained sin habits from our past. We have to die daily to the old self (1 Cor 9:24–27; Col 3:5; 1 Tim 4:7). We have to rise each day in the power of a resurrected life and stay on the alert. We have to pay close attention to our lives and our leadership. This requires solitude and reflection, learning from the difficult circumstances God places us in; learning from the people he places in our lives; and taking seriously the alternatives: the warning of a life without character. Eugene Peterson refers to it as "a long obedience in the same direction."[74]

Chris Lowney illustrates this in *Heroic Leadership*, which tells the story of the early Jesuit movement, the early Catholic leadership, and their long obedience. They recognized that a leader's most compelling leadership tool is who he or she is.[75] They held that "self-awareness" is the foundation of leadership. But they understood that mere technique cannot compensate for a disordered soul. Those who would lead must see the reality within and give themselves to deconstruction in order to construct heroic leadership.

This required a regular "ice water bath" of frank assessment. This enabled them to perceive any tangled affections and ungodly attachments. They saw their sin head-on, leading them to seek God's transformative work. Only then could they find any hope of discovering their true north, and tasting the fruit of a noble character. They understood that if there is no inner life, the amount of one's zeal and the intention of one's work will only lead to a life of barrenness.[76]

Bringing the Voices Together

Character matters. Without it, leaders are not credible. Acquiring character is a disciplined, lifelong pursuit. It's not about determining our values but discovering God's.

Reflecting the character of God is one of a leader's greatest goals. In the end, it means becoming like Christ. Having adopted his values, we then articulate and embrace them. We become principled leaders.

We must do this. The world is counting on such leaders! But this is only the first step to establishing credibility.

---

74. Peterson, *Long Obedience.*

75. Lowney, *Heroic Leadership*, 19.

76. Charles de Foucauld, "Meditations of a Hermit," quoted in Job and Shawchuck, *A Guide to Prayer for Ministers and Other Servants*, 34.

5

Sharpen Your Skills if You Want to Be Competent

In Andre Agassi's *Open*, he describes growing up in a home with a merciless father. His father had decided, long before Andre was born, that his son would be a professional tennis player. More than this, he would dominate the game. He would be number one in the world.

From his earliest years, Agassi was forced to stand on a tennis court and develop his skill. Every day, a ball machine fed him 2,500 balls. That's 17,500 each week, nearly one million each year. He was constantly moving, setting his feet, positioning his body and mastering his strokes. Meanwhile, his father screamed, "More topspin! Hit harder! Not in the net! Never in the net." He expected perfection.[1]

How long does it take to develop a skill? It depends on how good you want to be. From his research, Malcolm Gladwell concluded that the most successful people in the world – what he refers to as "outliers" – are driven by relentless discipline. The key factor is not natural aptitude, though this matters; it is the hours of hard work. It requires maybe 10,000 hours – three hours every day, for ten consecutive years – before one can become an "expert" in one's field.[2]

Is this true of leadership? Why would it not be? Are you ready? Your best attention here might be the difference between the goodness and the greatness of your leadership.

---

1. From the opening chapter of Agassi, *Open*.
2. Gladwell, *Outliers*.

The Voices We Hear

Leadership is both a gift and a learned skill. It has its own skill sets, regardless of the culture, that require their own development. There are requisite abilities that must be mastered over time. The world depends upon this. Just as . . .

- every soldier deserves someone adept at command;
- every athlete needs a coach skilled in training;
- every citizen hopes for a lawmaker proficient at governing;
- every corporate employee relies on a CEO good at organizing;
- every congregant prays for a pastor capable of shepherding;

. . . so every organization needs a leader who is competent to lead.

So what are the necessary competencies for leadership? Or, as someone has put it, "What are the technical skills needed to 'perform'?"[3] What are the abilities that, when teamed with character, lead to credibility? Is there a list that is applicable to every leadership context?

Out of a collection of leadership voices and a lifetime of observation, here are nine essential skills. Those who are accomplished have spent their lives honing each one.

Skill 1: The Skill of Thinking

It's not that leaders have to score at the highest level on an IQ test, but they do need to know how to use their minds. Leadership moments will call them to reason with others, analyze situations, and resolve issues. Leaders have to outthink others. They cannot afford to be mindless or dull, or, as Jordan Peterson puts it, a "walking cacophony of unintegrated experiences,"[4] always clearing their throats but never saying anything.

Followers don't want a vacuous leader, someone about whom people ask, "What if there is no 'there' there?" Leaders need to have a sound presence of mind, especially in an age when the speed of innovation and rapid change is redefining the norm. They must have command of the facts. As a New York Times journalist put it, "Leadership isn't all airy impulses."[5] It's more than a feeling. More than a visceral reaction to circumstances.

---

3. Schein, "Leadership Competencies," 261.

4. Peterson, *12 Rules for Life*, 231.

5. Noonan, "How to Find a Good Leader," *The Wall Street Journal*, November 1, 2018, http://www.peggynoonan.com/how-to-find-a-good-leader/.

There must be careful thought and sound judgment. All of this requires the habit of thinking deeply. Skilled leaders give some of their best time and energy to stretching their thoughts and expanding their imaginations. This leads to minds that are more agile and innovative; minds that are able to solve problems – and there are always problems!

Part of the skill involves determining what to feed the mind. The principle of GIGO (garbage in, garbage out) applies. Processing nonsensical data produces nonsensical output. Settling for information that only confirms one's thinking leads to narrow-mindedness. Leaders have to think critically if they are to respond to complexity and ambiguity with wisdom. There is no room to be shallow.

It's important to get beyond the morning news. Thinkers can see that the product of the news business is *change,* not wisdom. Wisdom has to do with seeing issues in their largest context, whereas news is structured in a way that destroys the larger context.[6] What is deemed newsworthy today is often treated as irrelevant tomorrow. Leaders have to see things within the greater whole. This requires uninterrupted mental space where those who lead can stretch their present awareness and expand their curiosity. They read the lives of other leaders and ask, "What was it that caused people to follow?" They look deep into the past and out into the future to discover patterns. They are attracted to ideas that take them to another level. There is little time for anecdotal fluff or articles that have short shelf lives.

This is becoming a greater challenge. Nicholas Carr, a writer on technology and culture, has been observing the results of recent technological advances. The immediacy of information is shaping the process of thought.[7] We used to have the ability to go deep, like submarines. Now, we skim across the shallow surface of Internet information. Our brains are more like hydrofoils, less equipped to read substantive books.

Leaders, however, can't afford to let their brains get reshaped in ways that diminish their thinking. If they are going to think deeply, leaders have to read deeply. They have to learn and keep learning. In a world "deluged by irrelevant information," leaders will need the discipline to find clarity, what futurists like Yuval Noah Harari equate with power.[8] They will need to slow down. To

---

6. Sommerville, "Why the News Makes Us Dumb."
7. Carr, "Is Google Making Us Stupid?"
8. Harari, *21 Lessons*, xiii.

discern what is essential, they will need to make the space to think. Only then can they apply highly selective criteria to the choices they make.[9]

Skill 2: The Skill of Exercising Wisdom

Leaders who make a difference are shrewd. In his book *Lead with Wisdom*, Mark Strom begins by noting that no one leads well (leads skillfully) without wisdom.[10] In a series of chapters, Strom notes that wise leaders . . .

- reflect on life as a whole;
- live in reality and create spaces where followers can learn to deepen their understanding of reality;
- pay attention to patterns, to behaviors and to consequences;
- learn from failure, knowing that this is where some of our greatest wisdom is hammered out;
- find wise counselors and expand;
- ask if it is time to lead or follow;
- admit when they do not know;
- pay attention to story, for stories bring us back to the things that matter;
- let go of status and hold on to grace.

Leaders who impress me with their leadership acumen are on a sapiential quest. They recognize that wisdom does not necessarily come with age; it's a lifelong, intentional journey. With enough practice, wise leaders learn such things as good judgment, which is critical. Leadership, at its marrow, is the chronicle of judgment calls.[11] Exercising sound wisdom in making them is one of the greatest skills of all.

A steady discipline of learning wisdom enables leaders to skillfully intuit. They can discern what is essential. They have a good read on situations and recognize what really matters. They are constantly processing internal questions like "What is the central purpose of my life?" "If I could excel at one thing, what would it be?" "What must I edit and possibly eliminate to get there?"[12] Externally, they are asking, "Is this a sensible course?" "Is this a reckless path or a prudent step of faith?" "Can we sustain this momentum?" "Is this the best use of our resources?" "Is this the right season?"

---

9. McKeown, *Essentialism*, 60.
10. Strom, *Lead with Wisdom*, loc. 467.
11. Tichy and Bennis, *Judgment*.
12. McKeown, *Essentialism*, chapter 13.

Part of wisdom is dealing with reality. Competent leaders are skilled at perceiving what is actual, and leading in light of this. We have a tendency to see what we want to see, holding on to images that may no longer be credible. To lead requires the skill to recognize what is actual.

In his book *Factfulness: Ten Reasons We Are Wrong about the World*, Hans Rosling speaks to our inclination to jump to swift conclusions without looking at the facts. This can be folly. When, for example, we speak about the gap between the West and the rest, are we working with current or outdated data? Are we aware of our tendency to focus only on the bad news, get things out of proportion and automatically categorize and generalize? We make reference to the Majority World, but what percentage of the world are we speaking about? Fifty-one percent? Ninety-eight percent? How accurate are our cultural maps? What statistics are we using? Are we developing the kinds of habits that will guard us from distorting what actually is?

A realistic, and wise, appraisal of the world sees a world that is changing at an unnerving rate. It is fast or last. We live in a cyber-realm where technology has made the world smaller and flatter. Cultural distinctions are not so black and white anymore.

Innovations in robotics, driverless cars, 3-D printers and drones may soon lead to societal upheaval transcending that of the industrial revolution. Globalism is redefining cultures. Will we have leaders with eyes wide open? Will they possess the wisdom to keep up with and generate ideas? Will an awareness of the present state of things press a leader to innovate? Will one do the things other people have not done?[13]

Skill 3: The Skill of Seeing through the Layers

Proficient leaders are good at comprehending what is before them. They can see multidimensionally. Every organization has layers, and it requires skill to read each one. According to Lee Bolman and Terrence Deal, every institution is made up of "social frames."[14]

The first frame reveals the *structure*, the architecture of an organization. It is through this lens the leader sees the goals and strategies, the vertical and lateral coordination, the time lines and accountability. Such awareness tells one how to allocate resources; clarifies one's authority and one's role in making decisions (am I in a high power distance culture where followers assume I have

---

13. Bennis, *On Becoming a Leader*, 143.
14. Bolman and Deal, *Reframing Organizations*.

authority, or in a culture where the structure is much more participative?); and explains why an organization is structurally functional or dysfunctional.

When an international church in the Netherlands called me to lead it, one of the first things I saw was a structural mess. Time to reframe. There were three boards and layer upon layer of committees. Like a plant whose tendrils went far beyond its intended boundaries, so the organization had morphed into an undisciplined bureaucracy. Committees pushed decision making from one group to another. We eventually restructured for greater effectiveness. Reframing set in motion policies and procedures that maximized efficiency for ministry.

The second frame exposes the *heart*. Organizations are made up of people, each of whom has strengths and weaknesses, hopes and fears. Successful leaders – those with intentionality to gain followers – pay special attention to this frame (especially in a high context culture where a premium is placed on harmonious relationships). Leaders decode the collective mood, the receptivity of hearts and the readiness of people.[15] Attention is given to feelings and the state of morale. You can't move forward without discerning these things.

The third frame is *political*. Though a community might be tight-knit on the surface, there are coalitions that lurk beneath. One discovers there are interest groups and tribal factions everywhere. They wrestle and compete. They bargain with one another and compete for influence, power and allocation of resources. It can feel like navigating through a jungle.

Skilled leaders know how to hack their way through the muddle. They understand the dynamics of power and the realities of politics. They effectively read nonverbal expressions. They discern who are the influencers, the troublemakers and the consensus builders. They map the terrain, categorizing the resistors and the supporters. Every group has them. Like effective politicians, skillful leaders know when to be direct, when to be subtle and how to be diplomatic.

Winston Churchill once defined diplomacy as the art of telling people to go to hell in such a way they ask for directions. Good leaders know how much leverage they have in negotiations. They recognize when to push forward and when to pull back.

The fourth frame is the *symbolic*. It is here that skilled leaders concentrate their focus. Every organization is a unique culture driven by stories, ceremonies, rituals and heroes. Seeing the past enables a leader to speak with credibility.

---

15. MacDonald, "I Have This Feeling . . ."

Celebrating former accomplishments anchors hope.[16] Most of the stories are accounts of people who dreamed, risked and sacrificed.

Take the shoe company Nike. Like most, this multinational corporation had a humble beginning. One reads about cushioned soles, initially created from rubber compounds that were poured into a wife's waffle iron. Or note the global mission of the Southern Baptists. It goes back to Lottie Moon, a woman who invested forty years of her life as a missionary in China. One cannot understand the success of Dallas Seminary without going back to its founder, Lewis Sperry Chafer, and a faith that conquered despair.

Smart leaders tap into these narratives. They see where others have lost sight. They put their goals and objectives aside and become the storytellers who point to past heroism. From here, they extend the narrative to the present and out into the future. If done skillfully, this has the potential to both endear and inspire.

The point is this: a leader does not have the luxury of seeing through one dimension. The leader must know, at any given moment, which frame demands the greatest attention. Above all, the leader must be able to see through all of the frames at the same time. It is a skill that requires constant practice.

Skill 4: The Skill of Reading the Readiness

Over time, leaders learn how to read the circumstances, the present and changing state of affairs. Those who are effective train their eyes to notice cultural shifts. They have to be adaptable and agile. They pay attention to the changing economics. They are aware of the politics. They study the demographics.

In what has historically been a white Anglo populace, my county will be 45 percent non-white within ten years. Millennials (those born between 1980 and 2000) are gradually replacing Boomers. This emerging generation has a different outlook on the world. They give greater weight to different values. Skillful leaders adjust their leadership, asking, "What are the cultural expectations?" "What kind of leader will be needed for tomorrow?"

One of the situations confronting leaders is the readiness of their followers. Paul Hersey, another voice out there, addresses this in his book *The Situational Leader*. He begins with the words "Read them, lead them, succeed with them." This became his leadership conviction: "Leadership is about influence, and we influence when we adapt our behavior to the performance needs of the

---

16. Bolman and Deal, *Reframing Organizations*.

individual or group."[17] To put it another way, skilled leaders read their followers and adjust their leadership styles to the readiness level of those they lead.

A person who is unable and unwilling to follow is at the bottom of the scale of readiness. A leader who wants to succeed will have to be more directive and less relational. As the person becomes a more willing follower, but is still ill-equipped to do the task, the leader must become more personal. There is less directive, more mentoring. When the follower becomes competent, but is lacking confidence to move forward, the leader must again adjust his or her style to focus less on the task and more on the need to encourage and empower. Finally, when the follower is both willing and proficient, the leader must pull back, delegate and monitor.

The ultimate aim is to empower others, moving them to a place of confidence and healthy independence. But leaders must learn the skill of reading the readiness level of those they lead. Situations sometimes regress, requiring another adjustment in leadership. Leaders must have an awareness of their own natural style of leading, and how this may enhance or detract from their ability to lead.

Are you aware of your situation? The demographics of the community you lead? The abilities and willingness of the people you lead? In the time you have led, how have things changed?

Skill 5: The Skill of Persuading Followers

Nearly everything leaders do is mediated through language. Some leaders are natural persuaders. They can sell beef to vegans and lawnmowers to apartment dwellers. For others, the art of persuasion is more difficult. Communication is hard. But no one wants a leader who bores the eyeballs out of one's lids.

A leader who cannot communicate clearly, powerfully and succinctly barely qualifies as a leader.[18] But given its comprehensive nature, skillful communication is a tall order. As one consultant puts it, "All forms of communication must be mastered by the effective leader: written and oral, electronic and digital, communication by graphics and behavior, by art and music, by expressed emotion and more. Such mastery often requires almost an entire lifetime to achieve."[19] Practice, practice, practice.

---

17. Hersey, *Situational Leader*.
18. Woolfe, *Leadership Secrets from the Bible*, 87.
19. Wilhelm, "Learning from Past Leaders," 226.

Leaders who have honed their communication skills must be able to gain one's interest. As Seth Godin notes, "Attention is a precious resource since our brains are cluttered with noise."[20] Skillful leaders value this, motivating, inspiring and making their case. They must wield a certain charismatic authority.[21] They do this by providing meaning and challenge, such that those who follow believe they are making a difference. They are changing something in their world. This is part of what gives people hope.

Konosuke Matsushita did this. He was the founder of Matsushita Electric Corporation, a major Japanese manufacturer. Although he was not personally impressive, he spoke words that called people to something bigger than themselves. Here's how John Kotter introduces him in his book *Matsushita Leadership*:

> By many standards, he didn't look like a great leader. Early pictures of Konosuke Matsushita show an unsmiling young man whose ears stick out like airplane wings. He never grew taller than five feet five inches nor weighed more than 135 pounds. Unlike his rival Akio Norita at Sony, he was neither charismatically handsome nor internationally recognized. Unlike most well-known Western politicians, he didn't excel at public speaking, and in his later years his voice grew increasingly frail. He rarely displayed speed-of-light intellectual skills or warmed an audience with hilarious anecdotes. Nevertheless, he did what all great leaders do – motivate large groups of individuals to improve the human condition.[22]

This is what skillful leaders do.

Effectual leaders appeal to common ideals, exude upbeat feelings and appeal from the heart. They know that people, at the deepest level, need a sense of meaning. Most people do not want to live in a harbor, sitting at anchor. US President John F. Kennedy tapped into this. On 25 May 1961, Kennedy stood before a joint session of Congress and made a bold ask. He shared his vision for sending a man to the moon. In just eight minutes, JFK changed the world.[23] His words moved a nation and launched a national effort. Hearers coalesced around a common idea, a common hope. This underscores that the skill of stirring the heart is necessary to complement a great vision.

---

20. Godin, *This Is Marketing*, 12.
21. Seidman, *How*, 284.
22. Kotter, *Matsushita Leadership*, 1.
23. Seidman, *How*, 269.

Historian Doris Goodwin writes: "John Kennedy understood the power of language, the importance of symbolism, humor, and image . . . He made millions of people feel they were part of the New Frontier. That's the mystery and art of leadership – the ability to mobilize people to feel included and to care about the tasks ahead."[24] In contrast, Kennedy's successor, Lyndon Johnson, was unable to mobilize the public at large. It was a matter of communication, and it was a failure of leadership. If a leader cannot persuade people to embrace the same mission and chase the same dream, ideas will never become realities.

Across every culture, inspiration is the skill of transformational leaders. Persuasive leaders speak words that unify, that bring people together. They use their political skills to help people network and to influence others.[25] They command situations and convert hearts. They know how to single out key influencers who, if motivated, can carry an organization forward. They aim for consensus, knowing the lines which compromise cannot cross.

Leaders have to learn this skill. They have to develop this astuteness. In his book on emotional intelligence, Daniel Goleman states that we often describe effective leaders as those who are strategic, visionary and full of powerful ideas. The reality, however, is much more primal: great leadership works through the feelings.[26] The leader has the maximal power to sway emotions, emotions that lead to amazing performance. Such skillful leadership instills a confidence that things will work out. It convinces others that they have the ability to achieve levels of performance beyond what they feel capable of. Able leaders infuse the organization with enthusiasm.

Judith Bardwick, another organizational consultant, adds that skillful leaders generate confidence, certainty, action, strength, expertise, courage, optimism and conviction. They build enthusiasm with a bounce in their step. All of this creates a passion in people to pursue the leader's strategy. With words similar to Goleman's, she writes: "In the end, leadership is not intellectual or cognitive. Leadership is emotional."[27]

But even here, part of the skill of persuasion is to know the boundaries of what to say and what not to say, when to be transparent and when to be private. A leader must preserve his or her innermost self from public appropriation.[28] A certain distance must be maintained, lest familiarity breed contempt.

---

24. Goodwin, "Lessons of Presidential Leadership."
25. Templer, "Why Do Toxic People Get Promoted?"
26. Goleman, Boyatzis, and McKee, *Primal Leadership*, 3.
27. Bardwick, "Peacetime Management and Wartime Leadership," 139.
28. Gergen, *Eyewitness to Power*, 46.

Charles de Gaulle once commented, "All religions have their tabernacles, and no man is a hero to his valet."[29] Skillful communication includes a measure of reserve, a certain unpredictability.

Skill 6: The Skill of Making Decisions

In their chapter on "Decision Making," John Shoup and Chris McHorney begin with these words: "One way to recognize the leader of any group is to identify who people go to for a decision."[30]

It is the nature of skilled leaders to get to the issues, define the problem, make a decision, convert the decision into action and communicate resoluteness in follow-through. Other leadership voices concur. Having observed numerous leadership moments, Useem concludes that skillful leaders exhibit an exceptional capacity to articulate a plan, lay out a way of achieving it and move forward with decisiveness.[31]

Part of the skill is knowing when it is time to decide. In a *Harvard Business Review* article, "What Sets Successful CEOs Apart," a ten-year-long study concluded that one of the core behaviors of flourishing leaders is an ability to decide with speed and conviction. They may not always make great decisions, but they are decisive. They have the skill to organize the data and the wisdom to make decisions earlier, faster and with greater conviction.[32] This may work in some cultures, but it won't work in all.

Skilled decision makers are good at other things. They know if there is a decision to be made, and if the decision is theirs to make. They recognize which decisions have to be a matter of collaboration. Out of years of practice, they can discern which decisions are consequential and which ones are not. They become good at framing the issues.

There is more. Part of good decision making is deciding when to say no. Skillful leaders reckon with the fact they can't do everything. They have an eye for editing and eliminating the trivial, the unimportant and the irrelevant. According to McKeown, the root of "decision" is *cis*, which literally means

---

29. Quoted in Gergen, 47.
30. Shoup and McHorney, "Decision Making," 197.
31. Useem, *Leadership Moment*, 264.
32. Botelho et al., "What Sets Successful CEOs Apart," 4.

to cut.[33] In his book, *Essentialism: The Disciplined Pursuit of Less*, he writes, "Saying no is its own leadership capability. It is not just a peripheral skill."[34]

Finally, good decision makers acknowledge that their perceptions have limitations. In most cases, we deal with incomplete data, and it is often distorted.[35] There is a human tendency to seek out information that bolsters preexisting beliefs. We assume we know more than we do.[36] It's essential to multiply options. The best decision is the one that has been selected from an array of potential outcomes.[37]

Skill 7: The Skill of Bringing Order

Leaders step in and bring calm out of chaos, direction out of misdirection, and stability out of instability. They are good at this. It begins with a leader's personal life. Steadiness requires that leaders not live with constant drama. We need leaders who emerge out of a certain quiet.

In Herman Melville's *Moby Dick*, there is a turbulent scene in which a whaleboat is in pursuit of the great white whale. The sailors are laboring fiercely. Behind it all is an ongoing cosmic conflict between good and evil: chaotic sea and demonic sea monster versus the morally outraged man, Captain Ahab. But there is a man who does nothing. He doesn't hold an oar; he doesn't perspire; he doesn't shout. He is quiet amidst the crash and the cursing. This man is the harpooner. He is poised and waiting. To ensure the greatest efficiency in the dart, the harpooner must start to his feet out of idleness, and not out of toil.[38] Skillful leaders step out of a similar stillness. This is necessary if they are to carry out their mission.

It's true that leaders must occasionally be revolutionaries. They may find themselves on ships trapped in the doldrums where everyone is calm, acting as caretakers of institutions that have all the order of a cemetery. Sometimes leaders are summoned to be a disrupting force. The work requires deconstruction.

But leaders must be skilled in knowing how to construct. Who wants a leader whose claim to fame is being a demolition expert? Effective leaders are those who have acquired the skills of an architect and the abilities of a

---

33. McKeown, *Essentialism*, 158.

34. McKeown, 142.

35. McKeown, 198.

36. See Heath and Heath, *Decisive*, chapter 1, for a great discussion on the four villains of decision making.

37. George, "Beyond the Firehouse Syndrome," 17.

38. Adapted from Peterson's *Contemplative Pastor*.

contractor. Leadership is about building organizations, creating efficiency and maintaining order.

This requires that leaders occasionally get into the details. It's not enough to be the big picture person; a leader must demonstrate some management ability, some organizational skill sets. You might have your head in the clouds, but your feet must be on the ground.

Management expert Ken Blanchard puts it this way: "The leader of the future has to manage the journey to effectiveness and efficiency to create an ultimate organization that knows where it is going and in which everyone is committed, organized, and ready to implement an agreed upon vision."[39] Otherwise, who will follow?

This is not to suggest that leaders and managers are one and the same. Managers tend to focus internally and get into the details. Theirs is a world of planning and budgeting, organizing and staffing, and driving for results. They are often behind the scenes. They have to ensure the organization is running at peak performance. In contrast, leaders tend to be less focused on the details. They are thinking out into the future, plotting the direction, aligning resources, focusing on strategic perspectives and inspiring followers. Both are essential, and they complement one another.

Still, competent leaders recognize that they can ill afford to be disorganized and chaotic. They are self-organizing. They read reports and prepare agendas. They cannot get lost in the minutiae, but they must be aware of the necessary particulars – if they want order.

Skill 8: The Skill of Stewarding Resources

A good part of what leaders manage is the available resources. Good leaders develop the ability to do this with excellence.

Time

Leaders, particularly in the West, recognize that time is part of the order and structure of leadership. Wisdom tells them that they need to have a sense of urgency. The clock is always running; it waits for no one. The older one gets and the longer one leads, the faster go the minutes. Time can feel like a tyrant, consuming choices left unmade. Leaders cannot afford to mismanage it. Skillful leaders act on the moments God serves up.

---

39. Blanchard, "Turning the Organizational Pyramid Upside Down," 82–83.

As I write this, author James Clear has just sent out his periodic tips for succeeding. Today's is about one's use of time:

- Be fully engaged in the task. Block out distractions and mind wanderings.
- If there is something important to do, do it first.
- Hold yourself to a schedule – not a deadline.[40]

Effective leaders know that if they are not careful, the repetitive and unproductive demands of others will occupy them.[41] They will respond to every emergency without stopping to ask, "Can this wait?" A critical part of time management is scheduling a weekly time to hide, to think, plan, focus on what is critical, re-prioritize, delegate and create processes.[42]

Leaders who do not manage their moments fail to build credibility with the followers they seek to attract.[43] Perpetual lateness, bungling the pace of meetings and wasting people's time with pointless demands put off followers. People respect those who value their time. Effective leaders arrange their most important tasks according to when they – and others – are most productive. They know when to wait and when to go forward with their goals.

It is a skill.

People

Urgency is critical, but one must also have the skill (and patience!) to steward the gifts of people. This requires that one pay attention to a person's strengths and weaknesses, allowing that person to flourish. It is about discerning a person's readiness level and, at the right moment, delegating responsibilities with judicious skill, and letting go. It might require repositioning those who are languishing, shifting them from their non-strengths and harnessing their abilities for what matters.

Such effective stewardship requires the heart of a servant. Effective management of people is not about command and control. Skillful leaders – servant leaders who steward the lives they lead – do not use followers as a

---

40. Clear, "3 Time Management Tips That Actually Work."
41. See Maciariello, "Peter F. Drucker," 12.
42. Azzarello, *Rise*, 111.
43. Ulrich, "Credibility x Capability," 218.

stepping-stone to their next assignment. They stay for the long haul, getting on their hands and knees, prepared to do what they ask of others.[44]

They let followers know that it is their privilege to serve those they lead. They promote others rather than themselves. They listen more than they talk and give more than they take. Servant leadership means they place the good of others and the organization over their own self-interest. Most of all, they put their lives on the line for those they lead.

Finances

Most leadership includes fiduciary responsibilities. Much of our day-to-day work is dominated by decisions surrounding incomes and expenses, debts and investments. It might be fair to say that every decision we make has financial implications.[45] One must be able to read budgets, wrestle with deficits and intuit when to step out and take risks – and when to cut back and wait.

Though I have often put this off, I have learned over time that leaders cannot ignore the data, delegating this to others. Figures help us to discern the difference between stepping out in faith and making a reckless decision. They tell us things we need to know. Those guided by them earn the respect of their co-leaders.

Energy

Leaders who are skilled in stewardship manage their drive. With time and practice, they discover when they are at their best. They recognize their high tide and low tide. Patty Azzarello, in *Rise*, writes, "It's hard to overstate the importance of managing energy."[46] Energy is a leader's currency. The true power of energy is unleashed when skillful leaders pay consistent attention to it.[47]

Leaders have to do this, for they tend to be high-energy types, ready for the next challenge. Discomfort is their comfort zone.[48] Leadership is also tough work, requiring an exorbitant amount of verve and vim. Crises will deplete us. Those who are effective triage their time and strength, focusing on the

---

44. Pollard has written a wonderful chapter, "The Leader Who Serves," 241–248. There are a number of powerful books on the theme, including Marshall, *Understanding Leadership*, and Greenleaf, *Servant Leadership*.

45. Rodin, "Christian Leadership and Financial Integrity," 230.

46. Azzarello, *Rise*, 118.

47. See Fleming's helpful chapter "Energy: The Currency of Leadership," 79–96 in *Leadership Wisdom from Unlikely Voices*.

48. Bryant, "How to Be a C.E.O."

consequential leadership in which they are most likely to excel.[49] They are aware of what energizes and what drains. The more focused one is, the better one's energy is spent.[50]

Presence

Finally, stewardship involves managing our presence. We can manifest ourselves in multiple ways. It might be through a letter, a text, an email, a phone call or a personal presence. The skilled manage the appropriate way.

This is especially true in crises. Leaders do not hide in their offices sending out memos. They do not delegate needed presence. True leaders are in the fight, wielding the necessary skill sets of a leader. "It is the leader who must feel the pressure first, hear the sounds first, smell the smells first, and sense the momentum of the way things are going long before anyone else."[51]

This brings to mind Peter Drucker's story of when he was in high school and asked to write a term paper on World War I. As the papers were presented, one of the students asked the history teacher, a World War I veteran, why the Great War was a war of total military incompetence. Without hesitating, the instructor responded, "Because not enough generals were killed; they stayed way behind the lines and let others do the fighting and dying."[52] Leaders, the skillful ones, choose to get in the fray. They skillfully manage themselves.

Skill 9: The Skill of Measuring Results

In the end, leaders are responsible for outcomes. The skilled attune everything to what will bring success. This means defining success. To get there will require a culture dedicated to superior performance. If things are not moving, skillful leaders set a course to generate movement. If an organization is showing signs of slowing, they are committed to reigniting. If things are moving, they do what is required to sustain advance. They know the threat of atrophy always lurks. It always happens at the top, where people often relax their grip.

What's needed is a way to measure how things are. Skillful leaders are wary of anecdotal stories. They do not build too much on soft data. They determine what the key performance indicators are. They can explicate what it means to

49. Stanley, *Next Generation Leader*, 11.
50. Fleming, *Leadership Wisdom from Unlikely Voices*, 93.
51. Hybels, *Leadership Axioms*, 161.
52. Drucker, "Not Enough Generals," xiv.

say, "We are getting great results." They have assembled the right evidence to demonstrate progress.[53]

The first measurement begins with ourselves. Effectual leaders ask probing internal questions. What outcomes have I established for myself, and what am I using to measure these? Am I building on my strengths? Am I developing the skills so necessary for effective leadership?

Skilled leaders also ask probing questions of the organization they lead. Are we making the necessary investments that will lead to success? Are we mimicking others, or writing our own story? Are we winning the battle but losing the war? Are we delivering effectively on our mission? Are we reaching our goals?

In the end, skillful leaders measure what matters. Leaders who succeed repeatedly are geniuses at grasping context.[54] This ability to understand – as well as to recognize and seize opportunities – is the "essential competence" of leaders.[55] They know what matters and what does not; what is the real situation, the state of things; when it is time to wait and time to act; what is a valid measurement and what is not.

Summarizing What We Hear

What does it take to become proficient at leading – or at anything, for that matter? It requires determining the necessary skill sets, and then practicing.

John Hayes, a cognitive psychology professor at Carnegie Mellon University, wanted to know what made certain musicians so skillful. He studied some of the most talented composers in history – people like Mozart. He investigated the choices and experiences that led to their success. The central question that drove his work was, "How long after one becomes interested in music is it that one becomes world class?"

What he discovered was that virtually every single "masterwork" was written after year ten of the composer's career. Not a single person produced incredible work without putting in a decade of practice first. Even a genius like Mozart had to work for at least ten years before he produced something that became popular. Professor Hayes began to refer to this period, which was filled with hard work and little recognition, as the "ten years of silence."[56]

---

53. Collins, *Good to Great and the Social Sectors*, 7.

54. Bennis and Thomas, *Geeks and Geezers*, 19.

55. Bennis and Thomas, 92.

56. Adapted from Clear's article "Lessons on Success."

Some of us might be in this time of silence. We are working on these skill sets, and sometimes we surprise ourselves with how proficient we are becoming – and how far we need to go! These are not born skills. Reading people like Bolman and Deal, Rosling, and Hersey can deepen our thinking, train our minds to see and help us navigate through the norms and expectations. We keep learning the dynamics within the organizations we are leading, the readiness of followers and the style of leadership required, as well as the organizational complexities and ambiguities. We keep sharpening our focus and developing our voice. And, hopefully, we compose.

The Voices We Need to Hear

Up to this point in the chapter, I have attempted to summarize skill sets critical to effective leadership. These, however, are not universal. Other cultures have their own lists. What leadership skills are required to successfully lead in Africa?

The Voice of Gideon Para-Mallam, Ambassador for IFES World Assembly, Nigeria

Meeting with Gideon Para-Mallam, one is impressed with his passion to train and mentor the next generation of young leaders across the African continent. More than ever, leaders of the future will need to lead with skills required by the context. His contribution underscores this.

The Nature of Leadership

There are similar and dissimilar competencies between Africa and the West. To understand these, I must first establish the African leadership context.[57] In my

---

57. The following are supplementary notes to Para-Mallam's contribution: (1) Leadership skills are an essential component in positioning executives to make thoughtful decisions about their organization's mission and goals and to properly allocate resources to achieve those directives. Valuable leadership skills include the abilities to delegate, inspire, and communicate effectively. See Rouse, "Leadership Skills"; (2) As to relational skills, see Goleman, Boyatzis, and McKee, *Primal Leadership*, which describes emotional intelligence as a person's ability to manage his or her feelings so that those feelings are expressed appropriately and effectively. Goleman further presents five categories of emotional intelligence. See also Walton, *Introducing Emotional Intelligence*; (3) Paul Borthwick writes, "Spiritual health demands a friend who will walk alongside us, speak truth to us (even when it hurts), and keep us honest in our relationships with God and with other people," quoted in an article by Rick Lawrence, "What Really Impacts Spiritual Growth," Group Magazine, February 1995; (4) For more on African leadership, see the entry "Kivebulaya, Apolo" in the *Dictionary of African Christian Biography* (internet resource); and Henry Kyemba, *State of Blood: The Inside Story of Idi Amin* (Kampala: Fountain Publishers, 1977).

culture, leadership begins at home with the father. We have certain expectations of how he should exercise leadership. Families make up clans, and the leader of a clan, the village chief, has similar familial responsibilities. Like a father, he is there to nurture a sense of belonging in the community. He promotes a common agenda, making sure that everyone has a sense of shared, collective responsibility. He takes upon himself the obligation to protect.

When you move to the tribal level, the tribal leader has more power than the leader of a clan, but his role as a leader is essentially the same. In the same paternalistic way, he leads by nurturing a sense of belonging, preserving people's identity, promoting a common agenda, encouraging collective responsibility and protecting those he leads. The chief works alongside the priest, who serves as a prophetic voice, speaking for the gods and performing healings.

There is a tribal leader who is the head of the other tribal leaders. He has paramount leadership importance. Still, followers look to him to carry out the role of a father. He works to harness the gifts and skills of those he leads. He is responsible to see that the community progresses and prospers. He connects with professionals and negotiates with civil authorities to make sure that the community progresses in socio-economic and other activities.

The Skills Required of a Leader

Given the context, some skills are valued above others. From what I have studied, observed, and experienced while serving as a leader here in Africa, the following are the seven necessary skills:

Strategic and Visionary Skills

To carry out this nurturing role, a leader must see beyond the present and out into the future. Visionary and strategic thinking is a critical, global skill. These are not Western concepts. As we are a storytelling culture, let me tell you some stories.

I think of four African church leaders, two from Nigeria and two from Uganda. Mari Habu and Panya Baba were ordained Reverends who served with the Evangelical Church Winning All (ECWA). Janani Luwum was an Anglican Archbishop of the Church of Uganda, and John Apolo Kivebulaya was an ordained Reverend Canon in the same Church of Uganda. These four men demonstrated visionary and strategic leadership skills, and this endeared them to many Africans.

Mari Habu had uncommon foresight, along with prophetic courage. He would always stand for the truth, regardless of the cost. This is part of the role of a leader as protector. Even with the tensions, he could see the future importance of building a relationship with Muslims. He preached to them, while showing respect for their different religious worldview. As a result, many Muslims supported the first flagship church building project in Kwoi, Kaduna State, Nigeria, in the 1960s. The church building was completed in 1971. Habu showed gratefulness to the Muslims for their support, telling them that one day this house of God would be their home. Up to his death in 2013 at the age of ninety-two, Muslims respected him as a man of God.

Panya Baba also envisioned a prosperous future. He would always encourage people, especially missionaries, to have a more progressive mindset. Leaders must always be about the future. He had the kind of foresight that most of his peers did not have. For example, when Abuja was emerging as the new capital city of Nigeria, he encouraged various mission agencies to buy land. He was Chairman of the Nigeria Evangelical Missionary Association (NEMA) and helped NEMA secure land in Karu, near Abuja. He also encouraged the Nigeria Fellowship of Evangelical Students (NIFES) to purchase land next to NEMA's in Karu in 1988. It proved to be a wise investment.

Like the apostles of old, Habu and Baba commanded respect and followership among fellow leaders, their followers and even those outside the Christian faith. They were leading counselors in traditional councils where elders meet in the village square to address issues which affect their communities. They worked to preserve a common agenda. People admired their vision and their strategic awareness of how the church should be a guiding light of the gospel to their communities.

John Apolo Kivebulaya of Uganda is another example of a man with visionary skills. He was once a rebel, participating in the insurrection against the British in the 1890s. He eventually came to faith, experiencing a conversion similar to that of the apostle Paul. Christ encountered Kivebulaya when he was a Muslim actively involved in persecuting Christians. He immediately began to share his convictions, traveling to Tooro (in western Uganda) and eventually to the Ituri forest in present-day Democratic Republic of Congo. Though uneducated, he was a powerful communicator and people listened to him.

The impenetrable forests of the Congo were largely a no-go area, but Kivebulaya could see God at work. He could see beyond the present. When, standing on a hilltop, he sighted smoke on the other side, he said, "There are people there for whom Christ died. I must go there." He preached to the people of Mboga at great cost. He was once beaten and left for dead. But, like Paul, he got up and kept preaching. The people were amazed at his communication skills, his courage and his perseverance. They began to believe his message. Today Mboga is a major center of Christian life.

Here is one more story that illustrates why we value leaders who are skilled in seeing a way forward. Like the others, Janani Luwum was a bold visionary and a skillful leader. He lived during the time Ugandan military dictator Field Marshal Idi Amin Dada was in power. Amin abandoned his responsibility to be the people's protector. He abused the rights of his citizens, eliminated the opposition, and silenced virtually all civil society voices in Uganda.

In contrast, Luwum was a true leader. He was a human rights advocate for the people of Uganda. He called on Amin to stop killing Ugandans. He believed that oppression and poverty had to be fought, for this is part of the vital mission of the church. For Africans, the church is to be a place of justice. This is its past, present and future role.

Luwum saw the church as the last voice left standing. He mobilized other Anglican bishops and together they wrote a pastoral letter to the nation. They called on Amin's government to observe the human rights of Ugandans. This put Luwum on a collision course with Amin, but while others fled, he stayed. Luwum faced execution, but he could see beyond his end. He had the unusual ability of seeing ahead. His final words were, "I see God's hand in this."

Effective Communication Skills

Effective leaders have to be skilled communicators, no matter the context. This is especially true in Africa. We are a strong communal culture. Leaders must have an ability to connect. Fathers need to be understood. Leaders must voice words of belonging.

Developing one's ability to relate begins with learning how to connect with God, how to talk to God in prayer. Prayer is dependence on God's absolute power through the continuing presence and influence of the Holy Spirit. Connecting with God is the leader's first responsibility. One must speak with God before speaking to people.

Key to communication is listening. The leader needs to develop the ability to hear God. One must allow the Word of God to speak, for this informs prayer. What does God have to say concerning future direction? Two biblical examples readily come to mind here: Nehemiah, the political and prophetic leader, who heard from God before speaking to the king (Neh 2:1–5); and the early leaders of the church, who sought to hear from the Holy Spirit before making their decisions (Acts 15:22–29).

Hearing from God and speaking to him enables a leader to listen to people. As the leader is intentional in hearing God, so the leader must be intentional in hearing the people. Listening leads to learning. It begins with God. It also begins at home.

Let me share another story, one that is personal. As a young itinerant staff worker and preacher, I usually returned home tired and drained. Visiting campuses, training, and preaching to students would wear me out. My wife, Funmi, would greet me and want to talk, but I would be so tired that I would simply nod my head to whatever she said. Sometimes she would say, "Darling, you are only hearing me – you are not listening to me." Over time, God used her gentle rebukes to teach me that, in all relationships, I need to work at intentional listening. I have to if I am going to fulfill the role of a leader. Listening skills translate into learning skills for the leader. The secret of learning is listening.

Mari Habu and Panya Baba were effective listeners. When you spoke with Habu, he would listen with care, praying at the same time and asking God for wisdom. His words of advice were like balm to those who sought his counsel. Both leaders gave attention to the less privileged. They heard their life concerns, prayed with them and conveyed a sense of belonging. Baba demonstrated the same reliance on the power of the Holy Spirit. He would listen to as many opinions as possible, but he would only act if such opinions were aligned with what he heard in Scripture. This skill – listening to God and to people – drew many followers to him.

In my leadership journey as National Director of NIFES, I have learned to enter the presence of God in prayer. I set aside time for personal retreats, when I am alone with God. I do this at the end and beginning of each year, as well as mid-year. The goal is to rest, retreat, and seek God's face regarding the many leadership issues before me. I pray for the work, the organization, my teammates and all of the stakeholders in NIFES.

I started this practice in 1982 when I was elected President of the Fellowship of Christian Students (FCS). When I am chairing team meetings, I encourage the same kind of listening. If we are unable to come to an agreement or consensus, I encourage everyone to sleep on the matter, waiting on God and listening to what the Spirit is saying. This is part of sharing a sense of collective responsibility.

As a leader in Africa, I have also learned to listen to my team. This involves asking teammates their thoughts and opinions. I ask others, too – drivers, gardeners and staff at every level. I want to know what they think. Because NIFES is a student-centered ministry, I have also sought the opinions of student leaders. I have found this leadership exercise invaluable for helping shape some of the policy recommendations I have made. This promotes a deep sense of ownership, often making policy implementation much easier. But it all begins with listening to God.

Strong Relational Skills

Communication without relational skills is unlikely to achieve the desired results in an African setting. Healthy relational skills help the leader experience an uncommon connectedness with followers. The most successful leaders are those who develop the skills to connect with their followers. They understand that true leadership amounts to friendship. People love and respect those leaders who engage in their lives and preserve the common good.

This begins with acquiring a healthy social intelligence. According to David Walton, social intelligence is the ability to be aware of yourself, understand yourself and understand those around you. It requires an understanding of everyone's need to be loved.

Can a leader lead without loving people? Can a father love without passion and empathy for the people? Can a leader be empathetic without feeling genuine compassion toward those he or she leads? No! True empathy is a function of effective listening in relational communication. Empathy flows out of a servant heart.

Aloofness hinders one's leadership effectiveness. Followers resent dictatorial types. They dislike impersonal leaders who keep their distance. These leaders distort the essence of leadership. Leaders creating space and seeing themselves as above everyone else is a key leadership pitfall in Africa. All too many fall into it. There is a strong temptation for leaders to view themselves as "superior" to their followers. Such leaders may be feared, but they are not revered.

Out of such fear, our culture does not confront ineffective, impersonal, and autocratic leaders. We are taught to respect our leaders and avoid giving criticism, even if the leaders show no desire for and demonstrate no skills in connecting. We tend to remain silent.

In other cultures, such as in Asia, followers hold their leaders accountable. There is a greater expression of honor and shame. Crooked, autocratic leaders are removed by public revolt. This may explain why corrupt and ineffective leaders tend to stay in power longer in Africa. Our culture of tolerance allows fraudulent, distant leaders to remain.

Thankfully, things are changing. Some are recognizing that a leader must demonstrate the skills of bridge-building and service. I go back to a leader like Panya Baba. He was a simple leader who demonstrated good relational and social skills. He came alongside and served others.

Efficient Management Skills

In a culture where followers look to the leader to guide, protect and draw people into a common responsibility, the leader must faithfully steward the resources. A good leader will put people first and resources second. As noted, this requires effective relational skills. How can you manage your followers effectively if you are not their friend? How can you manage the people if you come across as too spiritual, autocratic and beyond their reach? Human beings are not robots; they are flesh and blood. To be an effective leader, managing people must be devoid of manipulation. The day a single follower discovers you are controlling him or her, you have lost that person's trust and credibility to be his or her leader.

Managing people requires both diplomacy and firmness. Skillful leaders know how to direct their followers in times of crises. My late father, Para Kundi Nyam, was a devoted follower of Jesus. He was also a successful farmer and local businessman. He was full of wisdom and foresight. He was a disciplinarian to the core. Yet he attracted many followers, for his exemplary leadership earned him the trust of many people. His elders, peers and juniors responded, for his word became the rallying point of action for the community.

Skillful leaders are also known for how they manage material resources. This underscores their role as protector. One of the leadership strengths God has given me is the ability to mobilize and manage meager resources to achieve maximum results. I have never had large sums of money, but I have hosted key landmark transformational programs in which we have spent large amounts, with little or no deficit afterwards.

I think again of the example of Mari Habu, who demonstrated effective management of resources through seeking to empower people, including the daily laborers who worked on his farm. He would feed them and later pay them a little more. As a result, most people preferred going to work in his farms.

I have learned that managing resources means taking care of the people one leads. I determined that paying staff stipends would be a bottom-up priority policy. This means that we usually start by paying the lowest salary earner first, and then the next, and so forth, until it comes to me. Most times, others get paid and I might be owed until the funds come in, but this approach has helped me greatly in managing both people and resources.

Successful Mentoring and Coaching Skills

Leaders want the common good. They want to create a sense of belonging. They also want to share the responsibilities of leading. This requires a commitment to mentor the next generation.

Mentoring is the informal transmission of knowledge, social capital and the psychosocial support relevant for work, career or professional development. Hopefully, such imparting will clear the way and smooth out any bumps for those who are mentored. It involves caring for people and simulating their growth through affirmation. Mentors love, even if this entails tough love. This is OK. The aim is to help a protégé climb the ladder.

The work of mentoring enables older, more experienced leaders to use their lives as models for the younger ones. The skillful take into cognizance the intergenerational realities, gender issues and other sensitivities in the community. Mentoring involves delegation; that is the first point of mentoring in any organization. Many are ready. They have a deep sense of call and willingness to grow in their roles. Some have a strong passion to fulfill their mission. The duty of leaders is to help them achieve this through the passing on of responsibilities.

A personal experience in 2003 taught me that mentoring is a two-way experience. The one mentored and the mentor are both learners in the journey. Looking back at African leaders like Mari Habu and Panya Baba, I realize they were interested in delegating to and investing in younger people. Mari Habu personally showed keen interest in me and drew me close after he baptized me when I was twelve years old. We remained close until his death in August 2013.

Panya Baba also mentored several young, emerging leaders, drawing them close to him. He listened to and respected their views, which is invaluable in a culture where the younger person is expected to keep quiet and listen, without questioning anything the authority figure has to say.

Useful Networking Skills

Transformational leadership demonstrates an ability to create change through networking successfully with leaders in other spheres of influence. In a communitarian context like Africa, where leadership is less individualistic and tends to be communal and consensual, networking skills are vital.

Networking promotes deep togetherness and nurtures the spirit of unity. This enables a sense of ownership for joint group action. This is necessary, for effective leaders are committed to progress. Looking back, part of what made Janani Luwum an effective leader was his practice of partnering with other bishops. He realized that change could only happen if leaders came together. No wonder the late Bishop Festo Kivengere took up from where Luwum left. The death of Luwum did not end his advocacy group.

That is the power of network skills in leadership.

Good Problem-Solving Skills

Critical and creative thinking is vital for any leader in the twenty-first century. It prepares the leader to face unwelcome and unpredictable moments. Societal issues are complex, as are the theological and missional realities of our time. Secular and church leaders are struggling to find solutions to society's challenges, and they are in short supply.

What Africa needs today is skilled leaders who bring positive impact, regardless of the difficult contextual realities. We have a history of leaders known for their creative thinking and problem-solving skills. These include past and present leaders – Nelson Mandela of South Africa, Thomas Sankara of Burkina Faso, and Nigeria's Yakubu Gowon. But we need more. The church needs leaders with similar skills.

What we do not need is easy-believism, name-it-and-claim-it, money-grabbing leaders. Sadly, they make up part of our culture. Instead, we need leaders with a godly presence, with the skills to develop creative ministries that will reach the next generation. We need problem solvers who stand against theological heresies and lifestyles that counter the life of Christ.

Summarizing What We Hear

The seven leadership skills we have explored are critical leadership ingredients in Africa. When carried out effectively, they preserve the role of a leader. It's not enough to have charisma and character; an effective leader must be a skilled leader. Should a leader possess those skills mentioned, he or she will make an impact in the present and the future.

But it will not be easy. Today, leaders in Africa have to be skilled in navigating through a complex terrain. The trajectory of leadership in Africa is a combination of the relational, the communal and the dictatorial. On the one hand, a leader is expected to be the wise voice and protector of the community, while on the other hand, he or she is expected to have absolute power over the rest of the community. There are confusing cultural expectations that a leader must work through.

Lessons from an African World

As a Westerner, I find Gideon's leadership words so centering. In the main, the Western world thinks of leadership skills as they relate to performance; Africans think of leadership skills as they relate to relationships. My world loves a list of principles. The African world loves to hear stories. They draw them back to the community.

Years ago, I was invited to Europe to teach a course on preaching. All of my students were African. With precision, I laid out the principles – the necessary skill sets – required in what I considered to be effective preaching. We covered exegetical outlines, and how the homiletical outlines must build upon these. I emphasized the importance of effective introductions, illustrations and conclusions. We talked about finding the one main idea in the text.

The course assignment was to take these principles, apply them to preparation and then preach the sermon. So far, so good – until the students stood up to preach. One by one, they came to the pulpit and told stories.

Were they not listening? Where were the homiletical skills I had worked so hard to impart? Did they not hear a thing I had taught? But a more important question was this: Did I hear them? Did I notice that their skill sets involved storytelling? Not in the moment. I failed to understand that the skill of communication in their collective culture relies on narrative, as well as tone.

Did you notice how Gideon's descriptions of the seven skills were filled with stories? Storytelling is necessary when communicating.

Listening to Gideon, I was reminded how we in the West are trained to communicate as literally and explicitly as possible.[58] It's *what* you say. The listener must take things at face value. Leaders have to develop the skill to articulate their personal and organizational goals, and do this with intelligibility, clarity and credibility. Words need to align with the mission and goals, creating the kind of clarity that leaves little space for confusion, disorder and infighting.[59]

In other cultures, like in Africa, cutting to the chase is not a respected skill. Getting up, displaying your biblical knowledge and calling for decision may fall flat. It might come across as condescending, patronizing and insensitive. In much of the Majority World, communication is more of a dance. In a shame/honor environment, saving face is more important than speaking directly.[60] Good communication is more subtle.[61] Language is more internalized, nonverbal and indirect. It's *how* you say it.

Decision-making skills differ as well. In Gideon's world, leaders make the decisions. As much as I value collaboration, people in an African community might show greater respect to leaders who decide on their own. It is one example of how decision-making skills are different.

---

58. Meyer, "Being the Boss," 72.
59. Lencioni, *The Advantage*, 73.
60. Georges and Baker, *Ministering*, 52.
61. Meyer, *Culture Map*, 31.

Erin Meyer is a professor at one of the world's leading international business schools. Her exposure to cultures has enabled her to see how cultures differ when it comes to authority and decision making. Imagine leadership in four quadrants. In the first, authority is hierarchical, and decision making is top-down. Think Africa. Opposite this quadrant is a leadership culture where authority is egalitarian and decision making is consensual. Everyone knows best. Think Norway and Sweden. The USA represents another part of the map, where leadership is egalitarian, but decision making is top-down. Decisions are vested in the individual as opposed to the group. Opposite this is the final quadrant, where the authority is hierarchical, but the decision making is a collaborative effort. Japan exemplifies this.[62]

Effective leaders must read the map. Their skills must adjust to the quadrant they find themselves in. They can't assume their quadrant exemplifies the most effective way to skillfully lead. It is best to come as listeners, discerning when and how to exercise leadership. They must recognize that each culture has its own worldview, its own practices and its own values. Every global region has differing assumptions regarding such things as the way to manage crises, how to communicate, the need for goals, the use of power, the importance of community and the role of time.

Time management skills? I had better put them aside and focus on other skills when I visit Gideon. Flexible time trumps linear time. People are more relaxed when it comes to moments. Time is more elastic, open and less structured. The more important a person is, the later one arrives. Interruptions happen. Sit back and enjoy the ride. This takes skill as well. Practice, practice, practice.

The Voice We Must Hear

The task of theology is to ensure that we follow God's Word where it leads, with all our mind, heart, soul, and strength.[63] So where does it lead when it comes to leaders and their skills? How does Scripture contribute to the subject of leadership competencies? What does it tell us?

---

62. Meyer, "Being the Boss."
63. Vanhoozer, "Letter to an Aspiring Theologian."

God Requires That Leaders Exercise Certain Skills

Leadership is demanding. It requires certain skills. Unless we discover and refine them, our leadership will have a credibility gap. This is what Scripture tells us.

Imagine that you are standing in the midst of Joseph, Moses, Joshua, Samuel, Deborah, David, Solomon, Josiah, Jeremiah, Daniel, Nehemiah, Peter and Paul. What do you see? You might notice that all of them commanded followers. They had a vision for where they were going, and each had an influence that changed his or her world. Imperfect as they were (the biblical writers are often subtly deconstructing major characters, like Gideon and Solomon, exposing their flawed leadership),[64] they were still credible. They did not lapse into the idolatries of many of their contemporaries. They possessed both character and skills. Without one or the other, their leadership would not have been credible.

The skills outlined earlier in this chapter are found in their lives. They were proficient in reasoning (Paul, Acts 17:22–31); exercising wisdom (Solomon, 1 Kgs 4:29); seeing through the layers (Moses, Exod 2:11–13); reading the readiness levels of those they mentored (Paul, 1 Tim 4:11–16); persuading followers (Joshua, Josh 1:10–18); making decisions (Deborah, Judg 4:4–9); bringing order (Moses, Num 2); stewarding resources (Joseph, Gen 41:41–49); and measuring outcomes (David, 2 Sam 24:2–9). They used their skills to govern empires, lead armies, oversee projects, plant churches and shepherd people.

When Jesus walked this earth, he demonstrated all of the skills necessary for effective leadership. His mind was always at full press, ahead of every thought, for he alone has the mind of God (Luke 11:17). He exercised perfect wisdom because he came as one wiser than Solomon (Matt 12:42). In every context, he skillfully saw into every layer because he sees into the depths of every heart (John 4:29). He read every situation perfectly (Matt 9:36), delegating leadership as his followers grew in their readiness (John 21:15–20). He recognized reality. He knew to whom he could and could not entrust himself (John 2:24). He spoke the right words in the right moments. No one spoke the way he did (John 7:46). When he invited people to follow him, they dropped everything and came to him (Mark 1:17; 2:14).

Jesus was decisive in everything he did. Everything. He moved in a perfect rhythm of engagement and withdrawal, rest and action, prayer, and teaching.[65]

---

64. Copan, *Is God a Moral Monster?*, 67.
65. Oden, *Classic Christianity*, 371.

He was the great disruptor, yet skillfully brought order where there was chaos (John 2:13–17). He stewarded what the Father chose to give him (John 17:6). He determined the key performance indicators for everything that has been and will be done (John 9:39; 2 Cor 5:10).

The Skills to Lead Come from God and Are Ultimately for His Purposes

Whatever leadership skills we possess come from God. We are God's handiwork, with skills that come from above (Eph 2:10; 1 Cor 12:7, 11).

Most aspire to develop leadership skills in order to win championships, set record production goals, lead armies or govern nations. But theology liberates us from our small purposes. It is true that God has given us our skills so that we might live to our fullest potential and flourish. But there is more. He invites us to discover and develop our skills to carry out his will. This is why he created them.

In the end, it is his intentions that will stand (Isa 46:10). We have been called according to his purposes, not ours (Rom 8:28). God is working out everything for his mission (Eph 1:11). Leaders are ultimately for the furtherance of God's kingdom and the enhancement of God's glory (1:12). Every enablement goes back to God and is for God.

These initial paragraphs give a necessary theological perspective. Otherwise, we will be impressed with the wrong skills. Worse, we will think this is about us. What does it matter if we are skillful at making decisions with speed and clarity, if those decisions have nothing to do with the purposes of God? It does not matter much if we have an instinctive sense of timing, if we are using time for all the wrong reasons. If we have the skill of persuasion but we use it all for temporal purposes, who in heaven is listening?

When we come to grips with the fact that life is about God's will and not our own, our motives shift. We become even more intentional to discover our skills and yield to his ongoing refinement of them. We bring our abilities before God and, like Isaiah, declare, "Here am I. Send me!" (Isa 6:8).

It is critical to exercise *the skill of thinking*. Leaders have to be adept at pondering strategies, reasoning carefully, solving problems and thinking through how to employ the best tactics. God tells us it matters how we think. Those who follow God should be the world's greatest thinkers.

Our thoughts, however, must be taken captive to the obedience of Christ (2 Cor 10:5). This is necessary. Whatever we choose to ponder defines us (Prov 23:7). All of our thinking and planning must come out of minds fixed on moral excellence and set on what is honorable and pure (Phil 4:8). Each day, our minds must first be affixed to God. This will say a lot about our leadership. It will say a lot about us. Tozer makes the penetrating statement, "What comes into our minds when we think about God is the most important thing about us."[66]

This is what elevates the stature of a leader. It is the principal mission of our minds. John Piper writes, "The main reason God has given us minds is that we might seek out and find all the reasons that exist for treasuring Him in all things and above all things."[67]

When we use our *skills to reframe, to read the situation, and deal with realities*, we do so because we want to be in the center of God's will. We want to be in step with God's narrative. We want his will to be done. We want these skills to honor God, and so we wrap each one in the prayer, "Your will be done" (Matt 6:10).

In the same way, we work at *the skill of finding our voice* because we want to inspire people to do more than win championships and meet corporate objectives. As significant and right as these are, it does not end here. We find our voice and skillfully use it to help people find God and go hard after him.

We see how God has used this skill in others to accomplish his purposes. Joshua's words moved Israel to stare down the walls; Nehemiah instilled the kind of courage that moved men to build them. Deborah found her voice in the hill country of Ephraim, just as did Esther in the court of the king and Ezra before a disheartened crowd (Judg 4:4–5:31; Esth 8:3; Neh 8:5–12).

We practice how to be *skillful in decision making* because indecisive leaders do not achieve God's purposes. God is going somewhere, and in all of his choices he is inherently decisive. We must be certain because God is certain. He does not vacillate. He is not wishy-washy or slow in keeping his promises (2 Pet 3:9). When it comes to carrying out God's purposes, leaders cannot be anything other than resolute. God's decision making also shows us how to make decisions. Just as God's decisions are careful and not impulsive, timely and not late, so our decisions must reflect the same qualities.

Leaders are given *the skill of bringing order* because God is a God of order. He stepped into creation, and his first act was to bring order out of chaos (Gen 1:1–26). Stability is part of his purpose. Where there is sin, there is generally disorder and darkness. Where there is order, the right priorities are carried out (Acts 6:2–4). Lists are made, needs are fulfilled, tasks are delegated and function replaces dysfunction (1 Tim 5:1–25).

---

66. Tozer, *Knowledge of the Holy*, 9.
67. Piper, *Think*, 15.

Order can only come out of lives that are in order, and this requires times of quiet and solitude. This is where God does some of his most significant work in us. Moses spends forty years in the desert; David devotes years to the wilderness; and Paul logs time in Arabia. Out of this work, and out of their personal discipline, leaders step into the mess and bring stability.

Leaders are given *the skill to steward*, and whatever we steward we do to ultimately fulfill the purposes of God (Col 3:23–24). For this reason, we hold what we have been given with great respect. But there is more. We treat whatever we manage with value and dignity because it ultimately belongs to God.

God is the owner and he has created us to manage (Gen 2:15). Management is a skill that acknowledges from the start that we own nothing. Every resource ultimately belongs to God. We are placed on this earth as stewards to care for what is his, for his purposes (Deut 10:14; 1 Chr 29:12–14; Pss 24:1; 50:10–12; Luke 19:12–27; 1 Cor 4:1–2).

Time, as one example, is God's to give; our task is to use it well (Ps 90:12; Eph 5:16). This is a skill! Able leaders understand the times and know what should be done (1 Chr 12:32). More, they know there is only so much time to carry out this work – the work of fulfilling God's will. There is no time to waste! We are in a cosmic conflict where the adversary continues a relentless effort to deceive and destroy. There is a looming end point to time.

Stewarding finances is a necessary skill, but it is not only about the bottom line. In today's world, much of leadership is about generating income, making a profit, managing costs and satisfying shareholders. We tend to honor those who have this skill, as we should. But God has a higher purpose for the stewarding of finances. We take the resources he has given us and offer them back to God as part of our expression of worship. After all, God owns everything.

God also loves to give, but we must be careful. God's generosity can lead to our ruin. We might begin to love the gift more than the Giver. The desire for money and material things can get a grip on a leader's soul. The dimensions of money can get all out of proportion (1 Tim 6:9). We can attach our image to financial success, use wealth to build *our* kingdom, and play the owner and not the steward. These will serve to put us in bondage (6:10).[68]

A sound theology helps us to see that behind these are spiritual forces that energize and give finances a life of their own, creating a war for the heart (Matt 6:24). Generosity, kingdom investment and a heart of contentment keep money in its rightful place.

---

68. Rodin, "Christian Leadership and Financial Integrity," 235.

The Skill of Exercising Wisdom Is the Foundational Leadership Skill

I believe our theology argues that wisdom should be our standout skill. When Solomon was summoned to lead, he was at a loss: "I am just a youth with no experience in leadership" (1 Kgs 3:7). Solomon needed skills necessary for leadership. God responded by giving him a wise and understanding heart (3:12).

Wisdom is the virtue that regulates and balances all of the other virtues.[69] It is also the skill that regulates and balances all of the other skills. "Wisdom" (Heb., *hokma*) can be translated as "masterful understanding," "skill," or "expertise."[70] Possessing it enables one to hear, see, read, decide and speak; to cope with life. Wisdom recognizes that:

- if you scratch certain itches, they just itch more; this is reality;
- the more you talk, the less people listen;
- the more self-absorbed we are, the less there is to find absorbing;
- forbidden fruit has its brown spots;
- the grass is greener on the other side – but it also has its dead patches.

The book of Proverbs reinforces the truth that wisdom is the foundational ability of a leader. By wisdom leaders lead (Prov 8:15). But where is this wisdom to be found? Is it simply amassed by a lifetime of observation? Not necessarily. By reading lots of books on leadership? Partially. Writers on leadership will at least seek to convince us of this. Does it come by looking deep within? In our humanistic culture, this is a popular answer.

True wisdom, however, is found in God. He has made it available, but it requires a meticulous search to find it (Prov 2:1–5). It is his glory to conceal, our glory to discover (25:2). The Word of God serves as the raw material. It is God's instrument to form the mind. More than any other book in Scripture, Proverbs is a leadership manual enabling one to acquire understanding, knowledge and discretion (1:1–6).

Attending to the soul and meditating on wisdom's words enables a leader to think critically. It expands one's capacity to recognize and respond to the presence and activity of God.[71] This is what separates spiritual leadership from other models.

Biblical wisdom gets us in step with the most important realities:

---

69. Vanhoozer, "Letter to an Aspiring Theologian," 30.

70. Waltke, *Book of Proverbs*, 76.

71. Barton, *Strengthening the Soul of Your Leadership*, 192.

- No one is seduced except those who are in the market for seduction (7:6–8).
- How you respond to distress has everything to do with your heart's capacity (24:10).
- Words have the power of life and death (18:20).
- You are who you walk with (13:20).
- You become rich by becoming generous (3:9–10).
- Things are not always what they seem to be (14:12).
- A leader's greatest fear must be of God (1:7).

Leaders without the skill of wisdom often live in self-delusion.

Hampton Sides tells the story of the USS *Jeannette*.[72] It was the latter part of the nineteenth century, and people were obsessed with exploring the North Pole. Many were convinced that a warm Pacific current extended to the polar cap. Captains enticed crews by telling them they simply had to work through the outer crust to discover a paradise, a Shangri-la. But it was a fool's errand.

Unskilled leaders make decisions based upon unrealities. Skillful leaders focus on what is actual.

Whatever Skills God Imparts, He Empowers

Whatever skills we possess gain effectiveness as we practice them: Skills x Training = Strength of Performance. But in the kingdom of God, we are not left to our own strengths; God also infuses our skills with his empowerment. Dedicated to the will of God, a leader's understanding can grow to another level. Sight can replace blindness. Clarity can take the place of confusion. The Spirit can give us a sense of timing that transcends any internal instincts. God can fill our hearts with courage, moving us from hesitancy to decisiveness. His wisdom can enable us to discern in ways that go beyond our perceptions. His power can enable our words to move hearts. His energy can awaken us to chase after it.

At the base of our best resolve and determination, force of will and skill to administrate, initiative to bring order and voice to command, is divine authority. We can be a lot more who we already are (Eph 3:16–21).

---

72. Sides, *Kingdom of Ice*.

The Outworking of Our Skills Will Ultimately Be Assessed by God

The world tells us that skills matter. So does God's wisdom: "Do you see someone skilled in their work? They will serve before kings; they will not serve before officials of low rank" (Prov 22:29). God honors leaders who submit to the disciplines that will develop their skills and give them the edge.

It counts with people, and it matters to God. One day, he will judge our lives based upon what we did with our time, our gifts, our choices *and our skills* (2 Cor 5:10). Those who have made great use of their leadership skills will be entrusted with even greater kingdom responsibilities (Matt 25:14–30; Luke 19:11–27; John 12:26).

This should inspire us to aim for superior performance. But what does that mean? Theology gives us a centering answer – skillful leaders, take note! We should always assess our success relative to the person and mission of God. It begins with ourselves:

- Have I been faithful? (1 Cor 4:1–2)
- Did I serve with humility? (Acts 20:19)
- Did I follow the Spirit's leading? (Acts 20:22)
- Did I complete the work God called me to do? (Acts 20:24)
- Were my motives pure? (Acts 20:33)
- Did I finish the race? (2 Tim 4:7)
- Did I bring glory to the name of God? (1 Cor 10:31)

Those leading a church might ask:

- Are marriages being saved?
- Are people financially helping others?
- How well are we carrying out the "one-another" commands?
- Are people invited into each other's homes?
- Are people being restored from addictive behavior?
- Is there a marked statistical difference that differentiates the ethics of this community from the culture around us?
- Are people sharing their gifts?
- Is this a place where lives are being transformed?

Effective leaders know what to look for. They know how to calibrate success. Theology has taught them that outcomes cannot be measured with the same precision as they are in a business. Jesus warned against measuring as the world measures (Luke 16:15). God occasionally measures success by loss (see John 6:66). He called Isaiah to a ministry of unresponsiveness, and in this, Isaiah was a great success (Isa 6:9–11).

Those with the greatest skill in measuring know that, ultimately, if there are any successful outcomes, it is because of God (1 Cor 3:7). And where there is success, our theology warns us that we should be careful. Success can go to our heads. Successful leaders often implode. Achieving great outcomes can be one of our greatest tests (Prov 27:21).

Bringing the Voices Together

Leaders who maximize their credibility are perfecting their character, and honing and employing their skills. Those who are truly proficient look at skills through multiple lenses – personal, global, and theological. They then put them to use. But what does this mean?

Part II

Implementing Global Leadership for Twenty-First-Century Ministry

"Measure a thousand times and cut once."
Turkish proverb

6

Do It Together

In his riveting article "The White Darkness," David Grann tells the story of Henry Worsley. On 13 November 2015, this British explorer set out from the coast of Antarctica to achieve what his hero, Ernest Shackleton, had failed to do a century earlier: trek on foot from one side of the continent to the other. The journey, which would pass through the South Pole, is more than a thousand miles long. It is one of the most brutal environments in the world.

From the beginning, Worsley decided he would cross alone and unsupported. There would be no food caches deposited along the route to help him forestall starvation. He would haul all of his provisions on a sled, without the assistance of dogs or a sail. Without anyone. Even if he came across a scientific research station, he would not share a meal. He would maintain his self-imposed exile. This journey was a way to subject himself to the ultimate test of character.

Early on, Worsley experienced the awe of being little more than a speck in the frozen nothingness. Every direction he turned, he saw ice stretching to the edges of the earth. White ice and blue ice, glacial ice tongues and ice wedges. There were no living creatures in sight. Not a bear or even a bird. He was truly alone. Just as he planned.

Worsley pressed forward. In two months, he traveled eight hundred miles. By then, every part of his body ached. He had lost more than forty pounds. His legs and arms had thinned to sticks, and his eyes had sunk into shaded hollows. His hips were battered and scraped from the constantly jerking harness, and he had bleeding hemorrhoids. But he was inspired by the words painted on his sled, "Always a little further." So he kept at it. He kept on keeping on.

Worsley almost made it, but on 22 January 2016 his endurance gave way. Short of his goal, he was evacuated, only to die shortly after he was airlifted out.[1]

---

1. Grann, "White Darkness."

Going it alone. There is something of this "heroic" spirit in most leaders, regardless of the culture. We imagine ourselves as rugged self-starters crossing our own vast unknown by ourselves. Part of this goes back to our inclination to be independent and achieve goals on our own. It might go back to the myth of the great leader – the heroic, arms-crossed kingpin who can get the job done single-handedly. But this is irrational. Dynamic leaders, ones who are determined to use their skills and character to change their worlds, recognize the wisdom of building great teams.

The Voices We Hear

Looking at the leadership literature, the subject of teams inevitably comes up. Here are some sample chapter titles:

- "Building a Team to Get the Job Done."
- "It's Not Just the Leader's Vision."
- "Relationships: The Leader's Network."
- "The Team Message."
- "The Law of the Inner Circle."
- "Foster Collaboration."
- "Creating Organizations with Many Leaders."
- "Participative Premises."
- "Discipline 1: Build a Cohesive Leadership Team."

"Inevitably" might, however, be going too far. I have noticed that a number of works on leadership have little to no discussion on teams. I have also observed leaders who prefer to go it alone. Just how important are teams in carrying out successful leadership? Let's start at the beginning, with definitions.

What Is a Team?

Whether we are convinced or not that teams play an irreplaceable role, it helps to begin with meanings. In his work on teams, Patrick Lencioni observes, "The word team has been so overused and misused in society that it has lost much of its impact. The truth is, few groups of leaders actually work like a team."[2]

Here is what a team is not: a group of individuals driven by their own agendas to see who gets to the top. Jon Krakauer, in his book *Into Thin Air*, describes the tragedy of such a team. In 1996, a group gathered around

---

2. Lencioni, *Advantage*, 21.

one ultimate purpose: to reach the summit of Mt. Everest. Expedition mountaineering is about coming together as a crew, for it is an enterprise in which no one can reach the top without the unrelenting efforts of all.[3] But this was not the case for these mountaineers.

As Krakauer puts it, "We were a team in name only, I'd sadly come to realize. Although in a few hours we would leave camp as a group, we would ascend as individuals linked to one another by neither rope nor any deep sense of loyalty. Each client was in it for himself or herself. And I was no different."[4] As a result, eight climbers lost their lives.

In contrast, Ernest Shackleton led a band of twenty-eight men to Antarctica. They would be the first to cross the continent. When ice floes forced the crew to abandon ship, Shackleton reinvented the team's goals. He made it his mission to bring everyone back home. It would require an interdependent mindset, with everyone fixed upon the same goal. Any sense of "me" was replaced with "we." Personal goals were secondary to the collective welfare. All the members coordinated with the others to get there. Everyone survived.

Drawing on their study of 120 top teams from around the world, the writers of *Senior Leadership Teams* discovered the same essential characteristics of any true team. Those who make up a team . . .

- are behaviorally unified;
- have a collaborative spirit;
- are mutually dependent;
- have skills that complement one another's strengths;
- co-mission, charting the direction of an enterprise together;
- galvanize other's ideas and energy to cross the void;
- hold one another accountable.[5]

A definition must also take into account the fact that not all teams are the same. They have the same essentials, but different teams have different purposes and different work content. Some will be informational; others consultative; some coordinating; and some decision making.[6] Some teams will have a more strategic focus; others will be more tactical. Some will have no greater purpose

---

3. Useem, *Leadership Moment*, 105.

4. Cited in Perkins, *Leading at the Edge*, 72–73.

5. This represents a collection of statements from Ruth Wageman, Debra A. Nunes, James A. Burruss, and J. Richard Hackman in *Senior Leadership Teams*, xi, and Lencioni, *Advantage*, 19.

6. See a good summary of the different kinds of teams necessary for leadership in Wageman et al., 36–39.

than to generate ideas; others will be tasked to solve an ongoing problem. Each will have a different level of authority, from minimal to ultimate.

One of the more needful teams is an inner team of confidants, selected to share the load. Maxwell refers to this as "The Law of the Inner Circle."[7] They become an important sounding board, a restraint against impulsive acts.

One of my better decisions as a leader was to build a team that we called "Core Pastors." I bounced many ideas off them, and in time we began to collaborate and make decisions together.

How Essential Are Teams?

My leadership experience concurs with a number of leadership voices: teams are necessary if a leader wants to be successful. If you want to maximize your leadership potential, find others who complement you.

Kouzes and Posner begin the preface of their work on leadership by writing, "*The Leadership Challenge* is about how leaders mobilize others to want to get extraordinary things done in organizations."[8] In the opening words of his work *The Five Dysfunctions of a Team*, Patrick Lencioni states, "Not finances. Not strategy. Not technology. It's teamwork that remains the ultimate competitive advantage, both because it is so powerful and so rare."[9]

When teams are established, others in the organization develop their competence and confidence. Teams allow for greater buy-in. The vision becomes bigger than merely one person's. The work has a greater chance of getting done in a culture where the mantra of exemplary leaders is "You can't do it alone."

True, there are times I have preferred going it alone. An autonomous (dictatorial?) spirit resides deep in most of us. Teams slow things down. They can get messy. People will push back and disagree. Some will need more time, and it will challenge our patience. Moses formed a committee, and it got him forty years in the wilderness. Team meetings can be a waste of time, an interruption to the main work. Going it alone is much simpler and efficient. Right? Not really.

Any real movement forward begins with teams. A leader may occasionally have to go it alone. Leadership is a mix of the executive and the legislative. But going it alone is more the exception than the rule. Healthy organizations

---

7. Maxwell, *21 Irrefutable Laws*, 109–119.

8. Kouzes and Posner, *Leadership Challenge*, xi.

9. Lencioni, *Five Dysfunctions of a Team*, vii.

cannot afford to have "Lone Rangers." They need leaders who embrace the African proverb: "If you want to travel fast, go alone. If you want to travel far, go together."

It appears that more and more traditional cultures are realizing this. Individualistic leadership, often associated with top-down pyramidal hierarchies (high distance leadership), is becoming yesterday's leadership model. "Great leaders alone" is being replaced by "Great leaders who exist in a fertile relationship with a great group." Leaders are viewed as equals among titans.[10] Leadership is less and less about imposing the leader's solo dream, and more about developing a shared sense of destiny.[11] It's about participative leadership.

It's about leadership success.

In certain business sectors, leaders have been saying this all along. Peter Drucker writes, "The leaders who work most effectively never say 'I.' Not because they have been trained this way. They don't think this way. They understand their role is to make the team function. They don't sidestep responsibility, but 'we' gets the credit."[12]

There's good reason for this. Any leader who limits his or her organization to the talents and time of the leader seriously handicaps the group.[13] There can be no extraordinary effort, for one is too small a number to achieve greatness. "None of us is as smart as all of us."

Michael Useem's leadership stories (*Leadership Moment*) serve to illustrate. In every case study, a leader's use of teams determined their success or failure. Roy Vagelos could not have attacked river blindness without a team; Joshua Lawrence Chamberlain could not have defended Little Round Top without his officers; and behind the triumphant return of Apollo 13 was the leadership of Eugene Kranz and his staff. As Useem puts it, "Eugene Kranz, James Lovell, and their crews matched wits with technology failure, and they won."[14]

In contrast, behind one of the worst firefighting disasters in Forest Service history was Wagner Dodge and himself. He preferred to fight it alone, keeping somewhat to himself. There was no cohesion; just every man for himself.[15]

10. Bennis and Biederman, *Organizing Genius*, 3.

11. Kouzes and Posner, *Leadership Challenge*, 124.

12. Drucker, *Managing the Non-Profit Organization*, 18.

13. De Pree, *Leadership Jazz*, 118.

14. Useem, *Leadership Moment*, 79.

15. Useem, 43–64.

If anything, the times argue for the necessity of teamwork. Restructuring, global competition, expanding technologies and the rapid pace of change necessitate organizations that are flexible, effective at problem solving and excellent at decision making. This requires shared leadership. The demands on those who occupy the top roles are rapidly outdistancing the capabilities of any single person, no matter how gifted.[16]

This is becoming more obvious with modern-day presidencies. Writes one political observer: "The modern Presidency has gotten out of control."[17] No matter one's capacity, the work has morphed. Tasks need to be divided among others. We are at a moment where decision making needs to shift downward from a traditional hierarchy to more self-managed teams. Teams can process the rapidly changing data more quickly. They may actually speed the implementation.

Let's face it, we were built to do it together. We will not make it if we don't stop at occasional aid stations and find support. Better yet, start the journey as a team. We will fall short if we don't extend hands and travel as one.

What Makes for Great Teams?

Assuming you are a leader committed to teams, what are the essentials that make for a successful team? Here are three.

The Right People

Greatness starts with superb people. Our leadership strength is only as great as the people we build around us. Recruiting the most talented is the first task of anyone who hopes to create a skillful group. Useem gives this advice: "Pick your associates well, back them fully, empower them with both accountability and responsibility, and they will produce far more than you ever will achieve on your own."[18]

Using the metaphor of a bus, Jim Collins exhorts leaders to do whatever they can to get the right people on the bus, the wrong people off the bus, and the right people into the right seats. Greatness flows first and foremost from having the right people in the key seats.[19] This requires discernment, but that is what skillful leadership is about. Skillful leaders are "first-class noticers."

16. Wageman et al., *Senior Leadership Teams*, xiii.
17. Dickerson, "Hardest Job in the World."
18. Useem, *Leadership Moment*, 257.
19. Collins, *Good to Great and the Social Sectors*, 14.

They are able to look for next-generation leaders and size up potential. So what do they notice?

People with Credibility

We have defined credibility as a mix of character and skills. Great teams have credible people. This begins with principled hearts. Jack Welch, former CEO of General Electric, refers to values such as integrity, work ethic, dedication and trust as "the first acid test."[20] Members with integrity do not go against their convictions when it comes to team decisions. They follow through with what is expected and with what their consciences allow. They know when to keep things confidential. Their convictions earn themselves and the team respect.

Alongside their core values are the necessary core skills. They need to be learners, discerners and effective decision makers. They must be skilled in listening, in processing and analyzing, and in articulating their positions. They must have the power of analysis – the ability to solve problems and see the big picture. Most of all, they must have the skill of collaboration.

People Who Demonstrate Excellence

Building teams, great teams, requires not settling for mediocrity. Leaders have no time for teammates who go through the motions, who continually set fire to their shoelaces. Team builders have a nose for talent. They want to know a person's gifts. How developed are her skills? What is the depth of his knowledge, as well as the capacity of his growth? Is this person self-motivated and self-disciplined?

Leaders look for those who are compulsively driven to make whatever they touch the best it can be – not because of what they can get for it, but because they have a neurotic need to improve.[21]

In the early 1950s, Warren Bennis became interested in extraordinary collaborations. He recognized that the marriage of an able leader and an assemblage of extraordinary people could change the world.[22] To use the words of Steve Jobs, they have the potential to "make a dent in the universe." So he looked for commonalities – attitudes and behaviors that lead to great groups.

What constitutes the right people? Here are some of the characteristics Bennis came up with:

---

20. Welch, *Winning.*
21. Collins, *Good to Great and the Social Sectors*, 15.
22. Bennis and Biederman, *Organizing Genius*, xvi.

- Original minds: they create new forms rather than clone existing successes.
- Problem solvers: they identify opportunities rather than get bogged down in problems.
- Future-oriented: they want to do the next thing, not the last one.
- Deep generalists: as opposed to narrow specialists.
- Empathetic: they can paraphrase their colleagues' ideas and discern the meaning they have for them.
- Loyal: they see their goals as collective, and execute a decision as if it is their own.
- Initiators: they don't wait passively for instruction.
- Relational: they have the ability to work with others.
- Fire in the eyes: they are self-motivated, revealing hungry, urgent minds.
- Conceptual thinkers: they can synthesize complex information.
- Anticipatory: they can see around the corners and beyond the horizon.
- Delusional confidence: they do not know what is impossible.
- Tenacious: they have a drive to get things done and not give up.[23]

The one at the helm is not threatened by greatness. Those chosen may have the kinds of extraordinary gifts that might even cause a leader to temporarily follow – and that's OK. Great leaders thrive because of another's excellence and ability to do what they cannot do on their own.

People Who Have the Right Chemistry

A good leader builds a team where each member complements the others. Each one maximizes the strengths and minimizes the weaknesses of the others at the table. This requires the right harmony. A healthy group has the proper mix of personalities and temperaments. It's more important people fit together than fit in.[24]

Leaders look for people who connect and complement. They ask, "Will this person bring life and light into the meetings?" "Will her presence help boost the morale and unify the team?" "Does he have humor?" "Is he warm or standoffish?" "Does she have healthy emotional intelligence?" "Is there a sense of loss when she is not in the room?"

---

23. Bennis and Biederman, 196–218.
24. Sweet, *Summoned to Lead*, 76.

The right chemistry ensures the group will stay on task and flourish. The wrong mix, and a group will get off the rails.

A discerning leader is careful to avoid building teams with difficult and abrasive people, people who are humorless and thoughtless. No matter their intelligence or the political gain some may bring, good leaders will avoid adding any "derailers." These are people who are . . .

- toxic types who poison the team and deaden the spirit;
- egoists who always insist on their way, manipulate and pressure conformity;
- dividers who create mistrust and dissension, and withhold information;
- betrayers who triangulate and knife others in the back;
- subversives who appear to be in but are really not on board;
- high-maintenance types who need to be tightly managed and told what to do;
- sluggards who avoid responsibility and seldom volunteer for assignments;
- negativists who promote hopelessness and despair.[25]

In one of my first teams, I accepted a team member who disrupted the chemistry. Over time, his poisonous spirit led to leadership inertia. His withering criticism of others deadened the spirit. I found myself doing damage control. When you have people who increase, rather than lessen, your workload, it's time to make adjustments.

People Who Reflect and Celebrate Diversity
Monocultural teams may run more smoothly and predictably, but without a diversity of age, gender, perspectives and ethnicity, teams will lack depth and creativity.

Building teams comprised of dissimilar members, a leader recognizes there will be the potential for misunderstanding and conflict. What is right and acceptable in one culture or age group may be wrong and unacceptable in another. A leader will have to work for clarity and fight for unity. Multicultural teams will require patience and compromise, but it is a small price to pay for the gain. A team built of both left-brain (logical, analytical) and right-brain (creative, intuitive) types leads to a team that is whole-brained.

---

25. See Wageman et al., *Senior Leadership Teams* for a good description of derailers, 97–102.

Having the right people on the team is only one part of building great teams. There is a second essential:

The Right Leader

A great team cannot exist without a great leader, one who is organizing the genius of the others.[26] This is not easy. Even if a leader has brought together a group of high-performing, high-spirited thoroughbreds, can he harness their skills? Can she deal with the inevitable pitfalls that teams can fall into?

Lencioni warns of five "dysfunctions" that can be lethal for the success of any team: absence of trust, fear of conflict, lack of commitment, avoidance of accountability and inattention to results.[27] Working for functionality will require the right leadership.

Every year in one of my leadership courses, I ask students to sit in on a leadership team. It may be a board or a staff meeting. I want them to assess its health. I encourage them to use Lencioni's grid as one way of evaluating both teams and their leaders. More often than not, their field reports have been discouraging. I am astounded at how few leadership teams operate with any measure of health. What's wrong? Much of it goes back to a failure of leadership.

What kinds of team leaders are necessary?

Leaders Who Have Credibility

As with every other member on the team, leaders have to have the right character and competence. We owe it to our teams to be principled and skilled. Team members need to have respect for and confidence in their leaders.

Leaders Who Create and Sustain Meaning

A significant part of the leader's task is to keep before the team the purpose for its existence. Reading the minutes, reviewing financial reports and talking about present activities are needful, but a steady diet can dull the mind. Great teams have essential work to do and great goals to chase. They are about something consequential. Without these, energies will wane and members will look for other challenges.

Leaders who get this are those who recognize the immortal longings in people. They do not subject them to inconsequential meetings and trivial decisions. Teams need to believe they are about something significant and

---

26. Bennis and Biederman, *Organizing Genius*, 199.
27. Lencioni, *Five Dysfunctions of a Team*.

momentous – possibly earth-shattering! They are changing the landscape, tipping the balance and transforming the ethos. If not, why meet?

Great leaders tell great teams they are going to, in some respect, change the world. This is what Warren Bennis found that great teams have in common: they believe they are on a mission higher than themselves. They are doing something vital – even holy.[28]

Leaders Who Create and Maintain the Right Structure

In order to meet the objectives, teams must have a strong organization. Creating and maintaining this structure is the job of the leader.

Healthy teams have a defined number; a predetermined time frame for accomplishing their goals; a clear agenda that effectively uses the time; and the right procedures for carrying things out. These are critical issues, for many of the negative behaviors are symptomatic of poor team design.[29]

The following are some of the questions a leader must answer if a team is to be organizationally functional:

- What are the ground rules as to how discussions are carried out and decision making is done?
- Who is a member and who is not?
- Who votes and who does not?
- Will we insist upon unanimity or settle for consensus?

The editors of *Senior Leadership Teams* advise keeping teams small. "When team leadership gets into the double-digits, the space needed for real interdependence, meaningful contribution, and team decision making tends to be squeezed out."[30] It is harder to accommodate all the voices for robust discussions.

Effective leaders have a procedure for creating agendas (so strategic!) and have guidelines for how rigidly they should be followed. They have defined the outcomes, sorted out the motivations and defined the necessary constraints to keep the team on task. They keep a tight schedule, knowing that undisciplined meetings soon become counterproductive.

Sooner or later (better sooner), a leader will lead the team through an exercise that will determine the right norms of behavior. Healthy teams are proactive rather than reactive. Do not wait until the team becomes

---

28. Bennis and Biederman, *Organizing Genius*, 204.
29. Wageman et al., *Senior Leadership Teams*, 102.
30. Wageman et al., 19.

dysfunctional. Avoid putting off, lest destructive behaviors begin to hijack the meetings.

The following norms served us well on one board I led:

- *Inclusiveness:* we are a community where everyone has an equal voice.
- *Humility:* we acknowledge that on our own we can do nothing.
- *Integrity:* everything we do reflects honesty and trust.
- *Discernment:* we are determined to find God's will in everything we do, indifferent to anything less than his purposes.
- *Courage:* we are willing to take our stand and step out in faith.
- *Lovingkindness:* we are committed to showing grace, compassion and affection to one another.
- *Servanthood:* we are not above serving the most basic needs of one another.
- *Responsibility:* we are committed to carrying our weight, fulfilling the duties that come with being an elder.
- *Gratitude:* we hold to this value as a reminder to see God's blessing in our lives, thanking God always for one another.
- *Unity:* we will always seek for oneness, even through our conflicts.
- *Transformation:* we are committed to the disciplines that create greater spiritual maturity, as well as provoking one another to become more and more like Jesus.

Leaders Who Affirm and Protect

People thrive when leaders go out of their way to recognize excellence, communicate confidence and point out uniqueness. Wise leaders take time to celebrate victories and make public a team member's achievements. Astonishing accomplishments don't come easily, and they seldom bloom in barren and unappreciative settings.

At the same time, it is critical to diagnose problems, protect the team and discourage dysfunctional behavior. More than discourage it – oppose it. Rebuke disrespect, personal attacks, abusive control and subversive rebellion – and do it on the spot. Letting it slide leaves the team vulnerable. It suggests that such behavior is tolerable on the team.[31]

---

31. Wageman et al., 101.

Leaders Who Build Trust

It may not be an overstatement to say that mistrust is at the heart of most dysfunctional teams. Leaders have to work hard at building trust. A big part of creating trust is becoming vulnerable, going first when it comes to admitting mistakes or sharing weaknesses. Our flesh might scream at the thought. Sharing our real self might be as pleasurable as bathing a cat.

We have this misguided notion that real leaders maintain distance and keep private. We like it when people say of us, "It's hard to get close." But aloofness does not create an environment of trust. Better to be close – and transparent. Transparency means admitting to a misstep or acknowledging a wrong motive, sharing a childhood fear or a present anxiety.

Recently, my school hired a new dean. In his first formal meeting, he spoke about some of his early successes and failures. It was sobering. At times, it was funny. He shared the painful journey that he and his wife have been on with their son. Some of us asked ourselves, "Could I share that?" It was risky, as well as refreshing. He was being real. No, it was more than that: he was establishing trust.

Great leaders share their lives in a way that gets us thinking beyond the meetings. It reminds me of the legendary America filmmaker, Paul Schrader, who believes the best films start as you're walking out of the theatre. Great meetings, led by great leaders, start things that go beyond adjournment.

Leaders Who Create a Culture of Interdependence

A big part of a leader's work is to create a collaborative environment, a shared mindset, a common identity. Effective leaders invite people to weigh in. They respect the fact people have things to contribute, even if they are contrary. They draw out those who tend to be quiet, who might be culturally inclined to wait until their opinions are asked. Often, those who are silent have some of the greatest insights.

Max De Pree uses the metaphor of a jazz band. A leader will pick the tune, set the tempo and start the music. After that, it's up to the band to be disciplined and free, wild and restrained. Jazz band leaders know how to integrate the voices in the band without diminishing their uniqueness.[32] The aim is for everyone to emerge with a sense of ownership, each one depending upon the others.

Earlier, we mentioned Steve Kerr, the extraordinary coach of National Basketball Association champions Golden State Warriors. He stresses mutual

---

32. De Pree, *Leadership Jazz*, 103.

dependence. It is all about team. As his assistant coach puts it, Kerr has the authority based upon title, but the culture is by community. He is one of them. He doesn't look at himself as a figure the team has to defer to. He even allows for time-outs where the players decide what strategy they should implement for the next set of plays. It is all about interdependence.[33] This helps to explain why they have dominated other teams in the National Basketball Association.

Leaders Who Respect Boundaries

Within this interplay of interdependence, a leader must maintain lines of authority and appropriate points of access. It's important to be both available and unavailable. This is necessary to provide the necessary autonomy to achieve maximum results. If you are always available, you're not of much use when you are available. If you are always in their space, team members may not learn how to work things out on their own. And you may never get anything of significance done.

There are other boundaries. A healthy team establishes lines that discourage sexual misjudgment. Suggestive words, improper sharing or inappropriate touch cannot be allowed for any reason. A particular sin of leaders is to encourage out-of-control work hours. Accomplishing our goals at the expense of time with family or time for self creates its own sickness.

Leaders Who Leverage the Full Range of Team Members' Capabilities

Part of creating a culture of interdependence is to help people develop. Great leaders spot the strengths of those on the team and develop them. They are determined to help people do what they were born to do.

To put it another way, great leaders extract people's full capability. Liz Wiseman refers to these kinds of leaders as "multipliers."[34] They take the human capital, the most important asset of any institution, and make it more valuable for tomorrow's world. John Maxwell makes a similar point, using the following matrix:

- Wrong person in wrong place = regression
- Wrong person in right place = frustration
- Right person in wrong place = confusion
- Right person in right place = progression
- Right person in right places = multiplication[35]

---

33. Stein and Cacciola, "Why Do the Warriors Dominate the 3rd Quarter?"
34. Wiseman, *Multipliers*.
35. Maxwell, *17 Laws of Teamwork*, 33.

Wise leaders avoid the mistake of assigning the best-performing people to deal with the day-to-day problems. Peter Drucker refers to this tendency to fix the problems and starve the opportunities as the "deadly business sin."[36] Rather, put your best people onto the greatest openings, not your biggest problems. They need to be on the bridge directing the ship, not in the engine room putting out the fires.

Leaders Who Create a Culture of Accountability

Creating a culture of accountability is vital, but it is often avoided. Too many leaders like to be popular, to be liked. They are hesitant to hold people's feet to the fire. Yet leaders sidestepping holding people accountable is one of the biggest obstacles to teams reaching their potential.[37]

This was one of my biggest past mistakes as a team leader. I found it too easy to go through an agenda that covered everything from calendar dates to brief reports of plans for the week. Too often, we parked the operational plan to the side, avoiding the hard questions – "How is it this target did not get met?" "What is your strategy to accomplish the vision?" We will come back to this when we discuss tactics.

Leaders Who Communicate

There may be those on a team who do not have a high EQ, but leaders must possess keen emotional intelligence. They must be able to read their teams and communicate the necessary words at the right time. It is necessary to connect with hearts and minds. Interaction is critical to teamwork. It is the glue that holds an organization together. Effective leaders encourage two-way interaction. If people don't weigh in, they don't buy in.[38]

It's all part of clarity. Ambiguity undermines teamwork. Effective leaders move from the ethereal to the real. They get into the specifics. In the give and take, they gather the relevant facts and ideas and bring them together in a framework the team can understand and use.[39] They do not use communication as a weapon, punishing team members by ignoring or freezing them out.

Healthy leaders also know the appropriate form of communication – when to speak person-to-person, talk on the phone, use email or text. They never communicate emotional issues via email. They are deep listeners, seeking

---

36. Drucker, "Drucker On Management," *The Wall Street Journal*, November 18, 2009, online.

37. Lencioni, *Advantage*, 57.

38. Lencioni, *Advantage*, 48.

39. Wageman et al., *Senior Leadership Teams*, 188.

multiple perspectives. They also know the appropriate amount of sharing. They hold to the adage, "If you're not sick and tired of communicating, you probably aren't doing a good enough job."[40] Agendas must be clear, every item meaningful and outcomes clearly defined.

Leaders Who Ensure That the Necessary Resources Are Provided

One of the great morale builders is having the necessary means to go after the objectives. One of the great demoralizers is to have a great mission and vision, and the energy to go for them, but to lack the means. Leaders have to be the advocates who lobby for the necessary funds, people, space, training, access to data, and so on. This may require some of their greater energies. Leaders have to get the essential pieces in place.

Leaders Who Allow for Mistakes

The natural reaction to mistakes is criticism and conflict. Leaders can multiply the problem by insisting on their own mistake-free zone. But missteps are inevitable. Belasco formed a "Mistake of the Month Club" in his business to stimulate discussion and learning. He announced, "I expect everyone to make ten mistakes a day, but I expect originality in those mistakes."[41] Jim Burke of Johnson & Johnson notes that it's essential, in leading people toward growth, to get them to make decisions, and to let them make mistakes.[42]

Whenever we avoid mistakes, we lose lots of opportunities to learn. And leadership is essentially a lifetime of lessons. We can persevere through criticism if followers recognize we are generous when it comes to mistakes. We can also endure if we learn from the mistakes, gain from the criticism, weather the conflicts, regroup, and go on again with renewed conviction and confidence.

The Right Cause

Having the right team members and the right leader suggests a great potential. But it will not be realized if there is not a compelling direction. In their "Secrets of Great Teamwork," Haas and Mortensen identify this as the first secret.[43] Great teams are clear about what they are working toward. Leaders have helped them identify this, and they keep everyone "obsessionally focused."

40. De Pree, *Leadership Jazz*, 100.
41. Belasco and Stayer, *Flight of the Buffalo*, 320.
42. Bennis and Biederman, *Organizing Genius*, 97.
43. Haas and Mortensen, "Secrets of Great Teamwork."

People need to know where they are in the process and how to recognize when the objective has been reached. Great teams are not interested in maintaining the status quo. In the end, the only measure of a great team is whether it accomplished what it set out to accomplish.

The Voices We Need to Hear

Great teams have great people, great leadership and a great cause. Still, are teams necessary? What do voices from other parts of the world tell us?

The Voice of Elizabeth Sendek, Rectora, Biblical Seminary of Columbia (FUSBC), Medellín, Colombia

The exploration of how cultural tendencies affect leadership has become a focus of study in Latin America. It follows the results of the Hofstede and Globe projects.[44] It's necessary. In theological education and church contexts, we are not hearing the Latin American voice. Most literature on the topic reflects the thinking of North American authors. Elizabeth Sendek provides a centering voice. She has led BSC for a number of years, a school where she has also taught Greek and New Testament exegesis, we well as served as Academic Vice-President. All of this continues what she has devoted much of her life to doing – preparing the next generation of Latino leaders.

The Nature of Latin American Leadership
Before I discuss teams, I want to look at Latin American leadership and how it is perceived, reflecting on two sources. First, I want to look at how literature depicts leaders. Second, I will look at the results of the Hofstede study, giving some analysis and making application to Latin American leadership. Finally, I want to apply this, observing how cultural traits in the region affect leaders and teamwork.

Latin American Leadership Viewed from the Literature
The *caudillo* (strong man) leadership model, in Latin America, is one that has operated for generations. On the political scene, the role of the dictator epitomizes it. In Latin American literature, this genre is known as the "dictator

---

44. Hofstede, Hofstede, and Minkov, *Cultures and Organizations*; House et al., *Culture, Leadership and Organizations*.

novel." It is a narrative of power, and it is the effort of authors to rewrite part of our history.[45]

The genre started in the late nineteenth century and flourished in the twentieth. It was a time when political dictators were common in Latin America. Although dictators, as such, do not exist today, the exercise of political power reflects similar traits.

In her study of the Latin American dictator as a narrative prototype, Francisca Nogueral discusses the personal traits of this figure. Several are relevant for an understanding of power and teamwork dynamics in Latin America:[46]

- *Messianism:* the dictator relates to God as an equal. The historical figures behind the fictional characters ruled in Roman Catholic countries where their assumed close connection to God was a supernatural validation of their supreme power.
- *Saving patriotism:* the tyrant is indispensable for the good of the nation. He is the only one capable of making decisions, big and small. Without him there is no hope, no future. (This presumes the utter inability of others – even close associates – to carry out any responsibility in the functioning of the government and of the country.)
- *Paternalism:* the dictator is the benefactor of those who depend on him, the guarantor that their benefits will continue. This responsibility on his part demands reciprocity. His beneficiaries owe him total personal loyalty. This exchange of favors has its origins in the historical *hacienda* model where the "patron" did not only pay salaries to his workers, but provided a home, food, medical care for them and their families, and sometimes even schooling for their children.[47]
- *Love of death:* death is the dictator's most efficient instrument of power, the only friend who helps him deal effectively with enemies.
- *Hatred of others:* the dictator's utter contempt for others, even those around him. As a result, he is a solitary individual.

---

45. Gómez, *La novela del dictador*, 211–239.

46. Jiménez, *El dictador latinoamericano.*

47. Anabella Dávila and Martha Elvira, "Liderazgo en Latinoamérica: el poso de la historia," IESE Insight – Business Knowledge, 2012. http://www.ieseinsight.com/doc.aspx?id=1358&ar=17&idioma=1. Accessed 20 March 2018.

These dictatorial traits are still present in public and private dimensions of life in Latin America, including politics, business, education, economics, family, philanthropy, and church and faith-based organizations. This strong man, or *caudillo*, model of leadership affects how teamwork is conceived and carried out.

Latin American Leadership and the Hofstede Study

The 2010 edition of Geert Hofstede, Gert Jan Hofstede, and Michael Minkov's *Cultures and Organizations: Software of the Mind* presents the results of one of the most comprehensive studies on cultural influence and what distinguishes people. The study was carried out implementing a model that considers six dimensions of culture (6-D Model) and identifying how they are present in seventy-six countries.[48] The six dimensions are power distance, individualism, masculinity (called competitiveness here), uncertainty avoidance, long-term orientation and indulgence.

Table 6.1: Latin American Countries in the Hofstede Study

Dimensions of Culture Shaping Values in the Workplace				
Country	Power Distance	Individualism	Competitiveness	Uncertainty Avoidance
Argentina	49	46	56	86
Brazil	69	38	49	76
Chile	63	23	28	86
Colombia	67	13	64	80
Costa Rica	35	15	21	86
Ecuador	78	8	63	67
El Salvador	66	19	40	94
Guatemala	95	6	37	99
Honduras	80	20	40	50
Mexico	81	30	69	82
Panama	95	11	44	86
Peru	64	16	42	87
Uruguay	61	36	38	99
Venezuela	81	12	73	76

Fourteen Latin American countries were included in the study. Every one of these countries was listed under the first four dimensions. Ten of the fourteen

48. Hofstede, Hofstede, and Minkov, *Cultures and Organizations*.

were listed under the last two. All fourteen countries share similar results in three dimensions, with a wider diversity in the competitiveness dimension. This is reflected in table 6.1. The index value for each dimension in the table represents the relative position of the country in a scale ranging from 0 for little evidence of the dimension in a case to 100 for a lot of evidence of the same.[49]

To gain a better understanding of Latin American leadership, I will break these down and give some analysis. This will help us when we look at teamwork in Latin America.

Power Distance

This dimension refers to the extent to which people with less power expect and accept inequality in the distribution of power. Except for Costa Rica and Argentina, all Latin American countries in the sample show this acceptance and expect it both in private and in government institutions and organizations. This fits with the role of the leader in the dictator model, where objectives and programs of the organization are centered on the dictator's person.

Individualism

All Latin American countries in the study rank low in the individualism dimension, with Guatemala, Ecuador, Panama, Venezuela, and Colombia showing the lowest scores. These results put them in the category of collectivist societies with a high degree of interdependence between their members. Combined with the high scores in power distance acceptance, this means that it is through strong, cohesive in-groups that people obtain benefits and privileges.

Competitiveness

This is the only dimension in which these Latin American countries show a significant difference. Five score high in their orientation toward competitiveness and success, and nine in their tendency toward interdependence and in their people orientation.

In the first group, the focus is on achievement, assertiveness, and material success. These societies tend to be more competitive. The second group (a majority) stands for cooperation and care for others. Society here is more consensus-oriented.[50]

---

49. Hofstede, "Country Comparison."

50. Hofstede, Hofstede, and Minkov, *Cultures and Organizations*, 140.

It is important to note that competitive assertiveness goes alongside low individualism in Latin America. This explains why rivalry is focused on members of other groups and not toward members of one's in-group.

Uncertainty Avoidance

All Latin American countries in the sample have a high score in this dimension. Mechanisms are developed to deal with the anxiety uncertainty produces. Latin American societies resort to numerous and precise laws and regulations for every dimension of life. This also leads to social conservatism.

This does not mean that rules are inexorably obeyed, but their existence provides a sense of certainty and control. Combined with high scores in power distance and collectivism, it makes change difficult. Where there is change, it is led by a powerful figure of authority.

The tendency to avoid or minimize uncertainty does not necessarily mean lack of tolerance of ambiguity. For political and economic reasons, people in Latin America live with and tolerate uncertainty, while having a desire to minimize it. At the same time, tolerance of ambiguity, which is a great virtue of the culture, makes people less rigid and prone to improvisation. This makes it possible to live in the midst of the uncontrolled circumstances of their personal and work lives.[51]

The Application of Latin American Leadership to Teamwork

The cultural characteristics described above have both positive and negative implications for teamwork. The dictator, or strong-man, model leads to power distance and interdependence.

When forming a team and working within it, loyalty to the leader and to the team is fundamental. The leader's vision and thinking tend to shape those of the team and their decisions. Teams are not spaces for democratic participation; they exist to support the leader's vision. Members are not encouraged to express their own opinions or take interest in the opinions of others. Their role is to conform to the opinions of the leader as well as of powerful members of the group. The collectivist bent in the culture does not automatically imply awareness of group dynamics, except for the dynamics of power.

Loyalty to the leader is one side of the reciprocal relation between leaders and those around them. Though authority is not shared, the care of team members is expected. This goes beyond making sure the team is efficient and effective. A relationship of trust between the leader and team members, as well

---

51. Oligastri et al., *Cultura y liderazgo organizacional en 10 países de América Latina*, 29–57.

as among members of an in-group, is fundamental for a team to work. Successful leadership of teams requires the development of meaningful interpersonal ties. This takes time, and it does not automatically imply vulnerability on the part of the leader.

In this cultural context, the perceived benefit of belonging to the team goes beyond the achievement of goals. Personal relationships are more important than the task. When relationships are healthy, individuals are often willing to sacrifice personal time and rest to do their work. This works as long as team coworkers and leaders support it.

In Latin America, team members view the team as a context in which to compete with one another and shine. The focus tends to be on the individual role each member has in the group, but with support from team members. They band together to compete with those outside the team, who can easily be seen as adversaries.

This can produce a work environment where teams from different departments view each other as competitors defending their projects, precluding a unified approach to the overarching institutional mission and goals. The priority is not the common good, but the good of the in-group. This is an expression of individualism seldom overlooked.

A downside of the importance of loyalty is that leader and group avoid conflict to maintain group harmony. Members will aim for consensus, even if it is superficial and artificially attained, ignoring or eliminating dissenters. In Christian organizations, it is common to speak of unanimity in decisions, when in fact this means silencing dissenting voices. There tends to be little initiative to resolve disagreements and conflict.

The high value placed on loyalty to the leader, and the tendency to avoid uncertainty, discourages diversity. The tendency, especially in conservative circles, is to face differences by appealing to the authority of normativity. We do this rather than discuss the underlying sources of disagreements. Collaborative work to resolve differences – even by agreeing to differ – tends to be superseded by the search to eliminate conflict. We miss the richness that diverse opinions can bring to the conversation. Under pressure, differences will surface again.

In the strong-leader model, loyalty to an indispensable member takes priority over long-term agendas. This affects the potential of teams as a context to nurture successors for leadership positions. The lack of successors for top leadership positions is one of the main concerns of all types of organizations in Latin America.

This concern is not being addressed through the educational system, a key element in reproducing and reshaping cultural patterns. People are not being educated to be good team members. The results of the PISA Study 2015, sponsored by the Organization for Economic Co-operation and Development (OECD),[52] show that among fifteen-year-old secondary school students of fifty-one countries, Latin Americans rank low in their competency to work in collaboration with others, effectively pooling their knowledge, skills, and efforts in order to solve a problem. These results pose a great challenge for educational and other types of organizations involved in shaping the next generations of leaders for our societies.

Lessons from a Latino World

What do we hear when we listen to Elizabeth? What is gained by looking at Latino teamwork? There are positives and negatives.

In contrast to leaders in other cultures, a Latino leader does not shy away from exercising team leadership. There is no confusion as to who leads and makes the decisions. This can be good. A high distance culture, however, discourages transparency, closeness and trust, and this is not so good.

A collective culture helps shape an agenda that serves the people as a whole. This is much healthier than agendas that promote one's individual cause. Latino leaders tend to be paternalistic, viewing their leadership responsibility as one of care and protection. They might even view themselves as indispensable. But such "indispensability" can also go to seed. A leader might come to assume that a team exists to carry out his or her will. When this is unchecked, a team member's worth might be measured by loyalty and conformity to the leader's cause.

Those of us in North America might be impressed with our willingness to allow for disagreement and to mine for conflict. Who wants a compliant team? But this can also go too far. There is something to be gained from a more collective culture that works to honor one another and defer for the sake of unity.

I led a church where a significant core were Hispanic. For the most part, they were gracious, respectful and warm. Relationships were everything. I noticed, however, that few stepped up to become part of the leadership. I wonder if part of the reason was an assumption, made on their part, that their voices didn't really matter.

Leaders in my culture need to be asking, "How do we change this?"

---

52. OECD, *PISA 2015 Results*.

We tend to bring teams together to promote and facilitate change. One thing we learn from Latino culture is to respect voices that avoid uncertainty. While challenging people to step out into an unpredictable future can be good, it is also necessary to build teams committed to maintaining stability and creating a degree of certainty.

The Voice We Must Hear

In the grand narrative of Scripture, there appear to be numerous examples of heroic, standalone leaders – Abraham, Moses, Joshua, Gideon, numerous kings, and most prophets, as well as Paul, to name a few. Teams do not appear to have been a necessary part of their leadership. Are teams really necessary to effective leadership? Does God have anything to say?

God Never Works Outside of Teams

We should think about this – especially those of us prone to go it alone: from the very beginning, God has carried out the full extent of his will as a team. From Genesis to Revelation, everything God does is a team effort. As Van Gelder and Zscheile put it, "At the heart of our faith is a divine leadership community: the Trinity."[53] Creation is a team effort. Recounting the establishment of the heavens and the setting of the sea's boundaries, wisdom declares, "Then I was constantly at his side" (Prov 8:30). Wisdom personified is God's artisan, working alongside a committee of three. God stepped into creation and declared, "Let *us* make mankind in *our* image, in *our* likeness," (Gen 1:26). It's team all the way.

The redemptive mission of Jesus was a collective endeavor of Father, Son and Spirit (see Matt 3:16–17; 1 Pet 1:2). The Spirit empowered the Son, who came to glorify the Father. From eternity past, they have operated in partnership, always cooperating with one another. Writing on the Trinity, Tozer noted, "They work always together, and never one smallest act is done by one without the instant acquiescence of the other two."[54] Absent is any expression of rugged individualism on God's part.

It is not surprising, then, that God declared of man, "It is not good for the man to be alone" (Gen 2:18). No man is made to be an island. We were framed for society, not solitude. God made human beings to work as a team. He did not create us to work independent of one another. "Solo leaders" is an oxymoron.

---

53. Van Gelder and Zscheile, *Missional Church in Perspective*, 157.
54. Tozer, *Knowledge of the Holy*, 30.

Look beneath the heroic surface and it is clear that many, if not all, of the heroic leaders surrounded themselves with teams. God commissioned Moses and immediately commanded him to assemble the elders and carry out the will of God together (Exod 3:16–18). When Moses attempted to go it alone, he was rebuked by his father-in-law with words that serve to warn every leader: "The work is too heavy for you; you cannot handle it alone" (18:18). When Saul was called to be Israel's leader, God touched the hearts of brave men who went with him (1 Sam 10:26). The sheer strength of David's leadership compelled men, mighty men, to rally around him and carry out divine purposes together (22:1). So important are the members of a team that Scripture records their names as a memorial (2 Sam 23:15–39).

Nowhere are standalone leaders part of God's ways. There is no evidence that any leader is indispensable. Esther learned this. Elijah was rebuked for thinking he was a one-man show. Mutual interdependence is the norm; honoring the contribution of everyone is the standard.

Writing to emerging leaders, the sage speaks to the folly of going it alone: "An unfriendly person pursues selfish ends and against all sound judgment starts quarrels" (Prov 18:1). It is selfish and mindless to lead without a team. It also goes against who we are in our very being. Behavioral psychologists tell us this: "Rugged individualism, proud independence, chosen isolation violate the nature of our existence – as much as trying to breathe under water."[55]

Other wisdom passages affirm the necessity of working together. Using the metaphor of a rope, Qohelet makes the point that we are much stronger when there are multiple strands (Eccl 4:9–12). Teamwork requires work. Teams disrupt our independence and our convenience. Teams can, however, help us get through setbacks. They enable us to face certain adversaries, or lift us out of the mud. Teams can have our backs.

Nehemiah's success, in large part, is attributed to his initial step of assembling a team (Neh 2:12–18). Though Jesus is Lord and needs no one, he begins his ministry by building a team (Matt 10:2; John 1:35–51). In his public years of ministry, Jesus invests most of his time in his team. They live and work together, and he teaches them to depend upon one another. He sends them out in teams to preach the gospel (Luke 10:1). Jesus likens us to interdependent branches that are connected to the vine (John 15:1–8). There are no standalone shoots.

Like Jesus, Paul multiplies his leadership by building and empowering teams (see Acts 13:2; 16:1; 17:1; 18:1–5). Romans 16:3–16 underscores how

---

55. Crabb, *Connecting*.

connected Paul was, building networks wherever he went. Six of his letters were sent as a team (see 1 Thess 1:1). His concluding words in most of his letters underscore that his work was a collective effort (Eph 6:21; Phil 4:21; Col 4:7–15).

Paul called the church to establish teams in order to do ministry (see 1 Tim 3:1–13; Titus 1:5–7). Elders, not solo pastors, are the New Testament model. From heaven, God sent the church multiple leaders to work as a team (Eph 4:10–11). Each one is gifted differently, but all are driven by the same mission: to work as a team to equip the saints.

God gave the church apostles, those out on the point, leading the church into diverse cultures, going where old maps no longer work. He also sent prophets, those who discern God's mind and will and therefore speak for God. He mobilized evangelists, who are the recruiters of the cause, the infectious communicators of the gospel. He created shepherds, who care for and develop the people of God, leading, nurturing, protecting and making disciples. And he gave the church teachers, who clarify the Word of God so that people gain wisdom, the theologians who help people explore the mind and heart of God.

This is God's design, but most churches are inclined to call only one of the five: the pastor. Writers like Australian Michael Frost and American Alan Hirsch have sought to correct this approach.[56] They see a current system weighted in favor of teaching and pastoral care, directly marginalizing the apostolic, prophetic and evangelistic ministries. Churches are led without the full complement of team leaders. Hence, the emphasis of ministry has shifted from missional communities, releasing their missional imagination, to ministry focused on maintenance, caring for and teaching the congregation.

There is some debate over whether all five of these offices are still operative.[57] It's not the purpose of this book to defend one position or the other. But what should not be overlooked in the debate is that leadership of the church is not a one-man effort. It involves a team, and without the whole team the church will have significant deficiencies, be it in extending its mission or growing in depth. Five gifted leaders can bring a helpful synergy and the necessary checks and balances. The key to the formation of missional communities is a leadership of diverse gifts.

The overarching message of the Bible is: loners need not apply to be leaders. It will require teams to accomplish greatness.

---

56. See Hirsch, *Forgotten Ways*; and Frost and Hirsch, *Shaping of Things to Come.*
57. Johnson, "Is Apostolic Leadership the Key to the Missional Church?"

This is also the testimony of history. Consider this story. In the 1700s, John Wesley, a pastor, determined to build teams in his church. He called them Band Societies, and he believed this could turn the spiritual tide in England. These teams were mutually dependent, charting the direction of an enterprise together, and holding one another accountable.

Every time these teams gathered, they asked the hard but necessary questions:

- What is the state of your soul?
- Where have you moved away from God's will?
- What are the spiritual gains and losses you experienced this week?
- What known sins have you committed since our last gathering?
- What temptations are you experiencing?

What is astonishing is that their teamwork changed the world. Note these words from Wesleyan scholar Thomas Oden: "Out of these small bands came extraordinary energies for the behavioral change that affected the secular history of British and American culture, ultimately leading to the great revivals of the 18th and 19th centuries."[58]

In the counsel of God, teams matter!

Theology Underscores the Necessity of Building the Right Team

Just as almost every leadership book affirms that great teams are composed of great members and great leaders, so Scripture affirms the same. Choosing the right team determines our course (Prov 13:20).

God has built within us the potential to influence, to "overstate our wills," and to pass on to others our likeness. All the more reason to select our teams with care. Form the right group, and our leadership is sharpened (Prov 27:17). Surround ourselves with the wise, and they will literally "file the edges of our face." It's a way of saying they will sharpen our perceptions. Operating on our own, apart from a strong team, we become dull.

Proverbs has much to say about relationships, underlying the importance of building with the right material. Getting the wrong people on the team is as unpleasant as smoke to the eyes (Prov 10:26). You might as well cut off your feet (26:6). On the other hand, extraordinary teammates are as refreshing as flakes of snow on a day of scorching heat (25:13).

Shrewd leaders build excellence with excellence. Wise teams look for great leaders. But theology gives this caution: many of God's selections for his teams

---

58. Oden, *John Wesley's Teachings.*

are not always impressive, at least by the world's standards. Moses was not an imposing communicator. The Twelve, by most earthly measures, were a motley group full of flaws and weaknesses. Up to the end, some in their group doubted their leader. Peter denied Jesus. Judas disowned and betrayed the Son of God. And then there was Paul, the eminent church leader who, on the surface, was not too impressive (at least to the Corinthians).

So what do we look for? The better question is: What does God look for? Here's where theology transcends our human assumptions:

- Look for those who are courageous – yet fear God.
- Look for those who embrace life – the kind of life the gospel leads to.
- Look for those who are full of faith – in God, above themselves.
- Look for those who are wise – who demonstrate the kind of discernment, prudence, shrewdness, knowledge, and discretion that comes from God.
- Look for excellence – the excellence that meets God's definition.
- Look for those who are future-oriented – who see beyond and into eternity.
- Look for those who are loyal – but whose loyalty is always and ultimately to God and his will.
- Look for those who have fire in their eyes – but fire fueled by the Spirit.
- Look for those who are confident – but whose confidence is in God and not in themselves.
- Look for those who are tenacious – because they rely on power that passes all understanding.

In the end, we are called to honor the team God has given us to lead – to keep them, treasure them, help them become all that God intended and pray for them to be effective in the world.[59] Build the right team.

Theology Redefines the Reason for Teams

There are multiple kinds of teams and endless reasons for teams, but ultimately every team must have this as its reason for existence: to fulfill the will of God. This is a team's compelling purpose. The right leader keeps this before the team.

---

59. Lingenfelter, *Leading Cross-Culturally*, 156.

This objective explains the nature of teams. This is why Ruth Haley Barton prefers to call teams "discerning communities."[60] Teams come together to carry out their agendas, but they begin with discerning God's. This includes:

- preparing our souls;
- finding ways to be open to God's presence together;
- listening to God together – being attentive to his Word;
- creating space for the Spirit – allowing for times of silence;
- affirming our guiding values and living them out;
- putting the needs of others above our own;
- seeking to be indifferent to anything but the will of God.

Acts 15 serves as one biblical example. A team was formed. The team gathered to reflect upon the mind of God. They applied what they learned to the issue at hand. They listened to one another and related it all to what God had revealed. They made decisions that were world-changing.

Bringing the Voices Together

Anyone who is reading this and is working alone is on a perilous course. From every side, the message is deafening: to make your endeavor count, you need to find the right team to carry it out. Be the leader your team needs. Be the cord of multiple strands. Be the missional and visionary leader that changes the world. What does this look like?

---

60. See Barton, *Pursuing God's Will Together.*

7

Know Why and Where

"Simsups" is short for simulation supervisors. They are part of the training crew. Their job is to make the lives of American astronauts in training miserable. While these spacemen are preparing to fly to outer space, the simsups are devising creative ways to blow things up. A routine rehearsal runs for a while. Suddenly, without warning, these supervisors will shut down an engine when the rocket is only a thousand feet off the launchpad. These oppressors will kill the communications system five minutes after the crew has left earth's orbit. The simsups are merciless. They stay up at night devising fake disasters. They set the command module into a high-speed spin; they crash the spacecraft's environmental system.

But the astronauts do not whine, scream or give up. They are tenacious. They have their minds on something bigger.

In the book *Apollo 8*, Jeffrey Kluger tells their story. Dominating the narrative is Frank Borman. He leads this tenacious crew. Under his disciplined command, they enter the flight simulator and figure out how to work through every scenario. Day after day, month after month, they plan deeply, exhaustively and reflexively. Borman keeps their focus on what matters – the mission. They are learning to fly to the moon. And no one has ever done this before. This is their purpose. It is their goal.

Borman knows what every true leader understands: that the key to leadership is keeping everyone fixed on the mission and compelled by the dream.[1] Leadership studies underscore this.

---

1. Kluger, *Apollo 8*, loc. 2302.

The Voices We Hear

Every leader has to know the why and where of the community he or she leads. What is the mission? What is the vision?

If you are a leader, these define you. They constrain you. They must! Without ownership of these, your leadership will drift. But before we go too far, we need first to clarify what we mean by a mission and a vision. Many use the terms interchangeably, but they are not the same.

On Being Missional

The mission of a group is the broad philosophic statement that declares resolve: this is why we exist! It acts as the unifying principle that drives everything we do. Nothing precedes the mission. A clear statement determines the compass heading.

Missional lives approach life as an assignment. As Leonard Sweet notes, "A mission is what buys us life space. To be born is to be chosen – chosen for a mission. If you're alive, your mission on earth is unfinished."[2] This is especially true of leaders.

For a mission to have any impact, it must follow certain rules. Here are six:

Rule 1: An Organizational Mission Statement Must Begin with a Personal One

Before leaders lead anyone or anything, they must have a clear sense of their own purpose. How can leaders lead people toward a purpose they have not first embraced? A personal mission stabilizes. It enables leaders to overcome.

Friedrich Nietzsche once noted, "He whose life has a why can bear almost any how."[3] One way to discern your life purpose is to understand the meaning of key events in your life.[4]

Can you identify these events? Do you have a personal statement of purpose? Can you articulate it? Does it drive your life?

Rule 2: The Mission Must Be Embraced by All the Leaders

The mission is an organization's imperative and a leader's calling.[5] It gets to the philosophical purpose of why we are here. Why have we come into existence?

---

2. Sweet, *Summoned to Lead*, 105.
3. Quoted in Peterson, *12 Rules for Life*, loc. 1592.
4. George, *Discover Your True North*, 204.
5. Useem, *Leadership Moment*, 273.

It might also answer the question, "If we could be excellent at one thing, what would it be?"

The leadership team must be together when it comes to the answers. Has your team united itself around the mission? Do they see themselves as members on a pursuit? Does everything they do flow out of the purpose? Where is the evidence?

Like concentric layers, the mission must expand out to the whole. Leaders and followers must be about a cause, a commitment that everyone is passionate about – and learning to be great at.[6] It should connect to the resources and tactics that are available.

Gaining alignment is one of the greatest challenges leaders face, but face it they must. Why? Bill George answers, "The most empowering condition of all is when the entire organization aligns with its mission, and people's passions and purpose synchronize with each other."[7]

Rule 3: The Mission Must Be Accessible

Is there awareness of the mission? Is the organization's "reason for being" comprehensible? Those who follow need to know why they have come together. Otherwise, a sense of collective commitment will be lost. People will operate in a reactive, shortsighted way.[8]

Leaders are the catalyst for such efforts. They make sure people can answer questions like "Who are we?" "Why are we here?" "What is the point of our existence?" "What makes us unique?" "What will make us great?" "What is our collective purpose?"[9] Missional leaders are committed to clarity.

The mission cannot be a matter of guesswork. No one should be confused when it comes to answering the "why" question. A mission statement should be like a guiding star that shines brightly in the sky. Without clarity and well-channeled efforts, energy is diffused and power is dissipated.[10] So wording needs to be clear (not vague), as well as current (not archaic). Lencioni warns that the statement cannot be a "convoluted, jargony, and all-encompassing declaration of intent."[11] Leaders must work with a team to get to the center of things and bring precision.

---

6. Collins, *Good to Great and the Social Sectors*, 19.

7. George, 228.

8. Lencioni, *Advantage*, 83.

9. Harari, *Leadership Secrets of Colin Powell*, 124.

10. Myra and Shelley, *Leadership Secrets of Billy Graham*, 65.

11. Lencioni, *Advantage*, 75.

Conciseness helps bring clarity. Mission statements that require numerous paragraphs might impress some, but more often they depress people. No one will remember them. One's purpose statement should be succinct, such that people will be able to remember and articulate it.

The founder of Disneyland, Walt Disney, had a very simple mission statement: "Our mission is to make people happy." Talk about clearness! It's hard to forget it. Here is Nike's: "Our mission is to bring innovation and inspiration to every athlete in the world." Simple, but not to be confused with simplistic. And then there is Walmart's: "To give ordinary folk the chance to buy the same thing as rich people." Also memorable and to the point.

Rule 4: The Mission Needs to Inspire

A mission should emerge out of an imaginative context, one filled with large thinking. A group's purpose should rouse, captivate, and generate a powerful internal consensus.[12] Why settle for small, unimaginative and unoriginal statements?

After exploring the forces that fostered incredible collaboration, Warren Bennis made this observation: "people in Great Groups are different from those who spend countless hours in thrall to video games or other trivial pursuits. Their clear, collective purpose makes everything they do seem meaningful and valuable."[13] This is what a mission should do.

Roberto Goizueta, former CEO of Coca-Cola, had a simple but audacious mission: "A Coke within arm's reach of everyone on the planet." Talk about a purpose! Sure, it is idealistic, but an organization's core purpose should be expansive. Why should it not be an act of faith?

Still, Goizueta's mission seems rather small. The mission goes no further than seeking to satisfy appetites.

PepsiCo (I am giving equal time here) has its own mission: "To provide consumers around the world with delicious, affordable, convenient and complementary foods and beverages from wholesome breakfasts to healthy and fun daytime snacks and beverages to evening treats." It's nice, but not world-changing. Still, does a mission statement have to be?

Consider Japan General Electric. Its founder could have absorbed himself in a purpose no higher than providing energy to customers. Konosuke Matsushita thought further out. On 5 May 1932, he gathered his executives, reminded them of their collective achievements, and then unveiled this bold

---

12. Harari, *Leadership Secrets of Colin Powell*, 109.

13. Bennis and Biederman, *Organizing Genius*, 204.

proposition: "The mission of a manufacturer should be to overcome poverty, to relieve society as a whole from misery, and bring it wealth."[14] He determined to pursue a course that went beyond consumer needs, market share, or corporate profits; he wanted to change the well-being of a nation. It might take two, maybe three, centuries, but this became his reason to be.

Few mission statements are as grand and aspirational as Matsushita's. Many do not arouse. All too many are neither lofty enough nor descriptive enough to be helpful.[15] If this is what you have inherited, the best counsel is to rip it off the wall. Go back to the drawing board and let your imagination soar. Get your team off campus and into the solitude where they can reflect. Idealism is not off-limits. If the mission does not resonate deeply, you might be consigning your members to dull and monotonous routine.[16]

Rule 5: The Mission Needs to Be Realistic

While imaginative, the mission should be achievable. It should align with what the institution is actually doing. Otherwise, its words are empty. If it is out of reach, no one will take the mission seriously. It will only serve to create frustration, guilt and defeat. The mission has to be doable, even if it demands everything within one's soul.

In its early years, Merck Pharmaceutical developed this statement: "We are in the business of preserving and improving human life." It inspired a Roy Vagelos to step out and tackle river blindness in regions of Africa. This would stretch everyone from shareholders to logistical teams, but Vagelos knew they could do it. His team evaluated the risks and costs of developing and transporting Mectizan. It would require faith and courage, and cut into the bottom line, but it wasn't an option. The mission provoked them to move beyond their imagination, and they lived it because the words were achievable.

Rule 6: Leaders Must Lead through the Mission

Our purpose must be inseparable from our commitment to carrying it out.[17] It needs to define us. We should wear the mission like we wear our clothes: it's part of us, and people see it. There should be no mistaking who we are and what we have committed our lives to pursuing.

---

14. Kotter, *Matsushita Leadership*, 111.

15. Lencioni, *Advantage*, 82.

16. Rao, "Tomorrow's Leader," 175.

17. Harari, *Leadership Secrets of Colin Powell*, 109.

If the mission of your hotel is to make guests feel at home, then guests should walk into their rooms and find commonalities with home (a nice bed, Internet access, and availability of some hot tea). They should find that this is what drives you. If the purpose is to make people happy, then everyone – from the groundskeeper to those working graveyard, to the CEO – needs to be happy. If the mission is to win the world to Jesus, then a daily commitment to be available to the King of kings is essential. Achieving an organization's imperative is the leader's principal task.[18]

Still, in the day-to-day, the mission can get lost. Leaders can get bogged down in committee reports, budget deficits, personnel problems and corporate crises.

This can't happen!

Leaders need to continually call the organization to its purpose, using every opportunity to explain, clarify and teach it. Otherwise, it will become irrelevant. Worse, the organization will get off the rails and settle for mere survival.

The mission has to be too visible to hide, too obvious to miss and too forceful to become secondary. The purpose that unites us should be on the letterhead, on the signs, on the walls, on the napkins and, most of all, on the hearts. Effective leaders are those who make the mission so visible it feels redundant. They make sure each generation, each ethnicity and every team owns it. The mission is more than the originating impulse: it is the organizing principle.

On Being Visionary

As critical as the mission is, it is not enough. It is essential to answer the "why" question. That is the starting point. But missional organizations need to also be farsighted. They need to know how to answer the "where" question. Where are we going? The answer sets the direction. It generates the energy. It creates what everyone longs for: hope.

The Nature of a Vision
While the mission statement is a broad, generic definition of the key objectives, the vision statement is a clarification of the specific direction. It is more focused, detailed, customized and unique.[19] To be credible, the vision must flow out of

---

18. Useem, *Leadership Moment*, 273.
19. Barna, *Turning Vision into Action*, 39.

the mission. The mission is largely static, while the vision is more fluid. Groups need to review their dreams every two to three years.

A vision involves both eyes and ears. Some speak of vision as an "inner eye," a clear mental picture of what could be fueled by the conviction that it should be.[20] Others like Leonard Sweet refer to vision as something more audible, a summons that those with ears wide open hear.[21] Leaders should deploy both senses in discerning the future.

A vision worth pursuing contains similar elements to the mission. Bert Nanus, in his *Visionary Leadership*, lists the following:

- It is appropriate to the organization.
- It sets the standards of excellence.
- It clarifies the purpose and direction.
- It inspires enthusiasm and encourages commitment.
- It is understood.
- It reflects the uniqueness of the organization.
- It is ambitious.[22]

In sum, think of vision as a mental picture. If credible, it will take us out where we can see beyond the bends and curves of history.

The Necessity of a Vision

How important is vision? Warren Bennis notes that a guiding vision is the first basic ingredient of leadership. The leader has to have a clear idea of what he or she wants to do professionally and personally – and the strength to persist in the face of setbacks, even failures.[23] More than have the idea, a leader needs to communicate it. People need to see where things are going. They want to be part of a movement. A vision makes it easier for individuals to see how they fit. People feel empowered by a vision. Without it, they are less inclined to follow. Without a clear map, leaders and followers are apt to flounder.

A vision, however, is more than a conceptual map. As Northouse notes, the vision is what gives an organization meaning; it clarifies an organization's identity.[24] This is why it is so necessary. It is why leaders must own one. Kouzes

---

20. Stanley, *Visioneering*, 18.

21. Note Sweet's *Summoned to Lead*, in which he argues that the future needs ears more than it needs eyes.

22. Nanus, *Visionary Leadership*, 89.

23. Bennis, *On Becoming a Leader*, 39.

24. Northouse, *Leadership*, 145.

and Posner refer to envisioning as "the defining competence" of leaders.[25] In their research, they discovered that "forward-looking" ranks near the top of the most admired qualities of leaders.

Leaders who own a vision tend to make history. More than make a statement, they leave a mark. The following are some leaders who foresaw the trend lines of the world's future:

- Alexander the Great had a vision of a world united under one flag.
- Henry Ford could see a motor car large enough for a family, small enough for an individual and priced low enough to be affordable, and a day when roadways would be absent of horses.
- Walt Disney assembled his top animators and gave them a vision for a full-length animated cartoon.
- Postwar executives at Sony dreamed of a day when Japanese products would be known for excellence.
- John F. Kennedy had a mental picture of an American walking on the moon by the end of the decade.
- Bill Gates envisioned a personal computer in every home by the year 2000.
- Allen Neuharth saw what most of his contemporaries could not see: a national newspaper.
- Jeff Bezos, founder of Amazon, began with a dream to be the earth's most customer-centric company.

These were transformational leaders who had photographic images of the future which guided them toward a goal; hence they invested their time working out on the frontier where tomorrow was taking shape.[26]

Little wonder Canadian psychologist Jordan Peterson counsels his clients, "Don't underestimate the power of vision and direction. These are irresistible forces, able to transform what might appear to be unconquerable obstacles into traversable pathways and expanding opportunities."[27]

The Rules of a Vision

Like the mission, acquiring a vision has its own imperatives.

---

25. Kouzes and Posner, *Truth about Leadership*, 46.

26. Bennis, *On Becoming a Leader*, 5.

27. Peterson, *12 Rules for Life*, loc. 1592.

Rule 1: Visionary Leaders Must Have Their Own Dreams

It is not enough to live in the present; leaders must have the passion to embrace the future.[28] They have to if they are going to lead. Before leaders can urge others to envision their tomorrows, leaders must envision and articulate their own. They need to have dreams that awaken them in the night – maybe even keep them from sleeping.

Visions are about possibilities and desired futures.[29] Without a personal dream, a leader has little credibility to talk about organizational vision. People want to know the kind of future you see for yourself. Do you have a vision?

Be careful. It may sneak up on you.

You may find yourself opening up to possibilities you would never have considered earlier. Dreamers might be stepping into your life, inspiring you to ask of them, "What makes you tick?" "What explains your pulse?" Conditions might be unsettling your soul. You may find a passion forming, rising and gushing out – all of which is shedding light on your future.

Rule 2: Visionary Leaders Must Own the Task of Envisioning

Envisioning cannot be delegated to anyone but the one ultimately held accountable for it: the leader.[30] To pass the process on to others amounts to giving away one's leadership. Leaders envision what an organization can become. They spread their ideas with the aim of infecting others. Visions are top-down, not bottom-up.

Rule 3: Visionary Leaders Must Engage in Multi-Directional Thinking

The vision process requires that leaders live in three realms: past, present and future. To live in all three, a leader must find solitude, where noise and distractions are kept to a minimum. Out of silence and reflection, the inaudible becomes audible. The invisible begins to become visible. Perceptions expand in multiple ways.

Here in the quiet, it is important to look back. This is required to see ahead. Some refer to this as the Janus Effect. The further you look back into the past, the further you can see forward into the future.[31] The Roman god Janus was the god of doorways and passages. He had two faces, one looking forward

---

28. Marshall, *Understanding Leadership*, 10.
29. Kouzes and Posner, "Seven Lessons for Leading the Voyage to the Future."
30. Welch, *Winning.*
31. Kouzes and Posner, *Leadership Challenge*, 106.

and one looking back. To leaders he conveyed the idea that assessing the past enables one to make a plan for the road ahead.

Have you noticed how the greatest visionaries are often the greatest historians? Churchill could see beyond the range of ordinary perception. His clairvoyance is attributed to the fact he was schooled in history. He could rise above and see the arc of events. The American president Richard Nixon steeped himself in history. It enabled him to look in both directions. Writes David Gergen, "He was convinced that his very capacity to see the road behind enabled him to see where the road was heading. It is a priceless asset for a leader."[32]

Leaders must also look into another dimension: the present. To envision a future, one must have a grasp of present experience. Before one answers the question "Where do I want to go?" one must answer "Where am I?" Erwin McManus, pastor and artist, asks, "If you cannot engage present realities effectively, how can you lead effectively into the future?" In similar language, Dave Fleming writes: "To miss 'what is' frequently leads to a misperception of what could be."[33]

Leaders must have a keen awareness of what is around them. What has been the growth, or decline? How is present morale? What are people longing, hoping for? What is God putting on my heart? Is there a current crisis compelling us to move forward?

Often what we see is disconcerting. This is what has driven us into the quiet. It explains the growing discontent. Andy Stanley, author of *Visioneering*, writes: "Anyone who is emotionally involved, frustrated, brokenhearted, maybe even angry about the way things are in light of the way they believe things could be, is a candidate for a vision. Visions form in the hearts of those who are dissatisfied with the status quo."[34] They grow inside the heart like a fire.

Out of the stillness, looking past and present, a leader can more clearly see into the third realm: the future. One can think big, knowing that failure is not the crime – low aim is.[35] To extend their sight, leaders have to carve out the necessary time to peer into the distance and imagine.[36] What are the significant political, economic, cultural and global trends? What are credible predictions?

---

32. Gergen, *Eyewitness to Power*, 42.

33. Fleming, *Leadership Wisdom from Unlikely Voices*, 74.

34. Stanley, *Visioneering*, 17.

35. Bennis, *On Becoming a Leader*, quoting John Wooden, 194.

36. Kouzes and Posner, *Truth about Leadership*, 50.

Future-oriented leaders pay attention to technologies that will change lives. It is a safe bet that machine learning and robotics will change every line of work, "from producing yogurt to teaching yoga."[37] Leaders listening for tomorrow's trends will look for changing public perceptions, listening to cultural tones and moods, ones that can pivot the direction of history.[38] It's necessary to read unconventional thinkers and ponder their penetrating analyses. Visionaries hang out with high-energy pathfinders who cannot be held down by the present. They travel to see the world, not only for what it is, but also for what it is becoming. They look out at the fringes, where ideas yet to be adopted are forming.

They read statements by historians, like this one from Yuval Noah Harari: "As the pace of change increases, the very meaning of being is likely to mutate and physical and cognitive structures will melt."[39] Then they ponder how one hangs on and maintains some control.

Rule 4: Visionary Leaders Must Expand Envisioning into a Collaborative Experience

Leaders need to be dreamers, but what about followers? Do they simply wait for an enlightened leader to come down from the mountain with an inspired map? In some more hierarchical cultures, they do. A leader's vision is announced and imposed on his or her constituents.

It is not so in other global contexts. In some, it is a group effort from the start. In my culture, there is an expectation that what began as a monologue in the wilderness will expand to a dialogue in the community. It is here that a working vision is introduced, massaged, developed, tested, and expanded. The aim of this partnership is co-creation.[40]

In their chapter "It's Not Just the Leader's Vision," Kouzes and Posner observe that followers want to feel part of the process.[41] They want to dream with their leaders. The vision has to be something they care about as much as, if not more than, the leader.

How does this happen? A leader must take followers through the same long-term thinking. The function of leadership is to engage, not merely activate, followers. Together they commingle needs, aspirations and goals in

---

37. Harari, *21 Lessons*, 19.
38. Schwartz, *Art of the Long View*, 64.
39. Harari, "What the Year 2050 Has in Store for Humankind."
40. Ascough and Cotton, *Passionate Visionary*, 34.
41. Kouzes and Posner, "It's Not Just the Leader's Vision," 208.

a common enterprise, a common vision.[42] This begins with looking together at their history.

It is critical that leader and followers connect with the story that began and now continues. How did the organization begin? Why was it born? Someone had a dream. What were the faith steps taken by the earliest believers? What has been achieved? When did things plateau? Why? Does it matter? What do historic patterns and recurring life themes tell us?

A leader also takes people into the present to see things as they are – to see the good, but also to notice the things that might be missing. A leader has to know not only what wrecks him or her, but also what wrecks them. What is driving their discontent? Too many changes? Not enough changes? A harking back to the past? An impatience for the future? Are people as restless as the leader? Can they smell the stale air?

It may be that people are used to their musty trappings. They might even prefer them. The fresh air of the future might be discomforting to the senses. They may be satisfied with things as they are. Their response to the visionary process might be one of resistance. Some will stand and declare, "If it ain't broke, don't fix it."

Visionary leaders have to be bold and courageous. They must convince people that, while it may not be broken now, it will be in the future. They have to help people see that what got them here will not get them there. They have to hack away the overgrowth, untie the shades and open the doors to let people feel a crisp breeze. They must warn that, whether they realize it or not, entropy hovers over the organization, waiting for the slightest slackening of vigilance.[43]

Think of leaders as great blues players. For followers to see the present for what it really is, leaders must create a feeling of dissonance and discomfort. If we remain in an unchanged present, we will end up living in a dying past. More, they must create a sense of urgency; they must help people see the crisis that will come if things do not change. They must help them see that change is the only certainty.

This will not be easy. Crises are not self-evident to most. Leaders must help people see present realities. Without this, notes Covey, there is rarely enough motivation or humility to change.[44] And without change, there is nothing left for the system to do except to eventually wear down. Life goes on, but it is downhill.

---

42. Burns, *Leadership*, 461.

43. De Pree, *Leadership Jazz*, 34.

44. Covey, "Three Roles of the Leader," 149.

At some point, followers have to recognize that their institution was birthed in vision and risk. The past tells them to press on. A deeper realization of the present tells them there must be change. It is here that leader and followers engage in the final part of long-term thinking: the future.

Having shared his or her dreams, a leader invites people to share their dreams together. The leader invites them to finish the sentence: "What if we . . ." Together they wrestle with critical questions, such as:

- Where will new developments in science and technology, ecology and genetics take us?
- What will social media look like – and how is it shaping us?
- What is happening out on the fringe, the outer edge of ideas?
- How will the church of tomorrow reach a growing secular age?
- What cultural trends will shape tomorrow's world?

Successful leaders realize they and their people have to think ahead, with a willingness to let go. They have to do this together! Sometimes we fall in love with the past, and it inhibits us from stepping into the future.

Kodak was once the visionary leader of picture taking. It even created the digital camera. But it was so in love with film it refused to adopt the technological advances. Leaders have to convince a team that an organization will not thrive if there is no desire to step into the future, no matter the costs. They might have to break from something that they are attached to (or, more realistically, that has attached itself to them).

The reality is that few are prepared to die for the leader's sense of purpose and the leader's vision for the future. But they will die for something they own.

Rule 5: Visionary Leaders Must Cast a Vision That Is Both Imaginative and Realistic

There must be enough idealism to excite the heart but enough realism to convince others the vision is attainable. Visions that are credible look out only so far. Too far, and people will have no sense of how to get there. Credible visions also pay attention to the context. A vision divorced from the context of the times can produce very erratic and unpredictable results.[45]

---

45. Mayo, "Importance of Vision."

Summarizing What We Hear

A leader who has any hope of inspiring direction has to be able to stand up and ask, "Why are we here, and where are we going?" More than ask, leaders have to be the spark that moves people to engage in the answers.

In every organization I have led, I have begun with these two questions. Without answers to these fundamental questions, I am lost. I drift. Worse, the people I lead stray into meaningless activity. Having a purpose and a direction generates movement. People get on the same page. Hopefully, the world changes.

The Voices We Need to Hear

The voices we have just surveyed might suggest that missional and visionary thinking are Western concepts of leadership. But this reflects a certain deafness. Parts of the Majority World are thinking further out than us.[46] This is certainly true in the East.

In various regions of Asia, envisioning is a necessary part of culture. Much of this has to do with its long-term orientation. Sony Corporation is known for developing hundred-year strategic plans, but even these are short term when compared to the plans of other corporations, like Japan Electric, which, as we have seen, thinks in multiple lifetimes.

The Voice of Patrick Fung, General Director, OMF

I was privileged to have a recent conversation with this Asian leader. Patrick Fung has influenced lives through his medical practice, his leadership of a significant international ministry and his writings. One is immediately impressed with his missional heart and visionary spirit.

Given your experience as both a medical doctor and general director of OMF, with its focus on Asia, how would you contrast Asian leadership with Western leadership?
What immediately comes to mind is that those in the West give greater weight to goals and performance, while those in the East focus on relationships. This is not to suggest that Asians are not goal-oriented. We are very interested in setting objectives and aiming for execution. But it is not so necessary that these are communicated with the same clarity. Our goals are more internalized, whereas

---

46. Kouzes and Posner, *Truth about Leadership*, 47.

the emphasis in the West tends to be on goals that are clearly articulated and precise. Asians may not put their goals into words, nor is it essential that they are completely thought out at the beginning. We set goals and fine-tune them as we go along.

As a result, Westerners tend to perceive Asians as less missional, visionary or goal-oriented. But this is to misunderstand. Asians are better internalizing their goals rather than articulating their goals. Thus, they may pursue their goals with clarity in their minds but not necessarily in their words. They are processing, and drawing in others. It is a collective approach. If there is ambiguity – and there is – this is OK.

In your culture, how typical is it for a leader and an organization to be missional?

Asians appreciate missional and visionary leadership. There is, however, greater fluidity. We are OK with modifying these statements as we go along. Those in the West tend to develop these statements, write them down, seek agreement and then move forward. Asians are OK if things change. Again, flexibility is fine – even preferred.

When you think of visionary leadership, what does that look like?

I occasionally come across a visionary person. As in your culture, one sees a person who can paint a picture of the future. Visionaries are perceived as risk takers, hence leaders with courage. But even here, the vision is not the work of a single leader but is a collective work.

Hierarchical leadership tends to define Asian culture. Do you see this changing?

Perhaps, but often we see hierarchical leadership as something very positive. Hierarchical leaders are not necessarily autocrats and dictators. Those with godly character can accomplish great good. For example, most of the leaders in Scripture, particularly those in the Old Testament, were hierarchical.

What's essential is accountability. Those at the top who are not answerable for their decisions, who stop listening, tend to become autocratic over time.

In the traditional African culture, which is often tribal and hierarchical, the leader will get others around a campfire and listen, but the leader will always be the one to make the final decision. In Asian culture, which is deeply influenced by Confucian thought, the leader too must listen. He will bring the best and take note, and then make the the ultimate decision. Often the judgment is respected by the followers. What I observe is that a more hierarchical leadership functions well where there is much dialogue and relational building.

A more representative system, like democracy, has its advantages – particularly in a broken world. But democracies have their own abuses of power. Whatever the system, there need to be checks and balances.

Regarding accountability, those from the West tend to expect everything to be written in detail. Asians give more time to listening and talking. Whatever is written tends to be briefer.

What does an emerging Asian culture want most in a leader?

Above everything else, integrity. Passion and vision are critical, but Asians want a leader they can trust. This goes both ways. Younger leaders need senior leaders who will invest in them, prepare them, and trust them for future leadership. Younger leaders need leaders who have the kind of self-confidence that is not threatened, leaders who are not obsessed with protecting their power, but who have enough trust in younger leaders to gradually share it.

Looking from the other side, particularly as a medical doctor, what could the church learn from secular leadership?

Setting measurable goals and establishing key performance indicators are critical. The secular world tends to be better at this. Too many ministries perform at a sub-standard level because they do not hold one another accountable for carrying out the mission. This keeps them from being effective missional and visionary leaders. But it is not mere performance; there needs to be accountability for how one is developing character.

Lessons from an Asian World

Interviewing Patrick, it became clear that missional and visionary leadership will look different in Asian culture. Mission and vision statements may be more internalized and more fluid. A collective culture will require more dialogue, though a hierarchical leader will make the final call when it comes to purpose and direction.

Does hierarchical leadership work in our contemporary global context? Do hierarchical leaders tend to lead with a purpose and a clear vision? Not if they become autocratic. In a recent article, "The Myth of the Modernizing Dictator," historian Robert Kagan notes that leaders who are domineering are not reformers.[47] History underscores that, in the main, authoritarian governments, no matter the culture, cannot be trusted to set a course and lead their people into a great future. Overbearing leaders are not leaders who

---

47. Kagan, "Myth of the Modernizing Dictator." See also his book *Jungle Grows Back*.

make the right economic decisions or prepare society for an eventual transition to one in which more people have a voice. Authoritarian leaders do not create independent political institutions and representative government. They do not permit a vibrant civil society, because this will threaten their hold on power. Less energy is given to setting a course and holding out a dream. More energy is expended in holding on to their rule.

In contrast, those leaders who are hierarchical but not oppressive and high-handed can lead people into a future where the community flourishes.

The Voice We Must Hear

The voice of God does more than affirm what has been heard. It expands our imagination and takes us beyond our missional objectives and visionary dreams.

Some might choose to silence God's voice, moving him "upstairs" so that they can live without divine intervention or interference.[48] But God is here, answering both the ultimate "why" and the "where" questions. What is he saying?

Missional Leadership Is at the Heart of God's Leadership

Missional leadership does not originate with us. As we have often said, it would be foolish to begin and end with ourselves.

Consider this: God is the essence of mission. Mission is behind everything he does. Christopher J. H. Wright, who has written about this in depth, states: "The whole Bible itself is a missional phenomenon."[49] God has his mission statement nailed on a wall, and it supersedes every other purpose. The mission of God's kingdom is a mission of reconciliation and redemption of humankind. It is a mission to restore human flourishing and bring God glory. This stretches from creation to cosmic transformation, to the arrival of a new heaven and new earth. The whole of the Trinity is involved.

God's mission is more than a work of reestablishing a broken world; it is bringing creation to another level. It is bringing a purpose determined in eternity past to completion. There is no serpent in the next garden. There is no possibility of sin in God's future. He will bring the universe to the fullness of his purposes. We will enjoy his blessings for eternity and live for the glory of God (Ps 19:1; Rom 5:10; John 16:7; 1 Cor 10:31).

---

48. Wright, *Simply Good News*, 110.
49. Wright, *Mission of God*, 22.

Nearly every chapter of Scripture comes back to this. "The God who walks the paths of history through the pages of the Bible pins a mission statement to every signpost on the way."[50] It's impossible to exaggerate the point. Scripture is the grand universal narrative of the mission of God. It answers the ultimate "why."

Missional Leadership Must Be at the Heart of Our Leadership

Leaders who reflect the character of God are missional. More, they realize that whatever their personal or corporate mission statements declare, they are secondary to God's. There is no greater mission than his. It is the center of all existence, it is disturbingly subversive, and it uncomfortably relativizes one's own place and mission in the grand scheme of things.[51] Whatever our plans, in the end they must come back to this: they must ultimately further his plans. When they do, we realize he has liberated us from our small plans.

The world is filled with great missional stories. Here is a corporate story. Business giant Apple wants the world to know that its mission is to bring the best personal computing experience to students, educators, creative professionals, and consumers around the world through its innovative hardware, software, and Internet offerings. And it has been wildly successful. As I write, its market value is over $1 trillion. No other American company has accomplished this feat. Its commitment to its mission is inspiring. Announcing a new product makes headline news.

Shift to a personal story. In Grytvikin, South Georgia, a simple granite column marks the grave of polar explorer Sir Ernest Henry Shackleton. He is buried in a whalers' cemetery. On the column is inscribed a quotation from one of his favorite poets, Robert Browning: "I hold . . . that a man should strive to the uttermost for his life's set prize."

It's moving. It's missional. Crossing the Antarctic and traversing the South Pole was Shackleton's set prize. He was willing to lose his life for it, and he did. Shackleton died en route to Antarctica (his fourth trip to the polar region).

I love the missional spirit. But if the purpose of one's existence settles for one's set prize, things get tinny and thin. In the greater scheme of things, these are purposes that will pass. A missional God challenges us to seek his mission for our lives – which might include making iPads or crossing a barren continent – but our stories must ultimately fold into his greater, everlasting

---

50. Wright, *Mission of God*, 23.
51. Wright, *Mission of God*, 533.

mission. All of us must ask, "How does my narrative fit within this grand narrative?" This is what matters.

There's a better story. William Wilberforce had his own plans, but the purpose of God eventually dominated his life. On 28 October 1787 he wrote on a blank page of his diary, "God Almighty has placed before me two great objects, the suppression of the slave trade and the reformation of manners."[52] This would be his mission. It was where he would invest his best leadership. He would move with deliberate speed, no matter the cost, to convince the English Parliament to embrace the same mission and abolish this heinous practice. It would cost him both his health and his friendships, but twenty-six years later, and days before Wilberforce's death, slavery was abolished in England and throughout its colonies. Wilberforce listened for the divine "why."

Our theology points us to lives like the apostle Paul. He was all about going where others had not gone, but it was not for *his* life's set prize. It was about the prize promised by God's heavenly call in Christ Jesus (Phil 3:12–14). He pressed on to lay hold of that for which Christ had laid hold of him. This was his mission: to fit within God's intentions.

Every leader in Scripture was created and commissioned with this end in mind. Abraham was called to carry out God's mission, though he had no idea where he was going (Heb 11:10). Moses was apprehended in the desert to fulfill God's mission for Israel. One could add many more names: Noah, Samuel, David, Esther, Nehemiah, Jeremiah and the disciples. In the same way God summons and commissions some to lead (Isa 22:20–23), he removes from office those who live counter to his purposes (22:15–19).

Seizing this divine "why" is a lifelong venture. The tyranny of the urgent, the clamor of voices chasing other missions, the news of the day, the desires of the heart – all become secondary. If we do not step into his purpose, nothing else matters. This stands behind the words of Jesus, "What good is it if a man gains the world but forfeits his soul?" (Matt 16:26).

Some time back, the *New York Times* columnist David Brooks asked readers to send in essays describing their mission in life. He writes, "I expected most contributors would follow the commencement speech clichés of our high-achieving culture: dream big; set ambitious goals; try to change the world. In fact, a surprising number found their purpose by going the other way, by pursuing the small, happy life."[53]

Here is a typical reply:

---

52. Belmonte, *William Wilberforce*, 97.
53. Brooks, "Small, Happy Life."

I used to be one of the solid ones – one of the people whose purpose was clearly defined and understood. My purpose was seeing patients and "saving lives." I have melted into the in-between spaces, though. Now my purpose is simply to be the person who can pick up the phone and give you 30 minutes in your time of crisis. I can give it to you today and again in a few days. I can edit your letter. I can listen to you complain about your co-worker. I can look you in the eye and give you a few dollars in the parking lot. I am not upset if you cry. I am no longer drowning, so I can help keep you afloat with a little boost. Not all of the time, but every once in a while, until you find other people to help or a different way to swim. It is no skin off my back; it is easy for me.

Again, a small, happy life might be a worthy purpose, but only if it is wrapped within a larger divine purpose. God has called us to something more than ourselves and others. It's not about aligning God with our wills, but our wills with his. The English writer Evelyn Underhill notes: "He made us in order to use us, and use us in the most profitable way; for his purpose, not ours. To live a spiritual life means subordinating all other interests to that single fact."[54]

No one modeled this more than Jesus. He came to call sinners to turn from their ways and find life (Matt 9:13). His immediate mission was redemption, his aim was that we might experience life in all of its abundance, and his ultimate purpose was glorification (John 3:16; 10:10; 17:1). Everything he did was measured against these. Nothing would deter him. The will of the crowds did not dissuade him. The pushback of the religious did not get in his way, neither did even his own disciples and their mission for him (Matt 8:17; 9:11; 16:23). He would not invite men who preferred to carry out God's mission on their terms (Matt 16:18–22).

How does this apply to the church? If leaders are not careful, the churches they lead can get caught up in their own ideas of what a church mission should look like. In their quest to be missional, they can gather a team and ask, "What is *our* mission?" They might toss a number of ideas on a board and begin to craft a statement.

But any missional endeavor begins with discerning the mission of God. God is up to something in the world, something that is bigger than the church. This is what the church is to be about: it is an institution called to be a sign and witness to, and a foretaste of, God's mission.[55]

---

54. Evelyn Underhill, *The Spiritual Life*, quoted in Job and Shawchuck, *Guide to Prayer*, 86.

55. Roxburgh and Boren, *Introducing the Missional Church*, 20.

Leaders who have determined to reflect God and be missional must be guided by these words: "Our primary, indeed the very reason for our existence, is participation in the Trinity and their mission."[56] Only then will truth be pursued, God be worshipped, and people be reconciled and loved. Only then will leaders fulfill their purpose.

Missional Leadership Must Move from "Why" to "Where"

It's not enough for leaders to know *why* they and their organizations exist; they must know *where* they are going. We have underscored this, and Scripture affirms it.

God Is the Ultimate Futurist

We might be impressed with the scientists and historians of futurology, men like Alvin Toffler, Peter Schwartz, and Yuval Noah Harari, but no one knows the future like God. He is the Alpha and the Omega, the Beginning and the End, who sees the past and the future with the same clarity (Rev 21:6). His Word points to an impending end. It tells us both God and history are going somewhere. He alone can see into the future, and he is constantly inviting us into his future:

- "For I know the plans I have for you," declares the LORD, "plans to prosper you and not to harm you, plans to give you hope and a *future*" (Jer 29:11).
- "There is surely a *future* hope for you, and your hope will not be cut off" (Prov 23:18).
- "Now there is *in store* for me the crown of righteousness" (2 Tim 4:8).

Jesus came and gave his followers a picture of an open heaven, present and future (John 1:51).[57] He painted an image of a kingdom that would begin small but eventually overwhelm the world (Matt 13:32). Giving them a picture of his future kingdom in his Sermon on the Mount, he revealed what kingdom living can look like if people are willing to conform their lives to him.[58]

Jesus astounded the disciples with a bold vision when he declared that one day they would do the same things he did – and even greater things (John 14:12). He pointed to the future and spoke of a time when the Son of Man will come with power and glory, all things will be renewed and the Son

---

56. Van Gelder and Zscheile, *Missional Church in Perspective*, 162.
57. For an indepth look at this, note my book, *Under an Open Heaven*.
58. Langer, "Toward a Biblical Theology of Leadership," 79.

of Man will sit on the throne (Matt 19:28). He was the ultimate visionary, and his prediction rate is 100 percent.

Leaders Need to Be Futurists

God calls leaders to look into the future and dream. From God's viewpoint, "visionary leader" is a redundant phrase. Leaders, by definition, live out into the future. They impart a vision. They have to. Where there is no vision, there is no leader. Where there is no revelation of the future, people scatter (Prov 29:18). Followers without direction can fall into anarchy. They can end up following their own impulses (Judg 17:6). They can end up living in the past or living only for the present.

Leaders Need to Be Ultimate Futurists

It's not enough to think out five, ten or fifty years. Time is moving into God's future and toward time's end. Leaders who lead people toward this end are the ultimate visionaries. These are the leaders history remembers.

Pause and think about this. What does it mean?

Such leaders examine and assess everything in terms of potential – in terms of divine possibilities.[59] They are looking beyond the immediate, out into the far stretches of eternity. They are pointing people forward, urging them to invest in things that transcend current returns. They look for opportunities that outlast time (Matt 6:33). How large are your dreams?

Futurist leaders, informed by theology, tap into an eternal dimension that is resident in every human being. God has placed something of eternity in the human heart (Eccl 3:11). This means we live somewhere between time and time-without-end, in the already and the not-yet. Something compels us forward, though we are unable to fathom what God has done from beginning to end. This explains our restlessness. We long for something out there. This also explains our hope. Even creation waits in eager expectation (Rom 8:19).

Leaders Need to Submit Their Futures to God's Future

We step forward, with all of our preparations and prayers, into the unknown. There is a world full of possibilities, yet it is beset with futility, transitoriness, and contradiction.[60] This is what wisdom teaches. Our vision statements are tentative and vulnerable. We hold them with a certain looseness, knowing that

---

59. Marshall, *Understanding Leadership*, 15.
60. Zuck, *Reflecting with Solomon*, 13.

the future is incomprehensible and unchangeable (Eccl 3:14). The wise give them to God (Prov 16:1–3).

God, and his guiding, directing activity, saturates the historical process.[61] All we can do – and must do – is fear God, replace our dreams with his dreams and move into the future in faith, knowing that he is already there and his future is certain.

We might be impressed with our ability to shape tomorrow. One futurist boldly predicted, "once technology enables us to engineer bodies, brains and minds, we can no longer be certain about anything – including things that previously seemed fixed and eternal."[62] So compelling – and so wrong! We can be certain that God has a future, and it will not change.

The story of Scripture is one where God is urging leaders to step into *his* future, one that is fixed. In most accounts, God entered their lives and gave them a picture of the future, one that would further his story and move it to its completion. Sometimes they misread the map and lost their way. But history – his story – always moves toward an end technologies cannot change.

Abraham may have had his own short-term dreams, but God spoke into his life and gave him a vision of history's arc. Abraham would father a nation, one through which God would redeem the world, and it drove Abraham's life and defined his leadership (Gen 12:1–3). Along the way, God took Abraham outside, under the stars, and gave him more snapshots of the future (15:5). It may be that God is doing something like this with you.

In the depths of the night, God gave Joseph a dream. He would stand apart as a leader, ensuring Israel's survival. Like Abraham's vision, the road toward its fulfillment would be long and painful (Gen 37:5). God presented to Moses and the people a picture of a saved community (Exod 3:17). After Moses's death, Joshua received a vision of a conquered land (Josh 1:1–5), and he pursued it with the rest of his life.

Samuel was lying down in the house of the Lord when God began to impart a picture of a different future, one that would cause hearts to shake and tremble (1 Sam 3:4–18). God gave David a vision of an everlasting kingdom (2 Sam 7:10–16). His son Solomon gained a glimpse of a kingdom ruled by wisdom (1 Kgs 3:10–14). Nehemiah's was a world of politics and parties until God planted in his heart a far greater vision – one that would further the divine story (Neh 1–2).

---

61. Oden, *Classic Christianity*, 151.
62. Harari, "What the Year 2050 Has in Store for Humankind."

At the same time, God created a class of leaders, the prophets, who lived most of their lives exposed to the divine future. These were the visionaries, the "seers" of their day, whose words also caused hearts to tremble. The visions God revealed through them shattered old worlds and formed new ones, underscoring that these dreams were not of their making.[63]

In the New Testament, Paul recounted how his world was rocked by a vision of a completely different purpose (Acts 22:6–21). Suddenly, his own dreams seemed thin and worthless (Phil 3:7). Pursuing God's future drove him forward like a runner giving chase (3:12–14). He kept pressing forward, visualizing a ministry that would go to the edges of the known world (Rom 15:17–29). One day, John was in the Spirit (Rev 1:10) – a good place to be when seeking a glimpse into God's future – and received a vision of how the story of history would end. He was even able to see into timeless eternity (Rev 21–22).

As leaders dream and scribble their thoughts on a whiteboard, God is there. He is inviting us to think further out. He desires that our dreams coincide with his. Envisioning is about God's future, not ours. The important thing is to remain attentive. Our dreams may or may not come in the night. There may be a voice, audible or inaudible, that comes as it came to Samuel. One may have a burning bush moment as Moses did. Moses paused, and God revealed his future.

There's a cause and effect relationship. As Ruth Haley Barton puts it, "If spiritual leadership is anything, it is the capacity to see the bush burning in the middle of our own life and having enough sense to turn aside, take off our shoes and pay attention."[64] A voice might break the silence, as it did in Moses's and Paul's worlds.

However they come, dreams that matter are up to God. There will be the evidence of divine prompting. We won't be able to shake it. It may be a growing discontent with things as they are, mixed with a sense of divine calling to do something about it. An unbearable contradiction between what is and what should be collides. Here in the soul, where Spirit and spirit come together, we begin to sense a change is coming. Chaos may be about to replace order, which is OK because we have gotten terribly bored. He has sparked our imaginations. Out of prayer God is solidifying his invitation to enter into his future.

A vision will need to be tested. Does it contradict God's Word, or is it in line with God's Word? Does it reflect wisdom? Has it come out of deep prayer?

---

63. Brueggemann, *Like Fire in the Bones*, 7.
64. Barton, *Strengthening the Soul of Your Leadership*, 64.

Have I checked my motives (Prov 16:1–3)? Has it been worked through and confirmed by the community?

How do dreams show that God is in them? Here's a list of some indications:

- They will not go away.
- They have God's glory, not ours, as the aim.
- They fit with the larger narrative, the story God is writing.
- They have results that outlast time.
- They reflect God's character – his goodness, wisdom and greatness.
- They cannot be accomplished in our own strength.
- They have divine blessing written all over them.
- They have been fully submitted to God.

Leaders Need to Have Urgency in Their Vision Processes

A day is coming when time will end. There will no longer be a past, present or future. We will no longer dream. Casting a vision will be so yesterday. We will enter eternity and dwell with God, who is beyond time. He is the originator of time. He does not yearn for tomorrow or pine for the past. He is there in every moment. For God, the whole of time is viewed as now (Ps 102:27; 2 Pet 3:8).[65] Dream while you can!

God's futurists must also be urgent to live well in the present. The writer of Ecclesiastes urges visionary types to not be so obsessed with the future that they miss the now (Eccl 12:1–13). If all we do is think about tomorrow, we can become leaders who are irrelevant in the present. We may look back one day and realize we missed what God was serving up in the moment.

God has tasked leaders with a mission to guide people into God's moving current. Time does not stand still; it is always advancing forward. History is teleological, proceeding toward a "plausible, trustable end."[66] There will be a consummation of world history. In the future is eternal life, but we must lay old of it *now* (1 Tim 6:12).

Lay hold and make the most of the present (Eph 5:15). Solomon commands, "Whatever your hand finds to do, do this with all your might, for in the realm of the dead, where you are going, there is neither working nor planning nor knowledge nor wisdom" (Eccl 9:10). Now is our only time to act. Now is the only opportunity to choose to live according to God's will. When we die, deciding is past. Leading is past. So look forward and lead – now!

---

65. Oden, *Classic Christianity*, 43.
66. Oden, 151.

Summarizing What We Hear

That God still imparts his vision for our lives is verified by countless contemporary stories. Theologian J. I. Packer grabbed hold of God's vision for his ministry after one long afternoon with the Lord. Alone in the night, Cru founder Bill Bright could see a ministry that would take the gospel worldwide.

Billy Graham awoke at two o'clock in the morning with a vision to create a magazine called *Christianity Today*. Evangelist Luis Palau recounts how God spoke to him in his youth from John 14:12 with a summons to reach his hometown of Cordoba that expanded to Argentina, Latin America and, today, the world. And Bill McCartney was a successful collegiate football coach, when one day God expanded his imagination to see a different stadium, one filled not with rabid fans cheering on their teams, but men coming together to make promises to God. Promise Keepers was born, a ministry committed to empowering men to transform the world.

I never wanted to be a pastor. The dream of leading a church was nowhere on my radar screen. But over time, something stirred inside. Something ruined me. I was a cadet in military school preparing to attend the United States Air Force Academy. Every Sunday we marched to chapel, and every week I was embarrassed at the deplorable messages given by a retired Air Force officer.

He had no business being in the pulpit. He and others like him were "sideshow barkers," one step below the unemployed.[67] Over time, this disturbed me. I found my soul shouting, "This is not right! The pulpit has to be protected from faithless men who convince people God has nothing relevant to say to them. The church is supposed to be a movement, not a care center filled with sleeping attenders. We're called to be wide-awake missional saints!"

I began to pray about my future in ways that I had not prayed before. By my second year of seminary, it became obvious God was giving me a vision to lead churches to become thriving, missional, visionary communities. A vision brings a leader's world into focus and activates an energy, the sort that changes everything. Such leaders understand that to get what you've never had, you must do what you've never done.

God sanctions the envisioning process. We may see our dreams become reality, but it may be that others will take them to the end. Moses could only get a glimpse from Mount Nebo. Joshua would see the vision to completion, but it still wasn't the end. Hebrews speaks of those who gained what was promised,

67. Peterson, *The Pastor*.

but not everyone did. The vision they hoped to see did not materialize in their day. They could only watch from a distance (Heb 11:39–40).

I am still hoping to see resurrected churches. I get occasional glimpses.

The important thing is to dream. Helen Keller was once asked, "What would be worse than being born blind?" She replied, "To have sight without vision." What are your dreams?

Bringing the Voices Together

At its core, leadership is about determining a mission and chasing a vision. Present, past and global voices give us sound rules to be effectual. We should listen to them.

Following them will not guarantee smooth sailing. Missional and visionary types tend to disrupt. But this is necessary. To avoid either or both will miss the model of God.

Answering the "why" and the "where," however, is not enough. As we will see in the next chapter, purposes and dreams go nowhere without finding answers to two more questions.

8

Know How and When

In the introduction to his book *Good Strategy/Bad Strategy*, Richard Rumelt tells the story-behind-the-story of the Battle of Trafalgar.[1] In the early years of the nineteenth century, France and Britain were locked in a struggle for supremacy, both on land and on sea. The French general Napoleon was driven by a grand vision of military dominance.

By the time Napoleon was sixteen, he was a military officer rising up through the ranks. He distinguished his leadership on the battlefield with his speed of advance. Movement was part of his strategy. It was Napoleon's way of breathing. His army was always seeking a foe, pursuing new supplies and finding a way around fixed points.[2]

But all of this was threatened by the British, who were engaged in their own empire building. Lord Nelson was an admiral in the Royal Navy. He too demonstrated the skill, aggressiveness and charisma of a born leader.

On 21 October 1805, the two powers confronted one another off the southwest coast of Spain. Napoleon amassed a fleet large enough to take on England's flotilla. Thirty-three French and Spanish ships came together to attack the smaller fleet of twenty-seven British ships. Their strategy was simple: come alongside, fire away with full cannon force, and sink the enemy.

Commanding a smaller fleet, Nelson knew he would need a different strategy. He knew conventional warfare would lead to his defeat. So the admiral broke all the rules of tactics. He separated the British fleet into two columns and advanced against the Franco-Spanish fleet perpendicularly. The adversary had no game plan for this stratagem. Nelson broke the line and created confusion. In the end, the British lost no ships; the Franco-Spanish lost twenty-two.

1. Rumelt, *Good Strategy/Bad Strategy*, 1–2.
2. Wills, *Certain Trumpets*, 92.

This story illustrates a basic leadership truth, one that we will hear from multiple angles: missional and visionary leadership is dead in the water if there is not a forceful strategy and compelling tactics. The rise and fall of states, corporations, churches, teams, and so on, are the result of choices made by leaders about how, where, when and why to deploy resources to achieve objectives.[3]

The Voices We Hear

Ninety-seven percent of senior executives say strategic thinking is the most important skill for success.[4] The questions "Why are we here?" and "Where are we going?" go only so far (though, sadly, many organizations do not even ask these). Effective leaders, those who are strategic, also ask, "How will we get there?" "When?" "Who?" They want to know how this bold dream can become reality.

A mission and a dream have little relevance if they do not translate into something actual. As one leadership writer put it, "'Having the idea' is just a small part of the process, perhaps only 1 percent of the journey."[5] Strategies and objectives must be identified. Otherwise, the mission and vision will lack credibility. They will remain an aspiration, an illusion. And leaders will soon lose their voice. They will no longer be out in front.

A Model of Missional, Visionary, Strategic, and Tactical Leadership

In my international assignment to pastor a church in the Netherlands, I worked with a number of leaders who worked in the oil business. They included Dutch, British, Nigerian and Americans. At times, they invited me into their worlds. They included Royal Dutch Shell. It is headquartered in The Hague.

Like other successful corporations, Shell is committed to being missional, visionary, strategic and tactical. Their statements are out there for all to see. Their *mission* is to be an industry that satisfies its customers, achieves operational excellence, and employs an innovative results-oriented team. Their current *vision* is even more ambitious. Recognizing that climate change has the greatest potential to disrupt their industry, they dream of a day Shell and its customers will no longer add to the greenhouse gasses in the atmosphere.

---

3. Nagl, "'On Grand Strategy' Review."
4. Kabacoff, "Develop Strategic Thinkers."
5. Belsky, *Making Ideas Happen*, 1.

Like any vision, this one will require a *strategic* plan. This includes shifting the product mix from oil to gas, exploring alternative energy sources, selling enough biofuel to keep every car operational, providing enough electricity to meet power demands and capturing significant carbon by planting vast forests.

Some of the *tactics* include keeping operational expenditures highly disciplined, sustaining and developing cash engines (e.g. conventional oil and gas, deep water and chemicals, shale oil and gas) and recruiting excellent people.

All of this explains why it is a transnational market leader, one of the "supermajors" in the oil industry. For those of us in other fields, there is something to be learned.

Other Examples of Strategic Thinking

From the world of board games, to the sports world, to other corporate worlds, there are many illustrations of strategic thinking.

Monopoly is a game that has become a part of international popular culture. It is licensed in more than 103 countries and produced in more than thirty-seven languages. If your mission is to have fun and your vision is to be a reigning champ, you need a plan. Pundits suggest three core strategies: buy as much property as you can; never make a trade that gives the other a monopoly; and once you have a monopoly, mortgage everything to buy houses.

Here's another. For years, the American baseball team Oakland Athletics came up short of the goal. Winning the World Series was a distant dream. They had the right mission and vision, but their strategies had not worked. Like other teams, they depended upon the subjective opinions of scouts. It was time to choose a different strategy. The Athletics shifted to an analytical, evidence-based sabermetric approach in order to discover players. It transformed a losing franchise into a winning one. The movie *Moneyball* tells the story.

One more example, from the corporate world. While many airlines have struggled to make a profit, Southwest Airlines has been an ongoing success. Its mission is to be a low-cost airline, so its business plan reflects a careful strategy and shrewd tactics. Planes fly point to point (rather than using the traditional hub and spoke approach). They have reduced the costs of operation by utilizing one kind of plane, lowering costs in order to lower fares and fill planes. Finally, they provide frequent flights to fit people's schedules. These and other strategies help the airline accomplish its mission and get to its vision.

The Process of Becoming Strategic and Tactical

It's not easy to get beyond the aspirational, but looking at these examples helps us identify some critical steps. Here are five.

Listen and Assess

To be strategic, leaders must stop and listen. They need to set aside time regularly to think strategically. They must stay informed about trends, patterns and cultural changes.

It's important to observe, probe and question assumptions. In other words, leaders must first step sideways to move forward.[6] They must ask the questions that force people to think. There is necessary data that needs to be evaluated, and inquiries to be made that cause people to rethink notions.[7]

Questions are the language of strategy. "What does success look like?" "What are the challenges to forward progress?" "What must we overcome to realize the vision?" "What is the plan for winning this battle?" "What are the obstacles getting in the way of success?" "Is it an arrogance that sees no need for change?" "Could a faulty leadership model be blocking progress?" "Is a laziness at the center of the lack of energy to innovate?" A great deal of strategy work is trying to figure out what is going on.[8]

Assessment tools can be helpful, such as a SWOT analysis. Teams gather to look at where they are. They begin by identifying the organization's *strengths*. What is it we are good at? What are the resources making things possible? What enables us to experience present success? What sources of power are there to seize?

These questions set the tone, relax defenses, and build optimism. They enable a leader to guide a discussion that identifies *weaknesses*. What are the things we do not do so well? What are our limitations (resources, gift mix, etc.)? Who are our weak links? What apparent strengths might be giving us a false sense of security?

Acknowledging its shortcomings, a team needs to look in a different direction, assessing its present *opportunities*. What are the most promising possibilities that, if seized wisely and at the right time, will move us to our destination? What is changing that might work to our advantage? What are the circumstances telling us?

6. Ledbetter, Banks, and Greenhalgh, *Reviewing Leadership*, 137–138.
7. Wiseman, *Multipliers*, 116.
8. Rumelt, *Good Strategy/Bad Strategy*, 79.

Finally, a team needs to be aware of the *threats* – those obstacles that might hinder it (e.g. environmental changes, the readiness of people, emerging adversaries). What must we overcome to achieve our vision and accomplish our mission?

When I arrived in Europe to lead an international church, there was no clear mission, let alone a vision that was guiding the church's direction. We were at ground zero. Over time, we worked through the "why" and "where" questions. Eventually, we began to address the "how" question, but we had to first figure out what was going on.

We worked our way through a SWOT analysis. I have done this with every organization I have led, on a regular basis. It's important to ask: What are we good at? What is getting in the way?

One of the obvious issues in the church in Europe was a cumbersome structure – three boards and fourteen committees. Like barnacles that attached themselves in erosive ways, layer upon layer of boards and committees were added to the structure. No wonder the church could not be decisive. Proposals were passed from one board and one committee to another. Analysis turned into paralysis. Institution had replaced movement. Assessment was bringing all of this out.

Collaborate and Create

Strategic thinking has to be done as a team. Leaders cannot do this on their own. The best strategic plan emerges when leaders gather and create various strategies. The vital ones reflect an accurate assessment, draw upon the resources, tackle the challenges and anticipate the reactions.[9]

Collaborating gives the best chance for alignment, for a sustained synergy. For an organization to become more than the sum of its parts, individual strategies must be linked. This is why it is important to work together from the start. Otherwise, the parts will silo and form their own strategies, and any hopes of synergy will be lost.[10]

In working together, the final arbiters of which strategies to implement are the mission and vision. If the playbook will not get us to these, they are the wrong plays. If there are individual strategies, they need to align, cohere and build upon one another. This requires the oversight of disciplined missional and visionary leaders who harness individual ideas.

---

9. Rumelt gives a helpful chapter, "The Kernel of Good Strategy," 77–94.
10. See a helpful discussion in Kaplan and Norton, *Strategy Focused Organization*, 11–12.

One more illustration from my European ministry: out of our mission (which included reaching a lost world) and our dream (to be an English-speaking church ministering to the larger international community), we began to think strategically. How can we do this? What are the threats? One of the latter was the constant turnover of expatriates.

Nearly every week, corporations and governments were reassigning families, while the remaining members were left to say farewell. On the plus side, we were welcoming new people on a regular basis. Still, these losses were painful, even debilitating. When you live abroad, you become family with those who are away from home.

It was time to think strategically, to gather as a team and answer the "how" question. How do we turn a negative into a positive? Someone came up with a brilliant strategy: turn farewells into commissions. We began to use the occasion of a family's departure to send them out on their next assignment. We challenged them to fulfill a purpose larger than that of their corporation. We prayed over them, sending them out to live missional lives.

Over time, farewells became less a heartrending loss and more an opportunity for us to be what the church is called to be: a sending community to reach lost people. We were preparing people to go all over the world. And in most cases, the corporations were paying for the moves! It all came out of collaboration and creativity.

List and Reduce

The more strategies there are, the less gets accomplished.[11] Trust me. My team and I used to construct strategies that took up multiple pages. This, along with simultaneously setting a number of strategic initiatives in motion, led to confusion, frustration and deficits.

Rumelt cautions, "A long list of 'things to do,' often mislabeled as 'strategies' or 'objectives,' is not a strategy. It is just a list of things to do."[12] Too many, and teams lose focus and interest. Having fewer strategies, and giving attention to one or two at a time, gives the best chance of aligning every resource and activity.

Reducing ensures that a group determines what is essential. "Straddling" is a term used to describe the practice of keeping existing strategies while

---

11. McChesney, Covey, and Huling, *Four Disciplines of Execution*, 10.

12. Rumelt, *Good Strategy/Bad Strategy*, 53.

adopting other organizational strategies. This can lead to a strategic plan full of incompatibilities.[13] Stay lean. Stay with what is crucial.

There is one more piece to this. Reducing is not just about the number of strategies. One may have to downsize a particular strategy to ensure that it conforms to the existing and anticipated resources. Strategies that do not take advantage of the resources can mean missed opportunities; strategies that exceed the capacity can mean defeat. Aligning aspirations with capabilities is the very essence of strategic thought.[14]

As necessary as strategies are, effective leaders cannot afford to ignore the next step . . .

Adopt and Implement

Having a strategic game plan is not enough. What good is a strategy if it is affirmed and simply filed away? Who cares if it is an impressive statement on a website if it is irrelevant to the operation? Strategies are developed in order to be implemented. Leaders intending to take their organizations to the finish line see to it that operational plans flesh out strategies. Few accomplish this.

The real problem isn't bad strategies but poor execution.[15]

We are now into the tactics. Here leaders are assigning resources and establishing target dates. Critical questions are addressed: "What tactics, and how many?" "Who is going to carry these out?" "When must they happen?" "What are our measurable targets?" "What are our key performance indicators?" The failure to answer these questions is a sign of faltering leadership.[16]

At the level of objectives and tactics, things become more fluid. Assignments can change. Dates may need to be adjusted due to unexpected circumstances. Priorities alter. Side issues can push themselves to the front of the line.

All actions are not created equal.[17] Better tactics may emerge; goals may need reassessing. Here again, teamwork is critical. Some of the best work happens when those tasked work together. The best missional, visionary, strategic and tactical efforts are collaborative efforts.

---

13. Note McKeown, *Essentialism*, 53.

14. This point is developed in Gaddis, *On Grand Strategy*.

15. Kaplan and Norton, *Strategy Focused Organization*, 1.

16. Burns, *Leadership*, 455.

17. McChesney, Covey, and Huling, *Four Disciplines of Execution*, 11.

Review and Hold Accountable

Implementation requires regular review and accountability. Review keeps us from becoming so stuck to a strategy we miss the changes that might call for a new one. Even the best strategies have an expiration date. To the Amazons of the world: don't rest on your laurels. Learn from Sears.

Accountability means members of a team are willing to hold one another's feet to the fire "regularly and rhythmically." They must appraise their progress and ask one another: What are the one or two most important things we will do in the next week to achieve our goals and see our vision become reality?

Though difficult to do, leaders must have the courage to call procrastinators out. They must embolden one another. The next step may be unclear, but the best way to figure things out is to take some incremental action. Otherwise, goals tend to disintegrate into the wind.[18] But with accountability, with constant motion, execution happens.

Strategic and tactical thinking is a regular process. Strategic thinking and operation plans need to be seamless. For this to happen, teams must regularly review the plan, the performance, and the strategies that drive them.

This begins with leadership. Kaplan's words are worth noting: "If those at the top are not energetic leaders of the process, change will not take place, strategy will not be implemented, and the opportunity for breakthrough performance will be missed."[19]

Here is where we again must pause and ask some questions. Have we allowed the weekly meetings to descend into merely connecting? Have we lost sight of the mission and the vision? How intentional are we to keep the strategic plan in front of our teams? How willing are we to ask the hard questions and call people out for not performing?

Summarizing What We Hear

In the end, the leader's job is not merely to aspire – and inspire – but to act. One's purpose must be inseparable from one's commitment to achieving it.[20] It is not enough to be an architect; a leader must also be the general contractor who carries out the plan. But few leaders and few organizations follow through. One study reports that failure of execution ranges from 70 to 90 percent.[21]

---

18. McChesney, Covey, and Huling, 13.
19. Kaplan and Norton, *Strategy Focused Organization*, 16–17.
20. Harari, *Leadership Secrets of Colin Powell*, 109.
21. Kaplan and Norton, *Strategy Focused Organization*, 1.

What explains this? Too many leaders are reactive rather than proactive; isolated rather than curious; cautious rather than willing to take risks; inflexible rather than flexible; and content rather than creative.[22] Other leaders are simply in love with dreaming and strategizing, but they hesitate when it comes to execution. They have a difficult time making decisions, or finding the energy to tie the knot.

Sometimes we hide behind the constant analyses and assessments. We want everything answered. But when we mine and massage the data in pursuit of perfect knowledge (perfect certainty), we are edging toward the clinical condition known as "decidophobia": fear of facing a go point. Strategies that have substance will always carry some risk. Choosing a strategy does cut off options. One has to step out.

In a 1999 *Fortune* magazine article, "Why Leaders Fail," the authors point out that some leaders have the mistaken belief that being missional, visionary and strategic is enough. But it is the failure to execute that kills the organization, and this often comes from indecision, something the authors describe as a leader's fatal flaw.[23]

The words of James MacGregor Burns summarize well: "The ultimate test of practical leadership is the realization of intended, real change that meets people's enduring needs."[24] Realization. Dreams turned to reality. Possibilities becoming actualities. Strategies becoming accomplishments. This is the aim of great leaders.

The Voices We Need to Hear

In 2013, a large-scale global study evaluated the leadership practices and effectiveness of leaders in some 140-plus countries. Among the discoveries was that a strategic approach to leadership was, on average, ten times more important to the perception of effectiveness than other behaviors studied. It was twice as important as communication (the second most important behavior) and almost fifty times more important than hands-on tactical behaviors.[25]

Strategic leadership matters, whether you are leading in Africa, Latin America, Asia or Beirut. For over twenty years, I have witnessed the leadership strategies of Grant Porter. In one of the more challenging regions on earth,

---

22. Walsh, "Are You a Strategic Thinker?"
23. Welch, "Why Leaders Fail."
24. Burns, *Leadership*, 460.
25. Kabacoff, "Develop Strategic Thinkers."

he has invested thirty-five years of his life building teams and pursuing God-shaped objectives.

The Voice of Grant Porter, Former Leader of the Near East Initiative in Beirut, Lebanon

How would you define the differences between Western and Majority World leadership?

It is difficult to answer this without breaking down the parts. I have invested much of my life in the Arab world, where leadership is often patriarchal. The leader is the strong man who looks out for those he leads. Followers count on this, keeping him in power. It is a low-trust environment, requiring a dominant leader who will protect people's interests. In contrast to other cultures, there is often bravado attached to Arab leaders.

You have lived in three worlds – you grew up in Australia, spent thirty-five years in the Middle East and more recently have moved to the US. How would you define the differences in leadership?

My impression is that Australian leaders tend to understate themselves. In contrast, I have noticed that Americans are quicker to self-promotion, calling attention to their expertise and promoting their accomplishments. The Arab world has its own self-promotion. Much of this, however, is driven by a shame/honor culture. In many cases, self-promotion is necessary to cover for one's weaknesses.

When it comes to strategic leadership, what have you observed?

It's difficult to generalize, but I have noticed that in the Arab world, strategic thinking often begins with the community, the clan, the family. Strategies are less about achieving a goal, one informed by a concept or ideal. In a culture that is more collective and less individualistic, goals and strategies are driven by what will build the community. It is critical to think strategically, but I do not expect that every leader will think in strategic terms. Many think strictly in tactical terms, and they do a great job of leading. That said, I believe their effectiveness is multiplied when they collaborate with a strategic leader, one who is moving them toward a common goal.

You have done a lot of work and research with Muslims. How would you describe their basic approach to leadership?

In the Arab world, it's hard to see major distinctions between Christians and Muslims. Both are low-trust environments thanks to tribalism. There is a long history of enmity between one another – Christians in conflict with Christians, Muslims fighting Muslims, and Christians and Muslims at war with one another. All of this has necessitated a more autocratic leadership.

What is a common leadership mistake made by Westerners when they come to do work in the Middle East?
Arab leadership tends to be wrapped up in positional leadership. It is highly relational. Western leadership is more about reward, merit and achievement. There is an inevitable clash when a Western leader thinks his accomplishments and money give him the right to lead. One must have the position, and this must be earned – only by time, trust and connections.

How would you contrast team dynamics between an Arab and an Australian context?
Australians see themselves as equals at the table. Everyone has an equal voice. Arabs see distinctions at the table, defined by age, standing and position. Strategic and tactical planning needs to understand this.

In Arab culture, reciprocity is a huge word. Arabs often extend hospitality and help with the expectation that it will be reciprocated.

Westerners underestimate the place of reciprocity. Often, a patron–client relationship emerges in which the Westerner is the patron – and the expectation of a patron is to reciprocate. It is important to watch this, and one way is to spread yourself out in other relationships. Otherwise, you will be beholden to a few.

What has been your best team experience?
The best experience is the one I have had over these past ten years, working in a collaborative relationship with other Arab leaders to build a network of ministries. What has made the team strong is our commitment to be in this together, trust one another, enjoy comradery, have clear objectives and willingly sacrifice.

You have been impacted by Ori Brafman and Rod A. Beckstrom's book *The Starfish and Spider: The Unstoppable Power of Leaderless Organizations*. Do you believe leaders are necessary?
I believe leaders are critical. But this book has taught me that the real importance is not in the institution but in the movement. In the same way, it is leaders, not positions, that matter. This is especially true in the Middle East, where things are not so linear. Interconnection is what is valued.

Lessons from an Arab World

A recurring theme found throughout this book is the contrast between cultures that are relation-centered and those that are performance-oriented. In Grant's world, strategic and tactical leaders are necessary for effective leadership, but not at the expense of relationships. Taking the time to build these, however, can slow the process, creating tension in leaders driven by a sense of urgency and a determination to see successful execution. Rather than avoid the tension, it might be necessary to live and lead within it.

The Voice We Must Hear

Missional, visionary, strategic, tactical – it all sounds so Western, so corporate, so . . . theological. What? Are you serious? Consider this:

Every Act of God Is Strategic and Tactical

Let's review. We have noted that God is intentional. We awake to a world wherein its Creator is on an everlasting *mission*. The lover is on a mission to redeem and reconcile. "Redemption," as Oden puts it, "is the provision God makes to deal with a foreseen, permitted, restrained, condemned, and vanquished evil."[26] Reconciliation makes possible the restoration of relationships, the reestablishment of peace and the flourishing of creation (Rom 5:10; 8:18–25).

Ultimately, God's purpose is to exalt his infinite worth and splendor (Gal 1:5; Phil 4:20; 2 Tim 4:18). His aim is that in both general and special revelation, we see and savor his glory, "the greatest beauty and treasure of the universe."[27]

Alongside his mission, God has set a *vision* before us. One day there will be a new heaven and a new earth. People will be reunited with him, glorifying him in everything they do (Rev 22:1–5). We all look forward to a new Eden, when all things will be made new and all of the ancient promises will come true. God will make right what has been terribly wrong. Every knee will one day bow before the King (Phil 2:10–11).

All of this necessitates *a strategy and a tactical plan*. God is nothing if not strategic and tactical in everything he does. It would be inconsistent with what we know of the character of God to assume that in anything he does, it

---

26. Oden, *Classic Christianity*, 151.
27. Piper, *Expository Exultation*, 205.

is spur-of-the-moment, unplanned, and unstrategic. He has made *everything* for his own purpose (Prov 16:4). Everything.

God is directing everything toward its appropriate end for his own glory (Eph 1:9–12). In every moment and in every place, what God says and does is deliberate and calculated.

If this were not the case, his mission and vision would be mere aspirations. His vision of a new heaven and new earth would be a pipedream. The Bible would be nothing more than a book of wish lists.

Like his mission and vision, God's strategic plan is one determined in eternity past. Over the course of history, God has unfolded it. It's not that we can readily understand his schemes; he does things beyond our understanding (Job 37:5). We sometimes witness his ways, his stratagems, and like Paul we exclaim, "His paths are beyond tracing out!" (Rom 11:33).

What we know for sure is that there is a method to what can seem like a madness. His objectives are perfect, for God and his will are flawless (Matt 5:48; Rom 12:2). He is nothing if not wise and loving in the carrying out of every strategy and tactic.

Sin Necessitates a Redemptive Strategy

The kernel of a good strategy includes a diagnosis.[28] Here's what's going on: human beings have turned from God. Sin has obscured the glory of God. A strategy is required, and God has set in motion strategies that will lead to redemption and reconciliation.

In Genesis 3:15, God gives the first hints of a redemptive strategy, one that will deal with the obstacles and mark the direction. In Genesis 12, God begins to assign and give time lines. He will "undo the plight of the human race," redeeming the world through the seed of Abraham. As N. T. Wright puts it, "The call of Abraham is the answer to the sin of Adam."[29]

Abraham is the spearhead of God's rescue mission. Through Abraham, God will enable humanity to pick up again the threads of a project that had been theirs from the beginning: to care for the world, serve the Creator, experience perfect justice and peace, and bring glory to God.[30]

The Old Testament narrative is the systematic account of God executing his strategy through his people. Israel will be God's royal priesthood, a light to

---

28. Rumelt, *Good Strategy/Bad Strategy*, 77.
29. Wright, *How God Became King*, 73.
30. Wright, 86.

the nations (Isa 42:6).[31] Unfortunately, by the end of the Old Testament, Israel appears to be a failed strategy. Entrusted by God to be his agent to rescue the world, Israel itself is in need of rescue.[32]

It's all part of a larger redemptive strategy. One must step further out to see. Israel is simply the first piece.

God sends his Son Jesus to accomplish what he intended for Israel as a people. Jesus comes as part of the grander scheme to redeem his people and call them back to their original mission. Jesus comes as Israel's King and Redeemer, announcing that the kingdom is at hand (Matt 2:6; 4:17). Heaven has intersected with earth. We now live under an open heaven.[33]

God sends his Spirit as another part of his redemptive strategy. He comes to give birth to, indwell and empower the church. The Spirit's movements may appear random, like the wind, but the Spirit is intentional wherever he goes (John 3:8). There is alignment with the work of God's Word. Together they bring God's purposes to further completion. The Spirit makes effectual the redemptive work of Jesus in ways beyond our knowing and at a depth that cannot be expressed (Rom 8:26).[34]

God's Strategies Have Their Rules

God utilizes a number of plays in carrying out his will. What does this voice both affirm and add to what we already know about strategic thinking?

Up front, God is showing us that it is folly (and ungodlike) to be without a strategic plan. To put it another way, it is unlike God to settle for goals and values, and ignore strategies. Leaders are strategic for reasons that transcend winning or gaining profit; they are strategic because it models divine behavior.

Listen up! There is nothing spiritual about leadership that is undisciplined and ineffectual. God intends that every organization be strategy-focused. Here are his rules:

Strategies Need to Align

From Genesis to Revelation, the Trinity – Father, Son and Spirit – work in strategic alignment, turning divine mission and vision into reality. None works

---

31. Gentry and Wellum, *Kingdom through Covenant*, 247.
32. Wright, *How God Became King*, 178.
33. See Johnson, *Under an Open Heaven*.
34. Oden, *Classic Christianity*, 537.

apart from the others. They do not have individual strategic plans. They are the ultimate picture of synergy.

Everything in and outside of creation fits into God's blueprint. Lifeless matter, living plants, animals and humans are all under his divine governance. Nothing happens by chance. God has strategically coordinated all of the parts (Eph 1:11–14; Col 1:17). In similar ways, all of the pieces in our strategic plans need to cohere if they are to work.

Strategies Need to Be Timely

Good strategies pay attention to the clock. Our theology tells us that every moment of time has an order, a sequence, an ebb and flow (Eccl 3:1–8). "Time," as someone scrawled on a wall in a café in Austin, Texas, "is nature's way of keeping everything from happening all at once." Time is part of God's strategy, and its aim is to show his glory (Eccl 3:11).

God sends his Son to heal and transform the world at the perfect moment (Gal 4:4). Everything Jesus does is timed to fit with the Father's will (John 2:4; 7:6; 12:23). There is precision in the timing of the Spirit's coming and the birth of the church (John 16:7; Acts 2:1). Jesus's return will be at the right strategic moment (2 Pet 3:9–10).

The lesson: our strategies must not be behind the times, or ahead of the time – but on time.

Strategies Need to Be Shrewd

Everything God does coheres with reality. In putting together a strategic plan, he has diagnosed the critical factors and addressed the obstacles. Shrewd strategies solve problems. They take into account human behavior. They factor in the resources. They outthink the enemy.

As they set out to carry out God's operational plan, Jesus exhorts his disciples to be wise as serpents (Matt 10:16); to work from the inside out (Luke 13:21); to be as imperceptible as salt when it comes to engaging culture (Matt 5:13). Shrewd strategies are subversive. Our most effective tools are the "behind the scenes" work of Word and prayer.

Maximizing redemptive influence requires a series of careful stratagems: don't separate yourself from the world in ways that close you off from having any influence; avoid seeking to be like the world, trying to be so relevant you become irrelevant; and eschew any attempts to take over the world by aligning with political power. If you are to be strategic, be in the world, but not of it. Love the world, yet hate it. Serve one another, yet confront sin.

Our strategies have to be cunning. We will face resistance (1 Pet 5:8). The enemy has his own stratagems. His playbook is aimed at any forward progress (Eph 6:11). Deception is a core strategy. As Plantinga notes, to do its worst, evil needs to look its best. Vices have to masquerade as virtues (e.g. governmental tyranny as protective concern).[35] To be successful, evil needs to hijack goodness. Hijacked, love becomes lust; a shepherd heart devolves into an autocratic spirit.

It's all part of a strategy to relax a leader's defenses, to compromise his or her efforts. Our strategies must expose and frustrate the enemy.

Strategies Need to Maximize Resources

Good strategies leverage what is available. One of our most critical resources is people. One-man shows are not good strategies, especially when it comes to changing the world. Part of Jesus's plan for advancing God's kingdom was to find a team and pour himself into it (Mark 3:13). He looked for the right members. His inner core would have to have a sense of urgency and a willingness to be sacrificial. Otherwise, they would not make the team (Luke 9:58–62; John 13–17).

Think about it: Jesus called out twelve disciples, an intentional number that echoed the foundation of Israel as God's people (Matt 10:1–4). His strategy was that they should first be with him before he sent them out (Mark 3:14). This has always been God's strategy for all who serve on his teams. Sending them out, he gave them a strategy for where to go and not go, and how to handle the receptive and unreceptive (Matt 10:1–42).

Jesus also took advantage of his divine power. Miracles were one of his effectual strategies. More than a spontaneous response to people's needs, miracles verified his claims and led people to belief (John 1:47–51). They served to prove that Jesus is the Christ, and that by believing in him one might be restored to eternal life (20:31). But even here, he was strategic in their application. Misused, miracles could lead to the wrong outcomes.

Strategic leaders take inventory of who they are and what they possess. They maximize their divine assets (endless) and leverage the resources God has provided (the talents of people, money, the season one is in, the critical mass, etc.).

---

35. Plantinga, *Not the Way It's Supposed to Be*, 98.

Strategies Need to Be Birthed in Prayer

In his book on strategic thinking, Rumelt warns of bad strategies, those built upon mistaken foundations.[36] Here's one mistaken foundation: we can do all of this on our own.

Attempting anything apart from intercession is a strategy for failure. Prayer was part of everything Jesus did. As Yancey writes, "At such times he went aside and prayed, as if to breathe pure air from a life-support system that would give him the strength to continue living on a polluted planet."[37] He sent his team out with the same strategy: to pray without ceasing (Eph 6:18). Repeatedly he calls us to the same practice.

Prayer declares we need God. Summoning God's help is our acknowledgment that apart from him we can do nothing (John 15:5). Unless God builds the house – or anything, for that matter – we build in vain (Ps 127:1–2). Without prayer, our strategies will not get off the ground (Mark 9:29). With prayer, strategies become effective (Luke 11:5–13; John 14:14). Things beyond our imagination happen.

Strategies Need to Be Sequential

First things first. There is an order to what God does, so there needs to be an order to what we do. Jesus first went to the lost sheep of Israel (Matt 15:24). He commissioned his disciples to do the same (10:5–6). He mandated that the church begin local, and then work out in concentric circles (Acts 1:8).

Jesus told the initial twelve to wait for the empowering Spirit. If they were to do the same works, and even greater ones, they must wait for Jesus's ascension and the Spirit's descension (John 14:12; 16:7; Acts 2:1–4).

The early church followed a similar strategy. The apostle Paul went first to the Jews (Rom 1:16). This governed his missionary efforts. His initial step was to enter the synagogue (Acts 13:14; 14:1; 17:1; 18:4; 19:8). His constant aim was to demonstrate by word, power and life that Jesus is the Messiah, especially to the Jews (Rom 9–11).

God's strategies expanded. He extended his grace to all nations, and Paul and the church were commissioned to go to the Gentiles (Acts 15:6–21). Even here, leaders are to be strategic. The way to reach leaders is to first reach leaders (2 Tim 2:2).

---

36. Rumelt, *Good Strategy/Bad Strategy*, 7.
37. Yancey, *The Jesus I Never Knew*, 90.

Strategies Need to Be Counterintuitive

Our strategies do not always have to make sense. Like God's, some of our plans should reflect a depth not immediately seen on the surface.

A good plan often takes us beyond ourselves, so we should not feel threatened if the first response is, "Huh?" God's methods and God's values do not always cohere with the world's. His ways are not our ways. He is beyond us (Rom 11:33–36), and that is a good thing!

God sends his Son Jesus, employing a strategy that confounds most people. All of Jesus's movements are calculated and deliberate, but they sometimes go in directions we least expect. He goes to Samaria to find an outcast. He is not the king everyone expects. He does not come on a regal stallion, but rides into Jerusalem on a donkey. Some respond, but for the most part Israel turns its back on him (John 1:11). The people do not comprehend the strategy God laid out in the Old Testament.

It appears to be another failed strategy. In reality, it is a brilliant plan. The rejection of Jesus, leading to his death, had to happen (Luke 24:25–27). Israel's rejection brings reconciliation to the world (Acts 2:22–28; Rom 11:15). Christ's death, resurrection and ascension overcome the powers of darkness.

God launches a newly integrated way of life, one in which we have the capacity to do greater things than he did (John 14:12). A changed life is possible. Nothing can stand in the way of his long-planned new creation.[38]

Looking at God's broad strategic plan, it is clear that many of his strategies are counterintuitive. The strongest people are often the weakest (1 Sam 16:10–12; 1 Cor 1:26–29). The way to become big is to begin small (Luke 13:18–19). The path to wealth is to become poor (Prov 11:24–25). The way to the top is the way down (1 Pet 5:6). The first are those who are last. The best revenge is love.

The best strategies don't have to make sense. They just need to reflect God and his wisdom.

Strategies Need to Connect

God strategically accommodates to culture. As language shifts and literary forms change, so God's strategy changes. He sends his Son into our neighborhood in the form of man, that he might identify with us. Paul enters Athens and adapts his message to his audience (Acts 17:17, 28).

---

38. Wright, *Simply Good News*, 33.

What good are strategies if no one understands them? Jesus uses stories as an intentional way of reaching people, as well as a designed means to withhold truth from the unreceptive (Matt 13:11–15).

God's Tactical Playbook Is Designed for Optimal Returns

What do we learn about tactics? Theology tells us that God's strategies lead to operational objectives. His devices for accomplishing his ends are perfect. Here, where aspirations and plans translate into reality, God is at work. In the perfect moment, God is employing people, setting parameters and making things tangible. Here's what his ways show us.

Tactics Need to Be Timely

There is no time to waste. There is an urgency to God's plans (Eph 5:16). His assignments must meet his schedule. A day of reckoning is coming (2 Pet 3:10). There is no excuse for squandering the days. If we are serious about our mission and committed to our vision, we need to set goals and deadlines.

Tactics Need to Be Assignable

Scripture is the story of God summoning and assigning. With a strategy in play, he assigns Abraham, David, Esther, Paul and every other servant. The church is God's chosen instrument in the present to reach a dying world and call people to salvation. We are part of his operational plan. We need to be available, for we never know when he will call. And we need to make assignments.

Tactics Need to Be Measurable

We like to say that God is not into numbers. But is this true? His story of the talents tells us he is not impressed with those who are inattentive to results. He has no patience with those who play it safe (Luke 19:11–27). His return will be determined by the right number of responses (2 Pet 3:9).

And growth? It matters. He is the one who causes it (1 Cor 3:7). Faithfulness matters, but so does fruitfulness. It is all part of the mission: "This is to my Father's glory, that you bear much fruit, showing yourselves to be my disciples" (John 15:8).

God's measurables cannot be appraised with the same precision as in a business. He does not always measure as the world measures (Luke 16:15). Isaiah was given a ministry of unresponsiveness (Isa 6:9–11), and few listened to Jeremiah, but these prophets were successful. Success is sometimes measured by loss (see John 6:66). God has his own ways of measuring success.

Tactics Need to Be Reviewed

There will be a day of reckoning (2 Cor 5:10). The carrying out of the strategy and the employment of the tactics will one day be subject to review. It won't be up to us to measure. Human courts and personal evaluations will not be enough (1 Cor 4:1–5). The one who evaluates is God. He will bring out into the open things seen and unseen.

The parable of the talents tells us that God is serious regarding his investments. Leaders will have to give an account for people's souls (Heb 13:17). We will have to give an account for our own souls (Rom 14:12). This should prompt us to fear God, assess and reassess our tactics, and be about pressing forward (2 Cor 5:11; 2 Tim 4:7–8).

Accountability spurs execution.

Bringing the Voices Together

I find myself going back to a business writer – yes, a business writer – who writes to nonprofits. Addressing the church, this is his first line: "We must reject the idea – well-intentioned, but dead wrong – that the primary path to greatness in the social sectors is to become 'more like a business.'"[39] It's not business practices we should necessarily aspire to emulate; it's something much bigger. He goes on to describe what all great organizations have in common: discipline. "A culture of discipline is not a principle of business; it is a principle of greatness."[40]

I am convinced that what we have discussed in these last two chapters is all about discipline. Ordered leaders are missional, visionary, strategic and tactical. They reflect God and his ways. Those who experience the greatest success bring all of their missional thinking, visionary dreams and strategic plans to him. They know that implementation is ultimately up to him (Prov 16:1–3, 9).

Tactics and strategy, as it turns out, have nothing to do with whether one is from the West or the East, or is secular or religious. On every page, the Bible endorses and mandates that leaders be disciplined and intentional – be they admirals or coaches. If we are not, our leadership will become ineffectual and irrelevant. We will not make a difference, something we talk about next.

---

39. Collins, *Good to Great and the Social Sectors*, 1.
40. Collins, 1.

Part III

Sustaining Global Leadership for Twenty-First-Century Ministry

"If you take big paces, you leave big spaces."
Burmese proverb

9

Make a Difference

People fight over lots of things. In Delaware, Maryland, people fight over license plate numbers! There has been a decades-long obsession over tags with few digits. A low number signifies one of two things: deep roots or deep pockets. It tells everyone how "Delaware" you are. People bid, wait in line, and even pay close to a million dollars to have a tag with a single digit.[1]

We all have our loyalties – things we fight over or fight against. One of these is change. Some will do everything to keep things as they are.

To resist change amounts to resisting leaders. Leadership is, by nature, transformational. Hopefully, we have established this. True leaders are fundamentally restless. They relish change. They want to make a difference, as well as sustain their leadership. They see what is before them and ask, "Should this continue?" "Is there a better way?" "Are we settling for less?" "Is this an opportunity to modify and grow?" They carry within them a mandate to take a group of people from where they are to where they need to be. Studying leadership tells us this.

The Voices We Hear

Leadership Equals Change

Successful organizations look for change agents. Kouzes and Posner, and other writers on leadership, concur. "Leadership is inextricably connected with the process of innovation, of bringing new ideas, methods, or solutions into use."[2] Bringing change, real change, is what leaders do. Burns, in his book *Leadership*,

---

1. Calvert, "Pimp Your Ride."
2. Kouzes and Posner, *Leadership Challenge*, 165.

237

adds, "The ultimate test of practical leadership is the realization of intended, real change that meets people's enduring needs."[3]

Think about your leadership journey. Most likely, change has been a joint traveler. If a leader has determined to be missional, visionary, strategic and tactical, then predictability has gone out the window. Substantive alterations have moved in. There might even have been a revolution! Dreaming, strategizing and implementing can turn institutions upside down. Chaos may ensue, but this is OK. Chaos is the source of energy and momentum.[4]

Change Equals Tension

Most followers are of two minds when it comes to change. On the one hand, they hunger for new ideas and new directions. We are, by nature, restless. Sameness gets old; routine fatigue sets in.

For two months this summer, I sat at my computer writing this book, sometimes for eight to ten hours a day. I had things down to a routine. I began my day at 5:45 a.m. with a kayak paddle up the Pend Oreille River. It clears my head. Every morning I set out upriver, hugging the west side, then paddling left at the same cluster of trees.

One morning, something in me said to change it up. Go downriver and paddle along the east side. Suddenly it was a new world of sights and sounds. I was more observant. Different birds. Beaver dams. New obstacles. I was suddenly encountering new creatures for the first time. Adventure had replaced humdrum.

Sameness dulls us. Marketers get this. There's a reason "new and improved" or "fresh new taste" is occasionally (and strategically) added to the packaging labels.

When it comes to leadership, it is not enough to have a transactional leader intent on maintaining and managing. People want transformational leaders who will open the windows, change the antiquated landscape and disrupt the business-as-usual environment.

On the other hand, people are unsure they want to pay the cost that comes with change. Change is a mix of gain and loss. Doing something innovative will threaten the way things are. There's a good chance disruption and instability will replace tranquility and stability. Not everyone wants "new and improved."

---

3. Burns, *Leadership*, 460.
4. Bennis, *On Becoming a Leader*, 191.

People set in their ways might end up joining the resistance and miss the next approaching wave.

Charlie Chaplin, a comic film star during the era of silent movies, opposed filmmaking that included sound. In 1931, he predicted that the fad of talking pictures would pass on. Stuck in a passing art form, Chaplin missed the flow of history.

Leaders will confront their share of Charlie Chaplins, and if they are not tenacious for change, their organizations will become the equivalent of silent movies.

How do effective leaders – change agents – navigate through this?

There Is an Art and a Science to Change

Bringing change is a combination of creative imagining and careful analysis. Leaders have to listen to their hearts, their guts, and their intuitions. There are also certain disciplines and analytics to study. One must wrestle with questions of context. What is the history? Is there an ethos of trust? What is the feel? What are the non-negotiables? The negotiables? What comes first? How fast?

My first church was an eighty-year-old institution that had a history of resisting change. Members had become complacent. Absent of strong leadership, the congregation and its structures had gelled and hardened into place. Hanging on to traditions and surviving were the main goals.

Someone had to awaken the primal essence of what the church is. Rigidity had redefined its reason for existence. I learned that it is not easy to rouse a bear out of hibernation. Here I was, a young pastor ready to change the world! This church, however, was so entrenched in institutional order that changing bulletin covers was traumatic.

God had added Change 101 to my postgraduate curriculum. I had to learn the rules. Think of them as the "Twelve Commandments of Change":

First, Respect the Past

Before bringing necessary changes, study the story you have entered. This was one of my early mistakes. I was so interested in moving forward that I did not walk the halls, listen to the congregants and dig into the archives. Every person and every organization has a history, and it needs careful attention. People need to read their ancestors, and organizations need to read their pasts (see chapter 5, "The Skill of Seeing through the Layers").

In their enthusiasm, leaders have a tendency to ignore the past. We are anxious to scrap what's in place and charge into the future. But unless a leader goes back to the original vision, the initial steps of faith and the earliest dreams, and retells them, the leader will always be an outsider. One might charge into the future only to find that no one is following.

Michael Useem tells the story of TIAA-CREF, a huge pension fund created to service teachers. Over time, it had become cemented in outdated practices. Without change, emerging competitors would bury it. New leadership – the kind that would listen before leading – was critical. Clifton Wharton became chairman and chief executive, and he brought the institution back to the forefront. But not before he had listened.

After observing Wharton's intention to look back, Useem advises, "Criticism of the past is essential to see a better future. But honoring the past can be equally important to moving into the future."[5] Listening, acknowledging, celebrating and entering into a community's story go a long way toward establishing credibility. Helping people see that their past represents a story of faith and risk can become the fuel for pursuing change.

Second, Make Sure People Know Why Things Are Changing

Before initiating and implementing new directions, leaders must create a culture for change. They must model change, give pictures of change, then seize every opportunity to make the case for change. This requires deliberate and methodical preparation. One must size up the situation and see reality.

There is the hard work of removing the filters, filters that screen out the things people do not want to see. Leadership involves helping people acknowledge their shortcomings, admit losses and accept the need for change.[6] Like the leader, followers must become convinced that change and its risks are worth it.

They have to see that if they keep doing what they have been doing, they will keep getting what they have been getting.[7] They need to believe a new course will enable them to come closer to fulfilling their mission and vision.

When transformative leaders speak about these things, it must be with a conviction born of deep assessment. They must be able to explain why things cannot – must not – remain the same. Share the depth of your heart in such a way that what has been wrecking you will begin to wreck them. Help people see the benefits.

---

5. Useem, *Leadership Moment*, 171.

6. Tichy, *Leadership Engine*, 28.

7. Herrington, Bonem, and Furr, *Leading Congregational Change*, lx.

People in my first church resisted change. Ironically, many also lamented that the church was no longer reaching the next generation, which included their grandchildren. They weren't connecting the dots. Over time, some began to make the connection. It was worth the cost to have their routines disrupted.

It helps to tell stories of corporations that refused to change, as well as of the rewards they missed. Kodak fell in love with film and refused to market a digital camera. Today it is the shell of what it once was. Sears ignored the emergence of Amazon because Sears was big and successful. It owned the market share and did not believe there were things to learn from some upstart company. It has recently filed Chapter 11 bankruptcy.

Like Chaplin, these companies believed that their present would also be the future. In contrast, successful communities realize that there are moments in history when you have to change dramatically to rise to the next level. Miss the moment, and you start to decline.[8]

Third, Bring Real Change

If you are going to be a change agent, make it more than cosmetic; more than a small adjustment to the equilibrium; more than change for change's sake.

Be imaginative. Own the kind of vision that will change the structures and challenge people to achieve a higher moral purpose. Incrementalism – small changes to small things – is a waste of time. But know this: the call for significant change is risky. Leaders who depart from the established norms to lead groups into new futures will suffer undue attention, pressure, sanctions, and perhaps rejection.[9] Big changes to big things will cost.

Leaders who are true to the call never intend to play it safe. Substantial changes to things of consequence are what matter. Steve Jobs, founder of Apple, was not interested in cleaning out his inbox and calling it a day. He wanted to change the world, so he set out to revolutionize six (yes, six) industries: personal computers, animated movies, music, phones, tablet computing and digital publishing.

How does one explain this? Biographer Walter Isaacson described it as "an anarchic mindset" that refused to go with the flow and determined to imagine worlds not yet in existence.[10] It was not about making money or beating the competition. It was about doing something great. It was about revolutionizing the world.

---

8. Tichy, *Leadership Engine*, 37.
9. Burns, *Leadership*, 416.
10. Isaacson, *Steve Jobs*, 57.

For all of Jobs's personal weaknesses as a leader, his mercurial personality and abusive treatment of people, he got one thing right: he did not waste his time with small changes. He subscribed to the belief that those who are crazy enough to think they can change the world are the ones who do.[11] However, be careful. There is wisdom in beginning with a hurdle you can leap – and then move to the seemingly impossible.[12]

Fourth, Involve People through Change

Max De Pree notes that the quality of our relationships is the key to establishing a positive ethos for change.[13] Take the necessary time to know those you lead. Hear their hearts. Know where they are.

Behavioral research says people are at different stages relative to change:

- *Pre-contemplation:* they are unaware of the benefits of change. They underestimate the potential and have no intention of changing.
- *Contemplation:* they are ambivalent, distressed over things that are, but not sure they want to pay the price of change.
- *Preparation:* they have resolved their ambivalence and are both open to and ready for change.
- *Action:* they are motivated to make the effort to change and take the measurable steps.
- *Maintaining:* they are sustaining changes and stepping into the next ones.

Different stages require different leadership approaches, from encouraging to instructing, to exhorting, to involving. As you must include your followers through the mission, vision, strategic and tactical process, involve them in the outworking of change. Enter the undiscovered together.

How does a leader get people to venture into the unknown realms of change? By making the terrain familiar and desirable. Take people into their imaginations.[14] Urge them, especially at the first stage, to envision what it would be like if there was a surge of growth and a surplus of resources. Help them visualize people lining up to get into the community's story, the organization's vision.

Single out key influencers, those with disproportionate power due to their connections or their ability to persuade and explain change. Engage one person

---

11. Isaacson, 329.
12. Godin, *This Is Marketing*, 26.
13. De Pree, *Leadership Jazz*, 142.
14. Tichy, *Leadership Engine*, 174.

at a time, working systematically to create coalitions. Without them, change stalls and carnage grows.[15]

Involve if you hope the work will evolve.

Fifth, Create a Sense of Urgency

Successful organizations – be they governmental, religious or corporate – have a propensity to become satisfied, even smug. We have already illustrated this. Over time, we have a tendency to relax our grip. To coast. To rely on traditional practices. To lose all sense of time.

It's the role of leaders to sound the alarm and convey a sense of necessity for change. Something internal must say, "Now!" Atrophy occurs at the highest point. Once on the downward slide, a moment may come when the gravitational pull is impossible to correct.

John Kotter, an expert in business leadership, writes: "By far, the biggest mistake people make when trying to change organizations is to plunge ahead without establishing a high sense of urgency."[16] Changes of any magnitude will not occur until leaders point out reality, make people aware of the need for change, warn of the dangers of living in denial and call out the complacency. This has to be ongoing.

Do you sense the urgency? More than ever, almost every culture is in open, roiling and uncharted waters. People are losing their fixed points. Here's an example. Twenty-five percent of those living in American culture say they have no formal religion today. That's eighty million people! Philosophies at many universities have degenerated into relativism and nihilism; literary study has devolved into political correctness; and faith is viewed more and more as misguided myth.

It has become a fight over nothing less than who has the power to define reality.[17] Anti-religious elements are accumulating mass and creating momentum. On the rise is an increasingly systematic, zealous, secularist faith that views Christianity as a competitor to be vanquished, rather than as an alternative set of beliefs to be tolerated in an open society.

Meanwhile, too many churches do not sense the urgency. The church wrestles with decisions regarding the selection of music, the color of the carpet, or the best place to plant a community garden. It can sometimes feel like we are arranging chairs on the deck of the *Titanic*. There has to be change. We

---

15. Kotter, *Leading Change*, 66.

16. Kotter, 4.

17. Paul, "Culture War as Class War."

need leaders who can see that our relevance to society is slipping away. Who will sound the alarm and tell the church the world has changed for the worse because we didn't change at all?[18]

Leaders, whether they are in the corporate, religious or political world, have a high calling to awaken, point out the dangers just below the surface and call people to their stations. How does it make any sense to waste the time?

Sixth, Anticipate Resistance

There are numerous reasons for pushback. Change is discomforting for some. It amounts to disruption. Change is splashing cold water on one's complacency. Asking questions like "Why do we do this?," setting more effective procedures in place, and changing routines unsettle most people. Raising the possibility of a new future by asking "What if?" and "Why not?" can be unnerving. People will have to give up comfortable habits, and this is hard. We love familiarity and predictable patterns.

New ideas take time to cach on. Seth Godin, who runs TheMarketingSeminar. com, writes: "The best ideas aren't instantly embraced. Even the ice cream sundae and the stoplight took years to catch on. That's because the best ideas require significant change. They fly in the face of the status quo, and inertia is a powerful force."[19]

Change can signal a change of power and a loss of influence. Some will push back. Talk in the hallways might lead to subtle acts of subversion (avoiding interaction; holding back contributions). It might even lead to open warfare (calling for one's head). The greater the change, the greater the refusal to go along with it.

George Leonard writes, "Resistance is proportionate to the size and speed of the change, not to whether the change is a favorable or unfavorable one."[20]

People resist because change can stir up fears. Transformational leadership brings both possible opportunity and potential loss.[21] We are leaving the known and moving into the unpredictable; going from the security of the harbor to the unsettling high seas. Things once stable are becoming unstable. Things are now different. Disequilibrium, novelty, loss of control, surprise and risk can be scary. Fear brings its own emotions.

---

18. McManus, *An Unstoppable Force*, 28.
19. Godin, *This Is Marketing*, xii.
20. Quoted in James Clear's blogpost "The Paradox of Behavior Change."
21. Biehl, *Increasing Your Leadership Confidence*, 46.

Colin Powell, a blunt four-star general who served under four American presidents, found that changing things up will "piss people off."[22]

Seventh, Handle Resistance with Wisdom

It does no good to demonize opponents, take resistance personally, or simply ignore it and hope the pushback will go away. Listen and learn. Drill down to understand why some oppose change. Listen to their fears and anxieties.

Leaders need to give some room for apprehension and disbelief. There may be a history of stillborn change. A former leader called for change, believing he or she was summoned to transform the world. But halfway into the promised land, this person bolted for another opportunity, leaving people in the desert, worn out with unfulfilled vision statements and overwhelmed with debts.

Know the history you are getting into.

Part of wisdom is discerning the capacity of people to change. The room may need a major remodel, but people can get no further than a rearrangement of the furniture. It may be a matter of timing. It's important to know when to wait, how far to go, at what time to persuade, and at what point to draw a line in the sand and ask, "Are you in, or not?"

Some, ready to resist, might sign on if they know you empathize. You have entered into their pain. Admit that change can be uncomfortable, even for leaders. As Maxwell reminds us, if change doesn't feel a little weird, it's not really change.

Wisdom is also the ability to see the whole. Change tends to have a ripple effect. Modification in one area can have a major effect in another. Leonard Sweet writes, "You don't have to make big waves to make change. Small waves are potential tsunamis. Small inputs can have massive consequences."[23] Leaders with understanding anticipate what change in one area will mean for another, and how this might create resistance, even from unexpected quarters.

Some people may never come around. All of the explanations and all of the invitations to come on board have not calmed the waters. Patience and compassion have not moved hearts. There is a time when it is prudent to ask resistors to leave. Their presence may begin to steal away your best energies and discourage those ready to move forward. This will be hard. It will require the greatest wisdom.

I regret my youthful impatience that overran people's fears and dismissed the significance of cherished past events. At times, I misunderstood and

---

22. Harari, *Leadership Secrets of Colin Powell*, 20.
23. Sweet, *Aqua Church*, 97.

misinterpreted the refusals to join hands. But I also lament the times I should have said to obstructionists, "Enough! You are keeping the community from moving forward."

Leadership, change and resistance are all joint travelers on the same road. And sometimes you have to give less and less room for defiance.

Little wonder Maxwell refers to change as the ultimate test of leadership.

Eighth, Leave Some Things the Same

Sometimes, in our enthusiasm to change the world, we can carry out a form of scorched-earth policy. Fresh from the latest seminar, we are ready to make radical changes. Convinced that making small changes to small things is a waste of time, and certain that making big changes to big things is what builds the future, we come in with our flamethrowers and scorch anything that smells of yesterday.

Such all-or-nothing attitudes are unconstructive. They alienate.

Organizations sometime use the mantra: "Evolution is better than revolution." Better to begin one's leadership with some small but important upgrades, the sort that have minimal costs. Move some furniture, but leave other pieces in place. It is a leader's wisdom to recognize that people need both stability and change to function at their best.[24]

Navigating through this apparent contradiction requires wisdom. Sometimes leaders step into organizations that have lost their way. There is a need for restorative work. Get back to the mission. Recover the dream. Sometimes leaders need to push people to step into the unknown, attempt things untried and brave the black gulf of the unfamiliar. Neither will be easy, especially the latter. But even here, leave some things the same. Assure people that some things must never change (e.g. an organization's fundamental purpose, its values).

In their article "To Get People to Embrace Change, Emphasize What Will Remain the Same," the authors point out that change may pose a threat to people's subjective sense of continuity of organizational identity.[25] In other words, people may fear that change is destroying their uniqueness. Congregants may wonder if they will still be Baptists. Or still be a church. Presidents who pride themselves on being disruptors of the status quo may cause constituents to wonder if their system of government will survive.

---

24. Ledbetter, Banks, and Greenhalgh, *Reviewing Leadership*, 42.
25. Venus, Stam, and van Knippenberg, "Rresearch."

Wise leaders need to assure followers that, while some things will change, their identity will remain the same. Continuity without change comes with risk, but change without some continuity can be the higher risk.[26] Leave some trees standing.

Ninth, Aim for the 80 Percent

Michael Useem, in his book *The Go Point*, notes that every decision comes down to a go point, "that decisive moment when the essential information has been gathered, the pros and cons are weighed, and the time has come to get off the fence."[27]

At some point, the train of change does have to depart the station of status quo. Our tendency is to wait for everyone to get on board, but it rarely, if ever, happens. If we wait for everyone to buy in to the proposed changes, we may stay parked at the station. Worse, we will discourage and disempower those who are willing to risk and change. We may look back and discover they are switching trains. We may end up saddled with lost dreams and mediocrity.

When is it time to go? In part, when you find yourself repeating the same issues. Get going before windows close that will not reopen. If you have gained consensus, if 80 percent are ready to depart, push forward. On the other hand, maybe you prefer the way of the US Marines. They have a 70 percent rule: "If you have 70 percent of the information, have done 70 percent of the analysis, and feel 70 percent confident – move."[28] Most decisions are two-thirds fact, one-third step into the dark.

But the rules may be different in a collectivistic culture where the train waits until everyone is on board. Leaders have to know their context.

Tenth, Be Wise with Early Success

Change is a continuous, dynamic process. The hope is that the right changes are leading to better results. A can-do attitude toward new challenges may be happening. There has been an uptick when it comes to morale and confidence. Using this wisely, a leader can build a momentum for further changes.

Like climbing a mountain, however, there are moments to stop and enjoy seeing things from a new height. Let people catch their breath and celebrate their achievements. This will only motivate and accelerate more change.

---

26. De Pree, *Leadership Jazz*, 74.
27. Useem, *The Go Point*, 19.
28. Useem, 216.

One must also be careful with the data. Leaders can read too much into early successes. It is easy to assume everyone is on board for the next leg and depart too quickly for the next station. But leaders cannot afford to be naïve. Forces are always at work to get back to some equilibrium. Any quest for change contradicts stabilizing forces in one's life.[29] People might be getting off the train. Wisdom might say to slow down.

Alexander the Great led his army from victory to victory. He unified his people around his vision of conquering and ruling the world. He inspired men to believe they were unbeatable. Alexander, however, was not so wise with early successes. He equipped his army to defeat the known world, but not the unknown. He stopped listening to pushback. Pushing further and further east into uncharted stretches of India, his army finally refused to go any further. Alexander was forced to go home.

As we have underscored, strategic leaders pay attention to capacity. They have to know when to stop – or know when it is time to resound the alarm. John Kotter warns that the sense of urgency leading to early success can also lead to complacency.[30] The leader's job is to build a direction and a foundation for ongoing change, as well as to discern hearts. Sometimes the situation calls for pressing on.

Change agents who are wise with early successes also pay attention to how many chips are in their bank accounts. Most changes amount to withdrawals, and a leader can ill afford to overdraw. Give time for early successes to build a reserve. Migrate change.

Eleventh, Expect Losses

Change is a mixture of addition and subtraction, opportunity and loss. As already noted, some will not change with you. Change inevitably means the loss of some who will resist and then leave. Some will get impatient with the process or upset over a specific decision. With risk comes the potential for mistakes. There's no way a leader can make it perfectly safe to change.[31] Some will not stay to work through the setbacks.

Others who have been proponents of change may not like where the journey has taken them. They assumed a different outcome. Others did not consider the costs, and now they are not willing to pay them.

---

29. Clear, "Paradox of Behavior Change."

30. Kotter, *Sense of Urgency*, 170.

31. Kouzes and Posner, *Leadership Challenge*, 205.

Loss is hard for leaders. We are driven by a desire for things to grow, flourish and stay together. Change is risk.

If you have experienced – or are experiencing – loss, you are not alone. You are, in fact, in good company.

Twelfth, Be Willing to Reconsider

Sometimes the most important change is the change we need to make to change. On second thought, a careful analysis might reveal that this is not the right direction, or the right time. There may be a better strategy that is emerging.

Perhaps these are not the right people. It might all be preparatory for something God has in mind elsewhere. Those we lead need to see that we too are willing to be flexible, responsive and able to change.

Summarizing What We Hear

Following these twelve commandments will not guarantee successful change, but it will go some distance in helping leaders be successful change agents. "Change," as De Pree writes, "is essential to organizational survival. Followers are good at change when leaders are good at managing change."[32]

The Voices We Need to Hear

The rules of change are not consistent across cultures. As noted, those in the West may be fine with a 70 percent rule, while more collective cultures in the South may operate under a 100 percent rule. Unless everyone is on board with change, we wait.

Some cultures are more amenable to change and the uncertainty that comes with it. Leaders who bring change are perceived as innovative and forward thinking. Others are more averse. A high uncertainty-avoidance culture will tend to react to change agents with suspicion. Predictable structures and patterns, order and tradition are what matter.

What about the Middle East?

The Voice of Camille Melki, Executive Director, Heart for Lebanon, Beirut

How does Lebanese society view change? Camille Melki lives in a world constantly in flux. Upheaval might be a better word. Lebanon is a fragile culture.

---

32. De Pree, *Leadership Jazz*, 204.

Civil war and assassinations define its recent history. Lebanon is bursting at the seams with refugees. Because of infighting and civil wars, displaced people groups make up one-third of the population. At the center of the chaos, Camille oversees some of the best relief efforts I have ever witnessed.

Is change welcome? Not so fast.

We spoke recently; here is the interview.

How does someone from Lebanon view change?
While those in the West tend to embrace change as something healthy, as even the ultimate test of practical leadership, most Lebanese would resist such notions. A leader would not want to declare him- or herself an agent of change, not if he or she intends to lead for the long haul.

Why avoid change? Wouldn't the chaos call for change?
Not really. Change exacerbates the chaos, which, given the instability of the Middle East, is something to be avoided. Staying the course is what matters, especially if you want to lead long-term. And leaders in Lebanon tend to hold on to their leadership for life. This is especially true in the church.

While pastors in the United States tend to move every three to four years, Lebanese pastors rarely move at all. It's a sign of respect to allow leaders to remain. It would bring shame on the whole community to release a leader (or suggest a change in leadership), even if that leader was impaired.

What happens when people seek for change?
When people propose changes, such as a change in policy, a change in current practices or a change in leadership, a common response is, "You can do that when I die." Maintaining the status quo is what matters. This is why most people are content to leave things as they are. The cost is too high.

How do people respond to rigid leadership?
Unlike in the West, most followers will actually go along with and support inflexible leaders. People would rather stay with the known than step out into the unknown. In cultures like Lebanon, people fear the unfamiliar and the unidentified.

If they press for change, what follows might be more dangerous. Better to have constancy and the attendant complacency than risk and the ensuing turmoil. This is why many Syrians would rather stay with an Assad, or why some Iraqis miss Saddam Hussein.

Stability may be a good thing, but do people see a downside?
Yes, there is a downside, especially today. Let's take the church. Many of the younger generation are leaving the institution. They feel they have no voice and they see no future. Change seems impossible. To call for any kind of change is to risk dishonoring the present leadership. Better to leave than create trouble.

This will make matters far worse. There already is a gap in the middle. Many in their thirties to fifties have moved to other countries where there is greater stability, leaving thirty-somethings to deal with seventy-somethings, and there is a significant crisis in communication.

Are there exceptions? Are there leaders who are change agents?
Yes, some, but they are few. I believe I am one of them. I prefer change. I pay attention to trends. Because I travel, I am constantly exposed to new ideas. I see a future, and I am committed to reaching the next generation of leaders.

How do you avoid becoming a leader who resists change?
First, through lots of prayer. I must also check my own propensity to become rigid as I get older. If I am not careful, I can follow the models of those who have gone before me, leaders who resisted change. It is also important for me to hold myself accountable to my staff, most of whom are younger.

I don't want "yes-men" or cheerleaders to form some praise section. I want them to tell me what needs to change.

This is not easy. In our culture, where honor is so important, most are afraid to challenge me. They don't want to create any conflict. Still, I invite contradictory voices. Otherwise, there is a temptation to relax. I can soon become set in my ways.

What do you see, looking into the future?
I do fear that a number of younger leaders will follow in the footsteps of past leaders. Unless they find other models, there is a good chance they too will resist change. And this will be unfortunate, because Lebanon needs to be a catalyst for change in the surrounding region.

Lessons from a Lebanese World

For those of us who see ourselves as change agents, Camille's words are worth noting. Cultures like the Arab culture affirm a place for change. They teach us, however, to slow down and build relationships; to establish trust before setting out to discover a vision and a strategy; and to respect the place of stability. There is a strong sense of loyalty to family and cultural heritage, and this plays into the importance of steadiness. In a world of so much uncertainty, people will gravitate toward relationships and institutions that are predictable.

Any efforts to bring change must also esteem the role of leadership, especially in a patriarchal culture. Recognize the place of honor. Open challenges may derail the possibility of any immediate change. Be more attentive to the nonverbals than to the verbals. This means that any talk of change must begin with listening to the emotions of others, paying attention to others' body language.

Those who pride themselves on being agents of change can become wrapped up in trends, time lines and achievements. Having just read the latest book on urgency, they can run over people. Impressed with goals, performance and the change they will bring, they can miss that being is more important than doing.

The Voice We Must Hear

We've looked at change, hearing from multiple voices. How does God view change? Does Scripture reinforce the status quo? Fight for tradition? Can we build an argument for innovation, for a conviction that change is necessary and good? How does theology add to what we already know about change? We need to know. On this theme, many assume to speak for God. Here are several lessons.

Change Requires a Changeless Reference Point

In a world of change, there must be a constant. God is the one invariable. Nothing in his character shifts. Creation is in flux; human beings are like an evening shadow that quickly fades; but God, unlike shifting shadows, does not change (Ps 102:11; Jas 1:17). The heavens and the earth are likened to a garment that wears out, but God remains the same (Ps 102:26–27).

God does not get better or worse. He does not season with age, or decline over the years. "New and Improved" are incompatible with his nature. He does not undergo modifications. He is not in process. He is not different from who he once was. He always is. His name, I AM, tells us this. He is not only changeless himself; his plans do not alter. He never changes his mind (Num 23:19).

Why do we need to know this? Because change has to have some changeless reference point. If God, heaven and eternity were always in a state of flux, everything would always be chaotic. Change would have no meaning. It would only contribute to the mess. It would be like a soccer team constantly changing its strategies to place the ball in a goal that was constantly moving.

No wonder God, in the midst of instability, declares his immutability. Malachi speaks of a day of judgment when God will right the wrong. Out of this God testifies of himself, "I the LORD do not change" (Mal 3:6). In the context of trials, temptations and deceptions, James declares that, unlike the shifting shadows, God does not change (Jas 1:17). In the midst of exhortations against false teachings and marital impurity, the writer of Hebrews states, "Jesus Christ is the same yesterday and today and forever" (Heb 13:8).

The implication is that we as leaders are most effective at bringing change when we can trace the reasons back to God and his purposes. It also encourages us to have a similar constancy; to lead from a solid, changeless foundation. Erratic, impulsive and unstable leaders do not inspire change. Fitful flakes invite resistance.

Change Is the Ongoing Work of God

While it is true that God does not change, he is constantly changing things. Transformation is his work. In his *Confessions*, Augustine asks the question, "Who is God?" and answers, "You are most high . . . steadfast yet elusive, unchanging yourself though you control the change in all things, never new, never old, renewing all things, yet wearing down the proud though they know it not."[33] Change and changelessness work in a necessary tension.

It would be a mistake to assume that an immutable God validates the status quo. He is not some "stick-in-the-mud" Father, a dull and unadventurous Sovereign who resists change. He is the Creator whose first act is to bring change (Gen 1:1–2). He sets out to bring structure to chaos. He creates boundaries and sets in motion physical laws to govern the universe. He changes times and seasons (Dan 2:21).

From beginning to end, Scripture is the narrative of change. In most of its stories, God is summoning leaders to make the world different:

- Noah changes the slide of history.
- Moses changes how people perceive God's standards.
- Joshua changes Israel's boundaries.
- David changes the assumptions about kings.
- Solomon changes the definition of true wisdom.
- Isaiah changes despair to hope.

---

33. Saint Augustine, *Confessions*, 1.4.

- Paul changes exclusion to inclusion.
- Jesus changes everything.

Unlike the religious leaders of his day, Jesus did not come to stiffen things as they are. In his first public statement, Jesus declares that he has come to turn things right-side up. He proclaims release to the captives, restores sight to the blind, sets free the oppressed and proclaims the year of the Lord (Luke 4:18–19). He has come to restore physical health to the sick and spiritual life to the spiritually dead.

Jesus is not interested in preserving the existing state of affairs. He comes as the ultimate disruptor. The Leader of leaders shreds the status quo. "You have heard" is replaced with "But I say." In his Sermon on the Mount, Jesus reveals that his kingdom has radically different standards. He comes to fulfill an unfulfilled law (Matt 5:17); he shifts the emphasis from external to internal (vv. 21–22). In his kingdom, the first are last and the poor are now the rich (Matt 5–7). To save your life, you must lose it (Luke 9:24). Everything has changed.

Everywhere he goes, Christ's message and life defy tradition. He calls out hypocrisy and exposes rigidity (Luke 12:1). To the comfortable, he asks, "Do you think I came to bring peace on earth?" (12:51). To the complacent, he gives these urgent words, "Let the dead bury their own dead, but you go and proclaim the kingdom of God" (9:60). To those hanging on to their sin, Jesus demands an about-face, using the language of repentance.

To institutions bound by traditions, Jesus steps in and overturns tables, disrupting business-as-usual (Luke 19:45). To the rigid, Jesus announces that he is the new wine that bursts apart the old wineskins (Luke 5:35–39). To leaders seeking to be served, Jesus redefines leadership as serving others (Mark 10:45). And after investing three years in his disciples, he instructs his followers to go out and turn the world upside down (John 14:12).

Those who argue for constancy, who resist change of any sort, miss the nature and ways of God.

Change Has One Overarching Purpose

Theology underscores that change is not about us. Leaders bringing change must first ask, "Will this further the reputation of God?" Life is given that we might glorify God in everything we do (1 Cor 10:31). This includes change. Change is not simply about building up our egos, securing our happiness, raising profits, or impressing organizations. We bring change wherever it can better manifest God's greatness, goodness and wisdom.

God's own work of change is ultimately about glory – his and ours. The Spirit acts as a change agent, transforming those who are his from one degree of glory to the next – all for the praise of God (2 Cor 3:18).

Change Must Begin Inside

Leaders can devote their best energies to change and yet miss the most necessary change. If we hope to transform the world, change must begin inside us. Out of our own chaos of change comes the raw material for new creation.[34]

Humility admits that real internal transformation is the work of God. On our own, we are helpless to change an impatient spirit, a self-centered will and a bitter soul. Our internal wiring is a mess (Rom 3:10). We need a spiritual overhaul.

The work of the cross, the power of the resurrection, the present work of divine intercession and the coming of the Spirit make real change possible. Paul underscores this: "Therefore, if anyone is in Christ, the new creation has come. The old has gone, the new is here" (2 Cor 5:17). The principal reason for Christ's coming is so that we might experience change at the deepest depths. The change that matters most to God begins in the heart. Scripture calls it conversion.

The change God intends is ongoing. Our whole journey with God is an experience of change, what Scripture refers to as sanctification. Every leader used of God goes through a life of continual transformation and renewal (2 Cor 4:16). We cannot become what we need to become by remaining who we are. We all have a shadow side to our leadership. Our condition requires the ongoing transformative work of the Spirit (3:18). We must be intentional to give ourselves to his spiritual disciplines, whereby he breaks us down and builds us up (1 Tim 4:7).

Erwin McManus, author of *An Unstoppable Force*, summarizes it well: "When a person becomes a disciple of Jesus Christ, she is not simply accepting a new view of reality; she is not simply accepting new patterns of thinking; she is not simply accepting new habits for living; she is being radically and irreversibly changed."[35]

Out of this drastic work of change, leaders are able to see with disturbing clarity some of their motives for leading, their competitiveness for power, their tendency to manipulate and their desire to be noticed. Only in yielding to these changes can we hope to carry out the rules of change discussed earlier.

---

34. Fleming, *Leadership Wisdom from Unlikely Voices*, 111.
35. McManus, *An Unstoppable Force*, 80.

Bringing the Voices Together

Maintenance is not our mission. A summons to lead is a summons to bring change. Because change is the main work of God, it must be the main work of leaders. Without change, people and institutions . . .

- become rigid and set in their ways (Matt 23:4);
- become bored, setting themselves up for a myriad of temptations (2 Sam 11:1);
- remain as infants, ineffective and worldly (1 Cor 3:1–4);
- settle for small worlds and small lives (1 Sam 14:2).

It is our work to challenge one another to keep changing, beginning internally. We are to be like iron sharpening and changing iron (Prov 27:17). We are to exhort one another to enter a daily regimen of growth, exercising the spiritual disciplines. It is here that people are grounded in the presence of God at the center of their being.[36] In our practices, and in our encounters with God in the solitude and silence, God develops the heart.

If people are open to personal transformation, they will be more inclined to seek for the transformation of the organization to which they belong. They will hunger to see that it also is on a constant path of renewal, becoming all that God has intended it to become. There will be a shared urgency and tenacity.

Change agents, however, must exercise wisdom in their quest for change. There are rules to follow. Different cultures call for different changes.

William Barclay, in his *Prayers for the Christian Year*, has written a prayer leaders should pray daily for the church – and every other institution:

Protect the church
> From the failure to face new truth;
> From devotion to words and ideas
>> which the passing of the years has rendered unintelligible;
> From all intellectual cowardice
>> and from all mental lethargy and sloth.
Amen.[37]

But be prepared for what change brings

---

36. Barton, *Strengthening the Soul of Your Leadership*, 28.
37. Quoted in Job and Shawchuck, *Guide to Prayer*, 61.

10

Face Your Crucibles and Learn from Them

In his epilogue, biographer Evan Thomas reflects on the darker side of leadership by summing up the life of American President Richard Nixon. Nixon is an unfortunate figure in American history. Few presidents have been so reviled. He had a legion of sworn enemies committed to his end. You could compare the fall of this figure to the dramatic fall of a tragic hero in an ancient myth.

Nixon ran on five national tickets and won four. Behind his outward charm and his sentimental and generous spirit was a nasty side – one angry, vindictive, ill-tempered and mean-spirited. He was a storm of warring conflicts, and his enemies helped develop and deepen them.

To his detractors, he was "Tricky Dick," the deceiver, the malign faker. He was snubbed and slighted, scorned by the East Coast elite, the press, Wall Street, universities and the "Georgetown set." All were out to get him. Over time, Nixon became obsessed with them. After one painful defeat, Nixon growled, "You don't have Nixon to kick around anymore."

Like so many leaders, this man found himself in a titanic struggle between hope and fear. Ironically, though he was a public figure, time and relentless attacks made him a "lonely everyman." Events so overwhelmed Nixon he was on the verge of vanishing. Eventually, he did.[1]

---

1. A summary of the epilogue to Thomas, *Being Nixon*, loc. 9600–9668.

The Voices We Hear

Nixon is not unique. Those in leadership will eventually face some form of alienation, as well as conflict and attacks, and maybe even sabotage.[2] Chances are you are well acquainted with leadership's loneliness. There will be detractors and derailers. Setbacks and heartbreaks, difficulties and losses, mistakes and defeats are part of the landscape. Bennis refers to these as crucibles, "intense, transformational experiences."[3] One soon realizes that leadership is not for the timid, the placid and the weak of mind. *It's not for those who cannot take the heat.*

I also know something of this pain. There are days when the stress causes me to walk around with shoulders up to my ears. I look down to find that my shins are bruised and my knees are skinned. As De Pree notes, the leaders are the ones who typically are voted off the island.[4]

Sometimes I have been voted off. It comes with the territory. There are other ways to say this. Everyone has his or her own wall to climb.[5] Nelson Mandela, reflecting on his own arduous years, stated, "Every great leader must cross the desert."

The Reasons for Struggles

What is behind the scars most leaders eventually wear? Why are interpersonal conflicts and struggles an inevitable part of the leadership process? There are a number of reasons. Here are four, beginning with what we covered in the previous chapter:

Leaders Bring Change

Most organizations are comprised of four groups: radicals (innovators who start things); progressives (those who like risk and change); conservatives (those who prefer the status quo and reassurance); and traditionalists (those who prefer to hold on to the past). Leaders typically connect with the first two and fight with the last two.

Leaders arrive on the scene and begin rearranging things. Like new homeowners who repaint the walls and change the landscape, leaders start altering things. They modify procedures, reorganize staff and restructure

---

2. Clinton, *Making of a Leader*, 162.

3. Bennis and Thomas, *Geeks and Geezers*, 4.

4. De Pree, *Leadership Jazz*, 139.

5. Bennis and Thomas, *Geeks and Geezers*, 92.

systems. They confront and upend the status quo. Turbulence and tension are bound to arise.

Noel Tichy, a business consultant who has worked with a number of major corporations, notes that leaders are often hated and despised for this very reason. They take risks and show edge.[6] In times of crisis, they can be decisive straight-shooters, unafraid to tackle problems. This threatens people.

Mistakes, defeats, failures: these are bound to happen in a change environment. As Kouzes and Posner put it, "None of these are dirty words to leaders. Rather, they are signs that you are doing something tough, exacting, and out of the ordinary."[7] And sometimes costly.

Leaders Are Visible

When leaders are thrust into a prominent position, they are scrutinized, idolized and eventually criticized. It's natural. There is an instinctive rebellion against those in positions of authority. Leaders are those at the front of the pack. They stand out in a crowd and position themselves on the stage. They state their opinions and make public their positions on controversial subjects. Their victories and their failures, especially in an age of social media, are in full view – even before the morning news is printed.

For leaders, it can sometimes feel like open season, with no off-season. Over time, jealousy and envy collide with submission and respect. Visibility is exacerbated by the fact that leadership is confrontational by nature. Leadership is a serious meddling in people's lives.[8] There is a reciprocal engaging of two wills – one leading, the other following (often resisting).

As Garry Wills puts it, leadership is always a struggle, often a feud.[9] Leaders sometimes take people where they do not want to go. Why should people have to follow their lead? Why is it necessary to do another person's will? Why should people immolate their own needs and desires to the vision of some superior being?[10] A high profile has its price.

6. Tichy, *Leadership Engine*, 158.
7. Kouzes and Posner, *Truth about Leadership*, 102.
8. De Pree, *Leadership Jazz*, 7.
9. Wills, *Certain Trumpets*, 11.
10. Wills, 12.

Leaders and Followers Have a Different View of Reality

Leaders hear the anecdotal feel-good stories, but they start looking deeper into the organization. They tinker under the hood and find an engine that is not running to capacity. There are bolts that are loose and filters needing change.

While people might see stability, leaders see a different reality. Things are stuck. There is a mindless routine. For all of his popularity, a staff member is an underperformer. A movement has devolved into institutional inertia. Organization has become more important than organism, and it is clear that what got us here is not getting us there.

Followers may see growth, but they may be looking at different data. Leaders must look at what is actual, creating a sense of urgency that runs head-on into complacency. This begins a growing dis-ease between transformative leaders and stuck-in-the-mud followers. Tensions and disagreements rise. People push back against the "what if?" and "why not?" questions. They are confused and angry and fight back when someone is released.

But this can reverse. The clouds of conflict can also gather because a leader has a view of reality that says everything is fine, when, in reality, things are deteriorating. Followers are noticing what a leader no longer sees: that there is a loss of energy, creativity and vigilance. These creep into an organization when a leader fails to take with seriousness what makes important things go awry.[11] This ties in to the fourth reason.

Leaders Fail to Meet Expectations

People have a myriad of expectations of leaders. They need us to be missional, visionary and strategic. Followers hope we can fix their problems, produce growth and mediate in disputes. They assume we will lead like a CEO, manage like an executive and inspire in ways that radiate waves of energy. Some have idealistic expectations, even to the point of expecting perfection. They are sure we know the way to Shangri-la.

It can be so overwhelming it can make your brain freeze.

Sometimes leadership feels like a setup. This is especially so in politics. We crown the next king or queen, but, discovering they have feet of clay, we begin to criticize and condemn. Some of it is the fault of the leaders. They promise more than they can deliver, knowing that if they don't they will not get the vote. It's only a matter of time before they are vilified by the press and pilloried by their opponents for being . . . human.

---

11. De Pree, *Leadership Jazz*, 34.

Sometimes this confrontation will come with those from whom you least expect it. Those initially behind you, influencers in the organization who shaped the situation so that you might come, turn against you. Over time, they discover that you are not following their script; you have come with your own vision. It turns out you are demonstrating what you assumed everyone wanted: leadership.

What they really wanted was a facilitator to carry out their plans. This can lead to whispers that proliferate into full-blown attacks. Supporters become organizational pyromaniacs. All of this can lead to decreased productivity, increased stress, wasted energy, loss of revenue and ultimately organizational death.[12]

What Are Leaders to Do?

English writer Aldous Huxley once noted, "Experience is not what happens to a man. It is what a man does with what happens to him."[13] So what is one to do with the challenges that happen in life? Ignore them? Hide? Lose heart? Scale back ambitious plans? Go on the attack?

These are critical questions. If disagreements and arguments are handled ineptly or suppressed, unresolved tension can, over time, become very destructive. There will be increased stress, loss of confidence and heightened ineffectiveness. The leadership voices I have followed have taught me the following.

Face Your Challenges

No one likes conflict. Most avoid confrontation, and this is true of leaders. But none of us can hide from dissension and discord for long. Unresolved conflicts do not go away. If we shove them in a dark closet, they grow like poisonous mushrooms.

Effective leaders face their critics and look for solutions.[14] If necessary, they will mine for conflict, and do it directly. To use corporate metaphors, they "get the moose on the table," "acknowledge the elephant in the room" and "look for the thing in the bushes." They look for the problem behind the problem. They probe to discover what is behind the criticism.

---

12. Perkins, *Leading at the Edge*, 99.
13. Quoted in Bennis and Thomas, *Geeks and Geezers*, 94.
14. Bennis and Thomas, 102.

Facing one's challenges requires healthy emotional intelligence. One must be able to read faces. Read the culture. In your probing, ask such questions as, "How do our convictions differ?" "Why do they clash?" Ask yourself, "How did this person arrive at his/her conclusion?" "Do I truly understand?" "Am I seeing this only through my cultural eyes?"

To face the issues requires authenticity. Pretending to understand a person's perspective amounts to "pseudolistening."[15] Part of getting to the real issue involves a commitment to listen deeply. Facing challenges also includes meeting people directly. Circumventing issues by working through well-meaning intermediaries can make things more problematic. A fundamental rule of conflict is to go to the person, or insist that the person come to you. I have saved myself a lot of grief by letting it be known that I do not work through third parties.

Choose Which Battles to Fight

It's one thing to face our battles; it's another to know how much energy to expend. We have only so many fights in us. Healthy leaders know which cause is worth the energy and which cause is not; which one to engage with full force and which one to let go.

Leaders have to determine the true weight of criticisms. Are they coming from the core or the fringe? Is this isolated, or does it represent a movement? Is this critique a passing observation or a scream? A crisis or a concern? Voices have to be heard at their true decibel level.

Motives also have to be discerned. Is the intention to simply attack, or is there an honest desire to make everyone better at what they do? Are the statements petty or substantive? If the criticism comes from people who differ but who are committed to your success, try to build a bridge (rather than ignore or isolate them). This might mean bringing them into your leadership. If it comes from those committed to your failure, it's not worth your time.

If it comes from those who are divisive, intent upon poisoning others and sabotaging the mission, it will require confrontation. Sometimes it is not reforms that are needed but the expulsion of a member. Some represent a presence which will only heighten dissension, lower morale and disrupt the work.

Crises demand a balancing act. Significant energy may be required to douse the flames of conflict, and leaders may not always be the right people to do this. Those on the bridge can be drawn down to fight the fires in the engine

---

15. Muehlhoff, *I Beg to Differ*, 96.

room when they need to remain where they are, guiding the ship. Leaders like to fix things, but this might come at the expense of their leadership role. Infighting can suck the whole organization into the vortex of blame, dread and paralysis.[16] Leaders need to stop and ask which battles to fight and what role they need to play in the midst of conflict.

Keep the Main Thing the Main Thing

Sometimes challenges emerge because we are not keeping our focus, and the focus of those we lead, on the big picture. People can lose sight of what has brought us all together. Losing sight of the mission, no longer dreaming the dream and/or replacing urgency with complacency create greater possibilities for conflict. We begin to minor on the majors and major on the minors. Our interests become the dominating issue. Politics and territoriality take over. Behavioral problems start to prevent people from working together.

Silos, Politics, and Turf Wars describes the infighting that happens in organizations where the thematic goal has been lost.[17] When members rally around the overriding theme, confusion gives way to clarity. What might have been irksome may no longer matter in the bigger picture of things. Differences give way to the larger issue, and are reduced.

Discern the Difference between Healthy and Unhealthy Conflict

Lencioni describes a conflict continuum that moves from artificial harmony to mean-spirited personal attacks. Just to the left of the demarcation line (the ideal conflict point) is the optimal place. This is where constructive ideological conflict happens, and this can be good, even healthy (though this looks different in other cultures).[18]

Healthy arguments invite us to scrutinize and understand the differences. People take one another seriously, showing sensitivity, curiosity, and respect. Unhealthy disagreements, on the other hand, are those that are contentious and disrespectful. There is no interest in understanding the other side, only in arguing for one's position.

What makes confrontation work is trust. "When there is trust, conflict becomes nothing but the pursuit of truth, an attempt to find the best possible answer."[19] Trust takes the air out of insecurity and fear of personal attack. There

---

16. Welch, *Winning*, 148.
17. Lencioni, *Silos, Politics, and Turf Wars*.
18. Lencioni, *Advantage*, 38.
19. Lencioni, *Advantage*, 38.

is a spirited dialogue, one that often leads to the best decisions. Effective leaders set the guidelines and monitor the temperature.

Making efforts at building relationships, unpacking fears, and exposing misassumptions is the work of leaders. Patience and perseverance are the order of the day. An organization's health is not a given; it requires rigid intentionality.

Resist Responding Defensively

When leaders, or the organizations we lead, are criticized, the natural reaction is to become defensive. I know this from experience, and I am guessing you know this. Things can be said that seem so unfair. There is a tendency in people to assume the worst, and our immediate response is to fight back.

When I pastored an international church in the Netherlands, a small faction on the board challenged my leadership. Over the years, they were my constant critics. I loved my work, but there were days when Dutch life felt like a nineteenth-century Russian novel – unhappy and bleak.

On one occasion an elder grumbled, "You are the most autocratic man I know." It leveled me. I had never viewed my leadership in this light. If anything, I had wondered if I needed to be more assertive. The accusation left me feeling angry and defensive. Was this coming from his own insecurity, or was I leading in a manner that was domineering and high-handed? I challenged his assumptions.

Looking back, I wish I had been less protective of my leadership. Attacks require that we resist our natural, self-protective impulses, step back, and assess. Far better to respond to an accusation with words like, "I am not sure this is true, but let me take some time to evaluate myself, my actions, and my motives. Give me space to talk to those who know me best. I owe this to you – as well as to myself. And then let's continue this conversation."

And if it is warranted, admit mistakes. Own your part.

Aim for Resolution

Somehow, we have to look for common ground. Where can we agree? What are our common values? Can we affirm the same outcomes?

To be truly effective, a leader has to focus on what binds rather than what divides. If a leader wants to maintain a stable ethos, he or she must put mutual interest above self-interest. Ultimately, we should work for understanding. Resolving differences can strengthen a leader's effectiveness.

In his summary of leadership lessons, Useem has this closing thought for leaders: "Consistent, unrelenting efforts to hear and reconcile diverse positions, even when rooted in deeply entrenched and immensely powerful interests, are prerequisite to overcoming any conflict and mobilizing the resources that the contending parties are withholding."[20] Only when we come together can the mission and vision become reality.

Learn from the Challenges

Conflicts offer us a chance to grow. They lead us into the unknown where there is much to learn. This is good. If we fix the problem without learning from it, it opens the door for conflict's return.[21] And we stay at our present size – or become smaller. But learning from the challenges, and implementing the needed changes, will make us better leaders.

"Challenge," note Kouzes and Posner, "is the crucible for greatness."[22] We are forced to face and answer tough questions: Who am I? What is this doing to me? What am I becoming? What really matters? Can I adjust? Is there an opportunity here?

Bennis describes crucibles as dividing lines, turning points. Here, successful leaders adapt. How critical is this? Developing an adaptive capacity is "the essential competence of a leader."[23] Leaders must learn to bend and not break; to not give up when the doors slam shut. Brick walls might actually be doors to a new future.[24]

There will be times you will travel this road alone. Colleagues might pull back. Others won't understand. You may find yourself walking in the wilderness with a sense of abandonment. Out of these seasons, you might notice that you are changing. Over time, just as weather shapes mountains, so problems make leaders.[25] You might discover a depth, a patience, and a perseverance that would otherwise be missing.

David Gergen, reflecting on Richard Nixon and his early failures, noted that his banishment from politics was the best thing that happened to him. It prepared Nixon to lead.[26] The barren places may appear to be a path to oblivion, but if seized they can be an opportunity to deepen and broaden – and reflect. Gergen writes, "Gradually, he developed a more sophisticated,

---

20. Useem, *Leadership Moment*, 282.
21. Van Yperen, "Conflict," 250.
22. Kouzes and Posner, *Truth about Leadership*, 93.
23. See Bennis and Thomas, *Geeks and Geezers*, 87–120.
24. Kouzes and Posner, *Truth about Leadership*, 95.
25. Bennis, *On Becoming a Leader*, 146.
26. Gergen, *Eyewitness to Power*, 36.

tempered, longer-range view of world affairs that became the foundation for his presidency."[27]

If we are willing to submit and learn, the dark nights can develop us. They can separate the precious from the worthless, the spurious from the genuine. They can be the tipping points, where identities, values, and visions are thought and rethought.

The extraction of wisdom from the crucible experience is what distinguishes the successful from the broken.[28] If we stay at it, and learn from the challenges, we develop what all great leaders have in common: resilience.

The Voices We Need to Hear

Diverse cultures face challenges in different ways. If we listen to them, we may find that they teach lessons that can make us more successful at dealing with tests and trials. They can fill some of the conscious or unconscious gaps. I learned this while leading a multicultural church and working with a culturally diverse set of leaders. Men like Paul Choi, an up and coming Asian leader, pushes us past our horizons.

The Voice of Paul Kyu-Jin Choi, Pastor to Koreans at Village Church, Portland, Oregon

Facing Challenges in Asian Culture

No one likes confrontation – especially in my culture. There is a morbid antagonism toward conflicts. In a collectivistic culture like ours, Koreans view discord as a misfortune, the evidence of a dangerous crack in the community. The sacrificial silence of a minority for the sake of the majority is what is naturally expected. Agreeing with leaders is regarded as a virtue.

There is a certain beauty in collectivistic culture, for it values harmony and holds leaders with honor. There is also an unrealism. This same culture fails to acknowledge that conflicts are natural, part of having a free will. It fails to realize that challenges and conflicts can be an opportunity for healthier bonding.

In the Korean context, both on the peninsula and within the diaspora communities, the subject of conflict transformation demands attention, especially in the church. In his monograph "Why Did They Leave the Church?,"

---

27. Gergen, 37.
28. Bennis and Thomas, *Geeks and Geezers*, 94.

journalist Sook-Hee Jung concludes that conflicts are a major reason why people decide to no longer be a part of the church.[29] The results of research conducted among middle and high school students in Korean-American churches are also troubling. When asked the question "How many church conflict-schisms have you yourself ever experienced?," 68 percent of the respondents said, "Once"; 30 percent responded, "Twice or more."[30] Hardly any have experienced ongoing harmony.

What does this suggest? Are Koreans, by nature, more belligerent than other cultures? This would be unfair. What studies tell us is that Korean leaders do not handle conflicts effectively.

Tensions Leading to Conflict

What are the factors creating the tensions that lead to conflicts? Here are some:

Autocratic Leadership

Behind our "high power distance" culture is Confucian thought. Confucianism has long been the inner foundation in traditional Korean society, the metanarrative philosophy of life. According to Gallup research, Confucian values affect approximately 70 percent of Koreans worldview, regardless of their religion.[31]

Confucianism encourages an excessive use of authority and power. Leaders use their status and position to demand obedience. Positional power, "God-factor" power, and cultural power are the status-powers given to Korean leaders, especially pastors.[32] In this cultural system, pastor, elder, and deacon function as a power hierarchy. In their worlds, they assume that their decisions are ultimate.

Confucianism views disagreement with leadership as offensive. Harmony is expected, and it often comes from the weak and powerless.[33] There is little room for democratic dialogue and decision-making processes. This has hindered healthy conflict-transformation within Korean churches. To reject an idea is tantamount to rejecting the leader. It is an act that brings shame.

Chemyeon is an indigenous Korean term for a face-saving culture. It means "face to save in order to meet others with a dignified attitude without a sense

29. Jung, *Why Did They Leave the Church?*, 30–33.

30. Park, "Second Generation of Korean Churches Are Coming Back."

31. Kim, *Korean Cross-Cultural Communication*, 18–19.

32. Scazzero, *Emotionally Healthy Leader*, 245–247.

33. Lee, "Caring-Self and Women's Self-Esteem," 345.

of shame."[34] In other words, exterior relationships are more highly valued than one's inner concerns. A fundamental aim of Confucianism is collective welfare and harmony. The way to express honor and respect is to set aside personal interests. It is better to assimilate and pursue in-group benefits.[35]

The behavioral values of the Confucian cultural tradition may have been intended to honor leaders, as well as to honor the harmony of communities. But too many leaders have used the structures without appropriate kindness and benevolent care. It has been more about power and status than respecting one's constituency. This creates its share of challenges. Contemporary transformational leaders need to create a space for honest (but still relationship-honoring) conversations.

Mental and Emotional Stress

One of the great challenges facing leaders is the many stories of trauma. Traumas lead to negative behaviors, and leaders can make the mistake of focusing on people's conduct while missing the deeper story. An unhealthy environment continues because leaders are putting Band-Aids on deep wounds.

One of the traumas many in my culture live with is their immigration experience. This is not unique to Koreans. It affects other immigrant societies, with the degree of tension corresponding to the size of the cultural gap. Hyun Hur, a founding director of ReconciliAsian, finds that immigration is nothing less than a severe mental and emotional distress. It means that one is uprooted like a tree and replanted in new ground.[36] Like transplanted trees going through shock, so transplanted peoples go through their own devastation and disturbance. They need significant attention.

Sang-Kil Kwon identifies six major cultural shocks that immigrants encounter:

1. *Political visibility:* this leads to civil identity confusion;

2. *Economic conflict resolution:* one faces the need to survive economically in a new culture;

3. *Cultural visibility:* there are pressures to learn the new culture and language;

4. *Ethnic identity and awareness:* there is a disconnection from the home culture;

---

34. Choi and Kim, "Chemyeon," 33.
35. Ui-Chol Kim, "Individualism and Collectivism," 26.
36. ReconciliAsian.org, accessed 31 May 2018.

5. *Racism* against ethnic minorities;

6. *Generational conflict:* how will the next generation handle issues of identity?[37]

The greater the cultural gap the immigrant has crossed, the greater the tension. Having crossed to the other side, immigrants are people who live in the in-between. They find themselves between two worlds. It is difficult to describe their cultural characteristics in any definitive manner; instead, they can best be described in dynamic interactions between the home and host cultures.[38] This special context creates a unique situation when it comes to conflicts. Some immigrants will choose the "old" traditional way with regard to conflict resolution. Others in the same cultural group will choose the "new" way, namely, the ways in which the host culture handles conflict resolution.

There are other conflicts due to the subliminal cultural shocks that immigrants undergo. It is possible that these will result in the lowering of their self-esteem. Many already experience low self-esteem, due to the fact that they may have shifted from a professional role to a non-professional one. An Iraqi immigrant who once had a thriving medical practice is now driving a taxi in a host culture. He might seek to recover some dignity and self-esteem, sometimes in all the wrong ways – ways that challenge leadership. Effective leaders start with the deeper issues.

It is always dangerous to approach an issue with cultural presuppositions and prejudices. Leaders in an immigrant society (or in a cross-cultural context) must be aware of the complexity of conflict-resolution styles and the ones which are specific to the cultural group. Conflict-transformational leadership in the Korean immigrant church will not be the same as in the Korean church on the peninsula. Leadership in an immigrant context requires greater cultural sensitivity, the ability to employ complex approaches, an extra willingness to trust, and a greater compassion to embrace the hurts and diversity.

Cultural Shifts

Another leadership tension within Korean culture is ongoing change. Global trends and shifts heighten confrontation and clashes. The emerging cultures challenge traditional values. In particular, they push back against traditional leadership styles, preferring a more egalitarian style of leading.

---

37. Kwon, *Educational Ministry*, 63–66.

38. For further explanation, see Phan, *Christianity with an Asian Face*, 9.

Korea Research Institute for Mission (KRIM) conducted an empirical research on the leadership styles of Korean overseas missionaries. Of seven leadership styles – courage, impartiality, empathy, judgment, enthusiasm, humility, and imagination[39] – the younger generation of Korean leaders valued empathy as the most important virtue of leadership.[40] Of the respondents in their thirties, 40 percent chose empathy as the most important virtue in leadership, whereas only 24.4 percent of those in their forties and 13.5 percent of those in their fifties selected this as being critical.[41]

Younger Koreans value empathy over charisma. They are looking for leaders who will journey with them, leaders who are more egalitarian and democratic. Therefore, conflict-transformational leadership looks different for them than it does in the context of a traditional, older generation.

Summary

In the broader Asian region, including China and Japan, there has been ongoing relational turmoil. Because of prejudice and wars, people hang on to their traumas. Traditions are deep, and people resist change. In such a context, leadership faces many challenges.

Leaders also face a demanding environment. Asians expect much from them, and many of these expectations are unrealistic. Followers place those who lead on a pedestal, setting them up to disappoint. But we tend to hold back from saying anything. Given a leader's status, our culture avoids confrontation. As a result, unhealthy patterns can remain unresolved.

Lessons from an Asian World

As Paul notes, when it comes to conflict, those of us in the West can be direct and confrontational. In contrast, Asians are less aggressive, due in large part to their emphasis on maintaining social harmony. Relationships are everything.

The lesson for us is to moderate our stress on performance and expand our commitment to one another. We need to recognize that it is not only how one says it, and what one says, but also *who* says it. Have we made an effort to become a significant person in someone's life? Are we making the effort to build relational bridges?

---

39. Glanz, *Finding Your Leadership Style.*
40. Moon, "Research on Leadership Styles."
41. Moon.

We may see ourselves as strong and direct, but without some bond, some connection, cultures like those in Asia and Africa will not respect our voices. They will regard our words as rude and offensive. Challenging someone without trust-building will come across as offensive, even humiliating.

Asians respect their leaders. Even in disagreements, they are careful to uphold a leader's dignity and honor. This stands in contrast to contemporary American culture, where people seem to be in a contest to determine who can be most derisive of those in authority. Extending esteem and showing respect seem to be values of another era.

It is true that respectfulness can sometimes be misleading. A follower's demeanor might signal that everything is good. Without hearing the desires for change, leaders can assume there is nothing to adjust. Leaders in a high context culture might become oblivious to the fact that behind the pleasantries are unpleasant feelings. Still, there is something here to learn.

The Voice of Evi Rodemann, Germany

On the other side of the globe is another leader whose leadership also connects with the next generation. Evi Rodemann is a recognized global leader, and her context has taught her much about handling disagreements and discord.

Leadership, Conflict, and Past History

Leaders, and the challenges to leadership, is the story of Europe. I want to speak to this from multiple contexts.

It might be helpful to give a historical context. I live in Europe, a global region of forty-seven nations, twenty-eight of which belong to the European Union at this time. Europe hosts more than 730 million inhabitants. Most nations speak their own language, and almost all are culturally diverse. Even within each nation, we find multiple national and cultural groups.

Over the past decade, the European Union has tried to come up with a definition of European identity (the European Identity Project), but there has been little agreement. We tend to disagree and quarrel. Part of the problem is that Europe is not a continent on its own. It borders Asia, and most nations draw their own lines regarding where Europe lies and Asia begins. This has a lot to do with political circumstances, trade, and friendships. It helps explain why defining identity is difficult. Each entity has had its own thinking on what it means to be European.

I am from Germanic Europe. Our roots go back as far as the eighth century. As with other parts of Europe, conflict has been part of our history. There have been numerous wars between empires. Nations have fought nations. During the past hundred years, there have been two world wars, leaving many scars to this day. After World War II, Europe, as well as Germany, divided into East and West. Walls were built, separating nations and families. Ours has been a legacy of differences ever since.

Leadership, Conflict, and Recent History

During the past seventy years, Europe has experienced relative peace. The most recent regional war happened in the Balkans in the 1990s, but overall Europe has been stable.

With the influx of cultural groups, this is changing. There has been a rise in tensions all across Europe, as countries fight for their own borders and identities. To be a leader today is to face immense challenges. Confrontation is part of the landscape.

Religion and politics have shaped much of how we do leadership. Over the centuries, Protestants, Catholics, and Orthodox have combined with the state to exert power and influence. Much of the leadership style has been autocratic and authoritarian. Leaders and nations have had a long history of seeking to dominate others.

After the last world war, people became less embracive and more cautious of leaders. They became suspicious of boisterous and charismatic types. They kept their guard toward anyone capable of drawing large crowds. More, they became antagonistic and challenged any who wore the label "leader." It created a culture where people even apologized for taking the lead.

In recent years, the image of leadership has changed. It has become a more positive term. People today want to develop their leadership skills and attend leadership conferences. But there are still leadership challenges. People remain resistant to change. We still hold to many of our Germanic values, which include orderliness and straightforwardness. We prefer a leader who is low key, calm, attentive to structures, connects with others, seeks the common good, and listens to the past.

Leaders are still typically male and older in age. Chancellor Merkel is an exception, but her leadership has encouraged more and more women to have a greater leadership voice in culture.

This is true in the church, where women represent the greatest number of attendees. Still, it is harder for women to lead in the church. This is due to long-held theological understandings of the roles of men and women in leadership.

In the broader context, an emerging culture is challenging present leadership. The younger want a greater leadership voice. It is more secular and less bound to the past. Many are disillusioned with church, society, family, and politics. Younger people desire a different style of leadership, one that is more collaborative and less autocratic. They want to see distinctions in status flatten. The hope is for fewer structures and different lives, though this is not clearly defined.

All of this is creating tensions. There is still a strong history of predictability, order, and attention to protocol. Nonetheless, young people see themselves on a drive to see change, and while this is a threat to some, many view these calls for change as something positive.

We see this trend not only in Germany but across Europe. Younger people are taking the lead. This is becoming more evident in the church. Populists across Europe are on the rise. They are tired of old leaders and old systems. Millennials are more interested in being part of a movement. They are less inclined to become members of an organization with its positions and titles. It is more about vision, change, and leaving a legacy.

Leadership, Conflict, and the Church

This emerging shift in culture has forced the church and other institutions to reconsider and redefine the way they approach leadership. The church may be behind the curve at present, but not so long ago the church was on the edge of change. Behind the tearing down of the wall separating East and West were people who prayed. The younger generation, at great risk, marched in the streets.

This emboldened the older generation. It became an intergenerational faith project. People became more involved politically. They began to demonstrate, and the numbers grew. The church came out and took a stand for freedom. People of faith were willing to pay the price.

That was then. Forces, more internal, have challenged the church. Division always crouches at the door. The church today needs to recover its vibrancy and its leadership, and overcome its own conflicts. Faith needs to once again capture the imagination of a younger generation. It needs to help others see that, like communism, secularism is not the answer – not for the challenges that are emerging.

During the past three years, Europe (and the church) has faced a new crisis. There has been an extraordinary influx of refugees. This has led to many economic, national, political, and relational challenges – and conflict. A divided Europe has reacted in different ways. Germany has taken in more than one million refugees. Political and religious leadership has responded out of concern for basic human rights.

This has been an opportunity for churches once again to lead. Many have sought to help integrate, assist with legal procedures, and host people. For others, this crisis has been an unwelcome risk. Not everyone has been united in a common approach. But many refugees have found an open door in various churches. Some churches have doubled in size. Others that were dying are coming back to life, and there has been a new collaboration between churches. Still, it has created its own infighting. Assertive leadership can lead to this.

Leadership, Conflict, and Its Lessons

What have we learned from this brief history? Leadership and conflict seem to go together, regardless of the culture, regardless of whether the context is secular or religious. Great movements require great leaders, and where there has been such leadership, challenges emerge. And this is particularly true in a cultural ethos like that of Germany.

We may appear to other cultures to be abrupt, even abrasive and rude. We criticize and question our leaders. But other cultures must understand that it is inbred in a Germanic culture to discuss and debate. We are not afraid of conflict. We are competitive, so we sometimes debate for the sake of debating. Our teachers teach us to be reflective and discerning. We are trained to get to the root of things. We are not threatened if someone asks, "Why?" We instinctively want to dig deeper and challenge the context. Simply accepting things as they are is not acceptable.

It is obvious that we also like to go by the rules. We are decisive, and we tend to follow through with whatever is decided. We respect the past. If there is a call for change, one must marshal sound arguments. Otherwise, leaders must prepare to be challenged. If we see mistakes, we will confront them directly and openly. We will not tolerate them. We come from a guilt-oriented culture, one where people readily take the blame. Conflict is often part of our strategy to achieve something better. We do not seek conflicts, but neither do we avoid them. We address them with directness, and sometimes with force.

Lessons from a West European World

Evi's voice does not depart significantly from other Western voices. Still, there are things to learn. In conflict, there is value in being expressive. A Germanic culture would encourage leaders to be even more explicit and direct: don't be afraid to point out mistakes; let everyone have a voice, even if it is critical. These expressions do not necessarily connote dishonor.

There is a place for honor and respect, but these are not automatic: they should be earned. Leaders need to show that they deserve trust and a following. Just because they have been appointed does not mean that people should follow.

In cultures where there is a greater distance between followers and leaders, there is something to be said for deference and honor. We can learn from them. But from a European viewpoint – Germany in particular – such followers can appear to be passive and compliant, obedient to whatever is said from the top.

Because Germany is a less collective culture, where individualism is valued, personal goals and rights matter. It is OK to question authority. Its being an achievement-oriented culture means that relationships are important, but so is performance. Getting things done is valued. There is something fulfilling about seeing plans succeed. If necessary, people will be replaced by others to accomplish the goals. Objectives will not be sacrificed just to make sure that egos are pleased.

Summarizing Both Voices

How we successfully respond to challenges is not uniform across cultures. Each culture has its own imperatives. A culture governed by shame/honor (which is the predominant culture type) will find it more important to save face, avoid any direct confrontation that might cause embarrassment, and preserve the social harmony. In this case, acceptable communication will be more subtle, nonverbal, implied, intuitive, and indirect.[42]

On the other hand, a culture governed by a lower power distance will be more inclined to confront and question. Communication is more direct. Two personal illustrations come to mind.

Some years ago, in my role as Lead Pastor over a large staff, I confronted a former Korean pastor. He served on my staff and he was underperforming. Staff meetings can be a time for review, of looking at our progress and calling out those who are not meeting expectations. I called him out for failing to meet his goals. It was nothing personal; I really liked him as a person, but there were responsibilities he needed to address.

After speaking to his performance publicly, he shut down. A paralysis took hold. He could not look at any of us. He took my criticism as a personal attack. He felt shame. Looking back, I realize how culturally insensitive – actually obtuse – I was.

---

42. Webber, "Reflections," 9.

While I am bringing up my cultural missteps, I will mention a relationship I had with a German scientist in another church. It was clear that he did not agree with the direction in which I was taking the organization. Out of a desire to build some cohesion, I decided to visit him at his home. He was cordial and invited me in. After some pleasantries, I expressed my desire for a good relationship.

He proceeded to question some of my leadership decisions. It was nonstop. He spoke with passion, while I chose to remain silent and receive his criticisms. After some thirty minutes, the conversation ended. He shook my hand and politely saw me to the door.

I was confused – and devastated. He was kind, but painfully blunt. I took much of this as a personal attack, as a rebuff of my leadership. It felt as if he had little respect for my role and had little interest in building any friendship. But as I have grown in my understanding of global differences, I can see now that I misread him. He was simply wanting to be sure we did things in an appropriate manner. I am certain our relationship would have deepened had I understood this.

Conflict goes with the territory, and it is amplified in organizations that are multicultural. There will be misunderstandings and inevitable hurts. High context and low context, direct and indirect: it will not be easy. Some will not tell you what you need to hear; some will tell you more than you ever wanted to hear. Effective leaders listen to the verbal and nonverbal. They adapt and adjust to how they should confront or not confront, engage in conflict and resolve conflict. They listen to other cultures.

The Voice We Must Hear

If there is any manual on conflict and leadership, it is Scripture. The biblical narrative affirms that difficulties shadow leaders. Can you think of a leader in Scripture who did not face his or her crucibles? I can't.

Nothing has changed over the centuries. After his twenty-nine years as a pastor in Maryland, author Eugene Peterson spoke to his own challenges with a congregation he birthed: "I've never been anything but disappointed: everyone turns out to be biblical through and through: murmurers, complainers, the faithless, the inconstant, those plagued with doubt and riddled with sin, boring moralizers, glamorous secularizers . . . defeating all my utopian fantasies."[43]

---

43. Peterson, *Leap over a Wall*, 101.

The Reasons for Leadership Challenges

On the surface, it appears that leaders and followers in Scripture struggled for all of the same reasons noted earlier in this chapter.

People Struggle with Change

When God summoned leaders to interrupt the status quo (which would mean all leaders), the people often pushed back. They argued, quarreled, and fought. The aggression was sometimes overt (Neh 4:1–3) and many times covert (Mark 3:6; John 6:66).

People Struggle with Those Out in Front

God called Moses to step out of the shadows and be a voice for God. The people responded with complaints and pushback, hoping to cut Moses down to size. They cried out, "Isn't it enough that you have brought us up out of a land flowing with milk and honey to kill us in the wilderness? And now you also want to lord it over us . . . No we will not come!" (Num 16:13–14). Nehemiah was thrust into a visible role of leadership, and he was immediately mocked and despised (Neh 2:19).

The prophets were also prominent voices. They stood at the gates and on the ramparts and declared truth. Jeremiah was God's prophetic leader, called to speak to a nation. He was a leader of leaders. God literally set him *over* the nations to shatter and form worlds by his speech. He gave Jeremiah the authority to uproot, tear down, destroy, and replant (Jer 1:8–10). This required that Jeremiah hear, receive, and speak whatever God told him, and that he would have to live with the consequences.

Such a visible role invited rebellion, attack, and eventual arrest. This was the common lot of prophets (cf. Elijah, Elisha, Hanani). In Jeremiah's case, the people resisted to such a degree that he cursed the day he was born (20:14). He wanted out.

Scripture teaches that God will not put up with our hesitancies. He will overrule our protests, for he has an overriding and tenacious commitment to his own purposes.

Paul emerged to lead the church. He was the most visible apostle, and he was tested, threatened, and stoned. His letters reveal an early church often resistant to his leadership (see 2 Cor 11–12). As his influence grew, so did the potential for infighting (Acts 15:1–5; Gal 2:11).

People Struggle with Different Realities

Leaders challenge followers, and followers challenge leaders. They see the world differently from each other. Gideon clashed with different tribes because they had different views of what was actual (Judg 8:1–3). Jeremiah likened Israel and their lusts to a donkey in heat, but in Israel's eyes, they were innocent and pure (Jer 2:23–24).

What mattered for the religious of Jesus's day was the keeping of the law; Jesus saw a more important reality: the condition of one's heart (Matt 23:25–26). Peter argued with Jesus over his intentions to go to the cross. Peter saw the cross as an obstacle; Jesus saw it as his mission (Matt 16:21–23).

Paul and Barnabas argued over the reliability of John Mark. Paul saw John Mark as a failure, a coward disqualified to minister; Barnabas viewed John Mark as a man to be mentored and given a second chance. The conflict separated these two men from doing future ministry together (Acts 15:36–41).

People Struggle with Failed Leadership Expectations

Most leaders in the biblical narrative failed to measure up to people's expectations. In the eyes of many, Moses fell short. They didn't approve of his personal choices (Num 12:1); they questioned his call (12:2); they did not like the course he was taking them on (14:1–4); and they were quite sure that they could do the job of leading just as well (16:1–3).

Samuel failed to meet the hopes of Israel, so they begged for a different kind of leader (1 Sam 8:4–5). Kings, however, failed to live up to the hopes of the populace (13:13; 14:29). Shimei heaped abuse upon David for his failures (2 Sam 16:5), and much of Israel turned against Rehoboam for his refusal to live up to their needs (1 Kgs 12:16).

Even with the emergence of the Messiah, people turned away and no longer followed. Jesus did not meet their expectations of the King of kings (John 6:28–66).

When we listen to the voice of theology, we hear deeper tones. Behind conflicts, clashes, and challenges are deeper reasons why leaders face struggles.

All of Us Have an Internal Tendency to Fight

James raises the question, "What causes fights and quarrels among you?" (Jas 4:1). What is behind our acrimonious speech, our condescending words, our ungodly treatment, and our abuse of one another? What gives rise to the corporate friction, the church fights? Is it different philosophies, races, or leadership approaches? James exposes the deeper truth: "Don't they come from your desires that battle within you? You desire but do not have, so you kill" (Jas 4:1–2).

There is a self-centeredness that wants its own way. It is entrenched in all of us, the result of a sinful nature that runs like a fault line from Adam to us. Sin not only crouches at our door; it has taken up residence in our hearts (Gen 4:7; Rom 7:20). We are all under sin and its power (Rom 3:9; 7:23). It goes to the bone and all of the way to the heart.[44] Even our good acts are tainted (Isa 64:6).

Those who look deep inside themselves know this to be true. It corrupts our capacity to follow and our ability to lead. All of us have an innate propensity to break the law, trespass boundaries, rebel against authority, love self, and twist things.

The point here is that sin is the fundamental explanation for the breakdown in relationships between leaders and followers. This is not to say that all conflict is sin, but conflict is often the result of sin.[45] Left to itself, sin turns leaders into treasonous tyrants and followers into hardened rebels. When we yield to its power, sin suppresses any willingness on the part of leaders to serve, and any desire on the part of followers to follow.

When Adam and Eve sinned, the first thing they did was cover up. The second thing they did was engage in blame (Gen 3:7–12). Hiding and hurling have continued to be our mode of behavior ever since.[46] History is the story of humanity concealing and withholding, clashing and going to war. Twisted passions lead to coveting, conniving, and killing. As one writer put it, "To be alive means to be in conflict. People fight."[47]

Miriam and Aaron did not like the woman Moses married (Num 12:1). But the problem went deeper. Envy and jealousy, the fruits of sin, prompted them to grumble, "Has the LORD spoken only through Moses?" they asked. "Hasn't he also spoken through us?" (Num 12:2). Assessing the nature of humanity and the leadership experiences of Moses, Barton concludes that criticism of a leader is so predictable that it should be viewed as part and parcel of the leadership process itself.[48]

The same heart condition caused Saul to grow suspicious of David's growing status, the adulation of the population, and the evident favor of God (1 Sam 18:6–9). This also explains the rebellious behavior of Joseph's brothers,

---

44. Bird, *Evangelical Theology*, 675.

45. Van Yperen, "Conflict," 240.

46. See Howard, *Trauma of Transparency*.

47. Ortberg, *Everybody's Normal*, 130.

48. Barton, *Strengthening the Soul of Leadership*, 140.

the difficulties David faced with his sons, and the challenges Solomon faced near the end of his leadership.

The apostle Paul was summoned to lead the early church, but sin-driven upstarts sought to increase their status at Paul's expense (Phil 1:17). Envy is part of our wiring. It runs from Genesis to Revelation.

All of Us Are Assailed by Forces We Cannot See

Theology tells us that there is more than human nature at work; there is a full-blown cosmic conflict dedicated to creating turmoil in God's creation. We face a triad that gang up to do damage. They team up to break down and destroy our leadership and to separate friendships. They unite to keep us from making God's intentions in the world more luminous and God's reputation more lustrous.[49]

The first member is our sinful self. Every day is a battle with a self-centered disposition and an ego that clamor for control (Jas 4:1–3). The second member of the triad is the world and its pull to enamor us with its idols (4:4; 1 John 2:15–17). It too admits of no breathing time, no armistice, and no truce. In addition, leaders are in a fight with a third enemy, the devil and his forces of darkness (Eph 6:10–20). The adversary goes to and fro to devour and ruin souls, lure us away from finding our satisfaction with God, hem us in with his darkness, and alienate us from God's kingdom (1 Pet 5:8). This triad's best strategies are invisible and covert.

Hence, leaders – especially godly leaders – will face argumentative team members and disagreeable followers. It will at times feel like hell. Lovelace writes, "All who attempt for a single day to lead a life centered on God and His kingdom will discover they have a battle on their hands."[50] As long as institutions are made up of people, and as long as we are attempting great things for God, there will be mistakes, controversies, misunderstandings, and blow-ups; active and passive aggression – all the stuff of sleepless nights and churning pits.

Little wonder Jesus's leadership was challenged at every turn. His sanity was questioned by his own family; and religious leaders clashed with Jesus whenever their paths crossed (see Mark 3:21; John 5:18). In his closing words in the Upper Room, Jesus told his disciples that they too would suffer in this world (John 16:33). There would be antagonists who would resist their leadership and do harm (2 Tim 4:14). Attempting to provide the leadership that carries

---

49. Plantinga, *Not the Way It's Supposed to Be*, 37.

50. Lovelace, *Renewal as a Way of Life*, 65.

out God's mission and vision will stir up opposition. Detractors will deface, despoil, and destroy.[51]

What Are Leaders to Do?

Theology both affirms and adds to what has been heard.

Face Our Challenges

This side of heaven, everything is a fight. The good news is that it is a *good* fight (1 Tim 1:18; 6:12). The role of leadership is to keep perspective. Don't lose sight of the big picture. The ploy of the enemy is to preoccupy the leader with the small picture.[52] If we are not careful, we can become impressed with the power of this triad.

It is a fight that is good because, as J. I. Packer noted, "it is fought under the best of generals. The Leader and Commander of all believers is our Divine Saviour, the Lord Jesus Christ."[53] It is fought with the best help. None of us face our challenges on our own. We have the indwelling Spirit. We fight holding on to the best promises (e.g. "the one who is in you is greater than the one who is in the world," 1 John 4:4; "I can do all this through him who gives me strength," Phil 4:13).

God does not put up with fearful leaders who run from their challenges. He will not coddle us. Like he did with Jeremiah, he will call us to man up and run with the horses (Jer 12:5). He will expose us to this reality: "If you falter in a time of trouble, how small is your strength!" (Prov 24:10).

In one of my dark nights of the soul, I came close to capitulating. Giving up. Wimping out. Leaving the ministry. Darkness and depression did everything to get their claws into me. I will never forget the gloom that came over me. On that rainy night, all alone in my church office, God would have nothing to do with a spirit of defeat. He reminded me that he had never promised that leadership would be easy. He assured me of his power. That was enough.

Own Whatever Is Our Part

God calls us to be ruthlessly honest with ourselves. His Word acts as a mirror, and it exposes all of our blemishes (Jas 1:25). In the midst of conflict, God will show us the condition of our souls (if we let him). If we do the hard work of

---

51. Plantinga, 164.

52. Van Yperen, "Conflict," 243.

53. Packer, *Faithfulness and Holiness*, 167.

listening, he will reveal areas in which we may have contributed to the quarrel. He will lead us to ask, "Am I part of the problem?" "Have I played a role in this?" We all have our blind spots. Our first responsibility is to get rid of any logs before we can take out any specks (Luke 6:42).

Avoid Demonizing Our Opponents

Theology is our guide, but we can turn it into a weapon. We can use God-language to prove our position and assert our authority. "God told me" can be some of our more harmful language. We do this when we are certain God is on our side. Maybe he is. More likely, though, we have become so certain of our position and so full of ourselves that we give little space for differences of opinion. Worse, we turn these differences into something deeper, even sinister. We treat the issue as a wrestling match pitting evil against good, the will of vice versus the will of God. People become adversarial threats rather than colleagues who see things in a different way. This is not to minimize real threats, but my experience is that all too often we use this language to manipulate and shut off meaningful discourse.

Aim for Reconciliation

Reconciliation has to be our principal aim. This, before God, is our chief responsibility. If we don't aim for this, unresolved conflict has the potential to destroy relationships and organizations.

If we want to be functional, we must do this hard but necessary work. Dysfunctional strategies do the opposite. They include ignoring the existence of the conflict; developing a false compromise that gives the appearance of resolution; putting off conflict until we have marshaled more resources for a future fight; and making the other person suffer by making it about winning/losing.

Part of the good fight is fighting for the relationship. We must pursue peace, even with our enemies (Matt 5:43–47). Those leaders who do this are the true sons of God (5:9). Reconciliation and restoration are always the goal (5:23–26).

Paul tells us that reconciliation is the work God has given us to do (2 Cor 5:18). And it is work – some of our hardest work! Something in us wants to hang on to resentment. We don't easily let go of bitterness. But we must. We are to love without hypocrisy (Rom 12:10). We are to aim to be of the same mind (2 Cor 13:11; Eph 4:3). In a world of animosity, we are to be leaders who are known for our forbearance, gentleness, and generosity (1 Tim 6:11). The writer of Hebrews gives the same admonition: "Make every effort to live in peace with everyone" (Heb 12:14).

Learn from the Challenges

When we face rejection and unrelenting opposition, the pain can numb us. We can choose to withdraw, retreat, and close others out. Worse, over time we can grow a demanding spirit. We can find ourselves asking God to justify the pain he is putting us through. We can be like Job who announced, "I desire to speak to the Almighty and argue my case" (Job 13:1–28). This tension, these disputes, can be so unfair! But God is at work.

Conflict has a way of exposing our true selves. We become aware of our own character, our strengths and weaknesses.[54] It is often in our conflicts that God is doing his best work: forging us to be stronger leaders; smoothing the rough edges, the immaturities of youth, the impatience that needs to learn patience, and the arrogance that needs to learn humility.

The book of Proverbs affirms this repeatedly. Just as the refining pot purifies silver and the furnace refines the gold, so leadership struggles test us (Prov 17:3). It is out of the fire that a leader becomes usable (25:4). From the sparks, we become sharpened for the task (27:17). But it is more: God is shaping us to become more like him.

Bringing the Voices Together

There is so much to learn from all of these voices. What is certain is that leadership will come with its challenges. No one disputes this. The words of Leonard Sweet come back to mind: "Leadership is a high seas environment."[55]

The encouragement here is that none of us are alone. Criticism and conflict can cause us to feel painfully by ourselves. We begin to believe something is wrong with us. Maybe – probably – it is. But it is part of the calling. We are either leaving trouble, presently in deep trouble, or just about to enter into trouble. Our feet will be put to the fire.

As much as I hate conflict, pain, difficulties, and leadership challenges, I do love what they do in my life – if I let God use them to shape me . . . and, possibly, move me.

---

54. Clinton, *Making of a Leader*, 163.
55. Leonard Sweet, *Aqua Church*, 94.

11

Know When It's Time

Endings are not easy for most of us. American filmmaker Woody Allen once lamented, "I don't want to achieve immortality through my work. I want to achieve it through not dying."[1] Endings come with a sense of apprehension, as well as feelings of loss, anger, fear, depression, and confusion. It's hard to admit we have only so much shelf life. With each passing day, I feel this more deeply.

Whatever way endings come, they are inevitable. Every leadership post is transitory. Every leader is an interim leader.

Given this reality, perceptive leaders pay attention to time. They prepare for their departure. It might come because of the natural process of aging and dying; it might have everything to do with a new opportunity; it might be the result of a change of heart and needed redirection; it might happen because visions, strategies, change, and challenges have led to pushback; and it might come through underperformance and the need for termination.

No matter the cause, the aim behind every transition should be the same: to prepare, and then to exit the stage with grace and wisdom and favor.

The Voices We Hear

There is much to gain from looking at biographies and books on leadership. Those who are successful prepare for their succession earlier rather than later. Richard Vansel of the Harvard Business School states: "The process of managing the succession, handing over the baton of power, is one that begins soon after the CEO is named."[2] It's not a preoccupation, but neither is it ignored. After all, it's not changes that will do you in; it's the transitions.[3] A careful leader

---

1. Quoted in Bennis and Biederman, *Still Surprised*, 210.
2. Cited in Erickson, "Transition in Leadership," 299.
3. Bridges and Bridges, *Managing Transitions*, 3.

begins to think about a potential successor to mentor, as well as a plan that enables the organization to succeed without him or her.

Those who lead with a long view think this way. But most don't. Many leaders do not prepare for their departure, even late into their leadership. Succession becomes an event, when it should be a process. At times, this can be a disaster, both for the leader and for the organization. Alexander the Great astonished the world by conquering great empires. For a season, he was indispensable to his men. His conquests reached from Greece to the western border of India. But he had no succession plan. He did not mentor an heir to be king of Macedonia. When Alexander died in Babylon, his empire dissolved into a number of factious groups.

As I think about it, there have not been many successful personal transitions that are models worthy of emulation. Here's what I discovered after a quick perusal of biographies on my bookshelf:

- Abraham Lincoln was murdered at the height of his leadership and at a crucial moment when he was fixed upon healing the nation.
- Theodore Roosevelt died restless and frantic, unable to let go of the hope that he would once again grasp the reigns of leadership.
- Franklin Roosevelt died while leading the nation into a postwar world and preparing the nation for peace.
- Winston Churchill's leadership was eventually rejected, and his last recorded words were, "I am bored with it all."
- General Douglas MacArthur left a legacy that elicited respect, but little warmth. He was eventually dismissed from his command.
- Lyndon Johnson knew the nation no longer had confidence in his leadership, so he withdrew and died a bitter man.
- Richard Nixon was impeached in the end, and he died obsessed with his enemies and powerless to confront his weaknesses.

It's just a brief survey, but one sees a pattern. Most leaders find it difficult to let go. Most are too consumed with leading to mentor a successor.

What makes for a good transition? Most leadership books include the following:

Make Your Present Leadership Count

Before you begin something new, you have to end well. In Maxwell's twenty-first law of leadership, he notes that success is not measured by the size of your next post but by the health of what you are leaving behind.[4] It doesn't matter how impressive the next chapter is if the previous one has been left in disarray. There is wisdom in avoiding transitions until you can see you have done your best to leave the organization fit and confident in its future.

A leader contemplating change makes sure his or her followers can answer the following questions in the affirmative:

- Has the leader stayed true to the mission?
- Has the leader lived out his or her core values?
- Has the leader led the work to dream a new dream and move forward into the next phase of its development?
- Have present strategies been effectively executed?
- Has the leader finished what he or she set out to do?
- Are people confident they can move forward without this leader's presence?
- Has the leader created a leadership ethos?
- Has the leader poured him- or herself into a future successor?
- Has the leader crafted a good transition plan?
- Will the leader be remembered, not for what he or she did for him- or herself, but for what he or she did for others?[5]

An organization will need to be well prepared in the present, for successions are often hard on the community. Momentum can slow, fears may take hold, and the mission and vision can lose a certain clarity. A drawn-out process can drain energy and deplete morale.[6] People will become restless, and some may leave.

Solid leaders build organizations that can endure and weather these storms. Leaders owe this to them.

Know When It Is Time to Leave

Everything has a season. Organizations tend to have a life cycle, moving from dreaming, to launching, to organizing, to going strong, to institutionalizing, to entrenching, and to dying.

---

4. Maxwell, *21 Irrefutable Laws of Leadership*, 224.
5. This last question comes from the initial words of Kouzes and Posner, *Leader's Legacy*, 10.
6. Erickson, "Transition in Leadership," 298.

Leaders also have a life cycle. Smart leaders come to terms with this. They know that right endings represent the only way to protect the continuity into something bigger.[7]

Timing is everything. Depart too soon, and you will leave a work that is not completed. Stay too long, and your accomplishments may no longer matter. Leaders have to take long walks and ask the hard questions: Is it time to go deeper and take the organization to the next level? Is it time to retire or reposition? Is it becoming apparent that I can still reinvent myself, but it will not be here?

Transitions are more art than science. If it is time to move on, it is better that the leader be the first one to know. Leave while it is in your power to make the decision. Pass the baton while you are still able to run in full stride.

By God's grace, I retired from being a lead pastor before almost anyone else knew. When I announced my decision, I told the people that, when it came to transitions, I wanted to be the first to know. It's far better than being the last to find out!

But how does one know if the timing is premature or if it is the perfect moment? Here are some questions that serve as a needed checklist for a leader:

Have You Completed Your Mission?

It may be that you have stepped back, surveyed your work, and thought through your priorities. You have led well. You guided the organization into missional clarity. You brought everyone into the next chapter and witnessed the fulfillment of a vision. The institution finally understands what it means to be strategic and tactical, and this is how it operates. It's time for someone else to lead things forward from here.

Have You Run out of Energy?

Maybe you have lost the passion. Do you wake up and want to go back to sleep? Do the days drag? Are you going through the motions? Do you find yourself saying, "If I don't leave this place, I will die sooner than I have to"?[8]

Vitality is a precious commodity; it is the currency of leadership. Leadership coach Dave Fleming writes, "The true power of energy is unleashed when we pay attention – consistent attention – to it. It comes when we steward it

---

7. Bridges and Bridges, *Managing Transitions*, 41.
8. Barbara Brown Taylor describes her journey in her "memoir of faith," *Leaving Church*.

with intention and care. Great leaders know this either by instinct or through experience."[9]

There do come moments in any journey when we are at an energy loss. These can be episodic. You just need a cup of coffee, or a weekend away. But there is a kind of fatigue that Red Bull, Zipfizz, and DynaPep – as well as an occasional change of scenery – do not change. A weariness of soul hangs on, and on, and on. Your mind begins to coast like a car out of gas.[10]

Some years ago, Bobby Ross, coach of the NFL Detroit Lions, suddenly quit midseason. The team was on pace to make the playoffs, so everyone was shocked by his decision. For Ross, it was easy. He was physically and emotionally worn out. He realized he no longer had the energy, the passion, and the heart for the task of leading. There was nothing more to give.

If you feel this way, it is time.

Has the Organization Grown beyond You?

Has the time come when your unique abilities and experiences can no longer keep pace? Physical strength and mental quickness are running behind, and it is clear you are losing your effectiveness. Are you no longer able to keep up with the times and the trend lines? Maybe you are wired for a certain level, and that level has passed.

It could be something else. The cultural shift demands a different way of doing things, and you realize you did not sign up for this.

Perceptive leaders know when their value is diminishing, their influence is waning, or their willingness to change lies trapped under the weight of unwillingness.

Have You Grown beyond the Organization?

This is a fair question. Maybe you have experienced a season of powerful transformation. You have grown, and your passion to hold a tiger by the tail isn't going to be realized in your present context. The work feels like a governor, restricting the speed at which you are capable of moving.

Your organization may be in the "entrenchment" phase, and you feel stuck in the slow lane. Hopes of renewal are on hold, for people are unwilling to let go of their old ways.

It's no longer a good match. Move while you can!

---

9. Fleming, *Leadership Wisdom from Unlikely Voices*, 79.
10. Taylor, *Leaving Church*, 4.

Have You Lost the Support?

Has the leadership board lost confidence in your leadership? Are they no longer willing to cover your back?

Maybe you find yourself increasingly at odds with your staff. Or maybe you sense a loss of respect amongst your peers. Are they no longer embracing your leadership? Are they increasingly questioning your decisions? You may find increasing pushback at staff meetings. Plans are obstructed, and leading people forward has become a battle. American President Franklin Roosevelt once said, "It's a terrible thing to look over your shoulder when you are trying to lead – and find no one there."[11]

This could be the moment for a frank and open conversation; a time to sit down with those who will be honest and level with you. Leaders tend to judge their own leadership differently from others. Blind spots develop, and if we are not careful, we will only listen to our sycophants.

Is the Counsel of Those Closest to You Affirming the Decision to Move On?

Gaining the wisdom of others is vitally important. They must, however, be the right voices. Among them should be your spouse, your mentor, trusted colleagues and close confidants, your own internal sense, and God.

It works the other way as well. As much as you might be ready to move, these same voices might be saying "no." This has happened to me twice. Shrewd leaders take seriously the collective will of those they love and trust.

Is It Time to Pass the Baton to Those You Have Shaped?

Maybe it is time to give the organization the benefit of new blood. Is age speaking? To use Bennis's words, has there been the erosion of physical grace signaling that it is time?[12] Are you reckoning with your mortal fallibility? Are those you have led creating their own leadership? There comes a time to move aside and let emerging leaders have their day.

Likely, someone did this for you.

Has a New Opportunity Come Your Way?

This question requires careful discernment. We can read too much into open doors (and closed ones). Just as a crisis does not signal a time to leave, so another opportunity does not necessarily mean it is time to move.

---

11. Bridges and Bridges, *Managing Transitions*, 3.
12. Bennis and Biederman, *Still Surprised*, 200.

There may come a time, however, when you wake up and realize that things have changed. Something is stirring inside. It might be a growing restlessness, an unexpected discontent. At the same time, there is an unexpected inquiry, and the reasons for going far outweigh the reasons for staying. A dream is suddenly emerging. There is a growing sense that the work here is done.

Time to move.

Prepare the Organization to Succeed after You Have Left

Wherever you are at, there will come a time to leave. Wise leaders plan early on. They think beyond themselves; they invest in the future leadership. They must: future leaders represent the organization's leadership engine. Giving one's energies to this is the ultimate test of a leader.[13] Consultant Noel Tichy writes, "Institutions and movements succeed over the long term not because of their cultures, or their manufacturing competencies, or their use of modern management tools, but because they continually regenerate leadership at all levels."[14]

Existing leaders look for emerging leaders who are gifted and who have demonstrated leadership abilities. They give attention to those who reflect the essential values and skills of competent leaders.

Surveying those they lead, leaders look for those who are hungry, inquisitive, passionate, imaginative, and teachable. To these, leaders impart their lives, their ideas, their values, and their vision every chance they get. Gradually, leadership responsibilities – those that were once reserved for the leader – are delegated.

All of this requires an unselfishness spirit, a willingness to focus on someone other than oneself. There must be an interest in discovering the potential in others, a patience to tolerate mistakes, and a willingness to model what you require in others. Leaders must set expectations, be advocates for those they mentor, and have the grace and humility to pass on the baton.

Finish Well

"How we leave is how we will be remembered."[15] These words come from a leader who noted that people remember, with admiration and appreciation,

---

13. Tichy, *Leadership Engine*, 3.
14. Tichy, 43.
15. Hybels, *Leadership Axioms*, 214.

those who have been faithful to their calling to the end. He was a world-class leader who ran a great race. Unfortunately, he did not finish well. Misbehaviors led to his untimely resignation. He, like so many, forfeited a good legacy.

Leaders who transition successfully press hard right up to the end. They are careful to ensure that their early achievements don't lead them into pride. When leaders become full of themselves, they relax their guard. They ease their pace. Such leaders begin to make misjudgments, assume they are above the rules, and fall short of the finish line.

Those who make successful transitions stay the course, and when they come to the line and hand off, they do so running, hoping that those who follow are able to run in full stride.[16]

In my high school and early college days, I joined a group of harriers. It's another term for cross-country runners. Our coach was a disciplinarian. Every week he established a set of regimens that we carried out. It was not uncommon to run over 100 miles each week. There were good, and not so good, contests. I will not forget one of the not so good ones.

Our team was competing against our archrival, and for the first time I was running varsity. Though I felt ready, I wasn't. From the start, the pace was swift, and I decided I would stay with those at the front of the pack. I began well. A quarter of a mile out, I discovered I could not sustain the speed of the run. I had not properly paced myself, and it was the one race I finished dead last.

The lesson was clear: it's not how you start the race that counts, but how you finish – and if you finish. And the same is true in leading: it's not how your leadership endeavor begins, but how you close.

Step Aside with Integrity

One of the main rules of transition is to let go.[17] When it is time to leave, walk away and disconnect quickly. Let the board, staff, and members of the organization build a relationship with the next leader.

This is hard for both followers and leaders. Leaving amounts to a surrender of power and position. There is the real fear of leaving a certain stature, of plunging into "the abyss of insignificance."[18] Reflecting on Churchill and his transition, Roberts writes: "Winston Churchill stayed on in office too long. As with so many of his predecessors, he was too easily convinced by arguments

---

16. Vanderbloemen and Bird, *Next*, loc. 677.
17. Bridges and Bridges, *Managing Transitions*, 9.
18. Sonnenfeld, *Hero's Farewell*, 3.

about his own indispensability, despite the fact that they were being made by progressively fewer and fewer people."[19]

Some years ago, Jeffrey Sonnenfeld looked at the succession process in American culture. After five years of research, and interviews with fifty prominent retired CEOs, he found four patterns of departure that characterize four distinct executive types:[20]

Monarchs

Like aging athletes who won't give up, monarchs are the leaders most attached to their roles, believing they are not yet finished. Monarchs believe that no one can replace them. Some have a firm conviction that they have been chosen by God and are answerable only to God. If they leave, they leave bitter.

Sometimes these leaders do not resign until they are forcibly extracted. They often cling to their position until the last day they breathe, fearing that outside of their leadership role, they have no life. An inflated ego might have convinced them that they are indispensable and irreplaceable.

Some leaders hang on until there is nothing else. George Eastman, founder of Eastman Kodak, ran the organization for fifty-two years, and saw value in nothing beyond his position. He retired and left a suicide note that simply said, "My work is done, why wait?"

Generals

Like the monarch, a general's identity is intertwined with the trappings of office. These leaders love their stature and power. They gravitate to the stage and work to be the center of attention.

Unlike monarchs, they yield and leave office, even if it is with some reluctance. They choose a strong (but no one is as strong as they are) successor, and then they begin to plot a comeback. During the organizational turmoil that often ensues, they enjoy being the returning savior.

Ambassadors

While they might also have a strong affinity for their role, ambassadors see a life beyond their task. Their identity is not attached to the position.

These are leaders content with their accomplishments. They mentor strong successors, believing ministry can succeed without them. They do not believe the myth that they are indispensable. They step aside gracefully and remain

19. Roberts, *Hitler and Churchill*, loc. 3428.
20. Sonnenfeld, *Hero's Farewell*, 81–215.

as trusted confidants. They do not try to sabotage their successors. They have no real aspiration to return.

Governors

Governors also have little attachment to the office. These leaders serve a limited term of office, achieve their goals, and accept succession. They do not necessarily mentor a future successor. They break ties with the organization and leave willingly to pursue new interests.

These last two models describe leaders who determine, from the start, that there is life beyond their careers. They intend to keep evolving. Who knows what the next chapter holds? Life is too short to stay in one thing. They might experience some sadness for the past, but they seize new opportunities and make a new future. They have the sense to realize that someone once stepped aside for them, and now it is time to do the same.

The Voices We Need to Hear

Transitions can look very different depending upon the culture. Some leaders will hold on to their leadership positions to the end. In Bangladesh society, to take one example, the model is "leader for life." Leaders remain in place until they die, which often leaves a leadership vacuum. This is also true in other Asian cultures, where leaving means losing relationships, letting go of power, authority, and prestige, and losing face.[21] And face can be more important than life itself. Younger leaders end up bumping into rigid ceilings and must wait.

The following contribution from an African leader and interview with a Lebanese leader represent the larger global voices we need to hear. Julius Twongyeirwe has given his life to training pastors to be more effective leaders in Africa. Elie Haddad leads a flourishing seminary, equipping future leaders to serve in both the Middle East and North Africa.

The Voice of Julius D. Twongyeirwe, Leader of Proclamation Task, Kampala, Uganda

I am writing on leadership transition from an African perspective. The aim is to provide an understanding of the complexities and challenges of leadership change, taking into account the social, community, and institutional

---

21. Thura, "Losing My Face to Find My Soul," 16.

expectations. Specific examples will come from Uganda, in the region of East Africa, the place where I live.

The Traditional Identity of a Leader

Before looking at leadership and transition, it is important to understand how we have historically defined a leader in African culture.

Traditionally, leaders have played many roles. These include a custodial role, caring for the resources and working for the social development of their people. They have acted as judges, working to resolve disputes. They have been guardians of the traditional heritage, which includes norms, values, and principles. Leaders have also played a priestly role. They interpret and intervene in the spirit world, helping communities overcome misfortune. They mediate between the people and the higher spiritual powers, powers that are responsible for human affairs in connection with blessings and curses.

Identity is essential in African leadership. Identity includes one's status, one's possessions, and one's achievements – intended or accomplished. This means that, in our male-dominated, hierarchical culture, one's acquisition of leadership has much to do with who one is and one's heredity or ancestral origination (as opposed to a democratic vote). Thus in a typical transition, the son takes over leadership once his father dies. This occurs at the highest levels of leadership. This means that a single family can rule for decades.

For example, with President Gnassingbé's reelection, his family has run Togo for over 89 percent of its fifty-eight-year post-independence history. Gabon has a similar experience: a father and son have led for over 86 percent of the country's post-independence history. The son is still in power.

In the DRC, President Joseph Kabila came to power in 2001. This followed the untimely assassination of his father. Altogether, the Kabilas have ruled the DRC for a third of the country's post-independence history – over twenty years. The Rangoolam family of Mauritius has similarly ruled the country for over half of its independence history, for twenty out of thirty-nine years.

It has also been part of our culture to place leaders on lofty pedestals, viewing them as having multiple roles – king, priest, and warrior. These continue to occupy our contemporary imaginations in regard to their socio-spiritual redemptive role. More than political and religious, leaders are seen as saviors. They are king-fathers and queen-mothers. They have their councils and secret societies, their rituals and ceremonies. Leaders are elevated to the highest status, and as noted, a successor must meet the right hereditary requirements of approved or acceptable origination.

Wealth is a visible sign of status as a leader. A leader's possessions (culturally seen as his worth) affirm him as one with power, as one worthy to lead. In Uganda, possessions and power are indivisible in the leadership dynamic. What a man owns defines who he is. Hence, leaders give energy to acquiring and amassing possessions in order to prove their worth as guardians. They seek to impress with both their wealth and their achievements. The entire leadership dynamic is the platform for the leader's personal yearnings, dreams, and ambitions, tied to the need to be acknowledged and recognized as worthwhile.

Given a leader's stature, there is the expectation that followers will honor and obey. Just as the people in the Old Testament declared to Joshua, "Everything you have commanded us we will do, and everywhere you send us we will go" (Josh 1:16), many in Africa make similar vows to their leaders. It is expected that those who follow will express loyalty and appreciation. This serves to guard communal harmony and collective wellness.

Followers not only express devotion; they idealize their leaders because they need an ideal leader. A leader is a type of messiah. He must be magnetic and charismatic. Followers need leaders who can step into a room and sway people with their charm. They want leaders who carry themselves like triumphant warriors who ably defend their tribes. Followers want to see their leaders being assertive and self-confident – even aggressive.

What explains this? The harsh realities that come with diversity, resource sharing, and the general survival of the language and cultural expressions of each tribe require this. A domineering leader is preferable, for he brings assurance to those he leads. Whether through words or actions, leaders must be bold and fearless – especially when bargaining or confronting.

Having a compelling leader means there will be peace, prosperity, and security. Little wonder that tribesmen seek one of their relatives to lead. This will assure them of certain privileges in their glorious moment in power. If a leadership transition does not favor them, they must anticipate reprisals and punishment.

It is no surprise that transition is characterized by conflict. It is about fighting to win. There is less negotiation and fair competition, as in a democratic election process. Passive leaders are among the least respected and least desirable in our culture. They are perceived as weak and liable to submission in the face of challenges that will put a community or its values and heritage at risk.

The Shift to Colonialism and Post-Colonialism

During the colonial era, these traditional leadership assumptions were forced to adjust to a European value system (based upon a Judeo-Christian ethic) and political system (largely democratic). This had a profound impact, for existing leadership structures were flattened. Some of the first democratically elected leaders, such as Patrice Lumumba and Kwame Nkrumah, were nationalistic and charismatic leaders.

Leadership came to mean more than power; it meant loyal service to their nations and their continent. They had the trust of their countrymen as a backdrop against colonial rule. They were embraced as emancipatory leaders. Other leaders kept or took their positions of leadership as granted by the colonial powers who preferred them, and served their nations as the extension of colonial hands. Through them, former colonial powers have been exercising control over young African nations to this day.

Many of the previous roles of leadership have now been entrusted to local and state officials. Still, in various communities, the relationship between local authority and traditional authority remains complicated and can be confrontational. The institutions of traditional leaders in many African countries have persevered and resisted invalidation.

Leadership and Transition in Today's Africa

In many parts of Africa, leadership remains complex. Communities suffer from poor leadership models. This is at the root of many of the problems that plague African societies. Traditional roles of leadership remain in many parts, and these have defined the transition process. Reforming leadership has been delayed, and this has been to the detriment of society. It has created gloom for upcoming generations.

There are a number of reasons for this delay. First, leadership change is hard for the community, one brought up to show respect, loyalty, honor, homage, and fear toward leaders. Followers have historically rewarded their leaders with longevity in office. This has helped to preserve a collective feeling of worthiness and value.

It is against the norm for Africans to criticize or call for change, even if leaders are no longer effective due to age or incapacitation. It would be dishonorable and shameful to dislodge a leader. African culture is hesitant to confront leaders when they hold on to power too long. It is more important to protect the leader from shame, even if he maintains his leadership beyond its usefulness and does not pass his leadership role to the next generation.

A second reason why transitional reform has been delayed goes back to the leaders themselves. Leaders take advantage of a community's tendency to keep things as they are. They revise constitutions to indefinitely extend or strike off term limits. Leaders end up reigning as monarchical potentates and warlords. Given their near godlike status, leaders eventually assume that they are immortal. They feed off a collective opinion that sees them as indispensable and irreplaceable.

Leaders are disinclined to let go of leadership, in which their identity and worth are so entrenched, even when they have clearly outlived their usefulness. The thought of losing status, power, or possessions becomes the greatest threat to leaders and the cohort that thrives under the supreme leader. To relinquish power becomes too threatening for such a team.

This explains a leadership culture that gives little attention or effort to mentoring future leaders. Many leaders continue to fail to create the conditions for the evolution of a new generation of leaders with the capacity, integrity, vision, and commitment to take on leadership at all levels in non-threatening social environments.

Africa needs future leaders who have been mentored to honor human dignity, shun dictatorship, tackle conflict head-on, bring reconciliation, and take their stand against corruption. There is a dire need for leadership nurture that promotes the qualities of honesty, thoughtfully embraced loyalty, respect for knowledge, and justified pride in sacrifice as well as achievements and successes through hard work. But this need is not being addressed.

Leadership and Tomorrow

Regardless of how leaders perceive themselves, or how followers view their role, effective leadership transition is critical for a healthy tomorrow. Nothing is more crucial to a community's long-term health and survival than the cultivation of its future leaders and a preparation for the inevitable transition from one leader to another. This is not only vital, but it is also a test of the community's ability to renew itself perpetually.

In our cultural setting, effective transition can only be a reality when leaders begin to think of themselves as they ought to think, so as to have sound judgment (Rom 12:3). In a proper self-assessment, they need to acknowledge their flaws and admit to their vulnerabilities. In humility, they must see themselves as contributors to the wellness of communities rather than messianic originators of tranquility. They must see that those called of God are to give themselves to selfless service. They must determine to pour themselves into younger people for a guaranteed posterity.

Transitions that are planned and well managed will sustain and reinvigorate a community's cherished ideals, values, and productivity. When mismanaged, however, leadership transitions will continue to destabilize nations and communities to dislocate their prized tenets and aspirations.

The current generation of African leaders needs eyes that can fully see and comprehend the long-term implications of the local and global changes, the ever-shifting situational demands for leadership, the potential in the citizenry, and the need to adjust for competence to provide sustainable solutions. There is need for a fresh understanding of respect, reverence, and loyalty, and for a revisited description of tribal solidarity, communal responsibility, and clan obligations in order to create an environment that will enable the continuous evolution of succeeding generations of upcoming African leaders.

The Voice of Elie Haddad, President of Arab Baptist Theological Seminary, Beirut, Lebanon

Elie, talk about Lebanese culture and leadership transitions.
Traditionally, succession planning is not in the minds of most leaders, be they in the church or outside of the church. Local cultural norms and worldviews tend to infiltrate and impact churches, so leaders in both contexts typically lead for life.

Do pastors ever transition to other ministry opportunities?
Typically, this is not the case. The existing ministry would look upon it very negatively.

What happens when a leader grows old and is no longer able to lead the ministry into the future?
Leaders tend to believe they have unquestioned authority, and they often stay until they can no longer physically carry out their duties. It would be a dishonor to insist that a leader retire or leave. Unfortunately, this is creating a fair amount of frustration for an emerging generation.

What typically happens?
Some stay and wait a pastor out, while others leave. In some cases, an emerging leader takes a disgruntled faction and they begin another church. This helps to explain the divisive culture that characterizes much of the ministry.

What else is happening?

As you know, Lebanon is facing a huge humanitarian crisis. And contemporary churches can ill afford to simply maintain the status quo. Churches that are flourishing are reaching out to help the flood of refugees, and this is creating the need to train many leaders to carry out the tasks. Those who are oblivious to the crisis are simply maintaining ministry, while many of their emerging leaders are gravitating toward churches that are stepping out to meet the world's needs.

How is a school like ABTS addressing the problem?

First, we are intentional to correct a misguided ecclesiology. There should not be this clergy–laity divide that characterizes all too many churches. We are equipping future leaders to honor the priesthood of all believers, helping them to discover their gifts, and unleashing them to do ministry (1 Pet 2).

We believe ministry leaders must come back to the Ephesians 4 model, recognizing that they have been called to equip the saints for the work of ministry. Leaders have not been called to do everything while the followers watch. Unfortunately, most pastors are not doing this, and this creates a passive congregation whose future leaders are not mentored.

Second, we are training future leaders to be change agents. We want to see men and women sent out into the world, stepping into their ministries with the aim of influencing change. This will not be easy, especially in cultures that are entrenched and are tribal in orientation.

Why is mentoring so rare?

There are a number of reasons. Some pastors may feel threatened if they develop younger leaders. Some may explain that they are too busy. But in the main, pastors are not mentoring future leaders because they have not been trained to do this.

How does Lebanese culture view nepotism?

A fair number of leaders are in positions because they inherited them. In Lebanon, this can be good or bad; it depends. A future leader should not be disqualified simply because his father or some relative is the existing leader. On the other hand, someone should not receive preferential treatment and be hired simply because of family connections. Nepotism is a neutral term.

How do you view your future transition?

I am already intentional in pouring myself into tomorrow's leaders. God willing, I will eventually hand off the baton to my successor and remain to support and counsel. This, I hope, will serve as a model for future leadership transitions.

Lessons from Other Global Voices

Julius and Elie make it clear that transitions can look very different depending upon the culture you are in. Listening to their voices, as well as those we hear and others we need to hear, I wonder if they serve as stereo speakers, urging us to stand somewhere in the middle.

On one side is the sound of performance and execution.

Recently, I sat down with a leader who was essentially released from his role. It was announced as a resignation, but it was anything but; it was a forced departure. What troubled me was how matter-of-factly it was handled. He had served the community for over three decades, and then he was cast off. Where was the honor?

Those of us in the West tend to place great value on presentation, on keeping up with the trends and protecting the bottom line. Leaders are simply resources to get us there. If we are not careful, however, we can dishonor people and treat them with almost a callous disregard. We could learn from African and Arab cultures that respect roles, honor loyalty, and go to great lengths to protect a person's dignity.

On the other side is faithfulness and lifelong devotion.

This too has a negative potential. Roles, loyalty, and dignity can be used as weapons to keep followers in line. Leaders can assume it is their inherited right to lead, regardless of their gifts, their performance, or their effectiveness. They might eventually spend most of their energies protecting their power rather than mentor the next generation and pass it on. Over time, the community suffers.

There is a place for respect, as well as leadership accountability. Transitions should be the mutual work of leaders and followers, each respecting the needs of the other. If handled well, the baton is passed at full speed to the next runner, who is positioned and on pace.

In relays, the race is not won by those running the fastest, but by those who most effectively pass the baton. Teams can be disqualified by a bad pass. So, too, can leaders.

The Voice We Must Hear

We're again back to God. Back to looking past our immediate and long-range horizons. Back to the centering Word for one last time. It might still seem out of place in a leadership book. Especially in our times.

N. T. Wright captures something of this disconnect in his book *Simply Good News*: "The word *God* is a heavy, clunky little syllable. It drops like a lead weight into otherwise cheerful conversations. It sticks in the throat like a lump of undercooked dumpling. It comes up over the horizon like a sudden cloud, blotting out the sun. The very sound of the word in English (and in German, where the hard *Gott* has the same effect) reflects the way most people in Western culture now think."[22]

And yet, in every leadership chapter, I hope you have become convinced that God and his revelation are far more relevant than we might have assumed. His voice dominates the room and completes the testimony. No one understands leadership more than he. He has his own counsel regarding everything, from definitions to transitions. The Bible is full of stories of leadership change, and the exhortations that come with them. Let's begin with the obvious.

Acknowledge Your Limitations

Life Is Transitory

It can be hard for some leaders to admit, but all leadership is fleeting. Like life, leadership is a wisp of steam, a here-today-gone-tomorrow event. God hits us head-on with this truth. He compares our moments to a flower that emerges but which the wind blows over so that in an instant it is gone (Ps 103:15–16). We are immersed in our audacious endeavors, our strategies and plans, often oblivious to the fact that our days are but a "mere handbreadth" (Ps 39:5), a "mist that appears for a little while and than vanishes," as James describes them (Jas 4:14). Or as Peterson puts it, we're all puffs of air, shadows in a campfire.[23]

From story to story, Scripture is the broad narrative of leaders coming and going. In nearly every biblical story of leadership, the leaders move on. Their experiences reinforce the point that what leadership we have is transitory. Judges replace judges, kings succeed kings, prophets pass the mantle on to prophets, and church leaders raise up church leaders. To assume our leadership is an exception, or that we have all the time in the world, is folly.

Moses is not ready, but God orders him to face up to his limits. He is commanded to take Joshua, "a man in whom is the spirit of leadership," lay hands on him, and give away some of his leadership to him (Num 27:18–20). David hangs on to his kingship until the end. Only on his deathbed does he bless Solomon as the next king (1 Kgs 2:1–3). God appears to Elijah and

---

22. Wright, *Simply Good News*, 126.
23. Peterson, *The Message*, 960.

orders him to place his mantle over the shoulders of Elisha, signifying an investiture, a passing on of authority (2 Kgs 2:9–10). Jesus gathers his disciples and commissions them to carry forward his leadership (John 13–17). God sends Paul to Lystra, where he finds his successor and eventually hands his leadership off to Timothy (1 and 2 Tim).

Despite our sense of self-importance, we come and we go. We hope that what we have accomplished will last, but many of our accomplishments will go the way of sandcastles. Even this metaphor may be too solid and permanent.[24] Solomon describes much of our life and leadership as a chasing after the wind (Eccl 1:14).

This might sound discouraging, but it is actually centering. Knowing that life is short-lived gives us needed perspective.

Leadership Has Its Cycles

Transitions are as predictable as the rising and setting of the sun. The writer of Ecclesiastes observes this cycle and describes it in many of its phases in 4:13–16:

- Phase 1: like the sun coming up, leaders emerge.
- Phase 2: rising, they are accessible, flexible, fiery, and curious.
- Phase 3: after high noon, leaders begin to slow down, become rigid, even obstinate and set in their ways. There is this tendency to hold intractably to the past (v. 13).
- Phase 4: eventually, like the sun passing beyond the haze, they are gone.
- Phase 5: in time, new leaders emerge. They sometimes come out of nowhere. In this sapiential observation, the emerging star is a rags to riches story. He is an overcomer who enjoys his new popularity. He has captured the hearts of the masses and basks in the favorable headlines (v. 14).
- Phase 6: as quickly as the young leader has replaced the "has been," the people have turned to someone else – a fresh new face, someone with a new vision and better promises (v. 15).
- Phase 7: they will eventually turn on him as well (v. 16).

Ecclesiastes invites us to pause and reflect on transitions – on the nature of leadership itself. It is more than age and deterioration that lead to transitions; in this passage, it is clear that pride is a contributor to the rigidity. It comes with power. Leaders can become obsessed with their self-importance. They

---

24. Leithart, *Solomon among the Postmoderns*, 68.

can begin to misuse the authority we grant them. They stop listening to the counsel around them. They stop paying attention to warnings (v. 13). They think they are eternal. Eventually, they forfeit their role.

Followers also play a part. We have a human need to idealize our leaders. We project upon them our hopes, and leaders begin to believe all of this hype. Inevitably, they fall short of what has been projected on to them, and we fickle followers turn on them (v. 15). As quickly as we crown a king, we chase after another (v. 16).

What theology teaches, history affirms. Humanity likes novelty. Churchill was one of England's greatest wartime leaders, wielding more power than any other British prime minister had known. He was a statesman whose name rang across the world like that of no other Englishman in history.[25] But when peace came, the nation quickly voted him out of office. Even though Churchill was prepared to use his seasoned years of leading, people wanted a fresh face.

Time and familiarity have a way of taking their toll on leaders. Today's hope is tomorrow's call for change; this year's hero is next year's discard. It can become wearisome. It amounts to *hebel* – vanity, vapor, or smoke (Eccl 4:16). Finding the perfect leader and avoiding transitions are futile pursuits. Those expecting sustained continuity may as well chase after the wind.

And so the cycles continue. There might be wisdom in not taking our leadership too seriously.

Lead in Such a Way That People Will Lament Your Loss

There is a variety of successions in Scripture. Sometimes leaders pass on the mantle of leadership (Elijah); others lead until they die (Solomon); some are killed in battle (Ahab and Josiah); some take their lives in the midst of their leading (Saul); and some are murdered by political rivals.

The default succession plan for certain kings in the Old Testament was assassination (see 1 Kgs 15:29; 16:10–12).[26] In some cases, there is no record of succession. The story ends without a record of how a leader left his leadership to others (e.g. Nehemiah).

In some accounts, transition leads to order and life gets better. In others, leadership change is followed by chaos and disaster. In some stories, loss of leadership leaves a vacuum, and dysfunctional elements emerge. False prophets

---

25. Hastings, *Winston's War*, 478.
26. Weese and Crabtree, *Elephant in the Boardroom*, loc. 433.

fill the void left by a prophet who has passed. Paul warns the elders at Ephesus that his departure will open the door to savage wolves (Acts 20:29–30).

We will each have our own stories. What matters is to leave with people lamenting our leaving – not because we made them passively dependent, but because we made a difference. We influenced lives. Our leadership brought the community to another level. Imaginations expanded, lives flourished, and people became missional.

Solomon concludes that, in the end, leaving a good name matters more than anything else (Prov 22:1). Some in Scripture left a lamentable void (Joshua). In other cases, people celebrated and said, "Good riddance!" (Ahab). Some were lauded and extolled for their service, while others were condemned for their failure to lead.

In many stories, the transition of leadership had little emotional effect. This was true with most of Israel's kings. Scripture simply says they rested with their ancestors and were succeeded by the next king (e.g. 1 Kgs 11:43–45) – nothing more. David died in the midst of passing on his leadership, and there was no tribute, no memorial, and no lamenting the loss.[27] His last words were graceless and harsh, suggesting the transition had a note of bitterness (1 Kgs 2:9).

All of these transitions cause us to think about how we will lead and how people will respond to our passing. What am I doing to ensure that, in a healthy way, I will be missed? Did I make a difference?

Make Your Legacy about Having Served God's Purpose

Lots of questions come up concerning a transition:

Is It Time?

There are no statements about how long one should serve. Some leaders in Scripture served a matter of months; some led the same people for decades. There are potential dangers to both. Some leave at the first sign of discontent, and fail to learn the lessons God might be teaching. Some stay too long, and outlive their usefulness. There are stories of this in Scripture (1 Sam 8:5; 2 Kgs 20:3).

Who Should Follow Me?

How leadership is passed from one leader to the next has multiple options in Scripture. Nepotism is endorsed, even commanded in some cases. Kings

---

27. Peterson, *Leap over a Wall*, 218.

and Chronicles record the numerous successions of Israel's leaders, almost all from a father to a son. But some stories suggest that sons were not always the best choices.

Should I Have a Voice in Who Succeeds?

Maybe: many of Israel's leaders chose their successors. Maybe not: the wisdom of the community might be a better voice. But a leader's voice should be heard. Institutions can make the mistake of marginalizing leaders on their way out, relegating them to lame-duck status, and discounting any opinions they have to share. This can miss the unique wisdom that might be gained.

Is There Wisdom in My Handing off and Leaving?

Perhaps. Jesus did. But there might be wisdom in your staying to support your successor. For a season, Elisha was Elijah's servant (1 Kgs 19:21).

Is a New Opportunity the Will of God?

It could be. It could also be a distraction. Circumstances are only one piece of the will of God, and they are secondary to other, more important questions.

In the end, what matters most is that this one question is settled:

Have I Served the Purpose of God?

One of the greatest transition statements found in Scripture is recorded in Acts 13. Paul, reflecting on David's life, concluded: "Now when David had served *God's purpose in his own generation*, he fell asleep" (Acts 13:36). This is a verse that inspires one to reach for the summit. This should be our legacy.

No one else has probably lived the same range of humanness as David.[28] David was a combination of Napoleon Bonaparte, George Washington, Beethoven, Martin Lloyd-Jones, Michael W. Smith, and Robert Browning. He was everything from outlaw to military general, poet to composer, religious leader to musician, and sinner to saint.

There wasn't much of life that David did not explore. He seized the leadership opportunities that came because of God's calling. He demonstrated courageous leadership on the battlefield; he submitted to God's preparation in the wilderness; and he stepped up to his anointing and reigned for God in Jerusalem. He also made despicable choices that included adultery and murder.

But here is what mattered: amidst his flaws, David laid hold of the divine purpose set before him, prioritizing his life around it. In the end, if someone

---

28. Peterson, 5.

says of our leadership, "This leader completed the divine purpose for which he/she was sent," nothing else really matters.

What was said of David could be said of other leaders in Scripture. Elijah served God's purpose and made his present leadership count. He did what prophets do – take on the entrenched culture, expose the gods, and dress down the powers of domination. He maintained his passion to the end. In his twilight years, Elijah did not opt out of the race, confine himself to idleness, and give himself over to dryness, dullness, and barrenness.

Jesus is the ultimate model of a life that served God's purpose. He had a perfect awareness of his mission: "Let us go somewhere else – to the nearby villages – so I can preach there also. *That is why I have come*" (Mark 1:38). He had a perfect awareness of timing (see John 2:4; 7:6). His food was to do the will of the Father (4:34). His mission was to reconcile man to God. At the cross Jesus could say, "It is finished."

Let It Go

Serving a divine purpose does not mean we will see all of the way to the end. We may see the fruit of our faithfulness, or we may not. Moses did not see everything he had hoped. Having led Israel through the wilderness and on to the edge of the promised land, he did not go in. Some of us may have a similar calling. We might be summoned to lead a community through difficult years, but it will be for others to see our dreams come true. As God said to Moses, so he may say to us, "You will not enter the land" (Deut 32:52).

Eventually Moses came to a place where he could let go. He came to realize the true promised land is less a physical destination and more a spiritual entrance into the presence of God. This is where true contentment is found (see Exod 33:18–23). Will we? Barton asks, "Is it possible to get to a place where we are so given over to God that physical death is just one more step toward the intimacy and union we seek?"[29]

The apostle Paul came to this point. His walk with God brought him to such a state of intimacy that he could set aside all of his leadership goals. Life became all about Jesus, and dying was viewed as gain (Phil 1:21). The ultimate transition captured Paul, and he longed that it would come now. Nonetheless, he was committed to serving the purpose for which he was made:

- "I do not consider my life of any account that I might finish the course that I have received" (Acts 20:24).

---

29. Barton, *Strengthening the Soul of Your Leadership*, 215.

- "All of us run a race, but only one receives the prize. So run to win. Run not to be disqualified" (1 Cor 9:24).
- "I press on to lay hold of why God laid hold of me, forgetting what lies behind, pressing for the upward prize" (Phil 3:12).

The reality is that there is no such thing as tenure; God appoints for the time he ordains.[30]

Pass On Your Leadership

While it matters that we have lived out God's purposes for our lives, it also matters that we have enabled others to run after us. Who are we passing the baton to? There comes a time when our greatest usefulness as leaders is in passing on our leadership to others.

Scripture gives numerous examples of succession. Jacob passed on his blessing to his son and grandsons (Gen 48:15–16). Moses appealed to God to raise up a successor (Num 27:15–17). He did not want Israel to be like sheep without a shepherd. He invested himself in the leadership, not of his sons, but of his servant Joshua. Because of this, Israel did not lose a step when Moses died. The land was conquered.

The most detailed succession of one of God's servants to another is described in 2 Kings 2. Elijah passed on the work to the next generation of faithful men and women. He gave particular attention to shaping Elisha. He poured out a "double portion," which in Hebrew culture was the sign of being the firstborn, the prime inheritor (Deut 21:17). Elisha knew what he needed from his mentor: a spiritual power far beyond his own capabilities in order to meet the enormity of the task confronting him. He wanted what Elijah had: his boldness, his spirit, and his calling.

The transition from Elijah to Elisha foreshadows the succession from John to Jesus.[31] John declares, "He must increase, but I must decrease" (John 3:30). John poured himself into others and stepped aside with integrity.

Were it not for Jesus's determination to pour himself into twelve men, with the encouragement that they would do even greater things (John 14:12), there would not be a church. He increased their responsibilities over time, demonstrating that success in ministry is defined by successors.[32]

---

30. Langer, "Toward a Biblical Theology of Leadership," 68.
31. Leithart, *1 and 2 Kings*, 171.
32. Vanderbloemen and Bird, *Next*, loc. 401.

Like all effective leaders, Jesus expanded capacity and capability. Were it not for a Barnabas, there would not have been an apostle Paul. And were it not for a Paul, there would not have been a Timothy. Paul understood the necessity of passing leadership on. He taught Timothy, modeled Christlikeness, and laid out a pattern for developing future leaders: "And the things you have heard me say in the presence of many witnesses entrust to reliable men who will be qualified to teach others" (2 Tim 2:2).

When leaders do not mentor future leaders, their followers suffer the consequences. Joshua failed to pour himself into the next generation. There was no leadership engine, and the result was the book of Judges, an account of chaos and spiritual decline (Judg 21:25). In future days, many of the kings failed to invest their energies in preparing their successors. In most of these cases, those who followed nullified much of what was previously accomplished (cf. Rehoboam, Manasseh).

We can mentor and shape others, but ultimately we will one day leave our work for another, and who knows if it will be led with wisdom or folly (Eccl 2:18–19). Who knows if much of what we have built will be destroyed? What matters is that we have done our best to prepare those who succeed us.

Like David, who invested in his thirty future leaders, we must plead, "Even when I am old and gray, do not forsake me O God until I declare your power to the next generation, your might to all who are to come" (Ps 71:18).

Putting It All Together

Transitions help put things in perspective. As Oscar Romero, a martyred archbishop, wrote: "We accomplish in our lifetimes only a fraction of the magnificent enterprise that is God's work."[33] We will not see the end results because there will be no end results until the end of time. And in our humility, we need to accept that the next chapter can be done just as well, if not better, by someone else. And if not, this is no longer our problem.

The reality is that our lives are not our own. We are God's workmanship, created to do his will (Eph 2:10). We are not our own, for we have been bought with a price (1 Cor 6:20). We must die daily to this world and its expectations (1 Cor 15:31). Our lives are like a libation in the sanctuary, a drink offering poured out on the altar for the sake of those we lead (Phil 2:17).

---

33. Barton, *Strengthening the Soul of Your Leadership*, quoting Oscar Romero, Archbishop of San Salvador, 217.

This is what defines a godly leader: it is someone whose life is drained, expended, poured out on the altar of faith; someone whose body is presented as a living sacrifice (Rom 12:1); and someone for whom dying isn't the end of everything: it is actually the beginning.

"Only where there are graves are there resurrections."[34]

---

34. A quote attributed to Friedrich Nietzsche.

Conclusion

I recently completed my annual physical. Near the end, my doctor paused and whispered something in my ear. No, she wasn't making a pass at me. She was checking my hearing.

Think of this book as a checkup of sorts. I have written out of a conviction that many of us in leadership may suffer from a hearing impairment. Or is it selective hearing? We are tone-deaf when it comes to certain cultural sounds. Definitions of, and understandings about, leadership vary from one culture to the next, but ethnocentricity may be jamming our perceptions.

This was my condition when I moved to Europe in the early 1990s to pastor my second church. The first weekend, I remember sitting down to catch up on the news. I turned to CNN, where I assumed I would hear the latest about the president's summit, Supreme Court rulings, and the results of the primary in Ohio. Instead, it began with results from elections in Ghana, moving to troubling events in Somalia, and on to a weather-related tragedy in Finland.

Where was the news out of Washington, D.C.? Didn't they realize America is the cultural center of the world?

Ear surgery was required.

The psalmist in Psalm 40:6 talks about a similar procedure. He recounts a time when God needed to open his (the psalmist's) ears. The Hebrew is more graphic: "Ears you have dug." It was the writer's admission that he had gotten so caught up in the religious activity that he had become deaf to the voice of God. It became necessary for God to get a pick and shovel and dig through the cranial granite, opening a passage that would give access to the interior depths, into the mind and heart.[1]

Something like this was at work in me. Over time, God began to open my ears. I began to hear for the first time – hear the voices of the some thirty-five different nationalities that made up Trinity Church; hear their ways, their habits, their fears, their joys, their heartaches, and their prejudices. God was teaching me to get beyond my small horizons!

I was becoming what God defines as a leader.

There's something else that is problematic for many leaders. There are thunderous, even earsplitting sounds coming from heaven, but many of us are also oblivious to these signals. Call it hard of hearing (or is it hardness

---

1. Peterson, *Working the Angles*, 71.

of heart?). We may need to enter audio logic rehabilitation and recover our hearing. For others, it may be hearing for the first time.

My book, however, would fall short of the mark if it simply served to reveal a hearing loss. Instead, I hope it has helped to open passageways necessary to hearing the missing sounds. My argument throughout the book is that the study of leadership is incomplete if we leave out the contribution of global and theological voices. If we don't reach out to the horizon and beyond – and implement what we have heard – it will be difficult to make sense of what we claim to be familiar with.

Western voices have much to contribute to the subject of leading. We have seen this in the first part of each chapter. We have learned that effective leaders

- are, by definition, those who have followers, have influence, and have direction;
- are necessary, for they bring stability, sound the warning, sustain the momentum, and shape the ideals;
- take advantage of their gifts, invest in training, and respond to a summons;
- pursue core values and develop essential skills in order to be credible;
- build teams marked by excellence, chemistry, and diversity;
- are missional, visionary, strategic, and tactical;
- are change agents, disruptors who invent, explore, create, and inspire, pushing people forward while honoring the rules that come with change;
- face their challenges, keep their priorities, and aim for reconciliation;
- prepare for their departure, make ready the organization, finish well, and step aside with integrity.

Through reading and reflecting on the contributing global voices, here are some of the learnings that stand out from the second section of each chapter:

- While *low power distance worlds* demonstrate the value of mutuality, shared participation, and joint collaboration, *large power distance cultures* can teach us something about decisiveness, as well as honor and respect that should be accorded to leaders. There is wisdom in deferring to those with more knowledge and rationality than others who have less insight and are emotionally driven.
- While *individualistic worlds* reveal the importance of having personal goals, personal responsibility, and personal performance, *collectivistic cultures* underscore the importance of relationships, belonging, mutual care, and loyalty.

- While *low context worlds* demonstrate the value of things said, of being explicit, saying and hearing what is actual, and listening to ideas and concepts, *high context cultures* teach us the importance of things not said, of getting beyond words, paying attention to things around you, and hearing communication that is implied and internalized.
- While *low uncertainty-avoidance worlds* show the need for change, of taking organizations into the future and thinking through the strategies and tactics that might alter what is, *high uncertainty-avoidance cultures* draw attention to the need to keep agreements, avoid unnecessary risks, maintain order, and respect traditions.

No single region of the world has it together when it comes to leadership. There are strengths and weakness in every culture. One's assets can also become one's liabilities. For example: an overemphasis on individuality in the West has led to a fair amount of social disintegration. In other cultures, collectivism and hierarchical leadership have led to a high degree of unity, but at the expense of individual input and initiative.

We can learn from one another. It's time that the shelves in the Leadership Section of every bookstore and library were filled with books from every culture. Only then can we climb this mountain together and see beyond our own horizon.

By stepping into the theological world, we have discovered that Scripture is a leadership manual on its own. Among the main findings in this third section, we have seen that:

- Leadership begins with God. He is the essence of leadership.
- Leaders are ultimately instruments created and called to carry out his will.
- We need leaders, but God does not. He needs nothing, but he desires to use leaders as his main instruments.
- God is the original cause. Leadership is his to give. Ultimately, God shapes, gifts, and summons leaders.
- Character matters more than success. Character begins with God's character. His values inform our values, beginning with justice. Only the transformative work of Jesus can bring us to ourselves, give us our bearings, and keep us on track.
- Whatever leadership skills we possess are not generated on our own. They come from him, and are given to be developed and refined for

his purposes. Our greatest skill is wisdom, and our greatest power for leading comes from him.

- God never works alone, and neither should leaders. Fulfilling the will of God is a team effort. Standalone leaders are not heroes; they are fools.
- God is missional, just as leaders are to be missional. He is on a mission to repair and reestablish a broken world and bring honor to his name. His purpose is to be our purpose.
- God is visionary, just as leaders are to be futurists. His story has a beginning and an end, one written in eternity past. Leaders with vision are caught up in the same ultimate end.
- God is strategic and tactical in everything he does. Nothing is random. Leaders who reflect the ways of God are disciplined and intentional in everything they do.
- Change is the ongoing work of a changeless God. Transformation is his main work, and it begins with the heart. Those leaders who follow him realize that a summons to lead is a summons to bring change, change that will bring about his intentions.
- Many of our challenges are spiritual. Leaders are assailed by a triad of forces – the flesh, the world, and the devil. They gang up to create havoc in our leadership endeavors. But God's power is more than sufficient to help leaders overcome.
- Life is fleeting. Leadership is but for a moment. Knowing this encourages us to use our moments well, finish the race that God has called us to run, and pass on to others the task that was passed on to us.

Leaders who see the world as God sees the world discover that, in Christ, "fellow citizens" has replaced the language of foreigners and strangers. All of us – Asians, Latinos, Africans, Anglos, and so on – are built upon the same foundation. Though we have our differences, we are all being fitted together to grow into a holy sanctuary, a dwelling for God (Eph 2:11–22).

We all share the same home country, the kingdom of faith, and we're all ultimately about serving his purpose and building his kingdom. This is the essence of the leadership enterprise.

We all have a voice that needs to be heard, something underscored by one of this book's contributors. His words are a fitting close:

> My hope is expressed in this African hope. If we all can gain insights from our global perspectives, I will consider this book project

to have made a significant contribution to our understanding of leadership. The world is changing at a rapid pace. The emergence of technology and globalization has turned the world, not only into a global village, but into a hamlet – thanks or no thanks to social media. I hope that this book will inspire and create a new global understanding and practice of leadership. I hope it will help us to appreciate the contributions of other leaders, both from Western and non-Western worlds, and provide a global leadership development agenda.

Amen and amen.

Bibliography

Adjei, Solomon Nii-Mensah. "Education and Training among Fishing Communities in the Ga and Mfantse Coastal Towns." *Journal of African Christian Thought* 14, no. 1 (2011): 56–64.

Agassi, Andrew. *Open*. New York: Random House, 2009.

Ascough, Richard S., and Charles A. Cotton. *Passionate Visionary: Leadership Lessons from the Apostle Paul*. Ottawa: Novalis, 2005.

Augustine. *Confessions*. Translated by Henry Chadwick. Oxford: Oxford University Press, 1991.

Azzarello, Patty. *Rise: How to Be Really Successful at Work* and *Your Life*. [USA]: Newton Park Publishing, 2010.

Babu, Santhosh. "Ratan Tata: The Visionary." *Hindu Business Line*, 27 December 2012. https://www.thehindubusinessline.com/news/variety/Ratan-Tata-The-visionary/article20545504.ece.

Baldwin, Joyce G. *1 and 2 Samuel: An Introduction and Commentary*. Downers Grove: InterVarsity Press, 1988.

Bardwick, Judith M. "Peacetime Management and Wartime Leadership." In *Leader of the Future*, edited by Frances Hesselbein, Marshall Goldsmith, and Richard Beckhard, 131–140. San Francisco: Jossey-Bass, 1996.

Barendsen, Lynn, and Howard Gardner. "The Three Elements of Good Leadership in Rapidly Changing Times." In *Leader of the Future 2: Visions, Strategies, and Practices for the New Era*, edited by Frances Hesselbein and Marshall Goldsmith, 265–280. San Francisco: Jossey-Bass, 2006.

Barling, J., T. Weber, and E. K. Kelloway. "Effects of Transformational Leadership Training on Attitudinal and Financial Outcomes: A Field Experiment." *Journal of Applied Psychology* 81, no. 6 (1996): 827–832.

Barna, George. *Turning Vision into Action*. Grand Rapids: Baker, 1996.

Barton, Ruth Haley. *Pursuing God's Will Together*. Downers Grove: InterVarsity Press, 2008.

———. *Strengthening the Soul of Your Leadership*. Downers Grove: InterVarsity Press, 2008.

Bass, Bernard M. *A New Paradigm of Leadership: An Inquiry into Transformational Leadership*. Alexandria, VA: US Army Research Institute for the Behavioral and Social Sciences, 1996.

Belasco, James A., and Ralph C. Stayer. *Flight of the Buffalo: Soaring to Excellence, Learning to Let Employees Lead*. New York: Warner, 1993.

Belmonte, Kevin. *William Wilberforce: A Hero for Humanity*. Grand Rapids: Zondervan, 2002.

Belsky, Scott. *Making Ideas Happen: Overcoming the Obstacles between Vision and Reality*. New York: Penguin, 2010.

Bennis, Warren. *On Becoming a Leader*. New York: Basic, 1989.

Bennis, Warren, and Joan Goldsmith. *Learning to Lead: A Workbook on Becoming a Leader*. New York: Basic, 2010.

Bennis, Warren, and Burt Nanus. *Leaders: Strategies for Taking Charge*. New York: HarperCollins, 1985.

Bennis, Warren G., and Robert J. Thomas. *Geeks and Geezers: How Era, Values, and Defining Moments Shape Leaders*. Boston: Harvard Business School, 2002.

Bennis, Warren G., and Patricia Ward Biederman. *Organizing Genius: The Secrets of Creative Collaboration*. New York: Basic, 1997.

———. *Still Surprised: A Memoir of a Life in Leadership*. San Francisco: Jossey-Bass, 2010.

Biehl, Bobb. *Increasing Your Leadership Confidence*. Portland: Multnomah, 1989.

Bird, Michael F. *Evangelical Theology: A Biblical and Systematic Introduction*. Grand Rapids: Zondervan, 2013.

Blanchard, Ken. "Turning the Organizational Pyramid Upside Down." In *Leader of the Future*, edited by Frances Hesselbein, Marshall Goldsmith, and Richard Beckhard, 81–88. San Francisco: Jossey-Bass, 1996.

Bolman, Leo G., and Terrence E. Deal. *Reframing Organizations: Artistry, Choice, and Leadership*. San Francisco: Jossey-Bass, 1996.

Bordas, Juana. *Salsa, Soul, and Spirit: Leadership for a Multicultural Age*. San Francisco: Berrett-Koehler, 2012. Kindle.

Botelho, Elena, et al. "What Sets Successful CEOs Apart." *Harvard Business Review* (May/June 2017): 70–77.

Bowden, Mark. "The Worst Problem on Earth." *The Atlantic*, July/August 2017. https://www.theatlantic.com/magazine/archive/2017/07/the-worst-problem-on-earth/528717/.

Brafman, Ori, and Rod A. Beckstrom. *The Starfish and the Spider: The Unstoppable Power of Leaderless Organizations*. New York: Portfolio, 2006.

Branson, Mark, and Juan F. Martinez. *Churches, Cultures, and Leadership: A Practical Theology of Congregations and Ethnicities*. Downers Grove: InterVarsity Press, 2011.

Bridges, William, and Susan Bridges. *Managing Transitions: Making the Most of Change*. New York: De Capo, 1991.

Brooks, David. *The Road to Character*. New York: Penguin, 2015. Kindle.

———. "The Small, Happy Life." *New York Times*, 29 May 2015. https://www.nytimes.com/2015/05/29/opinion/david-brooks-the-small-happy-life.html.

Brueggemann, Walter. *Like Fire in the Bones: Listening for the Prophetic Word in Jeremiah*. Minneapolis: Fortress, 2006.

———. *Truth Speaks to Power*. Louisville: Westminster John Knox Press, 2013.

Bryant, Adam. "How to Be a C.E.O., From a Decade's Worth of Them." *New York Times*, 27 October 2017. https://www.nytimes.com/2017/10/27/business/how-to-be-a-ceo.html.

Burns, James MacGregor. *Leadership*. New York: Harper & Row, 1978.

Burns, John S., John R. Shoup, and Donald C. Simmons, Jr., eds. *Organizational Leadership: Foundations and Practices for Christians*. Downers Grove: InterVarsity Press, 2014.

Cacioppe, Ron. "Creating Spirit at Work: Re-Visioning Organization Development and Leadership; Part I." *Leadership & Organization Development Journal* 21, no. 1 (2000): 48–54.

Calvert, Scott. "Pimp Your Ride: Splurge on a Lower License-Plate Number." *The Wall Street Journal*, 19 September 2018. https://www.wsj.com/articles/pimp-your-ride-splurge-on-a-lower-license-plate-number-1537367204.

Caro, Robert A. *The Years of Lyndon Johnson: The Passage of Power*. New York: Alfred A. Knopf, 2012.

Carr, Nicholas. "Is Google Making Us Stupid?" *The Atlantic*, July/August 2008. https://www.theatlantic.com/magazine/archive/2008/07/is-google-making-us-stupid/306868/.

Charan, Ram, and Geoffrey Colvin. "Why CEO's Fail." *Fortune Magazine*, June 21, 1999.

Choi, Sang-Chin, and Ki-Bum Kim. "Chemyeon: Social Face in Korean Culture." *Korea Journal* 44, no. 2 (June 2004): 30–51.

Clear, James. "Lessons on Success and Deliberate Practice from Mozart, Picasso, and Kobe Bryant." Jamesclear.com. https://jamesclear.com/deliberate-practice.

———. "The Paradox of Behavior Change." Jamesclear.com. https://jamesclear.com/behavior-change-paradox.

———. "3 Time Management Tips That Actually Work." Jamesclear.com. https://jamesclear.com/time-management-tips.

Clinton, J. Robert. *The Making of a Leader*. Colorado Springs: NavPress, 1988.

Coenen, L. "Bishop, Presbyter, Elder." In *New International Dictionary of New Testament Theology*, Vol. 1, edited by Colin Brown, 192–201. Grand Rapids: Zondervan, 2002.

Collins, Jim. *Good to Great and the Social Sectors: Why Business Thinking Is Not the Answer*. New York: Harper Business, 2001.

———. *Good to Great: Why Some Companies Make the Leap . . . And Others Don't*. New York: Harper Business, 2001.

Collins, Jim, and Jerry I. Porras. *Built to Last*. New York: Harper Business, 1994.

Conger, J. A., R. N. Kanungo, and Associates. *Charismatic Leadership: The Elusive Factor in Organizational Effectiveness*. San Francisco: Jossey-Bass, 1988.

Copan, Paul. *Is God a Moral Monster? Making Sense of the Old Testament God*. Grand Rapids: Baker, 2011.

Covey, Stephen R. *The 7 Habits of Highly Effective People: Restoring the Character Ethic*. New York: Free Press, 1989.

————. "Three Roles of the Leader in the New Paradigm." In *Leader of the Future*, edited by Frances Hesselbein, Marshall Goldsmith, and Richard Beckhard, 149–160. San Francisco: Jossey-Bass, 1996.

Crabb, Larry. *Connecting: Healing Ourselves and Our Relationships*. Nashville: W Publishing Group, 1997.

Dávila, Anabella, and Martha Elvira. "Liderazgo en Latinoamérica: el poso de la historia." IESE Insight – Business Knowledge, 2012. http://www.ieseinsight.com/doc.aspx?id=1358&ar=17&idioma=1. Accessed 20 March 2018.

Davis, Scott. "Steve Kerr Explained How the Warriors' Offense Is Different Than the Rockets': The Juggernaut They're about to Face with the NBA Finals on the Line." *Business Insider*, 9 May 2018. https://www.businessinsider.com/steve-kerr-explained-warriors-offense-vs-rockets-2018–1.

De Pree, Max. *Leadership Is an Art*. New York: Dell, 1989.

————. *Leadership Jazz*. New York: Dell, 1992.

Dickerson, John. "The Hardest Job in the World." *The Atlantic*, May 2018. https://www.theatlantic.com/magazine/archive/2018/05/a-broken-office/556883/.

Dionne, Shelley D., Francis J. Yammarino, Leanne E. Atwater, and William D. Spangler. "Transformational Leadership and Team Performance." *Journal of Organizational Change Management* 17, no. 2 (2004): 177–193.

Dolan, Timothy G. "Called to Lead." In Burns, Shoup, and Simmons, *Organizational Leadership*, 15–34.

Dowd, Maureen. "Will the Blowhard Blow Us Up?" *New York Times*, 12 August 2017. https://www.nytimes.com/2017/08/12/opinion/sunday/dowd-trump-korea-kim-jong-un.html.

Drucker, Peter. "Drucker on Management: The Five Deadly Business Sins." *The Wall Street Journal*, November 18, 2009. Online.

————. *Management: Tasks, Responsibilities and Practices*. New York: Truman Talley, 1986.

————. *Managing the Non-Profit Organization: Principles and Practices*. New York: HarperCollins, 1990.

————. "Not Enough Generals Were Killed." In *Leader of the Future: New Visions, Strategies and Practices for the Next Era*, edited by Francis Hesselbein, Marshall Goldsmith, and Richard Beckhard, xi–xvi. San Francisco: Jossey-Bass, 1996.

Duckworth, Angela. *Grit: The Power of Passion and Perseverance*. New York: Simon & Schuster, 2016.

Eaton, Michael A. *Ecclesiastes: An Introduction and Commentary*. Downers Grove: InterVarsity Press, 1983.

Elmer, Duane. *Cross-Cultural Conflict*. Downers Grove: InterVarsity Press, 1993.

Emmanuel, Jeyakaran. "Breaking through the Barriers." In *Eastern Voices*, Vol. 1, compiled by Asian Access, 203–218. Cerritos: Asian Access, 2017.

Erickson, Wallace. "Transition in Leadership." In *Leaders on Leadership*, edited by George Barna, 297–316. Ventura: Regal, 1997.

Ferguson, Niall. "In Praise of Hierarchy." *The Wall Street Journal*, 5 January 2018. https://www.wsj.com/articles/in-praise-of-hierarchy-1515175338.

———. *The Square and the Tower: Networks, Hierarchies and the Struggle for Global Power*. New York: Penguin Press, 2018.

Fischer, Louis. *Gandhi: His Life and Message for the World*. New York: Signet Classic, 2010.

Fleming, Dave. *Leadership Wisdom from Unlikely Voices: People of Yesterday Speak to Leaders of Today*. El Cajon: EmergentYS, 2004.

Forbes, Dan V. "21 Quotable Definitions of Leadership and Leaders." Lead with Giants Coaching, 25 September 2014. http://leadwithgiantscoaching.com/21-quotable-definitions-of-leadership-and-leaders/.

Friedman, Edwin H. *A Failure of Nerve: Leadership in the Age of the Quick Fix*. New York: Seabury, 1999. Kindle.

Friedman, Thomas L. *The World Is Flat: A Brief History of the Twenty-First Century*. New York: Farrar, Straus, and Giroux, 2005.

Frost, Michael, and Alan Hirsch. *The Shaping of Things to Come: Innovation and Mission for the 21st Century Church*. Peabody: Hendrickson, 2003.

Fukuzawa, Yukichi. *Gendaigoyaku Gakumonnosussume ChikuwaShinsho*. Japan, 2009.

Gaddis, John Lewis. *On Grand Strategy*. New York: Penguin, 2009.

Gandhi, M. K. *An Autobiography or the Story of My Experiments with Truth*. Translated by Mahadev Desai. Ahmedabad: Navajivan, 1927.

Gates, Robert M. *Duty: Memoirs of a Secretary at War*. New York: Alfred A. Knopf, 2014.

———. *A Passion for Leadership: Lessons on Change and Reform from Fifty Years of Public Service*. New York: Alfred A. Knopf, 2016.

Gentry, Peter J., and Stephen J. Wellum. *Kingdom through Covenant: A Biblical-Theological Understanding of the Covenants*. Wheaton: Crossway, 2012.

George, Bill. *Discover Your True North: Becoming an Authentic Leader*. San Francisco: Jossey-Bass, 2007.

George, Carl F. "Beyond the Firehouse Syndrome." CT Pastors, 1997. https://www.christianitytoday.com/pastors/leadership-books/visionplanning/lldev02-15.html.

Georges, Jayson, and Mark D. Baker. *Ministering in Honor–Shame Cultures: Biblical Foundations and Practical Essentials*. Downers Grove: InterVarsity Press, 2016.

Gergen, David. *Eyewitness to Power: The Essence of Leadership; Nixon to Clinton*. New York: Touchstone, 2000.

Gerth, H. H., and C. Wright Mills. *From Max Weber: Essays in Sociology*. New York: Oxford University Press, 1958.

Gibbs, Eddie. *Leadership Next: Changing Leaders in a Changing Culture*. Downers Grove: InterVarsity Press, 2005.

Gladwell, Malcolm. *Outliers: The Story of Success*. New York: Little, Brown and Company, 2008.

Glanz, Jeffrey. *Finding Your Leadership Style: A Guide for Educators*. Alexandria: Association for Supervision and Curriculum Development, 2002.

Godin, Seth. *This Is Marketing*. New York: Penguin Random House, 2018.

Goleman, Daniel, Richard Boyatzis, and Annie McKee. *Primal Leadership: Learning to Lead with Emotional Intelligence*. 2nd ed. Boston: Harvard Business School Press, 2013.

Gómez, Gerardo. "La novela del dictador: summa histórica y persistencia en Latinoamérica. Sobre la diacronía del 'Primer Magistrado' carpenteriano." *Revista Iberoamericana* 22, no. 1 (2011): 211–239.

Goodwin, Doris Kearns. *Leadership: In Turbulent Times*. New York: Simon & Schuster, 2018.

———. "Lessons of Presidential Leadership." *Leader to Leader* 9 (1998): 23–30.

———. *Team of Rivals: The Political Genius of Abraham Lincoln*. New York: Simon & Schuster, 2005.

Gourevitch, Philip. "Kofi Annan's Unaccountable Legacy." *The New Yorker*, 18 August 2018. https://www.newyorker.com/news/daily-comment/kofi-annans-unaccountable-legacy.

Grann, David. "The White Darkness: A Solitary Journey across Antartica." *The New Yorker*, 12 & 19 February 2018. https://www.newyorker.com/magazine/2018/02/12/the-white-darkness.

Greenleaf, Robert K. *On Becoming a Servant Leader: The Private Writings of Robert K. Greenleaf*. Edited by Don M. Frick and Larry C. Spears. San Francisco: Jossey-Bass, 1996.

———. *Servant Leadership: A Journey into the Nature of Legitimate Power and Greatness*. New York: Paulist, 1977.

Grint, Keith. *Leadership: A Very Short Introduction*. Oxford: Oxford University Press, 2010.

Guiness, Os. *Character Counts: Leadership Qualities in Washington, Wilberforce, Lincoln, and Solzhenitsyn*. Grand Rapids: Baker, 1999.

———. *Prophetic Untimeliness: A Challenge to the Idol of Relevance*. Grand Rapids: Baker, 2005.

Gushee, David P., and Colin Holtz. *Moral Leadership for a Divided Age*. Grand Rapids: Brazos Press, 2018.

Haas, Martine, and Mark Mortensen. "The Secrets of Great Teamwork." *Harvard Business Review*, June 2016. https://hbr.org/2016/06/the-secrets-of-great-teamwork.

Hall, Edward T. *Beyond Culture*. New York: Anchor, 1977.

Harari, Oren. *The Leadership Secrets of Colin Powell*. New York: McGraw-Hill, 2002.

Harari, Yuval Noah. "Yuval Noah Harari on What the Year 2050 Has in Store for Humankind." *Wired*, 12 August 2018. https://www.wired.co.uk/article/yuval-noah-harari-extract-21-lessons-for-the-21st-century.

———. *21 Lessons for the 21ˢᵗ Century*. New York: Spiegel & Grau, 2018.

Hartog, D. N. Den, R. J. House, and P. J. Hanges. "Culture Specific and Cross-Culturally Generalizable Implicit Leadership Theories: Are Attributes of Charismatic/

Transformational Leadership Universally Endorsed?" *The Leadership Quarterly* 10, no. 2 (June 1999): 219–256.

Hastings, Max. *Winston's War: Churchill, 1940–1945*. London: HarperPress, 2009.

Hayashi, Masakatsu. *Genba o nameruna*. Tokyo: AsaShuppan, 2018.

Hayward, Steven F. *Greatness: Reagan, Churchill, and the Making of Extraordinary Leaders*. New York: Crown Forum, 2006.

Heath, Chip, and Dan Heath. *Decisive: How to Make Better Choices in Life and Work*. New York: Crown Business, 2013.

Herrington, Jim, Mike Bonem, and James H. Furr. *Leading Congregational Change: A Practical Guide for the Transformational Journey*. San Francisco: Jossey-Bass, 2000.

Hersey, Paul. *The Situational Leader*. New York: Warner, 1985.

Hersey, Paul, and Ken Blanchard. *Management of Organizational Behavior*. New Jersey: Prentice Hall, 1982.

Hesselbein, Frances. "The 'How to Be' Leader." In *Leader of the Future*, edited by Frances Hesselbein, Marshall Goldsmith, and Richard Beckhard, 121–124. San Francisco: Jossey-Bass, 1996.

Hesselbein, Frances, Marshall Goldsmith, and Richard Beckhard, eds. *The Leader of the Future: New Visions, Strategies and Practices for the Next Era*. San Francisco: Jossey-Bass, 1996.

Hesselbein, Frances, and Marshall Goldsmith, eds. *The Leader of the Future 2: Visions, Strategies, and Practices for the New Era*. San Francisco: Jossey-Bass, 2006.

Hirsch, Alan. *Forgotten Ways: Reactivating the Missional Church*. Grand Rapids: Brazos, 2006.

Hirsch, Alan, and Tim Catchim. *The Permanent Revolution: Apostolic Imagination and Practice for the 21st Century Church*. San Francisco: Jossey-Bass, 2012. Kindle.

Hjalmarson, Leonard. "Kingdom Leadership in the Postmodern Era." Christianity.ca, 2005. https://www.christianity.ca/page.aspx?pid=11722.

Hofstede, Geert. "Country Comparison." Hofstede Insights. https://www.hofstede-insights.com/country-comparison/.

Hofstede, Geert, Gert Jan Hofstede, and Michael Minkov. *Cultures and Organizations: Software of the Mind*. New York: McGraw Hill, 2011.

Hollinger, Dennis P. *Choosing the Good: Christian Ethics in a Complex World*. Grand Rapids: Baker, 2002.

House, R. J., and J. M. Howell. "Personality and Charismatic Leadership." *The Leadership Quarterly* 3, no. 2 (Summer 1992): 81–108.

House, Robert J., et al., eds. *Culture, Leadership and Organizations: The GLOBE Study of 62 Societies*. Thousand Oaks: Sage, 2004.

Howard, J. Grant. *The Trauma of Transparency: A Biblical Approach to Inter-Personal Communication*. Portland: Multnomah, 1983.

Hunt, James D. *Gandhi and the Nonconformists: Encounters in South Africa*. New Delhi: Promilla & Co., 1931.

Huntington, Samuel P. *The Clash of Civilizations and the Remaking of World Order.* New York: Simon & Schuster, 1996.

Huxley, Aldous. *The Perennial Philosophy.* New York: Harper & Brothers, 1945.

Hybels, Bill. *Leadership Axioms: Powerful Leadership Proverbs.* Grand Rapids: Zondervan, 2008.

Isaacson, Walter. *Steve Jobs.* New York: Simon & Schuster, 2011. Kindle.

Iyer, Pico. "'The Road to Character' by David Brooks." *New York Times*, 20 April 2015. https://www.nytimes.com/2015/04/26/books/review/the-road-to-character-by-david-brooks.html.

Ji-ho, Park. "The Second Generation of Korean Churches Are Coming Back." *Gyeonggi News*, 5 September 2007. http://www.newsnjoy.us/news/articleView.html?idxno=354. Accessed 31 May 2018.

Jiménez, Francisca Noguerol. "El dictador Latinoamericano: Aproximación a un arquetipo narrativo." *Philologia Hispalensis* 7 (1999): 91–102.

Job, Rueben P., and Norman Shawchuck. *A Guide to Prayer for Ministers and Other Servants.* Nashville: Upper Room, 1983.

Johnson, John E. "Is Apostolic Leadership the Key to the Missional Church?" Unpublished paper presented at the meeting of the Evangelical Theological Society, November 2009.

———. *Under an Open Heaven: A New Way of Life Revealed in John's Gospel.* Grand Rapids: Kregel, 2017.

Jones, E. Stanley. *The Christ of the Indian Road.* New York: Abingdon Press, 2014.

———. *Mahatma Gandhi: An Interpretation.* Lucknow: Lucknow Publishing House, 1963.

Jung, Sook-Hee. *Why Did They Leave the Church? Critique on Korean Diaspora Churches.* Seoul: Hongsungsa, 2007.

Kabacoff, Robert. "Develop Strategic Thinkers throughout Your Organization." *Harvard Business Review*, 7 February 2014. https://hbr.org/2014/02/develop-strategic-thinkers-throughout-your-organization.

Kagan, Robert. *The Jungle Grows Back: America and Our Imperiled World.* New York: Alfred A. Knopf, 2018.

———. "The Myth of the Modernizing Dictator." *Washington Post*, 21 October 2018. https://www.washingtonpost.com/opinions/the-myth-of-the-modernizing-dictator/2018/10/19/5f4bef0c-d30a-11e8-b2d2-f397227b43f0_story.html?utm_term=.d007c9dd7ddb.

Kapic, Kelly. *A Little Book for New Theologians: Why and How to Study Theology.* Downers Grove: InterVarsity Press, 2012.

Kaplan, Robert S., and David P. Norton. *The Strategy Focused Organization: How Balanced Scorecard Companies Thrive in the New Business Environment.* Boston: Harvard Business School, 2001.

Kellerman, Barbara. *Followership: How Followers Are Creating Change and Changing Leaders.* Boston: Harvard Business School, 2008.

Keltner, Dacher. *The Power Paradox: How We Gain and Lose Influence.* New York: Penguin, 2016.

Kennedy, John F. *Profiles in Courage.* New York: Harper & Brothers, 1956.

Kenyatta, Jomo. *Facing Mount Kenya: The Tribal Life of the Gikuyu.* Nairobi: Heinemann Educational Books, 1971.

Kim, Jung-Eun. *Korean Cross-Cultural Communication.* Seoul: Korean Culture, 2011.

Kim, Ui-Chol. "Individualism and Collectivism: Conceptual Clarification and Elaboration." In *Individualism and Collectivism: Theory, Method, and Applications,* edited by Ui-Chol Kim, Harry C. Triandis, Cigdem Kagitcibasi, Sang-Chin Choi, and Gene Yoon, 19–40. Thousand Oaks: Sage, 1994.

King, Stephen. *On Writing: A Memoir of the Craft.* New York: Pocket Books, 2000.

Kirkpatrick, S. A., and E. A. Locke. "Direct and Indirect Effects of Three Core Charismatic Leadership Components on Performance and Attitudes." *Journal of Applied Psychology* 81, no. 1 (1996): 36–51.

"Kivebulaya, Apolo." In *Dictionary of African Christian Biography.* https://dacb.org/stories/democratic-republic-of-congo/kivebulaya2-apolo/.

Klink III, Edward W., and Darian R. Lockett. *Understanding Biblical Theology: A Comparison of Theory and Practice.* Grand Rapids: Zondervan, 2012.

Kluger, Jeffrey. *Apollo 8: The Thrilling Story of the First Mission to the Moon.* New York: Henry Holt & Co., 2017. Kindle.

Kotter, John P. *Leading Change.* Boston: Harvard Business School, 1996.

———. *Matsushita Leadership: Lessons from the 20th Century's Most Remarkable Entrepreneur.* New York: The Free Press, 1997.

———. *A Sense of Urgency.* Boston: Harvard Business School Publishing, 2008.

Kouzes, James M., and Barry Z. Posner. *Credibility: How Leaders Gain and Lose It, Why People Demand It.* San Francisco: Jossey-Bass, 2003.

———. "It's Not Just the Leader's Vision." In *Leader of the Future 2: Visions, Strategies, and Practices for the New Era,* edited by Frances Hesselbein and Marshall Goldsmith, 207–214. San Francisco: Jossey-Bass, 2006.

———. *The Leadership Challenge,* 4th ed. San Francisco: Jossey-Bass, 2007.

———. *A Leader's Legacy.* San Francisco: Jossey-Bass, 2006.

———. "Seven Lessons for Leading the Voyage to the Future." In *Leader of the Future,* edited by Frances Hesselbein, Marshall Goldsmith, and Richard Beckhard, 99–110. San Francisco: Jossey-Bass, 1996.

———. *The Truth about Leadership: The No-Fads, Heart-of-the-Matter Facts You Need to Know.* San Francisco: Jossey-Bass, 2010.

Kruse, Kevin. "What Is Leadership?" Forbes, 9 April 2013. https://www.forbes.com/sites/kevinkruse/2013/04/09/what-is-leadership/#7fba219a5b90.

Kwon, Sang-Kil. *Educational Ministry for Diaspora 2nd Generation.* Seoul: Yea-Young, 2009.

Kyemba, Henry. *State of Blood: The Inside Story of Idi Amin.* Kampala: Fountain Publishers, 1977.

Lamott, Anne. *Bird By Bird*. New York: Anchor Books, 1995.

Langer, Rick. "Toward a Biblical Theology of Leadership." In Burns, Shoup, and Simmons, *Organizational Leadership*, 65–90.

Lawrence, Rick. "What Really Impacts Spiritual Growth." *Group Magazine*, February 1995. www.gmresourcer.com/Contexts.htm. Accessed on 3 January 2019.

Ledbetter, Bernice M., Robert J. Banks, and David C. Greenhalgh. *Reviewing Leadership: A Christian Evaluation of Current Approaches*, 2nd ed. Grand Rapids: Baker, 2004.

Lee, Boyung. "Caring-Self and Women's Esteem: A Feminist Reflection on Pastoral Care and Religious Education of Korean-American Women." *Pastoral Psychology* 54, no. 4 (2006): 337–353.

Leithart, Peter J. *1 and 2 Kings*. Grand Rapids: Baker, 2006.

———. *Solomon among the Postmoderns*. Grand Rapids: Brazos Press, 2008.

Lencioni, Patrick. *The Advantage: Why Organizational Health Trumps Everything Else in Business*. San Francisco: Jossey-Bass, 2012.

———. *The Five Dysfunctions of a Team: A Leadership Fable*. San Francisco: Jossey-Bass, 2002.

———. *Silos, Politics, and Turf Wars: A Leadership Fable about Destroying the Barriers That Turn Colleagues into Competitors*. San Francisco: Jossey-Bass, 2002.

Lingenfelter, Sherwood G. *Leading Cross-Culturally: Covenant Relationships for Effective Christian Leadership*. Grand Rapids: Baker, 2008.

Livermore, David A. *Expand Your Borders: Discover 10 Cultural Clusters*. East Lansing: Cultural Intelligence Center, 2013.

Lovelace, Richard F. *Renewal as a Way of Life*. Downers Grove: InterVarsity Press, 1985.

Lowe, K. B., K. G. Kroeck, and N. Sivasubramaniam. "Effectiveness Correlates of Transformational and Transactional Leadership: A Meta-Analytic Review of the MLQ literature." *Leadership Quarterly* 7 (1996): 385–425.

Lowney, Chris. *Heroic Leadership: Best Practices from a 450-Year-Old Company That Changed the World*. Chicago: Loyola, 2003.

Lui, Otto. *Development of Chinese Church Leaders: A Study of Relational Leadership in Contemporary Chinese Churches*. Carlisle: Langham, 2013.

Ma, Maiqi. "Leadership in China: Harnessing Chinese Wisdom for Global Leadership?" Paper. https://www.crcpress.com/rsc/downloads/Transpersonal_Leadership_Leadership_in_China.pdf.

MacDonald, Gordon. "I Have This Feeling . . ." CT Pastors, Summer 2008. https://www.christianitytoday.com/pastors/2008/summer/9.82.html.

Maciariello, Joseph. "Peter F. Drucker on Executive Leadership and Effectiveness." In *Leader of the Future 2: Visions, Strategies, and Practices for the New Era*, edited by Frances Hesselbein and Marshall Goldsmith, 3–30. San Francisco: Jossey-Bass, 2006.

Manchester, William, *The Last Lion: Winston Spencer Churchill; Alone, 1932–1940*. New York: Bantam, 2013.

Mango, Andrew. *Atatürk: The Biography of the Founder of Modern Turkey*. New York: Overlook Press, 2002.

Marshall, Tom. *Understanding Leadership*. Grand Rapids: Baker, 1991.

Martin, Thomas R. *Ancient Greece: From Prehistoric to Hellenistic Times*. New Haven: Yale, 1996.

Matsushita, Konosuke Shidosha no Joken. *Real Leader's Requirements*. Japan: PHP Institute, 1975.

Maxwell, John C. *17 Indisputable Laws of Teamwork*. New York: HarperCollins, 2013.

———. *The 21 Irrefutable Laws of Leadership*. Nashville: Thomas Nelson, 1998.

Mayo, Tony. "The Importance of Vision." *Harvard Business Review*, 29 October 2007. https://hbr.org/2007/10/the-importance-of-vision.

Mbigi, Lovemore. *The Spirit of African Leadership*. Randburg: Knowres, 2005.

McChesney, Chris, Sean Covey, and Jim Huling. *The Four Disciplines of Execution*. New York: Free Press, 2012.

McKeown, Greg. *Essentialism: The Disciplined Pursuit of Less*. New York: Crown Business, 2014.

McManus, Erwin. *Seizing Your Divine Moment: Dare to Live a Life of Adventure*. Nashville: Thomas Nelson, 2002.

———. *An Unstoppable Force: Daring to Become the Church God Had in Mind*. Colorado Springs: David C. Cook, 2013.

Meacham, Jon. *Thomas Jefferson: The Art of Power*. New York: Random House, 2012. Kindle.

"Measuring the Return on Character." *Harvard Business Review*, April 2015. https://hbr.org/2015/04/measuring-the-return-on-character.

Meyer, Erin. "Being the Boss in Brussels, Boston, and Beijing." *Harvard Business Review*, July–August 2017. https://hbr.org/2017/07/being-the-boss-in-brussels-boston-and-beijing.

———. *The Culture Map: Breaking through the Invisible Boundaries of Global Business*. New York: PublicAffairs, 2014.

Millard, Candice. *Hero of the Empire: The Boer War, a Daring Escape, and the Making of Winston Churchill*. New York: Anchor, 2016.

Miller, Calvin. *The Empowered Leader: 10 Keys to Servant Leadership*. Nashville: Broadman and Holman, 1995.

Miller, Christian B. *The Character Gap: How Good Are We?* Oxford: Oxford University Press, 2018.

Montefiore, Simon Sebag. *Stalin: The Court of the Red Tsar*. New York: Vintage, 2005.

Moon, Steve Sang-Cheol. "A Research on Leadership Styles of Korean Overseas Missionaries." Krim Presentation, Seoul, 25 March 2015.

Moore, Russell. "How Frederick Buechner Blessed My Life." *Christianity Today* 16, no. 8 (October 2017): 44–48.

Morris, Edmund. *The Rise of Theodore Roosevelt*. New York: Coward, McCann, & Geoghegan, 1979.

Morrow, Lance. "The Gravitas Factor." *Time*, 14 March 1988. http://content.time.com/time/magazine/article/0,9171,966995,00.html.

Muehlhoff, Tim. *I Beg to Differ: Navigating Difficult Conversations with Truth and Love*. Downers Grove: InterVarsity Press, 2014.

Muller, Roland. *Honor and Shame: Unlocking the Door*. Bloomington: Xlibris, 2001.

Murray, Alan. "After the Revolt, Creating a New CEO." *The Wall Street Journal*, 5 May 2007. https://www.wsj.com/articles/SB117831845901692745.

Muthoni, Faith. "Accelerating Women Leadership: Lessons from Kenya Leaders in Non-Profit Organizations." Thesis, International Leadership University, Nairobi, 2016.

Myers, Bryant. *Engaging Globalization: The Poor, Christian Mission, and Our Hyperconnected World*. Grand Rapids: Baker, 2017.

Myra, Harold, and Marshall Shelley. *The Leadership Secrets of Billy Graham*. Grand Rapids: Zondervan, 2012.

Nagl, John. "'On Grand Strategy' Review: The War against Decline and Fall." *The Wall Street Journal*, 16 April 2018. https://www.wsj.com/articles/on-grand-strategy-review-the-war-against-decline-and-fall-1523915579.

Nanus, Bert. *Visionary Leadership*. San Francisco: Jossey-Bass, 1992.

Ng'ang'a, John N. *The Leader's Source of Influence*. Nairobi: Taruma Vision Creators, 2006.

Nitobe, Inazo. *Bushido*. Hong Kong: Tuttle, 1969.

Noonan, Peggy. "How to Find a Good Leader." *The Wall Street Journal*, November 1, 2018. http://www.peggynoonan.com/how-to-find-a-good-leader/.

———. "Churchill's Adversaries Weren't His Enemies." *The Wall Street Journal*, December 22–23, 2018. https://www.wsj.com/articles/churchills-adversaries-werent-his-enemies-11545350705.

Northouse, Peter G. *Leadership: Theory and Practice*. Los Angeles: Sage, 2016.

Nouwen, Henri. *In the Name of Jesus*. New York: Crossroad, 1989.

Oden, Thomas, *Classic Christianity*. New York: HarperOne, 2009.

———. *How Africa Shaped the Christian Mind: Rediscovering the African Seedbed of Western Christianity*. Downers Grove: InterVarsity Press, 2007.

———. *John Wesley's Teachings, Vol. 3: Pastoral Theology*. Grand Rapids: Zondervan, 2012.

OECD. *PISA 2015 Results*, Vol. 5: *Collaborative Problem Solving*. Paris: OECD Publishing, 2017.

Oligastri, Enrique, et. al. "Cultura y liderazgo organizacional en 10 países de América Latina. El estudio Globe." *Revista Latinoamericana de Administración* 22 (1999): 29–57.

Opuni-Frimpong, Kwabena. *Indigenous Knowledge and Christian Mission: Perspectives of Akan Leadership Formation on Christian Leadership Development*. Accra: SonLife, 2012.

Orr, Deborah. "Paul Schrader on First Reformed." *The Times*, 12 July 2018. https://www.thetimes.co.uk/article/paul-schrader-on-first-reformed-it-was-time-to-make-the-movie-i-swore-i-never-would-wgl0j5h5r.

Ortberg, John. *Everybody's Normal Till You Get to Know Them*. Grand Rapids: Zondervan, 2003.

Packer, J. I. *Faithfulness and Holiness*. Wheaton: Crossway Books, 2002.

Paul, Darel E. "Culture War as Class War." *First Things* 285 (August/September 2018): 41–46.

Peckham, Jeremy. "Relational Leadership." *Evangelical Focus* (blog), 12 April 2016. http://evangelicalfocus.com/blogs/1527/Relational_Leadership.

Perkins, Dennis N. T. *Leading at the Edge: Leadership Lessons from the Extraordinary Saga of Shackleton's Antarctic Expedition*. New York: American Management Association, 2012.

Peterson, Eugene. *The Contemplative Pastor: Returning to the Art of Spiritual Direction*. Grand Rapids: Eerdmans, 1989.

———. *Leap over a Wall: Earthly Spirituality for Everyday Christians*. New York: HarperSanFrancisco, 1997.

———. *A Long Obedience in the Same Direction: Discipleship in an Instant Society*. Downers Grove: InterVarsity Press, 1980.

———. *The Message*. Colorado Springs: NavPress, 2002.

———. *The Pastor: A Memoir*. New York: HarperOne, 2011.

———. *Working the Angles: The Shape of Pastoral Integrity*. Grand Rapids: Eerdmans, 1987.

Peterson, Jordan. *12 Rules for Life: An Antidote to Chaos*. Toronto: Random House Canada, 2018. Kindle.

Phan, Peter C. *Christianity with an Asian Face: Asian American Theology in the Making*. New York: Orbis, 2003.

Piper, John. *Expository Exultation: Christian Preaching as Worship*. Wheaton: Crossway, 2018.

———. *Think: The Life of the Mind and the Love of God*. Wheaton: Crossway, 2010.

Plantinga, Jr., Cornelius. *Not the Way It's Supposed to Be: A Breviary of Sin*. Grand Rapids: Eerdmans, 1995.

Plueddemann, James E. *Leading across Cultures: Effective Ministry and Mission in the Global Church*. Downers Grove: InterVarsity Press, 2009.

Pollard, William. "The Leader Who Serves." In *Leader of the Future*, edited by Frances Hesselbein, Marshall Goldsmith, and Richard Beckhard, 241–248. San Francisco: Jossey-Bass, 1996.

Prior, Karen Swallow. *On Reading Well: Finding the Good Life through Great Books*. Grand Rapids: Brazos, 2018. Kindle.

Puryear, Jr., Edgar F. *American Generalship: Character Is Everything; The Art of Command*. New York: Random House, 2000.

Rah, Soong-Chan. *The Next Evangelicalism: Freeing the Church from Western Cultural Captivity*. Downers Grove: InterVarsity Press, 2009.

Rao, Srikumar S. "Tomorrow's Leader." In *Leader of the Future 2: Visions, Strategies, and Practices for the New Era*, edited by Frances Hesselbein and Marshall Goldsmith, 173–182. San Francisco: Jossey-Bass, 2006.

Richards, E. Randolph, and Brandon J. O'Brien. *Misreading Scripture with Western Eyes*. Downers Grove: InterVarsity Press, 2012. Kindle.

Roberts, Andrew. *Hitler and Churchill: Secrets of Leadership*. London: Phoenix Publishing Group, 2004.

Roberts, N. C. "Transforming Leadership: A Process of Collective Action." *Human Relations* 38 (1985): 1023–1046.

Rodin, R. Scott. "Christian Leadership and Financial Integrity." In Burns, Shoup, and Simmons, *Organizational Leadership*, 229–252.

Roe, Earl. *Dream Big: The Henrietta Mears Story*. Ventura: Regal Books, 1990.

Rosling, Hans, and Anna Rosling Rönnlund. *Factfulness: Ten Reasons We Are Wrong about the World – and Why Things Are Better Than You Think*. New York: Flatiron Books, 2018.

Rost, Joseph C. *Leadership for the Twenty-First Century*. Westport: Praeger, 1991.

Rouse, Margaret. "Leadership Skills." TechTarget. https://searchcio.techtarget.com/definition/leadership-skills.

Roxburgh, Alan, and M. Scott Boren. *Introducing the Missional Church: What It Is, Why It Matters, How to Become One*. Grand Rapids: Baker, 2009.

Rumelt, Richard. *Good Strategy/Bad Strategy: The Difference and Why It Matters*. New York: Crown Business, 2011.

Sahu, Sangeeta, Avinash Pathardikar, and Anupam Kumar. "Transformational Leadership and Turnover: Mediating Effects of Employee Engagement, Employer Branding, and Psychological Attachment." *Leadership & Organization Development Journal* 39, no. 1 (2018): 82–99.

Saidi, Farida. *A Study of Current Leadership Styles in the North African Church*. Carlisle: Langham Monographs, 2013.

Sanders, J. Oswald. *Spiritual Leadership: Principles of Excellence for Every Believer*. Chicago: Moody, 1967.

Sarkar, Leor. "Sharing Credit in a Guru-Centered World." In *Eastern Voices*, Vol. 1, compiled by Asian Access, 85–100. Cerritos: Asian Access, 2017.

Scazzero, Peter. *The Emotionally Healthy Leader: How Transforming Your Inner Life Will Deeply Transform Your Church, Team, and the World*. Grand Rapids: Zondervan, 2015.

Schein, Edgar H. "Leadership Competencies: A Provocative New Look." In *Leader of the Future 2: Visions, Strategies, and Practices for the New Era*, edited by Frances Hesselbein and Marshall Goldsmith, 255–264. San Francisco: Jossey-Bass, 2006.

Schwartz, Peter. *The Art of the Long View*. New York: Currency Doubleday, 1991.

Seidman, Dov. *How: Why How We Do Anything Means Everything*. Hoboken: John Wiley & Sons, 2007.

Shamir, B., R. J. House, and M. B. Arthur. "The Motivational Effects of Charismatic Leadership: A Self-Concept Based Theory." *Organizational Science* 4, no. 4 (Nov. 1993): 577–594.

Shoup, John R., and Chris McHorney. "Decision Making." In Burns, Shoup, and Simmons, *Organizational Leadership*, 197–228.

Sides, Hampton. *In the Kingdom of Ice: The Grand and Terrible Polar Voyage of the USS Jeanette*. New York: Anchor, 2015.

Sire, James W. *The Universe Next Door: A Basic Worldview Catalog*. Downers Grove: InterVarsity Press, 1976.

Sommerville, C. John. "Why the News Makes Us Dumb." *First Things*, October 1991. https://www.firstthings.com/article/1991/10/why-the-news-makes-us-dumb.

Sonnenfeld, Jeffrey. *The Hero's Farewell: What Happens When CEOs Retire*. New York: Oxford University Press, 1988.

Stanley, Andy. *Next Generation Leader: 5 Essentials for Those Who Will Shape the Future*. Colorado Springs: Multnomah, 2003.

———. *Visioneering*. Colorado Springs: Multnomah, 1999.

Stein, Joel. "What I Learned about Leadership from Leading Leaders." *Time*, 21 September 2017. http://time.com/4951213/what-i-learned-about-leadership-from-leading-leaders/.

Stein, Marc, and Scott Cacciola. "Why Do the Warriors Dominate the 3rd Quarter? Consider Their Halftime Drill." *The New York Times*, 31 May 2018. https://www.nytimes.com/2018/05/31/sports/warriors-third-quarter.html.

Stogdill, R. M. *Handbook of Leadership: A Survey of Theory and Research*. New York: Free Press, 1974.

Strom, Mark. *Lead with Wisdom: How Wisdom Transforms Good Leaders into Great Leaders*. Brisbane: Wrightbooks, 2014. Kindle.

Sweet, Leonard. *Aqua Church: Essential Leadership Arts for Piloting Your Church in Today's Fluid Culture*. Loveland: Group, 1999.

———. *Summoned to Lead*. Grand Rapids: Zondervan, 2004.

Taylor, Barbara Brown. *Leaving Church: A Memoir of Faith*. New York: HarperOne, 2006.

Taylor, Bill. "If Humility Is So Important, Why Are Leaders So Arrogant?" *Harvard Business Review*, October 15, 2018. https://hbr.org/2018/10/if-humility-is-so-important-why-are-leaders-so-arrogant.

Taylor, Kate. "How Howard Schultz Went from Living in Brooklyn Public Housing to Ending His Decades of Starbucks Leadership as a Billionaire with Rumored Political Aspirations." *New Haven Register*, 6 September 2018. https://www.nhregister.com/technology/businessinsider/article/Starbucks-CEO-Howard-Schultz-reveals-what-it-felt-6347215.php.

Templer, Klaus J. "Why Do Toxic People Get Promoted? For the Same Reason Humble People Do: Political Skill." *Harvard Business Review*, 10 July 2018. https://hbr.org/2018/07/why-do-toxic-people-get-promoted-for-the-same-reason-humble-people-do-political-skill.

Thiselton, Anthony C. *The First Epistle to the Corinthians*. New International Greek Testament Commentary. Grand Rapids: Eerdmans, 2000.

Thomas, Evan. *Being Nixon: A Man Divided*. New York: Random House, 2015. Kindle.

Thomson, Mark. *Gandhi and His Ashrams*. Bombay: Popular Prakashan, 1993.

Thura, Wesley Kyaw. "Losing My Face to Find My Soul." In *Eastern Voices*, Vol. 1, compiled by Asian Access, 7–22. Cerritos: Asian Access, 2017.

Tichy, Noel. *The Leadership Engine: Building Leaders at Every Level*. New York: HarperBusiness Essentials, 1997.

Tichy, Noel M., and Warren G. Bennis. *Judgment: How Winning Leaders Make Great Calls*. New York: Portfolio, 2007.

Tozer, A. W. *The Knowledge of the Holy*. New York: HarperCollins, 1961.

Ulrich, Dave. "Credibility x Capability." In *Leader of the Future*, edited by Frances Hesselbein, Marshall Goldsmith, and Richard Beckhard, 209–220. San Francisco: Jossey-Bass, 1996.

Ulrich, Dave, and Norm Smallwood. "Leadership as a Brand." In *Leader of the Future 2: Visions, Strategies, and Practices for the New Era*, edited by Frances Hesselbein and Marshall Goldsmith, 141–152. San Francisco: Jossey-Bass, 2006.

Useem, Jerry. "Power Causes Brain Damage." *The Atlantic*, July/August 2017. https://www.theatlantic.com/magazine/archive/2017/07/power-causes-brain-damage/528711/.

Useem, Michael. *The Go Point: When It's Time to Decide; Knowing What to Do and When to Do It*. New York: Three Rivers, 2006.

———. *The Leadership Moment: Nine True Stories of Triumph and Disaster and Their Lessons for Us All*. New York: Three Rivers, 1998.

Van Gelder, Craig, and Dwight J. Zscheile. *The Missional Church in Perspective: Mapping Trends and Shaping the Conversation*. Grand Rapids: Baker, 2011.

Van Yperen, Jim. "Conflict: The Refining Fire of Leadership," In *Leaders on Leadership*, edited by George Barna, 239–260. Ventura: Regal, 1997.

Vanderbloemen, William, and Warren Bird. *Next: Pastoral Succession That Works*. Grand Rapids: Baker, 2014. Kindle.

Vanhoozer, Kevin J. "Letter to an Aspiring Theologian: How to Speak of God Truly." *First Things*, August/September 2018. https://www.firstthings.com/article/2018/08/letter-to-an-aspiring-theologian.

Venus, Merlijn, Daan Stam, and Daan van Knippenberg. "Research: To Get People to Embrace Change, Emphasize What Will Remain the Same." *Harvard Business Review*, 15 August 2018. https://hbr.org/2018/08/research-to-get-people-to-embrace-change-emphasize-what-will-stay-the-same.

Wageman, Ruth, Debra A. Nunes, James A. Burruss, and J. Richard Hackman. *Senior Leadership Teams: What It Takes to Make Them Great*. Boston: Harvard Business School, 2008.

Walsh, Peter. "Are You a Strategic Thinker? Test Yourself." *Harvard Business Publishing*, 20 May 2014. http://www.harvardbusiness.org/blog/are-you-strategic-thinker-test-yourself.

Waltke, Bruce K. *The Book of Proverbs, Chapters 1–15*. New International Commentary on the Old Testament. Grand Rapids: Eerdmans, 2004.

Walton, David. *Introducing Emotional Intelligence: A Practical Guide*. London: Icon, 2012.

Wan, Enoch. *Diaspora Missiology: Theory, Methodology, and Practice*. 2nd ed. Portland: IDS, 2015.

Wan, Enoch, and Mark Hedinger. *Relational Missionary Training: Theology, Theory, and Practice*. Skyforest: Urban Loft, 2017.

———. "Transformative Ministry for the Majority World Context: Applying Relational Approaches." *Occasional Bulletin* (Spring 2018): 4–17.

Webber, Malcolm. "Reflections on Chinese Conceptions of Leadership." Unpublished paper.

Weese, Carolyn, and J. Russell Crabtree. *The Elephant in the Boardroom: Speaking the Unspoken about Pastoral Transitions*. San Francisco: Jossey-Bass, 2004. Kindle.

Welch, Jack. *Winning*. New York: HarperCollins, 2005.

Westberg, Daniel A. *Renewing Moral Theology: Christian Ethics as Action, Character and Grace*. Downers Grove: InterVarsity Press, 2015.

Wheatley, Margaret J. *Who Do We Choose to Be? Facing Reality, Claiming Leadership, Restoring Sanity*. Oakland: Berrett-Koehler, 2017.

Wilhelm, Warren. "Learning from Past Leaders." In *Leader of the Future*, edited by Frances Hesselbein, Marshall Goldsmith, and Richard Beckhard, 221–226. San Francisco: Jossey-Bass, 1996.

Willard, Dallas. *Renovation of the Heart*. Colorado Springs: NavPress, 2002.

Willimon, William H. *Pastor*. Nashville: Abingdon, 2002.

Wills, Garry. *Certain Trumpets: The Nature of Leadership*. New York: Touchstone, 1994.

Wiseman, Liz. *Multipliers: How the Best Leaders Make Everyone Smarter*. New York: HarperCollins, 2010.

Woolfe, Lorin. *Leadership Secrets from the Bible: Management Lessons for Contemporary Leaders*. New York: MJF Books, 2002.

Wright, Christopher J. H. *The Mission of God: Unlocking the Bible's Grand Narrative*. Downers Grove: InterVarsity Press, 2006.

Wright, N. T. *After You Believe: Why Christian Character Matters*. New York: HarperOne, 2010.

———. *How God Became King: The Forgotten Story of the Gospels*. New York: HarperOne, 2012.

————. *Simply Good News: Why the Gospel Is News and What Makes It Good*. New York: HarperCollins, 2015.

Yancey, Philip. *The Jesus I Never Knew*. Grand Rapids: Zondervan, 1995.

Yukl, Gary. "An Evaluation of Conceptual Weaknesses in Transformational and Charismatic Leadership Theories." *The Leadership Quarterly* 10, no. 2 (Summer 1999): 285–305.

Zaccaro, Stephen J., and Deanna Banks. "Leader Visioning and Adaptability: Bridging the Gap between Research and Practice on Developing the Ability to Manage Change." *Human Resource Management* 43, no. 4 (November 2004): 367–380.

Zuck, Roy B. *Reflecting with Solomon*. Grand Rapids: Baker, 1994.

Contributing Voices

Emmanuel Bellon, Vice President of Scholarleaders International, Executive Network, Kenya. Emmanuel also directs the Vital Sustainability Initiative (VSI), a project designed to facilitate theological institutions in Latin America, Africa, the Middle East, Eastern Europe, and Asia to strategically plan for institutional sustainability.

Paul Kyu-Jin Choi, Pastor, Korean Fellowship, Village Church, Portland, Oregon. Paul is part of a multicultural church on the west side of Portland, leading efforts to reach and train leaders to lead multicultural churches.

Patrick Fung, Director, OMF International. Patrick is a Singaporean medical doctor who today provides spiritual leadership for OMF, which currently has more than 1,400 workers from over twenty-five countries serving among East Asia's peoples.

Omar Gava, Founder and Director of Recursos Estratégicos Globales (Global Strategic Resourses), and Regional Director (Latin America) for People International, Argentina. Omar is also ambassador for COMIBAM International, and a member of the International Missionary Training Network of WEA.

Mark Greene, Executive Director, The London Institute for Contemporary Christianity, UK. Mark leads efforts to change the culture of the UK church, helping Christians flourish and the church to fulfill its disciple-making responsibility.

Paul Gupta, President and Director of Hindustan Bible Institute, Chennai, India. Paul (Bobby) also pastors New Calvary Bible Church, is the founder of the Indian National Evangelical Fellowship, and heads up HBI Global Partners.

Elie Haddad, President of Arab Baptist Theological Seminary, Beirut, Lebanon. Elie has invested the past ten years of his life leading an evangelical seminary in a turbulent yet strategic part of the world. ABTS was founded to develop and equip both present and future leaders for the ministry challenges arising in the Middle East and North Africa.

Alex Kulpecz, Executive Chairman of Kerogen Exploration, a North American Oil and Gas Company, Houston, Texas/London, UK. Alex is a geologist and former Managing Director of Royal Dutch Shell responsible for Central Europe, Russia, Africa, and South America. He participates on various energy company boards for private equity.

Camille Melki, Founder and CEO, Heart for Lebanon, Beirut, Lebanon. Camille leads an effort to provide humanitarian aid, relief, and capacity building for marginalized people groups, with a particular concern for children.

Luis Palau, Evangelist, Founder and Director of Luis Palau Association, Beaverton, Oregon. Luis heads a ministry that has shared the gospel with millions of people through evangelistic events and media around the world. He has spoken in person to more than 30 million people in seventy-five countries, and has counseled business leaders, political leaders, and heads of state around the world.

Gideon Para-Mallam, IFES Regional Secretary for English and Portugese-speaking Africa, Nigeria. Gideon has been involved in leadership with the International Fellowship of Evangelical Students (IFES) for over thirty years. His most recent position was as Regional Secretary for IFES in Africa. He currently serves as Ambassador for IFES World Assembly 2019.

Samuil Petrovski, National Director of the International Fellowship of Evangelical Students, Serbia. Samuil has a demonstrated history of working in international affairs. He is skilled in negotiation, analytical skills, government, and volunteer management.

Grant Porter, Former Middle East Director, Operation Mobilization, Head of Near East Initiative, and Current Program Director, Cornerstone Trust, Grand Rapids, Michigan. Grant is an Australian who has spent much of his life leading ministry initiatives in the Middle East, bringing together diverse leaders and guiding them to become a unified front.

Evi Rodemann, former CEO of Mission-Net, currently with the Lausanne Movement, Hamburg, Germany. Evi is a self-proclaimed cheerleader of the next generation. She has a huge passion for Europe, young people, and younger leaders. She heads up and leads various European youth mission projects.

Elizabeth Sendek, Rectora, Biblical Seminary of Columbia (FUSBC), Medellín, Colombia. During the past eight years Elizabeth has served in leading the

FUSBC, where for twenty-five years she has served in teaching Greek and New Testament exegesis, and as Academic Vice President. She served for fourteen years in evangelism and discipleship of college students prior to joining FUSBC.

Dan Sered, Chief Operating Officer, Jews for Jesus, Tel Aviv, Israel. Dan is a leader of Jews for Jesus, the largest Jewish mission in the world today. He oversees Missionary Teams in Israel, Europe (Russia, Ukraine, Hungary, Germany, France, Switzerland, and the UK), South Africa, and Australia. Dan also pastors an Israeli International Church Community in a suburb of Tel Aviv and is an adjunct lecturer at Israel College of the Bible.

Takeshi Takazawa, Asian Director, Asian Access/Japan, Tokyo, Japan. Takeshi also currently serves on the Asian Access International Ministry Leadership team. He has headed the creation of the *Eastern Voices* project, a compilation of Asian leaders dedicated to making an impact across Asia.

Julius D. Twongyeirwe, Leader of Proclamation Task, Kampala, Uganda. Julius is an African leader devoted to equipping pastors and teachers to be effective leaders in the church.

General Index

Scripture Index

NEW TESTAMENT

1 John

Revelation

Langham
PARTNERSHIP

Langham Literature and its imprints are a ministry of Langham Partnership.

Langham Partnership is a global fellowship working in pursuit of the vision God entrusted to its founder John Stott –

to facilitate the growth of the church in maturity and Christ-likeness through raising the standards of biblical preaching and teaching.

Our vision is to see churches in the majority world equipped for mission and growing to maturity in Christ through the ministry of pastors and leaders who believe, teach and live by the Word of God.

Our mission is to strengthen the ministry of the Word of God through:
• nurturing national movements for biblical preaching
• fostering the creation and distribution of evangelical literature
• enhancing evangelical theological education
especially in countries where churches are under-resourced.

Our ministry

Langham Preaching partners with national leaders to nurture indigenous biblical preaching movements for pastors and lay preachers all around the world. With the support of a team of trainers from many countries, a multi-level programme of seminars provides practical training, and is followed by a programme for training local facilitators. Local preachers' groups and national and regional networks ensure continuity and ongoing development, seeking to build vigorous movements committed to Bible exposition.

Langham Literature provides majority world preachers, scholars and seminary libraries with evangelical books and electronic resources through publishing and distribution, grants and discounts. The programme also fosters the creation of indigenous evangelical books in many languages, through writer's grants, strengthening local evangelical publishing houses, and investment in major regional literature projects, such as one volume Bible commentaries like *The Africa Bible Commentary* and *The South Asia Bible Commentary*.

Langham Scholars provides financial support for evangelical doctoral students from the majority world so that, when they return home, they may train pastors and other Christian leaders with sound, biblical and theological teaching. This programme equips those who equip others. Langham Scholars also works in partnership with majority world seminaries in strengthening evangelical theological education. A growing number of Langham Scholars study in high quality doctoral programmes in the majority world itself. As well as teaching the next generation of pastors, graduated Langham Scholars exercise significant influence through their writing and leadership.

To learn more about Langham Partnership and the work we do visit **langham.org**

Lightning Source UK Ltd.
Milton Keynes UK
UKHW021832290120
357829UK00005B/15